Information Reuse and Integration in Academia and Industry

Tansel Özyer • Keivan Kianmehr • Mehmet Tan
Jia Zeng

Editors

Information Reuse
and Integration in Academia
and Industry

 Springer

Editors

Tansel Özyer
Department of Computer Engineering
TOBB University
Sogutozu Ankara
Turkey

Mehmet Tan
Tobb Etü Economics and Technology
  University
Ankara
Turkey

Keivan Kianmehr
Department of Electrical Engineering
University of West Ontario
London, Ontario
Canada

Jia Zeng
Baylor College of Medicine
Houston, Texas
USA

ISBN 978-3-7091-4842-6   ISBN 978-3-7091-1538-1 (eBook)
DOI 10.1007/978-3-7091-1538-1
Springer Wien Heidelberg New York Dordrecht London

Preface

We are delighted to see this edited book as the result of our intensive work over the past year. We succeeded in attracting high-quality submissions of which we could only include fourteen papers in this edited book. The present text aims at helping the readers both researchers from academia and practitioners from industry to grasp the basic concepts of information integrity and reusability which are very essential in this rapidly growing information era. Over the past decades, huge volumes of data have been produced and stored, large number of software systems have been developed and successfully utilized, and various products have been manufactured. Not all these developments could have been achieved without the investment of money, time, effort, and other resources. Over time, new data sources evolve and data integration continue to be an essential and vital requirement. Further, systems and products should be revised to adapt new technologies and to satisfy new needs. Instead of building from scratch, researchers in the academia and industry have realized the benefits of and concentrated on building new software systems by reusing some of the components that already exist and have been well tested. This trend avoids reinventing the wheel, however, comes at the cost of finding out the best set of existing components to be utilized and how they should be integrated together and with the new nonexisting components which are to be developed from scratch. These are nontrivial tasks and have led to challenging research problems in the academia and industry. Some of these issues have been addressed in this book, which is intended to be a unique resource for researchers, developers, and practitioners. In addition, the book will cover the latest developments and discoveries related to information reuse and integration in the academia and in the industry. It contains high-quality research papers written by experts in the field. Some of them are extended versions of the best papers which were presented at IEEE International Conference on Information Reuse and Integration, which was held in Las Vegas in August 2011.

The first paper "Mediators, Concepts and Practice" by Gio Wiederhold studies mediators, their concepts, and practice. Mediators are intermediary modules in large-scale information systems that link multiple sources of information to applications. They provide a means for integrating the application of encoded knowledge into information systems. Mediated systems compose autonomous data and information services, permitting growth, and enable their survival in a semantically diverse and rapidly changing world. Constraints of scope are placed on mediators to assure effective and maintainable composed systems. Modularity in mediated architectures is not only a goal but also enables the goal to be reached. Mediators focus on semantic matching, while middleware provides the essential syntactic and formatting interfaces.

The second paper "A Combination Framework for Exploiting the Symbiotic Aspects of Process and Operational Data in Business Process Optimization" by Sylvia Radeschütz, Holger Schwarz, Marko Vrhovnik, and Bernhard Mitschang addresses the optimizing problem of a company's business process. A profound analysis of all relevant business data in a company is necessary for optimizing business processes effectively. Current analyses typically run either on business process execution data or on operational business data. Correlations among the separate datasets have to be found manually under big effort. However, to achieve a more informative analysis and to fully optimize a company's business, an efficient consolidation of all major data sources is indispensable. Recent matching algorithms are insufficient for this task since they are restricted either to schema or to process matching. They present a new matching framework to (semi)automatically combine process data models and operational data models for performing such a profound business analysis. They describe the algorithms and basic matching rules underlying this approach as well as an experimental study that shows the achieved high recall and precision.

The third paper "Efficient Range Query Processing on Complicated Uncertain Data" by Andrew Knight, Qi Yu, and Manjeet Rege investigates a special type of query, range queries, on uncertain data. Uncertain data has emerged as a key data type in many applications. New and efficient query processing techniques need to be developed due to the inherent complexity of this new type of data. They propose a threshold interval indexing structure that aims to balance different time-consuming factors to achieve an optimal overall query performance. They also present a more efficient version of their proposed structure which loads its primary tree into memory for faster processing. Experimental results are presented to justify the efficiency of the proposed query processing technique.

The fourth paper "Invariant Object Representation Based on Inverse Pyramidal Decomposition and Modified Mellin-Fourier Transform" by R. Kountchev, S. Rubin, M. Milanova, and R. Kountcheva presents a new method for invariant object representation based on the Inverse Pyramidal Decomposition (IPD) and modified Mellin-Fourier Transform (MFT). The so-prepared object representation is invariant against 2D rotation, scaling, and translation (RST). The representation is additionally made invariant to significant contrast and illumination changes. The method is aimed at content-based object retrieval in large databases. The experimental results obtained using the software implementation of the method proved its efficiency. The method is suitable for various applications, such as detection of children sexual abuse in multimedia files, search of handwritten and printed documents, and 3D objects, and represented by multi-view 2D images.

The fifth paper "Model Checking State Machines Using Object Diagrams" by Thouraya Bouabana-Tebibel discusses that UML behavioral diagrams are often formalized by transformation into a state-transition language that sets on a rigorously defined semantics. The state-transition models are afterwards model-checked to prove the correctness of the models construction as well as their faithfulness with the user requirements. The model checking is performed on a reachability graph, generated from the behavioral models, whose size depends on the models' structure and their initial marking. The purpose of this paper is twofold. The author first proposes an approach to initialize formal models at any time of the system life cycle using UML diagrams. The formal models are Object Petri nets, OPNs for short, derived from UML state machines. The OPNs marking is mainly deduced from the sequence diagrams. Secondly, an approach is proposed to specify the association ends on the OPNs in order to allow their validation by means of OCL invariants. A case study is given to illustrate the approach throughout the paper.

The sixth paper "Measuring Stability of Feature Selection Techniques on Real-World Software Datasets" by Huanjing Wang, Taghi M. Khoshgoftaar, and Randall Wald studies the stability of different feature selection techniques on software data repositories. In the practice of software quality estimation, superfluous software metrics often exist in data repositories. In other words, not all collected software metrics are useful or make equal contributions to software defect prediction. Selecting a subset of features that are most relevant to the class attribute is necessary and may result in better prediction. This process is called feature selection. However, the addition or removal of instances can alter the subsets chosen by a feature selection technique, rendering the previously selected feature sets invalid. Thus, the robustness (e.g., stability) of feature selection techniques must be studied to examine the sensitivity of these techniques to changes in their input data (the addition or removal of instances). In this paper, authors test the stability of eighteen feature selection techniques as the magnitude of change to the datasets, and the size of the selected feature subsets are varied. All experiments were conducted on 16 datasets from three real-world software projects. The experimental results demonstrate that gain ratio shows the least stability while two different versions of ReliefF show the most stability, followed by the PRC- and AUC-based threshold-based feature selection techniques. Results also show that making smaller changes to the datasets has less impact on the stability of feature ranking techniques applied to those datasets.

The seventh paper "Analysis and Design: Towards Large-Scale Reuse and Integration of Web User Interface Components" by Hao Han, Peng Gao, Yinxing Xue, Chuanqi Tao, and Keizo Oyama studies the reuse and integration of Web user interface components. With the trend for Web information/functionality integration, application integration at the presentation and logic layers is becoming a popular issue. In the absence of OpenWeb service application programming interfaces, the integration of conventional Web applications is usually based on the reuse of user interface (UI) components, which partially represent the interactive functionalities of applications. In this paper, they describe some common problems of the current Web-UIComponent-based reuse and integration and propose a solution: a security-enhanced "component retrieval and integration description" method. They also discuss the related technologies such as testing, maintenance, and copyright. Their purpose is to construct a reliable large-scale reuse and integration system for Web applications.

The eighth paper "Which Ranking for Effective Keyword Search Query over RDF Graphs?" by Roberto De Virgilio presents a theoretical study of YAANII, a novel technique to keyword-based search over semantic data. Ranking solutions is an important issue in information retrieval because it greatly influences the quality of results. In this context, keyword-based search approaches use to consider solutions sorting as least step of the overall process. Ranking and building solutions are completely separate steps running autonomously. This may penalize the retrieving information process because it binds to order all found matching elements including (possible) irrelevant information. The proposed approach presents a joint use of scoring functions and solution building algorithms to get the best results. The author demonstrates how effectiveness of the answers depends not so much on the quality of the scoring metrics but on the way such criteria are involved. Finally it is shown how YAANII overcomes other systems in terms of efficiency and effectiveness.

The ninth paper "ReadFast: Structural Information Retrieval from Biomedical Big Text by Natural Language Processing" by Michael Gubanov, Linda Shapiro, and Anna Pyayt discusses methods for retrieving information from large-scale text datasets. While the problem to find needed information on the Web is being solved by the major search engines, access to the information in Big text, large-scale text datasets, and documents (biomedical literature, e-books, conference proceedings, etc.) is still very rudimentary. Thus, keyword-search is often the only way to find the needle in the haystack. There is abundance of relevant research results in the Semantic Web research community that offers more robust access interfaces compared to keyword-search. Here authors describe a new information retrieval engine that offers advanced user experience combining keyword-search with navigation over an automatically inferred hierarchical document index. The internal representation of the browsing index as a collection of UFOs yields more relevant search results and improves user experience.

The tenth paper "Multiple Criteria Decision Support for Software Reuse: An Industrial Case Study" by Alejandra Yepez Lopez and Nan Niu reports a case study that applied SMART (Simple Multi-Attribute Rating Technique) to a company that considered reuse as an option of reengineering its Web site. In practice, many factors must be considered and balanced when making software reuse decisions. However, few empirical studies exist that leverage practical techniques to support decision-making in software reuse. The company's reuse goal was set to maximize benefits and to minimize costs. They applied SMART in two iterations for the company's software reuse project. The main difference is that the first iteration used the COCOMO (COnstructive COst MOdel) to quantify the cost in the beginning of the software project. In the second iteration, they refined the cost estimation by using the COCOMO II model. This combined approach illustrates the importance of updating and refining the decision support for software reuse. The company was informed the optimal reuse percentage for the project, which was reusing

76–100 % of the existing artifacts and knowledge. This study not only shows that SMART is a valuable and practical technique that can be readily incorporated into an organization's software reuse program but also offers concrete insights into applying SMART in an industrial setting.

The eleventh paper "Using Local Principal Components to Explore Relationships Between Heterogeneous Omics Datasets" by Noor Alaydie and Farshad Fotouhi analyzes the relationships between a pair of data sources based on their correlation. In the post-genomic era, high-throughput technologies lead to the generation of large amounts of "omics" data such as transcriptomics, metabolomics, proteomics that are measured on the same set of samples. The development of methods that are capable to perform joint analysis of multiple datasets from different technology platforms to unravel the relationships between different biological functional levels becomes crucial. A common way to analyze the relationships between a pair of data sources based on their correlation is canonical correlation analysis (CCA). CCA seeks for linear combinations of all the variables from each dataset which maximize the correlation between them. However, in high-dimensional datasets, where the number of variables exceeds the number of experimental units, CCA may not lead to meaningful information. Moreover, when colinearity exists in one or both the datasets, CCA may not be applicable. In this paper, the authors present a novel method to extract common features from a pair of data sources using Local Principal Components and Kendall's Ranking (LPC-KR). The results show that the proposed algorithm outperforms CCA in many scenarios and is more robust to noisy data. Moreover, meaningful results are obtained using the proposed algorithm when the number of variables exceeds the number of experimental units.

The twelfth paper "Towards Collaborative Forensics" by Mike Mabey and Gail-Joon Ahn proposes a comprehensive framework to address the efficacious deficiencies of current practices in digital forensics. This framework, called Collaborative Forensic Framework (CUFF), provides scalable forensic services for practitioners who are from different organizations and have diverse forensic skills. In other words, this framework helps forensic practitioners collaborate with each other, instead of learning and struggling with new forensic techniques. In addition, the fundamental building blocks for the proposed framework and corresponding system requirements are described.

The thirteenth paper "From Increased Availability to Increased Productivity: How Researchers Benefit from Online Resources" by Joe Strathern, Samer Awadh, Samir Chokshi, Omar Addam, Omar Zarour, M. Ozair Shafiq, Orkun Öztürk, Omair Shafiq, Jamal Jida, and Reda Alhajj presents researchers with an analysis that summarizes data collection and evolution features in the World Wide Web. Authors have reviewed a large corpus of published work to extract the research features supported by advanced Web features, i.e., blogs, microblogging services, video-on-demand Web sites, and social networks. They have presented summary of their review and analysis. This will help in further analysis of the evolution of communities using and supporting the features of the continuously evolving World Wide Web.

The fourteenth paper "Integration of Semantics Information and Clustering in Binary-class Classification for Handling Imbalanced Multimedia Data" by Chao Chen and Mei-Ling Shyu proposes a novel binary-class classification framework that integrates the video semantics information and the clustering technique to address the data imbalance issue which is a major challenge in the classification task. Experiments are conducted to compare the proposed framework with other techniques that are commonly used to learn from imbalanced datasets. The experimental results on some highly imbalanced video datasets demonstrate that the proposed classification framework outperforms these comparative classification approaches about 3 % to 16 %.

Last but not the least, we would like to mention the hard workers behind the scene who have significant unseen contributions to the successful task that produced this valuable source of knowledge. We would like to thank the authors who submitted papers and the reviewers who provided detailed constructive reports which improved the quality of the papers. Various people from Springer deserve large credit for their help and support in all the issues related to publishing this book.

Ankara, Turkey   Tansel Özyer
Ontario, Canada   Keivan Kianmehr
Ankara, Turkey   Mehmet Tan
Houston, Texas   Jia Zeng

Contents

Chapter 1
Mediators, Concepts and Practice

Gio Wiederhold

Abstract Mediators are intermediary modules in large-scale information systems that link multiple sources of information to applications. They provide a means for integrating the application of encoded knowledge into information systems. Mediated systems compose autonomous data and information services, permitting growth and enable their survival in a semantically diverse and rapidly changing world. Constraints of scope are placed on mediators to assure effective and maintainable composed systems. Modularity in mediated architectures is not only a goal, but also enables the goal to be reached. Mediators focus on semantic matching, while middleware provides the essential syntactic and formatting interfaces.

Overview

We first present the role of mediators and the architecture of mediated systems, as well as some definition for terms used throughout this exposition. Section "Conceptual Principles" deals with mediators at a conceptual level. Section "Operations and Managing Volume" presents the basic functionalities, and section "Integration" presents the primary objective of mediators, information integration, including the problems of heterogeneous semantics, and the modeling of knowledge to drive integration. Section "Related Topics" points to related topics, not covered as such in earlier chapters. A final summary reviews the state of the technology, indicating where research is needed so that the concepts will support composed information systems of ever greater scale.

G. Wiederhold (✉)
Prof. Emeritus, Computer Science, Electrical Engineering, and Medicine, Stanford University, Stanford, CA 94305, USA
e-mail: gio@cs.stanford.edu

T. Özyer et al. (eds.), *Information Reuse and Integration in Academia and Industry*, DOI 10.1007/978-3-7091-1538-1_1, © Springer-Verlag Wien 2013

1

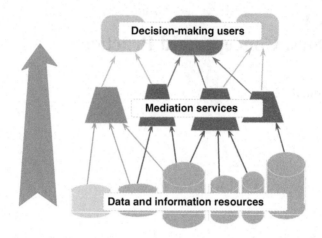

Fig. 1.1 Place and role of mediation

Architecture

Mediators interpose integration and abstraction services in large-scale information systems to support applications used by decision-makers, where the scale,
diversity, and complexity, of relevant data and information resources are such that
the applications would be overwhelmed. Augmenting databases and other base
information sources with adequate functionality to directly serve the broad demands
of applications is does not scale beyond specific application types, as computer-
aided design [48]. Multiple, autonomous resources cannot support all the possible
combinations of application requirements, especially as they expand in the future.
Figure 1.1 sketches the basic layering of mediation.

Any single mediator will focus on a specific domain, say finance, logistics,
clinical care, manufacturing specific types of goods. Such specialization introduces
governance by domain experts, creating reliability and trustworthiness.

The mediator architecture hence partitions resources and services in two dimensions [58]:

- Horizontally into three layers: the client applications, the intermediate service
  domain modules, and the base servers.
- Vertically into multiple domains or areas of expertise.

The result is a modularization which enables effective maintenance of the
mediated system. For any specific application the number of domains it exploits is
best limited to 7 ± 2 [38]. For each domain the number of supporting servers should
be limited similarly. But the combination allows applications to easily obtain access
to several dozen sources, while the components can participate in a much larger
network.

Internally mediators provide semantic services and transformations, but delegate syntactic bridging among at other levels components to middleware [3]. More complex layerings are envisaged in section "Complex Architectures", but in general it is best to keep architectures simple.

Motivation

Today, few large information systems are built from the ground up. Instead, they are constructed from existing components and systems. Without an architectural structure system integrators supply the functionalities necessary to make the pieces work together by augmenting the applications and insisting on compliance with standards for their sources. Their integration effort can take place at several levels of granularity. Much work has been focused on schema integration [41]. Composition of basic software modules is the approach used in object-oriented (OO) software engineering [31]. Transformations are needed when modules come from distinct libraries. Composing webservices is the approach when the modules are remote, and perhaps owned by other parties, but must impose standards to assure compatibility [10]. Combining services provided in clouds will requires shipping control information and results among them. While there are commercial products, no broad framework exists as of now [14]. In all these efforts, first of all middleware has to resolve format incompatibilities, transforming data among differing standards, including proprietary conventions [42].

Mediation attacks the next level of inconsistency encountered in composition, where large systems depend on services that were independently developed. Such resources, not having been designed from the outset as services or components, cannot be expected to be compatible in any dimension. The incompatibilities will involve representation, to be resolved by middleware, and semantics, requiring mediation. An example of a semantic mismatch occurs when diagnosing patients, where sources used for billing use different terms, scopes, and aggregations than those needed for epidemiological research. Semantic differences exist anywhere where objectives differ, say among a householder trying to fix a plumbing problem and a professional installer. Just insisting that we all use the same terms will not work. Section "Integration" will expand on these issues.

Semantic differences are hard to resolve [36]. Any standards, where they exist, depend again on terminologies that are hard to pin down. Ontologies can enumerate and classify these terms [17]. Ontologies typically introduce abstract hierarchies, but those hierarchies are based in application models and cannot be imposed on independent sources. Only when the definitions are finally reduced to enumerated real objects can full agreement be assured [39]. But a world that is ever growing in unpredictable directions cannot be limited to existing objects. The use of abstract concepts brings a power to information systems that we cannot do without [33]. Gaining access to such diversity is the objective of mediation.

Fig. 1.2 System interfaces

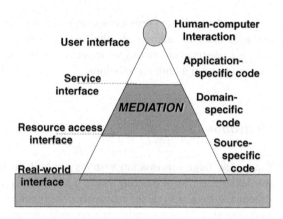

Interfaces

For a system composed of modules interfaces are crucial. Mediation requires interfaces at two levels, as sketched on Fig. 1.2. Information technology has a surfeit of interface standards, and we cannot cover specifics in this exposition. Today, XML is the prime candidate for delivery of information to an application [8]. Its hierarchical structure supports a useful model, as described in section "Modeling the Knowledge in a Mediator". Early applications often used CORBA [46]. It is important to note that there is no need for a user-friendly interface for mediators, at this level we need a machine- and communication-friendly interface.

For obtaining information from the data resources one has to adapt to what is available: SQL, XML, OQL, search engines, data mining programs, etc. [31]. Wrappers are needed to achieve commonality.

By formalizing and implementing mediation a partitioned information systems architecture is created. The modules are now internally consistent, of manageable complexity, and, in combination, can deliver the power that technology makes available. The partitions and modules map into the distributed hardware concepts of servers, webservices, and clouds.

Complex Architectures

Structuring mediators themselves into hierarchies should not lead to problems. Low-level mediators only have knowledge about database or information resource contents, and understand little about application domain semantics. High-level mediators may take on well-defined decision-making functions as expected from staff in human organizations. The experts that control such mediators must be willing take on corresponding responsibilities.

There are also secondary roles for mediators. Search ad discovery mediators can inspect and propose mediators for application use. Such service discovery is envisaged for web-based service, but even assuring that the required metadata is available within a single domain is a daunting problem [5].

In general, it is wise to gain experience with simple architectures, before starting to generalize concepts and create layers that make systems hard to understand. Keeping the structure of any application system clear to the users engenders trust. In any extant application domains human experts and agents are available today that perform the task manually. To gain manageability organizations are willing to structure and constrain interactions among its members, even at some lost-opportunity cost. Similarly, it is wise to impose constraints on the broad information systems we wish to deploy.

From Facts to Knowledge

We must introduce some definitions for this chapter, since the world of information technology (IT) has become so broad that identical terms are used – and misused – in a variety of contexts, often obvious to the reader, but confusing when trying to build semantic bridges.

Databases are best viewed as retainers of observed and recorded facts. Ideally each stored data value should be verifiable by comparing it with a real-world artifact. In practice observations and recording is imprecise, has occurred in the past, so that validation becomes impossible. Ideally any data element should have a timestamp associated with it [30]. But that ideal is rarely reached.

Having access to facts is a prerequisite for information processing, but other resources exist as well. Most databases also contain summary data, aggregations computed by their owners. The volume of all the detail may have been overwhelming, or the factual detail was not be relevant to the prime user of the database. Since a single source database would live within a single context, there should be few problems due to semantics, and all users can accept all if its contents as facts.

There are databases that have been built only by combining data from disparate databases. We regard them as less trustworthy, as was shown using some analyses performed on the CIA factbook [28]. The convenience of using such aggregated databases – everything you want to know is in one place, is offset by errors due to temporal inconsistencies, changes in classification, and simplistic semantics. We will cite some problems encountered later as examples of mediation tasks.

Information is created when data are being processed, such processing requires knowledge. Having knowledge is primarily a human capability, but can be encoded in programs. Common operations are summarizations, here knowledge is needed about the structure of that data. Should facts about sales be aggregated by location, by type, by producer, or by customer? What is information is hence determined by the receiver. The technical definition if information [51] is yet more narrow: information should be novel to the reader, otherwise it is of no import.

Indeed, stored information does little good until it is transmitted to a reader who can exploit it. Then information will augment the readers' knowledge, and perhaps cause the reader, if in the role of a decision maker, to initiate some action.

Information can also be further processed, creating information further removed from the source of the data and subjected to more assumptions, based on the knowledge of any intermediaries. The representation of information changes during such processing, typically becoming more complex and less amenable to simple aggregation. Information in the form of written text, such as this article, is very far removed from its many sources, We try to validate it by giving references, but tracking all the real world facts that contributed to it is impossible, although a topic of current research [43]. The intent of this article is to contribute to the readers' knowledge, and it depends on their prior knowledge how much of the information will augment that knowledge.

Knowledge is required to process data or information. It is acquired by learning. Learning from existing text is attractive, but hard. For human processing the limits are education and to some extent their ability to profit from education. Programs are the prime means for representing knowledge in computing, but maintaining knowledge in that form is painful and costly to update [15]. The choice of computable representations for knowledge remains a prime issue of artificial-intelligence research; it is inextricably bound to the processing algorithms that operate on those representations. Mediators do embody knowledge to carry out their functions. In mediators that knowledge is focused and domain specific, making it easier to represent and maintain. Mediators can learn during their operation from the data they access.

Actionable information is information that actually causes a decision-maker to carry out an action, as purchasing something, choosing among alternative in an operation, investing in a new venture, or even abandoning an ongoing project. It is only when information becomes actionable, i.e., does more than just increase one's knowledge, that economic value is generated. Previously received information increased the decision-maker's knowledge, enabling the capability to understand the crucial increment of information. Without prior knowledge actionable information will be lost.

We summarize these definitions below:

Concept	Definition
Data	Recorded facts about the state of the work
Information	Data or processed data not currently known to the recipient
Knowledge	Personal or encoded information that can drive processing of data or information
Actionable information	Information, that when combined with knowledge can be used to change the state of the world

In some settings direct access to fact-based data does not exist. Then low-level information is treated as data.

Since people have a limited capacity to retain knowledge, some information will just help them to recall what they should have known. In general it is easier for us to record facts we don't want to lose as information, and then trust that our processing capabilities will reconstruct the knowledge.

There is also information that amuses, and as such is worthwhile. Being able to recall useless knowledge can be source of pride. But, for a business information should be potentially actionable, even while it increases one's general knowledge.

There are feedback loops, which when closed, create growth of capabilities. Actionable information leads to actions, say, a purchase of a piece of hardware. That action changes the facts in the world: after some time there is one fewer unit of hardware in the store, and more in your hands. That fact can be recorded, and becomes part of the data cycle. The action will also increase knowledge, immediately because it validates the purchase process you constructed, and over the longer term, as the new piece of hardware satisfies expectations and understanding of its catalog description.

In a business environment, actionable information is easy to recognize.

- A factory manager needs sales data to set production levels.
- A sales manager needs demographic information to project future sales.
- A customer wants price and quality information to make purchase choices.
- A manager of a healthcare plan has to balance investments in preventive, urgent, episodic, and palliative care.

Most of the information needed by the people in these examples can be derived from factual data and should be available on some computer somewhere. Communication networks can make data available wherever it is needed. However, to make the decisions, it must be transformed to manageable volumes of actionable information, a considerable amount of knowledge has to be applied as well. Today, most knowledge resides within the administrative and technical staff in an institution, and human-mediated intermediate steps are interposed between the databases and the decision makers [56].

Conceptual Principles

Knowing that information exists in the myriad of resources available on the Internet creates high expectations by end-users. Finding that it is not available in a useful form or that it cannot be combined with other data creates confusion and frustration. The task of mediators is to provide functionalities that extract actionable information for those resources.

> Mediators embody in software functionality that selects, transforms, aggregates, integrates, and summarizes data from multiple sources, in order to support information needs of decision makers.

While this is an ambitious statement there are simplifying conditions that make the creation and maintenance of mediators feasible.

One-Directional Flow

We expect mediators only to process data only in one direction, towards the end users. Since we assume that the sources are truly independent, the consumers have no authority to alter them. If inconsistencies are found they will have to be reported to the decision-making programs. Mediators may include knowledge about the credibility of the sources, and uses such information to select or weigh the trust in the information. Trust affects the preference for selecting data sources.

It is up to the receivers to provide feedback to inconsistent sources, if they desire. Often inconsistencies are a natural outcome of the sources having different origins, and no feedback is needed. For instance, if one source obtains more recent data, it will be preferred, and only major inconsistencies will be of concern.

Delegation of Technical Incompatibilities

So that mediators, and their creators and maintainers, can concentrate on issues at the semantic level, matching to transmission and representation standards is carried out by lower-level modules, i.e., middleware [3] or specialized wrappers [22]. Textual data especially requires processing that is best delegated [25].

Note that these low-level modules need only support a one-way match at the two interfaces, that of a source and that of the mediator. Where multiple sources have identical interfaces those modules can be reused or replicated. There is no need to support n-way interaction at this lower level.

Limiting Scope to Commensurate Semantics

Mediators must carry out reliable computation, so that they can be trusted by the decision maker. That means that data that are inherently not comparable cannot be included in one mediator. An example in healthcare would be cost of patient services and quality of patient services. We expect that in this case two mediators would be required, one managed by the CFO of the institution and the other by the chief medical physician. The financial mediator aggregates cost and revenue detail and presents them as net cost per type of patient. The clinical mediator aggregates the variables that are indicators of quality of care for the patients. The decision-maker receives both types of data and must make the difficult choices in balancing the two objectives. The decision-making application will focus on a clear presentation and rapid assessment of the alternatives being considered. Modeling the decision-maker's reasoning is task beyond the scope of the mediator architecture.

The number of mediators required to serve a decision-making application will vary from one to several. One mediator suffices if all the information being obtained from the sources can be reduced to common units. The number of mediators supporting an decision-making application remains small in practice, since few decision-makers will be able to balance more than several incommensurate inputs. In complex situations there might be hierarchies of decision makers, each receiving input from multiple mediators, perhaps sharing the use of some of them. We have not seen practical examples of such hierarchies.

No Requirement for Automation

No requirements for automatic generation or maintenance are imposed on mediator technology. Having automatic discovery, linking to sources, and adaptation when sources change to facilitate mediation is exciting, but hard. Such automation is the goal of artificial intelligence research, and as progress is made in that arena, that technology should transition [66]. But gaining experience with a new technology is essential for learning how to automate it, and such experience is gained by actual building and maintaining mediators [37].

Much of the logic in mediators can be placed into tables, simplifying ongoing maintenance. In section "Maintenance" of this chapter we discuss what type of maintenance will be required.

What Is Left?

These four conditions listed here limit the issues that mediators and their creators have to deal with. The central, very hard issue remains: the conversion of voluminous data from many disparate and autonomous sources into integrated actionable information. Autonomy implies that no standards enforcing consistency of representation, nor content, nor abstraction level, nor vocabulary can be imposed on the sources. Having consumers of information within a system creates a setting that encourages consistency. Now participants can observe the benefit from consistent semantics. Over time they may adopt standards or at least document the formats, intent, and scope of their data.

Even those four conditions listed are not cast in silicon. Many researchers and some implementers have gone beyond the conditions and worked on extensions of the mediator architecture. Researchers have worked on automated matching, two-way communication, automated knowledge acquisition, and tracking of data. But, in the process of becoming more ambitious, many projects have not covered the basic functionalities that are needed to make mediation effective.

Mediators Versus Data Warehousing

An alternative data integration technology is data warehousing [29]. Warehouses collect data from multiple sources, and will store large volumes. The warehouses maintainers cannot worry greatly about semantic consistency. Submitting queries to a warehouse does not require the costly intermediate processing expected to occur in mediators. However, keeping a warehouse complete and up-to-date also requires costly a priori maintenance, since every change in a contributing database should be reflected in the warehouse. This cost limits the scope of warehouses in practice. Mediators can hence cover a wider range of sources than warehouses, but pay for that by slower execution times.

Conceptually, mediators select the required intersection of the source information, while warehouses provide the union. While mediators are hence quite distinct from data warehousing, it seems feasible to design mixed systems, using warehousing technology for relatively static data and mediators for dynamic information. Mediator queries can be treated similar to warehouse view queries, if the warehouse is consistent [55].

Operations and Managing Volume

A decision-maker can only absorb a modest amount of actionable information at any time. Making all of the underlying sources available in an attempt to produce 'all the possibly relevant information' causes information overload. The role of the mediators is hence to greatly reduce the volume that arrives at the decision maker, while losing little of the information the decision-maker needs.

Reductions in volume are made by

1. Selection of relevant data records to be obtained from the sources.
2. Projection, i.e., selection of relevant columns of the data.
3. Aggregating the selected data to the level of abstraction needed for integration.
4. Reducing the integrated and aggregated data further.
5. Pruning the results to reduce application overload.

If the sources can handle queries at the complexity of SQL, then reduction tasks 1, 2, and 3, can be combined, and the mediator itself will have less data to cope with. For less competent sources a priori reduction of volume is limited to selection and retrieval of relevant records. The sources must inform the creator of the mediator what functionalities are available. For automation, that information must be in machine-processable form, as discussed in section "Modeling the Knowledge in a Mediator" of this chapter (Fig. 1.3).

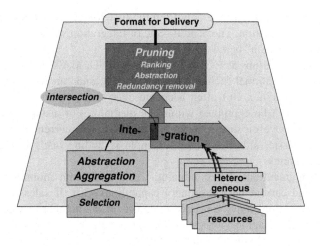

Fig. 1.3 Functionalities within a mediator

Selection and Projection

It is not coincidental that SELECT is the principal operation of relational database management systems, since this their most important functionality. Getting only the relevant rows, or in OO terms, the relevant objects, typically reduces volume by several orders of magnitude, especially for voluminous sources. Sometimes an adequate tactic for providing the required information is sampling [45]. To select from textual sources, selection requires exploiting indexes, limiting retrieval to records where terms intersect, and other relevancy metrics to further reduce the volume [16].

Projection reduces the number of columns or the number of attributes. In a relational setting projection can also reduce the number of rows if key attributes are projected out. Getting rid of key attributes is rare though for early stages of mediating processing, since they are often needed for integration. Often data not needed for the decision maker must be forwarded to the mediator to enable integration. In the end projection may reduce volume by an order of magnitude.

Aggregation

Selected data is typically at too fine a level of detail to be useful for decision making. Especially when the sources are operational databases, where every transaction is logged to assure completeness, the amount of detail is overwhelming. Distinct sources may also provide data at different abstraction levels, say sales data by store from one source and income level by municipality from another source. Aggregation from store to municipality of the data from the first source will be needed prior to combining the information. The central issue of integration will be described in its own section "Integration" below.

Aggregation operations as COUNT, AVERAGE, SD, MAX, MIN, etc., provide within SQL computational facilities for abstraction, and can reduce the volume of input to the mediator. But often adequate query capabilities do not exist and the abstraction must be computed within the mediator. For instance, abstractions that require recursive closures cannot be specified with current database query languages. A classic, although trivial, example is finding one's grandfather via transitivity of parents.

Temporal aggregations, say combining weekly data into monthly summaries are also beyond current database query capabilities [30]. If sales data is to be aggregated, corrections may be needed to adjust for the number of weekends in a specific month. Geographic aggregations present similar problems, say information coded by postal-code versus town-limits [69].

Common computations which convert data to a more useful abstraction are summarization over hierarchies, changing temporal granularity, performing seasonal adjustments, enumerating exceptions, and recursive path computations. Diverse mediator modules will use these functions in various combinations to provide the support for user applications at the decision-making layer.

Abstraction

Abstraction is the process of reducing data to more meaningful units. Abstraction is often required prior to integration, since source data, collected in distinct base systems, will likely differ in representation. After integration, data should be aggregated and abstracted according to the user's information needs

Numeric measures are often too specific to serve decision-making and also are hard to match during integration. It is unlikely that even very similar data will match. Non-essential differences may even due to the precision used or the choice of metrics, as 3.14 versus 3.14159265358979323846264338832795, or 1 mile versus 1.609 km. In general, numeric data is converted to categories, as tiny, small, medium, large, huge. Category breaks may be based on multiples, as 0, 10, 100, 1,000, etc. In medicine the categorization of subjective observations ranges from 0 to 10, for absent to expected death. In general, seven categories provide adequate distinctions [38]. Categorization reduces data volume greatly, but can rarely be requested to be computed within the sources, so that input volume will remain large, and be a major task in mediation.

Categorization criteria are to create groups of roughly equal amounts of contents, as voting districts, or application significance, as *newborns, babies, children, teens, young, middle-aged, senior, old, bedridden*, for healthcare. Middle-age may be defined as age from 30 to 60, and comprise most of the population, but members of this category will all be treated similarly. The selection of categories could be provided by the application. In many application domains there are accepted categorizations

When results are based on historical records, the detail is likely to be voluminous. Detailed historical data often have to be summarized to permit integration, since time intervals have to be mapped. An initial abstraction is to derive temporal interval representations from time-stamped event data. There are two major styles for representing intervals, open and closed, which have to mapped to match; open intervals support further algebraic operations best [67].

Prior to integration, the largest common temporal interval is to be chosen. After integration further abstractions are useful, as determining and combining intervals over periods of growth or improvement versus periods of loss or deterioration. Those intervals can then be parameterized by length, delta, and variance. The applications can then present the reduced results in graphical form [12]. Mediators should not perform the actual conversion to graphics, to allow applications the choice of presentation.

Removing Redundancy After Integration

Integration, described in section "Integration", brings together information from multiple sources. The result is likely to contain redundant information. There will be information only used for matching data elements. For instance, if integration involved matching on price, only the categories need to be retained and monetary amounts, currency designations, and inflation correction factors can be removed. Identical data can obviously be omitted. Some matching may have been performed that required matching fields based on object identity, say the town names of 'Bangalore', now 'Bengaluru'. Again only one entry should be reported, the choice would be based on relevance to the decision maker, typically the most recent one should be provided.

The integrated information may be further aggregated. Then many more columns can be omitted, for instance, all town names if the result is a summary of national software industries.

Ranking

Information for a decision maker can often be ranked, and then results that are ranked low can be omitted from the result, or presented only by specific request. Ranking and pruning also reduces volume greatly; a rule of thumb is that a decision-maker should not be presented with more than seven choices [38]. But such choices should be different in a meaningful way.

For instance, when scheduling travel from Washington, DC to Los Angeles, significantly different alternatives to be presented to a travel application for a given day are:

Alternative S1: UA59: depart IAD 17:10, arrive LAX 19:49.

Alternative S2: UA199: depart IAD 9:25, arrive LAX 11:52.

giving the traveler a choice to get some work done at home or having time to get settled in Los Angeles and avoid airline food. A poor qualitative difference in travel scheduling is shown by:

Alternative P1: UA59: depart IAD 17:10 p.m., arrive LAX 19:49.

Alternative P1: AA75: depart IAD 18:00 p.m., arrive LAX 20:24.

But some travelers may wish alternative rankings, by price, by frequent-flier bonuses, by minimal time in the air, etc. Neither list now includes flights with stopovers. A ranking by price would list them, and perhaps not show pricey non-stop flights at all. It should also include other airports in the Washington and Los Angeles area. A listing of all possible ways to get from Washington to Los Angeles, via any and all U.S. cities within a day would be very long and useless.

When search engines rank results, they have had no input from the users or their applications. A mediator can receive such directions, and since the volume to be ranked is much less, can compute the ranking to order, and comply with the preferences of the application.

Integration

Once source data is at a common conceptual level it can be integrated. If there are no semantic mismatches then the data can be combined, typically creating longer records and bigger objects.

At the integration step relational data are often transformed into object or XML formats [18]. For complex information the redundancy created by relational join operations or their programmed equivalents can be confusing. If the requesting applications can manage information in object format, such a presentation is a better choice.

Heterogeneous Sources

Much of the benefit from combining distinct sources is that in that process valuable information can be generated, information not actionable from the distinct sources by themselves. However, there is no reason that terms from such distinct sources should match. The terms we must be concerned with are [20].

1. Terms used in schemas: SQL column names and XML category names
2. Terms used to identify objects, as database keys and XML entry headers, as names, product identifiers, service types

3. Terms used to match data on criteria other than keys, as location, price, quality, etc.

Terms will likely match when the experts that defined the sources have been educated together or have been communicating over a long time. For instance, in medicine, the use of shared textbooks has created a consistent ontology at common levels. But within specialties and recent topics terminology diverge, as in pathology and genetics.

Import of Heterogeneous Semantics

In simple search and retrieval semantic mismatches are often ignored. Synonyms may be employed to assure broad coverage. Search engines leave the resolution of inconsistencies to the reader.

For the business applications that motivate the building of mediators (and warehouses) the occurrence of mismatches creates problems, especially if the results must be delivered to applications that do not have the insight of human readers. A central issue for mediators used in business is hence the resolution of heterogeneous semantics.

Four Common Types of Mismatches

1. **Synonyms** present the simplest problem. The country which is formally The Netherlands is also referred to as Holland. Gambia is listed formally as The Gambia. Name changes can also be seen as synonyms, as Mumbai and Bombay. Simple tables can match these entries. Some matches are context dependent. The airport for Basel, a Swiss city, is located in France, at Mulhouse. Old documents refer to that town as Mullhausen.
2. **Homonyms**, the use of the same letter sequence for different objects, are the bane of search engines. China is both a country and dinnerware. But the domain constraints in mediation resolve those problems, since relevant sources will be distinct. Attaching the domain or column name to a term can keep terms distinct if there is a chance of false matches.
3. **Differences in scope** are best resolved by prior aggregation. For instance information on Czechoslovakia now requires aggregation of the Czech Republic and Slovakia. To avoid losing information an object with subsets for the two current parts may be created. If historical data for Slovakia only is needed, then its eight lower level component regions have to be aggregated when those regions were reported with Czechoslovakia.
4. **Inconsistent overlaps** are the hardest to deal with. A personnel file, showing the human resources available to a company may list contract consultants that

do not appear on the payroll, since those consultants are reimbursed by contract charges. The payroll file may list retired employees, who are paid pensions, but those are no longer part of personnel. Rules to resolve such mismatches depend on the objective of the mediator results. If the average pay of active workers is needed, retired employees should be omitted, but consultants should be included with an equivalent pay rate.

The resolution of such mismatches often requires obtaining data from the sources that will not be needed as part of the delivered results. After integration such data can be omitted, reducing the volume of information delivered to the decision maker. Some sources may be used only to provide data to enable a match, say a table that links salary levels to employee ranking.

Futility of Fixing the Sources

Integrators often blame the sources for being inconsistent. But those sources must first of all satisfy their primary objectives, as getting checks into the mail for the payroll, or locating employees that can perform certain tasks for the personnel file. More insidious are differences in data quality in distinct sources. The payroll file may not keep the employees work location with care, and the personnel file may ignore errors in the social security number. The count of a workers' children should be the actual number in the personnel file, but the payroll just keeps a number for tax deductions.

Researchers on webservices have implied that they will be truly successful when all sources become consistent [2]. But such a state is actually not globally desirable. The quality of a source depends on the competency and interest of its maintainers. A project oriented towards billing for healthcare services cannot be relied on to give a full account of diagnoses and clinical problems encountered in a case. The billing personnel cannot be forced to improve their data, and getting clinical personnel involved in improving billing data will be very costly and not help the institution.

In general, it is not feasible to impose on autonomous sources a requirement to report information to a depth that is not within their scope. A blog by a homeowner can talk about what nails were used in a project, perhaps stating their size and shape. A carpenter uses many specific words: *sinker, boxnail, brad,* etc. Enforcing a common vocabulary is futile and will, in the end, lead to loss of information.

Public data sources often restrict themselves to aggregated data in order to protect privacy of respondents. No recourse exists to fix such databases, although often the data maybe biased or incomplete. When the objective is understood, say to convince people to support some political initiatives, the likely bias has to be taken into account.

Mediating Knowledge

Mediators, because of their focus on commensurate domains and the intersection of the source data, provide an opportunity to deal effectively with heterogeneous semantics. If the application area to be supported already used information from both sources, then there was typically an expert who understood the intersection.

The knowledge of the expert can then be used to devise rules that handle problems due to having synonyms and scope overlap. If data from two sources appear to be redundant an expert will know which source is more trustworthy.

Such rules are best incorporated in rules that can be inspected by all the participants. The maintenance of such knowledge should be assigned as well, best to the specific experts on the intersecting domains. At times a committee may be required, but in general having a committee slows the process of rule maintenance. If the assignment to a committee is too broad then it is likely that compromises will be made and that precision will be lost. Such loss of precision has been seen in warehouse maintenance, where source heterogeneity is not constrained by domain limits.

Rules devised for mediation should be validated by going back to the source databases. Applying rules devised to obtain a consistent scope to each of the sources should create a perfect match [65]. If the databases are large, just obtaining counts of the matches provides a validation. Since databases always have errors, having differences on the order of a few percent may not invalidate the rule, but it will be useful to check those exceptions. Sometimes one will find surprisingly large differences. The reason should be tracked down and an additional rule devised. For instance, in one case highway patrol records and vehicle registration records did not match. It turned out that the cause was that the vehicle registrations included boats. Obtaining another data element and adding a rule to the mediator restricted the match to roadworthy vehicles.

Keeping Incommensurate Information Distinct

For a mediator to be trustworthy requires that it does not try to integrate data that are intrinsically incomparable. In general, balancing cost factors, expressed in monetary units, and quality, expressed in terms of customer satisfaction, should be handled by two distinct mediators. Both can integrate data, sharing some sources, each using its own metrics. The decision maker will receive both types of information. Understanding how costs, incurred now, will affect customers' perception of product quality over time, is a task best not automated.

Exploiting Human Capabilities

To build a mediator, knowledge is needed from diverse sources. A top-level expert will be used to working with abstractions that are not sufficiently precise to allow constructing effective mediators. But human knowledge is effective at all levels. The required knowledge is related to the roles that humans perform in the processing of information:

(a) A technician will know how to select and transfer data from a remote computer to one used for analysis, such information is essential for constructing wrappers.
(b) A data analyst will understand the attributes of the data and define the functions to combine and integrate the data [11].
(c) Agents often deal with integration: A travel agent will be able to match airports and cities, a hardware store customer requests and stock-on-hand, a broker with monetary units and values [60].
(d) A statistician can provide trustworthy procedures to aggregate data on customers into groups that present distinctive behavior patterns [50].
(e) A psychologist may provide classification parameters that characterize such groups.
(f) An experienced manager has to assess the validity of the classifications that have been made, forward the information to allow the making of a decision, and assume the risk of that information is adequate to the task.
(g) A public relations person may take the information and present it in a manner that can be explained to the stockholders, to whom the risk is eventually distributed.

In the process of constructing the mediator, much knowledge is obtained and recorded. That knowledge remains available for maintenance. The mediator provides a corporate memory, one of the goals of corporate knowledge management, in a focused and more thorough fashion [24].

Uncertainty

Abstraction and integration introduce uncertainty. Some source data, especially if they include projections about the future, are inherently uncertain. Observations and their representations also induce uncertainties. Researchers in artificial intelligence have dealt with many aspects of these issues [21]. A variety of methods to represent uncertainty are available, based on differences in domain semantics. Perhaps all uncertainty computation can be subsumed by probabilistic reasoning [6]. Uncertainty increases during integration of information [13]. Only recently has traditional database research attempted to integrate uncertainty into its processing model [43].

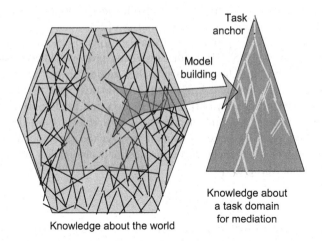

Task anchor

Model building

Knowledge about a task domain for mediation

Knowledge about the world

Fig. 1.4 Knowledge for task modeling

Mediators should be able to obtain data from sources, use provided or external ancillary data to establish confidence ranges, integrate the results, including metrics of confidence, and provide those results to the decision-makers. Decision-makers are used to operating with uncertainty, since they typically must project the findings into the future, using their knowledge, information from databases, spreadsheets, planning tools, etc. These tools still await effective integration [64]. Decision-makers also obtain advice from colleagues, and likely employ some intuition, a reason why the final phase can typically not be automated.

Modeling the Knowledge in a Mediator

The knowledge required for mediation can either be explicitly programmed, formulated as rules, or encoded in decision table. The conditions placed on a mediator in section "Conceptual Principles" also simplify a formal knowledge representation. Mediators have a specific, application-oriented objective. While unconstrained knowledge requires a complex network representation, the knowledge needed to support a specific task domain can typically be represented in a hierarchical manner, as sketched in Fig. 1.4. The application task provides the anchor which becomes the root for the hierarchy and the criteria for subsequent matches [40]. Object oriented technology and XML schemas are adequate to structure the required knowledge.

Much of the knowledge collected when designing a mediator is not formally captured when mediators are implemented by code [32]. Entity-relationship models can provide some formal documentation, but ignore semantic differences [7]. The use of rule engines allows representation of rules in a consistent formalism [35]. These can then be interpreted by engines as CLIPS [26].

Ontologies, if available, provide the meta-data for the description of data and information resources [19, 52]. If distinct resources have associated ontologies, the discovery of semantic matches and mismatches among distinct resources can be facilitated and partially automated [53]. The technologies match those that are used for ontology-based integration [44]. For mediation one needs only to obtain the candidate intersections, and human pruning is desirable to limit the number of articulations and avoid unnecessary complexity. As the semantic web develops, more resources will have adequate ontologies, and automation of model-based mediation can make progress [9].

Sharability of Mediator Knowledge

The mediator modules will be most effective if they can serve a variety of applications [23]. The applications will compose their tasks as much as possible by acquiring information from the set of available mediators. Unavailable information may motivate the creation of new mediators.

The mediation module which can deal with inflation adjustment can be used by many applications. The mediation which understands postal codes and town names can be used by the post office, delivery services, and corporate mail rooms.

Sharing reinforces the benefits of vertical partitioning into domains. A mediator which only deals with commensurate data can be maintained by an appropriate and trusted expert. The knowledge inserted and maintained in such a mediator will be reused by many applications. Just as databases are justified by the shared usage they receive, sharable mediators will justify an investment in formally capturing knowledge.

Trusting the Mediator

An important, although not essential, requirement on mediators is that they can be inspected by the potential users. Much depends here on the knowledge representation. A coded mediator can have an associated description, but code documentation is notorious for being deficient and poorly maintained. When software is being reused, uncertainties arise, if the original designers made assumptions that will not match the new context.

Having formal models, inherent when rule-systems are in use, will enhance the trustworthiness of a mediator. For instance, the rules used by a mediator using expert system technology can be inspected by a potential user [57]. Still, having access to the human maintainer of the mediator seems to be essential. Providing knowledge for information systems by maintaining may be a viable business, but that has not been proven. The expectation that Internet services should be free hinders the development of quality services that require ongoing expenses.

Maintenance

To allow systems to survive over time they must be able to deal with continuing change. Data change over time because the world evolves and knowledge changes over time because we learn things about our world. Rules that were valid once eventually become riddled with exceptions, and a specialist who does not adapt will find his work to become without value. Any information system must deal explicitly with data and knowledge maintenance.

In mediation the data remains in the resources and will be changed independently. But knowledge is required to access, process, and assess those data sources. We know that software maintenance has annual costs of about 15 % of the initial investment. While distinct mediators may share software tools, their uniqueness is in the knowledge about the resources and the domain they process. It is likely that mediator maintenance, even if software is shared, will require similar expenditures to maintain that knowledge. Keeping mediating modules focused, small, and simple will allow their maintenance to be performed by one expert or at most by a coherent group of experts. In that manner the problems now encountered in maintaining large integrated information systems are ameliorated.

Triggers for Knowledge Maintenance

Since the knowledge in the mediator must be kept up-to-date, it will be wise for mediators to place triggers or active demons into the databases or their wrappers [54]. Now the mediators can be informed when the database, and, by extension, the real-world changes. Induction from triggers carries an excessive cost when any state-change must be forwarded through all possible forward chains. For most changes immediate relevance to a user is unlikely. By not carrying induction through to the decision-making layer, but terminating forward chaining in the mediator, that cost can be reduced [47]. Having intermediate results available in the mediator avoids excessive latency during inquiry. The owner of the mediator should ensure that structural and semantic changes are in time reflected in the mediator's knowledge base.

In a rule-base mediator the certainty factor of some rule can be adjusted. If the uncertainty exceeds a threshold, the mediator can advise its creator, the domain expert, to abandon this rule. The end-user need not get involved [49].

Eventually mediators may be endowed with learning mechanisms. Feedback for learning may either come from performance measures [27] or from explicit induction over the databases they manage [68].

Related Topics

Mediation, just as information technology in general, impinges on many topics of system sciences. We will touch on them briefly in this section, but for discussion in depth other sources must be studied.

Private Versus Public Mediation

Mediation provides a means of portioning information systems by level and by domain. Effective maintenance should be a major benefit, but required maintenance efforts must be assigned and supported. When mediators are constructed, specialists contribute their knowledge about data resources in a manner that applications can effectively share the information. That knowledge may pertain to public or private resources. If the capabilities of the mediators provide a competitive advantage they may well be kept private, even if the mediators access public resources. Such knowledge formalizes the corporate memory, and some mediation technology has in fact been used to capture knowledge of experts that were about to retire.

There may be an incentive for independent specialists to develop powerful, but broadly useful mediators, which can be used by multiple customers. Placing one's knowledge into a mediator will allow rapid exploitation of one's knowledge, and perhaps more rewarding, the writing of a book on the topic.

Partioning Versus Centralization

Mediators are oriented towards partitioning of function and knowledge. In that sense they do not follow the database paradigm, where larger often implies better. While warehouses can provide rapid access to massive data collections, they do not deal well with dynamic data and information. And, the knowledge required to understand the data remains outside of the warehouse managers.

Partitioning that knowledge avoids the knowledge centralization, and the associated bureaucracy that ensues when a notion of having corporate information centers is promoted [1]. It will be impossible to staff a single center, or a single mediator for that matter, with experts that can deal with all the varieties of information that is useful for corporate decision-making.

Security and Privacy

Mediators gain access to much information, some of which should be protected. The summarization process greatly reduces linkages to individual source data, and can protect privacy. But assuring that such privacy is protected requires first of all that the mediator, which accesses such data, is kept secure, and that the aggregation is sufficient so that no incriminating identifications escape. Assuring a priori that no results can be used to infer individual source data fatally weakens information processing over irregular data [34]. In a mediator dynamic functions can be implemented that analyze results and adapt aggregations to assure privacy protection [63]. For this function, since a high level of security is required, a distinct mediator should be employed, adding a layer to the architecture.

Efficiency and Reliability

In actual systems efficiency is always a concern. Each layer in a mediated system should add enough value to overcome the cost of an interface. Standard techniques as caching will be effective where data change less rapidly than application requests. Use of a local warehouse for static data is the ultimate cache. Since information emanating from a mediator has much less volume, the caches can be much smaller than the source information.

In pure mediation every component has to work for the system to work. Mediators can easily be copied and executed at alternate sites. Caches, warehouses, and redundant sources can provide backup when source resources are not available. If the sources cannot be accessed, the delivered data should be identified as being out-of-date. Requirements of data security may impose further constraints. Dealing with trusted mediators, however, may encourage database owners to participate in information sharing to a greater extent than they would if all participants would need to be granted file-level access privileges.

Summary

Information systems are becoming available now with the capabilities envisaged by Vannevar Bush for his MEMEX [4]. We can discover and retrieve documents kept in remote repositories. We can present the values on one of multiple windows. We can select and scroll information on our workstations, we can copy documents into our files, and we can annotate text and graphics. We can reach conclusions based on this evidence and advise others of decisions made [59].

But actual integration of information, beyond simple data aggregation, as needed for decision-making support, is still uncommon [61]. Most actual decision makers depend on human analysts to provide summaries, aggregate information, and rank and present recommendations. A variety of staff and colleagues peruse files and prepare summarizations and documentation, aided by databases, statistical tools, spreadsheets, etc. The associated tedium means that decisions, once made, are

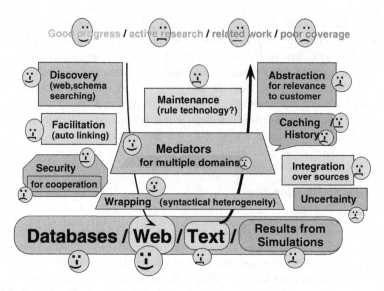

Good progress / active research / related work / poor coverage

Fig. 1.5 State of meditation technology

rarely withdrawn, even if facts, documented in updated databases, would indicate otherwise [62].

Mediators are information processing modules that transform source data from distinct sources into actionable information. They automate a process within decision-making support that mimics activities carried out manually. The intent of the architectural model is not to be exclusive and rigid. It is intended to provide a common framework under which many new technologies can be accommodated.

By automating the function within mediators such tasks are automated, and can be performed rapidly when the need arises, allowing the decision-makers to have access to the most recent information. The rules that drive mediation can often be obtained form experts that carried out such tasks in the past. Figure 1.5 conveys an impression of the current state of Mediation technology. As the systems become larger, responsiveness and efficiency must be addressed, but this issue is shared with the entire database community.

The resolution of semantics using terms from diverse sources is a task without end. That does not mean that no progress has or will be made. It is just that, as we learn to deal with one level of issues, further, finer shades of meaning become visible. The knowledge-based paradigms inherent in intelligent mediators indicate the critical role of artificial intelligence technology foreseen when implementing mediators. Mediators may be strengthened by having learning capability. Derived information may simply be stored in a mediator. Learning can also lead to new tactics of data acquisition and control of processing.

The technologies and issues presented in this chapter are and will be seen in many information systems, independent of the names and architectures used. In any case, a clear focus and organization can make such information systems effective, reliable, and maintainable.

References

The references chosen are biased, because they are derived from work that we are familiar with. More references can be found in the cited works.

1. Atre S (1986) Information center: strategies and case studies, vol 1. Atre International Consultants, Rye
2. Berners-Lee T, Hendler J, Lassila O (2001) The semantic web. Sci Am 284:28–37
3. Bernstein PA (1996) Middleware: a model for distributed services. Commun ACM 39(2): 86–97
4. Bush V (1945) As we may think. Atl Mon 176(1):101–108
5. Caceres C, Fernadez A, Oosowski S, Vasirami M (2006) Agent-based semantic service discovery for healthcare: an organizational approach. IEEE Intell Syst 31(6):11–20
6. Cheeseman P (1985) In defense of probability. In: Proceedings of the IJCAI, Los Angeles. AAAI, pp 1002–1009
7. Chen MC, McNamee L (1989) A data model and access method for summary data management. In: IEEE international conference on data engineering, Los Angeles, vol 5
8. Connolly D (ed.) (1997) XML: principles, tools, and techniques. O'Reilly, Sebastopol, CA
9. Davies J, Fensel D, van Harmelen F (2003) Towards the semantic web: ontology-driven knowledge. Wiley, Hoboken, NJ
10. Decker S, Hauswirth M (2008) Enabling networked knowledge. In: Comparative information agents, Prague. Springer, Berlin, pp 1–15
11. DeMichiel L (1989) Performing operations over mismatched domains. IEEE Trans Knowl Data Eng 1(4):485–493
12. DeZegher-Geets I, Freeman AG, Walker MG, Blum RL, Wiederhold G (1988) Summarization and display of on-line medical records. M.D. Comput 5(3):38–46
13. Fagin R (1999) Combining fuzzy information from multiple systems. J Comput Syst Sci 58(1):83–99. Academic
14. Furht B, Escalante A (2010) Handbook of cloud computing. Springer, New York
15. Glass RL (2003) Facts and fallacies of software engineering. Addison Wesley, Boston
16. Grossman DA, Frieder O (2004) Information retrieval, algorithms and heuristics. Springer, Dordrecht
17. Gruber TR (1995) Toward principles for the design of ontologies used for knowledge sharing. Int J Human Comput Stud 43(4–5):907–928
18. Grust T, van Keulen M, Teubner J (2004) Accelerating XPath evaluation in any RDBMS. ACM Trans Database Syst 29:91–131
19. Guarino N (1998) Formal ontology in information systems. IOS, Amsterdam
20. Halevy AY, Ives ZG, Suciu D, Tatarinov I (2003) Schema mediation in peer data management systems. In: Proceedings of the 19th international conference on data engineering, Bangalore. IEEE, Piscataway, pp 505–516
21. Halpern JY, Koller D (2004) Representation dependence in probabilistic inference. J Artif Intell Res 21:319–356
22. Hammer J, Garcia-Molina H, Nestorov S, Yerneni R, Breunig M, Vassalos V (1997) Template-based wrappers in the TSIMMIS system. In: Proceedings of the ACM SIGMOD international conference on management of data, Tucson. ACM, New York, pp 532–535
23. Hayes-Roth F (1984) The knowledge-based expert system: a tutorial. IEEE Comput 17:11–28
24. Holsapple C (ed) (2004) Handbook on knowledge management: international handbooks on information systems. Springer, Berlin
25. Ipeirotis PG, Agichtein E, Jain P, Gravano L (2006) To search or to crawl? Towards a query optimizer for text-centric tasks. In: ACM SIGMOD, Chicago
26. Jackson P (1999) Introduction to expert systems, 3rd edn. Addison Wesley Longman, Harlow, UK
27. Jain R (1991) The art of computer systems performance analysis. Wiley, New York

28. Jannink J, Pichai S, Verheijen D, Wiederhold G (1998) Encapsulation and composition of ontologies. In: Proceedings of the AAAI summer conference, Madison. AAAI
29. Jarke M (2003) Fundamentals of data warehousing. Springer, Berlin
30. Jensen CS, Snodgrass RT (1999) Temporal data management. IEEE Trans Knowl Data Eng 11(1):36–44
31. Kim W (ed) (1995) Modern database systems: the object model, interoperability and beyond. ACM/Addison Wesley, New York/Reading
32. Knoblock C, Minton S, Ambite JL, Ashish N, Muslea I, Philpot A, Tejada S (2001) The ARIADNE approach to web-based information integration. Int J Cooperative Inf Syst 10(1–2):145–169
33. Koller D, Halpern JY (1992) A logic for approximate reasoning. In: Proceedings of the third international conference on principles of knowledge representation and reasoning (KR), Cambridge, MA, pp 153–164
34. Lin Z, Owen AB, Altman RB (2004) Genomic research and human subject privacy. Science 305(5681):183
35. Maluf DA, Wiederhold G (1997) Abstraction of representation for interoperation. In: Ras Z, Skowron A (eds) Foundations of intelligent systems. Lecture notes in computer science, vol 1315. Springer, Berlin/Heidelberg
36. McIlraith S, Son TC, Zeng H (2001) Semantic web services. IEEE Intell Syst 16(2):46
37. Melnik S, Garcia-Molina H, Paepcke A (2000) A mediation infrastructure for digital library services. In: Proceedings of the fifth ACM conference on digital libraries, San Antonio. ACM, New York
38. Miller G (1956) The magical number seven ± two. Psychol Rev 68:81–97
39. Mitra P, Wiederhold G (1994) An ontology-composition algebra. In: Proceedings of 1994 Monterey workshop on formal methods, Monterey, pp 93–113
40. Mitra P, Wiederhold G, Kersten M (2000) A graph-oriented model for articulation of ontology interdependencies. In: Zaniolo C et al (eds) Extending database technologies. Lecture notes in computer science, vol 1777. Springer, Berlin
41. Mork P, Rosenthal A, Seligman LJ, Korb J, Samuel K (2006) Integration workbench: integrating schema integration tools. In: ICDE workshops IEEE, Atlanta, p 3
42. Muslea I, Minton S, Knoblock C (1999) A hierarchical approach to wrapper induction. In: Third international conference on autonomous agents, Seattle. ACM, New York, pp 190–197,
43. Mutsuzaki M, Theobald M, de Keijzer A, Widom J et al (2007) Trio-one: layering uncertainty and lineage on a conventional DBMS. In: Proceedings of the CIDR conference, Asilomar. VLDB Foundation
44. Noy NF, Musen MA (2000) PROMPT: algorithm and tool for automated ontology merging and alignment. In: Proceedings of the national conference on artificial intelligence, Austin. AAAI
45. Olken F, Rotem D (1986) Simple random sampling from relational databases. In: VLDB 12, Kyoto
46. OMG (1991) The common object request Broker: architecture and specification (CORBA). Report 91.12.1, The Object Management Group
47. Orman L (1988) Functional development of database applications. IEEE Trans Softw Eng 14(9):1280–1292
48. Prabhu CSR (1992) Semantic database systems. Universities Press, Hyderabad
49. Risch T (1989) Monitoring database objects. In: Proceedings of the VLDB 15, Amsterdam. Morgan Kaufmann, Palo Alto
50. Rowe N (1983) An expert system for statistical estimates on databases. In: Proceedings of the AAAI, Washington, DC
51. Shannon CE, Weaver W (1948) The mathematical theory of computation. Reprinted by The University of Illinois Press (1962)
52. Staab S, Studer R (eds) (2004, 2009) Handbook on ontologies. Springer, Berlin
53. Staab S, Schnurr H-P, Studer R, Sure Y (2001) Knowledge processes and ontologies. IEEE Intell Syst 16(1):26–34

54. Stonebraker M, Rowe LA (1986) The design of POSTGRES. In: Proceedings of the ACM SIGMOD'86, Washington, DC, pp 340–355
55. Ullman JD (2000) Information integration using logical views. Theor Comput Sci. 239: 189–210. Elsevier
56. Waldrop MM (1984) The intelligence of organizations. Science 225(4667):1136–1137
57. Wick MR, Slagle JR (1989) An explanation facility for today's expert systems. IEEE Expert 4(1):26–36
58. Wiederhold G (1992) Mediators in the architecture of future information systems. IEEE Comput 25(3):38–49
59. Wiederhold G (ed) (1996) Intelligent integration of information. Kluwer, Boston
60. Wiederhold G (1999) Mediation to deal with Heterogeneous data sources. In: Vckovski A, Brassel KE, Schek H-J (eds) Interoperating geographic information systems. Lecture notes in computer science, vol 1580. Springer, Berlin, pp 1–16
61. Wiederhold G (2000) Future needs in integration of information. Int J Cooperative Inf Syst 9(4):449–472. Intelligent integration of information. World Scientific
62. Wiederhold G (2000) Information systems that really support decision-making. J Intell Inf Syst 14:85–94. Kluwer
63. Wiederhold G (2001) Collaboration requirements: a point of failure in protecting information. IEEE Trans Syst Man Cybern 31(4):336–342
64. Wiederhold G (2002) Information systems that also project into the future. In: Bhalla S (ed) Proceedings of the second international workshop on databases in networked information systems, Aizu. Lecture notes in computer science, vol 2544. Springer, New York, pp 1–14
65. Wiederhold G (2002) Obtaining precision when integrating information. In: Filipe J, Sharp B, Miranda P (eds) Enterprise information systems III. Kluwer, Dordrecht
66. Wiederhold G, Genesereth M (1997) The conceptual basis for mediation services. IEEE Expert 12(5):38–47
67. Wiederhold G, Jajodia S, Litwin W (1993) Integrating temporal data in a heterogenous environment. In: Tansel A, Clifford J, Gadia S, Jajodia S, Segiv A, Snodgrass R (eds) Temporal databases, theory, design and implementation. Benjamin Cummins, Redwood City, pp 563–579
68. Wilkins DC, Clancey WJ, Buchanan BJ (1987) Knowledge base refinement by monitoring abstract control knowledge. Int J Man Mach Stud 27:281–293
69. Wolfson O, Mena E (2005) Applications of moving objects databases. In: Spatial databases. Idea, Hershey, pp 186–203

Chapter 2
A Combination Framework for Exploiting the Symbiotic Aspects of Process and Operational Data in Business Process Optimization

Sylvia Radeschütz, Holger Schwarz, Marko Vrhovnik, and Bernhard Mitschang

Abstract A profound analysis of all relevant business data in a company is necessary for optimizing business processes effectively. Current analyses typically run either on business process execution data or on operational business data. Correlations among the separate data sets have to be found manually under big effort. However, to achieve a more informative analysis and to fully optimize a company's business, an efficient consolidation of all major data sources is indispensable. Recent matching algorithms are insufficient for this task since they are restricted either to schema or to process matching. We present a new matching framework to (semi-)automatically combine process data models and operational data models for performing such a profound business analysis. We describe the algorithms and basic matching rules underlying this approach as well as an experimental study that shows the achieved high recall and precision.

Introduction

"Information integration is a vibrant field powered not only by engineering innovation but also by evolution of the problem itself" [2]. The increasing number of web services available within an organization raises a new integration task: The warehousing and analysis of processes for fast adaption and optimization of processes [25]. However, these methods usually fall short or require significant manual labor [5] when it comes to integrating process data with related operational data from other business applications such as ERP systems. For example, when trying to optimize the process of a car rental company illustrated in Fig. 2.1, a highly relevant question to a business analyst is: How do trainings and work experience

S. Radeschütz (✉) · H. Schwarz · M. Vrhovnik · B. Mitschang
Universität Stuttgart (IPVS), Stuttgart, Germany
e-mail: sylvia.radeschutz@ipvs.uni-stuttgart.de; holger.schwarz@ipvs.uni-stuttgart.de; marko.vrhovnik@ipvs.uni-stuttgart.de; bernhard.mitschang@ipvs.uni-stuttgart.de

T. Özyer et al. (eds.), *Information Reuse and Integration in Academia and Industry*,
DOI 10.1007/978-3-7091-1538-1_2, © Springer-Verlag Wien 2013

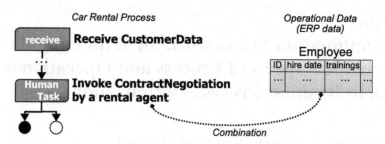

Fig. 2.1 Combination of process and operational data

affect the execution time as well as the outcome of the rental process? Answering this question requires both process data (execution data, paths taken) as well as operational data related to the employee executing the *ContractNegotiation* activity in the process (hire date, trainings). In such a situation, an effective integration of ERP data with process data makes a valuable contribution by ensuring that all relevant data is taken into account.

Our approach provides a solution to this matching problem combining process data models with operational data models of a company. It is novel, because it goes beyond mere schema or process matching. Instead, operational data models are matched with process data models. Content and structure of process models and audit trails that record process data significantly vary from operational data models, which adds complexity to the matching task. Thus, typical schema matching rules will fail. In order to distinguish our approach from these classical matching rules, we call our approach "combination". In particular, the main contributions of this paper are:

- We introduce a combination framework for processes and operational data and explain its processing pipeline covering pairing and filtering steps.
- We elaborate on the main steps of the processing pipeline and the used set of combination rules. This includes rules that are specific to the combination steps as they consider process structures (e.g. process variables as well as control and data flow structures underlying a process) and schema structures.
- Our rules benefit from the technologies developed for semantic web services and reuse their semantic annotations for variables. The fact that a standard for annotating messages and services is available [24] emphasizes the pragmatics of our approach.
- We discuss the benefits of the combination framework and describe a detailed experimental evaluation. The evaluation shows that our technology provides both high recall and high precision.

This paper extends the work presented in [16] regarding the following aspects: More details related to the combination framework and the main steps of the processing pipeline are presented. Concerning the pairing and the filtering phase, the focus of this paper is on the algorithms that allow to efficiently apply the combination rules. Furthermore, additional experimental results as well as a more extensive discussion of related work are covered here.

The paper is organized as follows: In section "Related Work", we discuss related work. We introduce our combination framework in section "Combination Framework" and illustrate main aspects by means of an extensive sample scenario. Sections "Pairing" and "Filtering" introduce the rules and algorithms for the pairing and filter phase. In section "Evaluation", we discuss the benefits of the combination framework and present experimental results, before section "Conclusion" concludes.

Related Work

The optimization of business processes plays a major role in many companies. Business performance management [3, 6, 19, 20] or process mining [1, 18, 21, 22, 27] allow to analyze process data and to discover new workflow models out of the audit logs. Related operational data sources are typically neglected. One of our previous research work was concerned with the optimization of processes including SQL statements in BPEL/SQL activities that were executed on operational data [23]. We developed techniques to analyze and thus to understand control and data flow. This provides one basis for reusing it here for combining process variables to related operational data.

Finding combinations between process variables and operational data models is closely related to many other matching problems. The highest similarity can be found compared to schema matching or web service matching. The database community considers the problem of automatically matching schemas [8–10, 17]. The work in this area has developed several methods that try to capture clues about the semantics of the schemas and suggest matches based on them. Such methods include linguistic analysis, structural analysis, the use of domain knowledge and reuse techniques. However, the search for matching operational data with process variables differs from schema matching in three significant ways. First, content and structure of the input sources are different: our combination copes with variables that are nested within other non-matchable process elements while in pure schema matching all elements might be combinable. Furthermore, the audit trails vary significantly from operational data storage. Secondly, not every variable is combinable. It makes no sense to match technical parts of a variable with operational data. Pure name matching produces misleading results. Thirdly, the process variables are typically much more loosely related to each other than tables in a schema, and each web service in isolation has less information than a schema. Hence, we lose tremendous semantic preciseness if we only rely on techniques for schema matching in this context.

Recent work for matching web services [4, 12] proposes annotating web services manually with additional semantic information, and then using these annotations to compose new services automatically. But there, the goal is to ease the modeling and monitoring of business processes by support of domain ontologies. In [7, 11], non-annotated web services are combined. However, all approaches refer to web services only. A combination of business process artifacts with operational data, as we describe it here, has not been suggested so far. Furthermore, they only focus on web service interfaces and not on the process itself, as we do. We consider process semantics, since we go deeper into the process structure by looking into control and data flow issues to find relationships.

Approaches in [5, 26] combine process and operational data models by hand. However, this is very cumbersome and error-prone for such huge data amounts. We think it is worthwhile to face the challenge of automatically combining this data and developed a technology for exactly this.

Combination Framework

In this section, we briefly describe the pipeline approach of our combination framework and present its input models, i.e., the process model, the operational data model as well as the annotation model. We also define the combination results of each step and the final combination result.

Pipeline and Processing Overview

The processing pipeline shown in Fig. 2.2 creates a set of combinations (*COM*) between process variables (*PV*) and operational schema elements (*S*). Each step requires a different fraction of input sets: partially-annotated process variables (*PV*) and schema elements (*S*) or their annotated components (PV_{Ont}, S_{Ont}), the annotation ontology (*Ont*), and the annotated (P_{Ont}) or partially-annotated process context (*P*) of the variables.

In order to reflect the different input data, we distinguish two basic processing pipelines: (i) partially-annotated Pairing $\rightarrow$ structure-based Filtering $\rightarrow$ manual Filtering and (ii) annotated Pairing $\rightarrow$ structure-based Filtering $\rightarrow$ manual Filtering. *Partially-annotated pairing* covers the pairing of partially annotated process context, process variables and schema elements. If all elements involved in a pairing step are annotated, we consider it as *annotated pairing*.

After being converted to the internal representation format of the framework, the process models and schema models are traversed in the pairing phase to determine at least one matching schema element for each process variable with a similarity value between 0 and 1. If different rules estimate a combination, the highest value is taken. One pairing step performs reasoning over *Ont* and annotated elements. For this *annotated pairing* a reasoner determines an intermediate combination result consisting of semantically annotated variables and corresponding semantically annotated schema elements with a similarity value. It applies combination

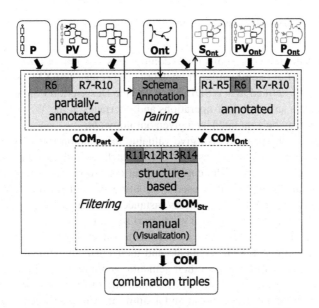

Fig. 2.2 The combination framework covers rules for annotated and partially-annotated pairing and structure-based filtering. It provides combination triples that consist of combinations of process variables and schema elements as well as a similarity value between 0 and 1

rules R1–R5. The *partially-annotated pairing* step finds combination results for combinations of annotated and non-annotated elements. In R6, we exploit well-known matching techniques using names of schema elements or process variables. R7–R10 are essential to consider the ontology, the data flow or other process features for combination. They are applied in both pairing steps. The framework also supports an easy adaption of exiting rules and the extension with new rules.

In the *structure-based filtering* step the results from the pairing steps are refined by considering element hierarchies in *PV* and *S* or process features contained in *P*. It uses well-known structural matching techniques (shaded in dark-gray) with features like the elements' path or data types (R11, R14), but also needs novel rules R12 and R13. The *manual filtering* step derives the final result by user interaction. Process variables are visualized together with their proposed combinations for changing them manually. For a pure automatic combination this step is skipped or just serves as a visualization output.

Schema Annotation is executed when the process side is semantically annotated but the operational data elements are not. This is quite often the case as the trend goes towards semantic web services but database annotations are still not widely-used. As our framework applies common schema matching algorithms to find matches between ontology *Ont* and partially-annotated schema elements *S*, we do not go into detail here. After matching, the results are stored as semantic annotations into the operational metadata S_{Ont}. Then *annotated pairing* is executed using these annotations together with the given variable annotations PV_{Ont}.

Input and Output Models

BPEL process models consist of various components, e.g. *process variables PV* that are in the focus of our combination framework. They consist of XML schema types, or their types are defined in a WSDL (Web Service Description Language) file. All process variables and also their operations and interfaces in the WSDL description of the process may be annotated by a given ontology *Ont*.

Other parts in the process also give valuable information for the combination. This includes names of activities and both data flow and control flow aspects modeled by these activities. The correlation set also supplies context information with its name and structure. It is used for routing subsequent messages between two web services to the correct process instance. How this process knowledge is exploited in the framework is shown in the next sections.

We consider an *operational data model S* as a collection of relational tables and views or a collection of XML elements and their attribute elements. Operational data models can be available with their semantic annotations as described in [14]. The combination result *COM* is a set of combination triples of a process variable element, an operational data element and a similarity value between 0 (dissimilar) and 1 (very similar) indicating the plausibility of their correspondence.

Definition 1. Let $COM = PV \times S \times sim$ be a set of *combination triples*. One triple indicates that the process variable element $v_r \in PV$ corresponds to the operational schema element $s_j \in S$ with a similarity value *sim* from an interval [0,1] of rational numbers.

Combination triples cover directed combinations because the goal is to find all match candidates for the variables of a process while accepting that schema elements may remain unmatched. This goal is different to schema matching where the elements of both sources aim to find a match partner. Without having to combine all the schema elements, the combination problem is simplified, as the amount of process variables is usually smaller than the set of schema elements. A combination is an n:m-relation, because a variable may map to many schema elements and a schema element may map to many variables. According to the combination pipeline from Fig. 2.2, our framework applies various combination steps to determine the following subsets of *COM*:

Definition 2. Let $COM_{Ont} = PV_{Ont} \times S_{Ont} \times sim_{Ont}$ be a relation whose domain is the Cartesian product of PV_{Ont}, S_{Ont} and an interval that includes rational numbers between 0 and 1. Then, the *combination set* $COM_{Ont} \subseteq COM$ contains combination triples of annotated process variable nodes in $PV_{Ont} \subseteq PV$ and annotated schema elements in $S_{Ont} \subseteq S$ and their similarity value sim_{Ont}. COM_{Ont} is created by making use of an ontology *Ont*.

Definition 3. Let $COM_{Part} = PV \times S \times sim_{Part}$ be a combination set $Com_{Part} \subseteq COM$. Then COM_{Part} contains combination triples between process variable nodes in *PV* and schema elements in *S* and their similarity value sim_{Part}.

Definition 4. Let $COM_{Str} = PV_{Str} \times S_{Str} \times sim_{Str}$ be a relation that refines the combination sets COM_{Ont} and COM_{Part} that contain $sim_{Ont} > 0$ or $sim_{Part} > 0$ by estimating the structural similarity sim_{Str} of the nodes in Com_{Ont} and Com_{Part} respectively. Then, the *combination set* $COM_{Str} = COM_{Ont} \cup COM_{Part} \subseteq COM$ contains combination triples of process variable nodes in PV_{Str} and schema elements in S_{Str} and their similarity value sim_{Str}.

COM_{Ont} is the combination result of the annotated pairing step, whereas partially-annotated pairing leads to the result COM_{Part}. In the partially-annotated pairing step the pairing rules do not require annotations of the variables and schema elements, so it can be applied for S and PV. Structure-based filtering can be applied to both result sets COM_{Ont} and COM_{Part} and leads to COM_{Str}.

Definition 5. Let the value sim_i be a weighted mean of the similarity of sim_{i_P} received from the pairing step and $sim_{i_{Str}}$ received from the filtering step: $sim_i = w_{weight} * sim_{i_P} + (1 - w_{weight}) * sim_{i_{Str}}$, where the constant w_{weight} is in the range of 0 to 1 and sim_{i_P} is the maximum value of sim_{Ont} or sim_{part}.

A final combination triple com_i is created by calculating a weighted similarity sim_i based on the similarity values from the pairing step and the filtering step. Definition 5 defines this in analogy to [13]. We accept triples for a combination of v_r and s_j where the calculated similarity value exceeds a certain threshold ($sim_i > $ threshold).

Sample Scenario

This section describes the input and output sets of the combination framework for the sample scenario shown in Fig. 2.3. This fragment of a car rental process describes the selection of a rental car. It is supposed to be optimized in a sense that expensive long running process parts must be analyzed and revised. All process variables are marked by # in Fig. 2.3. The process receives its input data by activity *CustomerData* with information about a customer and his preferred car model and checks in activity *RentalService* if it is available. If no car is available during the desired rental period, an employee executes the human task *ContractNegotiation* to prove if the customer would also accept another car class. The task is assigned to one of the available roles. Thus, *ContractNegotiation* can be claimed and executed by all agents from departments A, B or C. If the customer does not accept an alternative car the process is canceled. Otherwise, the car is handed over to the customer by an employee of department D in human task *CarHandOver*. The operational data in our scenario (shown in tables *Customer*, *Automobile* and *Employee*) includes useful data for optimization as well. Thus, these data models are combined with the elements of the process data models: Element *custID* of variable *inputData* with *CID* of *Customer* table (1), table *Employee* with the executing roles of *ContractNegotiation* in *TaskVar* (2), and variable *ServiceInfo* with *Model* of table *Automobile* (3).

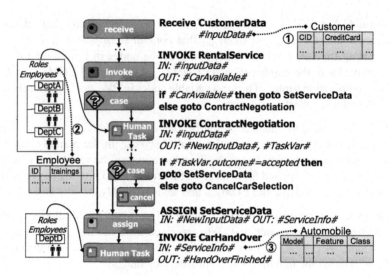

Fig. 2.3 RentalCarSelection scenario

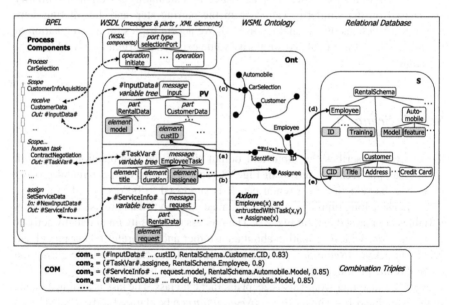

Fig. 2.4 Input and output data models of sample scenario

All input and output sets of our combination pipeline are illustrated in Fig. 2.4. In the left part of this figure, the process and its variables *PV* are shown. The variables *inputData*, *TaskVar* and *ServiceInfo* are illustrated referring to activities in the *CarSelection* process where they are used. The relevant components of a variable for the combination procedure are marked in gray. Tree components are defined in different sources: BPEL, WSDL and variable definitions in XML. On the right side, a relational operational schema S is illustrated via a tree-structure with the columns as leaves. Some components on both sides are annotated by *Ont*. The concepts in *Ont* are represented as a graph and are connected via equivalent, subconcept or object property relations. *Ont* further contains axioms like the definition of an assignee as an employee that is entrusted with a task.

The bottom of Fig. 2.4 illustrates four output triples received by our combination rules. Each triple com_i shows a process variable element and an operational schema element and their similarity value calculated by our rules. To calculate sim_i for all com_i, we choose a weight $= 0.6$ (Definition 5) and a threshold $= 0.7$.

Pairing

This section describes annotated and partially-annotated pairing. Depending on whether there is an annotation on none, one or both process and schema input models, different rules are applicable. Some of these rules are taken from other matching approaches, some of them are applied to our case, and some are new. Table 2.1 shows all pairing rules and the similarity value they calculate. Rules and algorithms for annotated pairing (R1–R5) are further explained in the following two sections, whereas non-annotated and partially-annotated pairing (R6–R10) is the subject of sections "Partially-Annotated Pairing Rules" and "Partially-Annotated Pairing Algorithm".

Annotated Pairing Rules

All combination rules for annotated pairing are based on reasoning over a given annotation ontology *Ont* and calculate a similarity value between annotated elements. They adapt existing approaches [2, 13] that find matches between names based on semantic relations defined in a lexicon. Our rules use an ontology instead and the respective elements are explicitly annotated. Thus, these relations carry even more weight. Rule R1 (*sameConcept*), rule R2 (*equivalentConcept*), rule R3 (*subConcept*) or rule R5 (*union*) combine those elements in PV_{Ont} and S_{Ont} that are annotated by the same ontology concept or that have a synonym, sub Conept or union relation modeled between their ontological concepts. In the sample scenario, rule R2 combines *custID* with column *CID*, as they are annotated by equivalent concepts in *Ont* (see com_1 and arrows (a) + (e) in Fig. 2.4). Rule R4 (*axiom-based*) makes use of axioms that are defined in the ontology using logical expressions. At least one antecedent of the axiom may consist of a domain concepts c_r while a consequent consists of c_j. If c_r and c_j are used for annotation like c_r for v_r and c_j for s_j and if both atoms refer to the same parameter x, the elements are combined. The similarity calculation uses the amount (#) of occurrences of concept c_j and c_r in the domains of the axiom divided by the total amount of atoms. For com_2, rule

Table 2.1 Rules for annotated pairing (R1–R5) and partially-annotated pairing (R6–R10)

Rule	Rule name	Novelty	Similarity value
R1	sameConcept	Adapted	1 (match found) or 0 (no match)
R2	equivalentConcept	Adapted	1 (match found) or 0 (no match)
R3	subConcept	Adapted	$\dfrac{\#c_i \ in \ subconcept \ definitions \ of \ concept \ c_k}{\#subconcepts \ of \ c_k}$
R4	axiom-based	New	$\dfrac{\#c_r \ and \ \#c_j \ in \ domain \ of \ atoms \ in \ axiom \ a_t}{\#atoms \ in \ axiom \ a_t}$
R5	union	Adapted	1 (match found) or 0 (no match)
R6	linguistic	Old	$\dfrac{2*\sum_{t1 \in v}[\max_{t2 \in s} similarity(t1,t2)]}{\#token_v + \#token_s}$
R7	tokenOntology	Adapted	$\dfrac{2*\sum_{t1 \in c}[\max_{t2 \in s|v} similarity(t1,t2)]}{\#token_c + \#token_{s/v}}$
R8	elimination	Adapted	0
R9	dataFlow	New	sim_i
R10	correlation	New	sim_i or cf. R6 or R7

R4 combines *TaskVar.assignee* annotated by (b) with *Employee* annotated by (d)
exploiting the given axiom in *Ont*. A third atom in the axiom models the relation
entrustedWithTask. The relation is based on the domain concept *Employee*. Thus,
rule R4 calculates $sim = \frac{3}{3}$ as all atoms are based on one of the concepts used for
annotation.

Annotated Pairing Algorithm

Algorithm 1 illustrates the annotated pairing procedure. It gets annotated process
variables PV_{Ont}, annotated operational schema models S_{Ont} and the referred ontology *Ont* as input. It finds all meaningful combinations and stores them together
with a similarity value in a triple set COM_{Ont} as output. The concepts used for
annotation in PV_{Ont} and S_{Ont} must come from the same ontology to be able to apply
the following rules.

In a first step, the algorithm identifies all used concept groups (*Groups*) within
ontology *Ont*. Concept groups are sets of ontology concepts which are used for
annotation of one or more variables or models containing equivalent concepts in
one group. The algorithm calls function *getEquivalentAndUnionConcepts* in order
to find all concept groups for the given annotation sets with elements referring to
the *equivalent* or *union* concepts.

Algorithm 1: Annotated pairing

Input: AnnotationSet PV_{Ont}, AnnotationSet S_{Ont}, Ontology *Ont*
Output: CombinationTripleSet COM_{Ont}
  Groups ← *getEquivalentAndUnionConcepts*(PV_{Ont}, S_{Ont}, *Ont*)
  for all concept in Ont **do**
    cG ← *findGroup*(*concept*, *Groups*)
    if |*cG*| is not empty **then**
      COM_{Ont} ← *addSameUnionEquivalentTriples*(*cG*)
      COM_{Ont} ← *addSubConceptTriples*(*cG*, *Ont*)
      COM_{Ont} ← *addAxiomTriples*(*cG*, *Groups*, *Ont*, COM_{Ont})
    end if
  end for

Then *Ont* is traversed. For this traversal, we build a spanning tree of the ontology graph with view to its subconcept structure. The name of the ontology defines the root. To obtain the tree we only use simple subconcept relationships, i.e., concepts that are deduced only from one concept branch. Complex subconcepts (concepts with more than one parent from different ontology branches) are allocated to the first referred sub concept in the description.

Function *findGroup* estimates for each concept in *Ont* whether it belongs to a concept group. If so, we store the concept group in *cG* and apply our rule set for *cG*. This way, all combination triples are determined in an iterative way, until we have processed all rules. First, combination triples in a concept group are searched (rules R1 (*sameConcept*), R5 (*union*) and R2 (*equivalentConcept*)) with their similarity value. If a concept group contains both variable and operational model annotation sets, each variable is combined with each schema element in this group (*addSame-UnionEquivalentTriples*). Afterwards function *addSubConceptTriples* finds triples where the variable concept and the operational model concept are located in different concept groups in the path from the leaf to the concept group *cG* in *Ont*. As this algorithm works on models instead of data instances, we use simple subconcept relations in rule R3. For complex relations, we mark these combination triples and prove the combinability later in the cleansing phase on the instance data.

Function *addAxiomTriples* is based on rule R4 and parses all axioms in *Ont*. Axioms create new relationships between concepts in an ontology with the use of logical expressions. The function seeks axioms that have one of the concepts in *cG* in the antecedents and a concept of the consequences in another concept group and that are not yet in COM_{Ont}. For simple axioms that consist only of different concepts, compatible elements can be combined, if one concept is used in the annotation set PV_{Ont} and the other one in S_{Ont} and if both axiom concepts contain the same parameters. In complex axioms containing also properties, domain and range concepts of the properties are extracted before concepts of different annotation sets can be correlated if they refer to the same parameters in the axiom. In rule R4, the results are also marked and validated on instance data in the cleansing phase.

Partially-Annotated Pairing Rules

The partially-annotated pairing aims to find combinations between elements in PV and S, which are not or only partially annotated. Rule R6 (*linguistic*) applies common matching techniques to the names of the elements as discussed in other papers. See [13] for the similarity calculation. Rule R7 (*tokenOntology*) adapts R6 and compares the element names with concept names that are associated with one of these elements. This enables the usage of *Ont* for further derivations.

Rules R8–R10 do not obey Definition 5, but have their own similarity calculation. Rule R8 (*elimination*) discards defined elements like preposition and articles [13]. We extend this idea to exclude variables with pure controlling purpose from the result. All combinations containing such an element are eliminated, i.e., their similarity value is set to 0. Rule R9 (*dataFlow*) exploits data dependencies considering assign activities that copy data from one variable v_i to a variable v_j. From the found triples derived for v_i, rule R9 copies an operational match partner and similarity value sim_i to the variable v_j. For com_3 in Fig. 2.4, rule R9 uses com_4 that was found by other combination rules. Rule R9 copies *Automobile.Model* and the similarity 0.85 to *ServiceInfo... request* and receives com_3, due to the assign activity *SetServiceData*. Rule R10 (*correlation*) considers shared aliases referenced in a correlation set of the process. The alias contains property labels for different variables v_i, v_r. If v_i is already in *COM* its matched element s_j and sim_k are copied to v_r. Otherwise, the labels of the alias and the properties are tried to be matched to all $s \in S$. Finding a partner s_j leads to the triples (v_i, s_j, sim_k) and (v_r, s_j, sim_k).

Partially-Annotated Pairing Algorithm

Algorithm 2 illustrates the partially-annotated pairing procedure based on a *RuleSet* consisting of rules R6–R10. It gets process variables PV and operational schema models S that contain also the annotated sets PV_{Ont} and S_{Ont} as input as well as the referred ontology *Ont* and the process context in P. It finds all meaningful combinations together with their similarity value and stores them in a triple set COM_{Part} as output.

We linearize the given variable and schema trees (function *getList*). Algorithm 2 traverses the given linearizations of the input set PV. We apply our rule set for each variable and schema node. This way, all combination triples are determined in an iterative way, until we have processed all rules.

First, it checks if the current node pv can be skipped by rule R8 (*elimination*). Otherwise it traverses the linearizations of the input set S and the rules in the rule set until a combination is found or all rules have been traversed. Once a rule can be applied by function *applyTokenRules*, the combination triple is stored in COM_{Part} with its similarity value calculated by the rules. Finally, the rules R9 and R10 are applied for all found combination triples in COM_{Part} and—if we do not separate the

---

Algorithm 2: Partially-annotated pairing

Input: VariableSet PV, SchemaSet S, Ontology Ont, Process P
Output: CombinationTripleSet COM_{Part}
   $COM_{Part} \leftarrow \emptyset$
   for all pv in getList(PV) **do**
      if (R8(pv)) = false **then**
         for all s in getList(S) **do**
            repeat
               $rule \leftarrow getNextRule(RuleSet)$
               $COM_{Part} \leftarrow applyTokenRules(pv, s, rule, Ont)$
            until RuleSet fully traversed
         end for
         for all com_i in $COM_{Ont} \cup COM_{Part}$ **do**
            $COM_{Part} \leftarrow applyR9(pv, P, COM_{Ont}, COM_{Part})$
            $COM_{Part} \leftarrow applyR10(pv, P, COM_{Ont}, COM_{Part})$
         end for
      end if
   end for

---

execution of both partially-annotated and annotated pairing rule sets—in COM_{Ont}. They evaluate the process context P if pv is able to be combined with a schema element s that was used in com_i.

Filtering

The filtering steps refine the received combination triples by taking the context of the elements into account and allowing users to adjust false and missing combinations. At the end, our framework calculates a weighted *sim* value (Definition 5) and returns the final triple set *COM*.

Structure-Based Rules

The structure-based rules exploit the context of the variable and the operational schema elements given in a combination triple to achieve higher accuracy for the found triples in *COM*. By using the similarity values in Table 2.2, we define a combined structure-based similarity value $sim_{str} = \alpha * sim_{R11} + \beta * sim_{R12} + \gamma * sim_{R13} + \delta * sim_{R14}$ with the weights $\alpha, \beta, \gamma, \delta \geq 0$ and $\alpha + \beta + \gamma + \delta = 1$. In the sample scenario all these weights are equally set to 0.25. The rule R11 (*path*) and the rule R14 (*dataType*) are based on [13]. R11 refines results in *COM* by considering matches between their parent elements, e.g., between their parent names. Rule R14 inspects the similarity between elements by their data type category. Rule R12 (*processStructure*) looks for hints in the control flow. It considers e.g., the names

Table 2.2 Structure-based rules

Rule	Rule name	Novelty	Similarity value
R11	path	Old	$\dfrac{\textit{combined sim of parent matches of } v_i \textit{ and } s_i}{Min(\#pathToRoot(v_i),\#pathToRoot(s_i))}$
R12	processStructure	New	$\dfrac{\textit{combined sim of matches}(controlflow(v_i),\ path(s_i))}{\#controlFlowParents(v_i)}$
R13	WSDLAnnotation	New	$\dfrac{1}{minDistance(c_p,\ c_s)}$ or 0 (if not annotated or $sim_i > 1$)
R14	dataType	Old	1 (same datatype group) or 0 (different datatype)

of partner links or activities that work on the respective variable. Furthermore, it estimates the similarity via matching the names of these process components to the operational partner element or its parents. Rule R13 (*WSDLAnnotation*) exploits the annotation c_p of a process component that employs a variable v_i of a combination $com_i = (v_i, s_i, sim_i)$. It traverses the ontology subtree below concept c_p to find the minimum distance between the annotations c_p and c_s of s_i. sim_{R13} calculates the fraction using this distance between the concepts c_p and c_s.

In com_1 of Fig. 2.4 structure-based similarities $sim_{R11}=\frac{1}{2}$, $sim_{R12}=\frac{1}{2}$, $sim_{R13}=\frac{1}{3}$, and $sim_{R14}=1$ are combined to $sim_{Str1} = \frac{7}{12}$. Rule R11 calculates the minimum path (#pathToRoot(CID)=2) to root *RentalSchema* and summarizes the similarity of parent matches, i.e., of *Customer* and *RentalSchema* with parent element names of *custID* in the variable tree *inputData* and receives 1 (*CustomerData* matches *Customer*). R12 counts three control flow parents that use *custID*: *CustomerData*, *CustomerInfoAquisition* and *CarSelection*. As only the first two match with the operational parent *Customer*, we get a combined $sim = 1 + \frac{1}{2} + 0$. Rule R13 results in $\frac{1}{3}$, as the distance in *Ont* from the concept *ID* of *CID* (e) and the concept *CarSelection* that annotates the WSDL operation *initiate* (c) that uses *custID*, adds up to 3. sim_{R14} is *1*, because both *custID* and *CID* have the same datatype integer. The overall similarity sim_1 results in $0.6 * 1 + 0.4 * \frac{7}{12} = 0.83$.

Structure-Based Algorithm

Algorithm 3 illustrates the structure-based filtering procedure. It gets as input the process P with its variables PV and an operational schema model S. Both may contain annotated sets. Further inputs are the referred ontology *Ont*, the annotation set of further process description elements P_{Ont} as well as already found combination triples in COM_{Ont} and COM_{Part}.

The goal of the algorithm is to receive a refinement of these combinations as output COM_{Str}. It traverses the given combinations in $COM_{Ont} \cup COM_{Part}$ found by Algorithms 1 and 2. First, it extracts the variable node pv by function $getPV$ and the schema node s by function $getSValue$ of the combination triple com_i with

---

Algorithm 3: Structure-based filtering

Input: Process P, VariableSet PV, SchemaSet S, COM_{Ont}, COM_{Part},
Ontology Ont, AnnotationSet P_{ont}, weights $\alpha, \beta, \gamma, \delta$
Output: CombinationTripleSet COM_{Str}
  $COM_{Str} \leftarrow \emptyset$
  for all com_i in $(COM_{Ont} \cup COM_{Part})$ **do**
    if $sim_i > 0$ **then**
      $pv \leftarrow getPV(com_i)$
      $s \leftarrow getSValue(com_i)$
      $psim \leftarrow applyPathRule(pv, s, P, S)$
      $csim \leftarrow applyProcessStructureRule(pv, s, P, S)$
      $osim \leftarrow applyWSDLAnnotationRule(pv, s, S, Ont, P_{Ont})$
      $dsim \leftarrow getDatatypeSimilarity(pv, s, sim_{Str})$
      $sim_{Str} \leftarrow getSimValue(psim, osim, dsmin, \alpha, \beta, \gamma, \delta)$
      $COM_{Str} \leftarrow mergeSimilarity(com_i, COM_{Str}, sim_{Str})$
    end if
  end for

$sim_i > 0$. For each triple, all structure-based rules are applied and a similarity value is calculated in all rules: $psim$ (R11), $csim$ (R12) and $osim$ (R13). *Csim* is estimated by *applyProcessStructureRule* between pv and s using their related process P and schema set S to find relationships between further process parts and schema elements. *Psim* is estimated by the function *applyPathRule*. The more levels there are in the two tree paths, the more valuable becomes this rule.

Function *applyWSDLAnnotationRule* is illustrated in Algorithm 4. It returns *osim* by extracting all annotated description elements in P_{Ont} that use pv via function *getDescriptionElements* and stores them in $P_{Ont|pv}$. Function *getSchemaParents* extracts all parents of the given schema element s. For each description element p_i annotated by c_k and all parents in *sParent searchOntologyMatches* aims to find the nearest concept c_j that annotates *sParent*. If it is successful ($c_j \neq \emptyset$), *calculateOntologySimilarity* estimates *osim* as distance between c_j and c_k. Function *getDatatypeSimilarity* applies R14 to determine the correspondence of the datatypes of the found combination elements.

At the end of Algorithm 3, function *getSimValue* calculates the similarity sim_{Str} of the current triple com_i combining all received structural similarity values using the given weights alpha, beta, gamma and delta. Then function *mergeSimilarity* estimates the combination triple set Com_{Str} by merging com_i in conjunction with sim_{Str} with all triples in Com_{Str} watching that one (variable – schema) combination exists only once, namely the combination with the highest similarity value.

Manual Filtering

Given the fact that no fully automatic solution is possible, a user-friendly interface is essential for the practicability of a match system. The graphical user interface of the editor described in [15] provides the user with many ways to influence the

---

Algorithm 4: applyWSDLAnnotationRule

Input: VariableNode pv, SchemaElement s, SchemaSet S_{Ont}, Ontology Ont, AnnotationSet P_{Ont}

Output: osim

osim $= 0$

$P_{Ont|pv} \leftarrow getDescriptionElements(pv, P_{Ont})$

for all $p_i(c_k)$ in $P_{Ont|pv}$ **do**

    $sParent \leftarrow getSchemaParents(s, S_{Ont})$

    $c_j \leftarrow searchOntologyMatches(sParent, c_k, Ont)$

    if $c_j \neq \emptyset$ **then**

        osim $\leftarrow calculateOntologySimilarity(c_j, c_k, Ont)$

    end if

end for

---

match process. It allows to configure the reasoners before combination, to iteratively refine the proposed correspondences during combination, as well as to manipulate the obtained match results after combination. To provide feedback, the user can remove false matches or add missing ones. The manually added combinations are automatically provided with the highest similarity 1 and are stored in *COM*.

Evaluation

In this section, we discuss the benefits of the combination framework and analyze the effectiveness of the combination rules.

Benefits of the Combination Framework

Pure schema matching would not find any matches at all if we apply it to the raw source process without extracting the XML variables from the BPEL process. In our sample scenario, standard schema matching would perhaps be able to find com_1, if it is able to work on ontology mappings. However, com_2 and com_3 would not be found, as user-defined ontology axioms and process context are usually not considered during schema matching. Instead, we would find a wrong match between *TaskVar.title* and *Customer.title*. Rule R8 excludes this combination.

Applying the pairing and structure-based algorithms to the sample scenario reveals multiple combination triples shown in Fig. 2.4 that turn out to describe the useful relations marked in Fig. 2.3. We may discover in (1) a correlation between the assets of customers (type of credit card) and canceled processes. In order to win wealthy customers, they should be routed to special services. The performance of *ContractNegotiation* in (2) depends on the employee and his skills. To increase the number of accepted tasks, a reorganization of these roles is needed. In (3), an adequate provisioning of resources is needed for cars with certain features.

While for non-annotated attributes our framework provides partially-annotated combination rules, for annotated process and operational data it critically depends on ontologies and annotations. At the moment we still have an overhead of annotating this data. However, more and more web services will be provided with annotations for enabling a semantic service detection at runtime. So our framework will also benefit from these ambitions.

Experimental Setup

The experimental setup consists of the data models of the business processes, the operational database schema and an ontology for semantic annotation. For evaluation, we used 20 different BPEL processes averaging 10 variables each with 4–10 matchable elements and one schema with about 400 attributes. Processes and schemas come from the car rental domain. The ontology was modeled in WSML and contained all concepts needed for annotation.

To evaluate the quality of our rules, we compared the manually determined real combinations R with the combinations T returned by our tool. We determined the correctly identified combinations C. Based on the cardinalities of these sets, two quality measures are computed (cf. [8]): $Precision = \frac{|C|}{|T|}$ estimates the reliability of the combination predictions, $recall = \frac{|C|}{|R|}$ specifies the share of real combinations that is found. Because of sparse element interrelations in the variables, the structural results are lower weighted as the rest and w_{weight} (see Definition 5) is set to 0.6. Our tool determines T by applying our rules with a threshold of 0.7 that was set based on a significant number of test runs.

Results

In a first set of experiments, we focused on the annotated pairing rules and the structure-based rules applied to annotated elements. Figure 2.5(a) shows the combination results. As expected, the recall is very high because all models are correctly annotated. A detailed analysis reveals that the missing 5 % comes from some axioms defined in the ontology that contain five predicates and some even more in their antecedents resulting in a similarity value below the threshold. The precision results are almost just as well, but some wrong combination results have been found. Due to the missing check via instance data, the rules R3, R4 and R13 found combinations that cannot be validated with concrete data values. A later cleansing phase could improve this result.

Fig. 2.5 The evaluation of combination rules compares precision and recall for using (**a**) all annotated paring rules and all structure-based rules, and (**b**) subsets of the partially-annotated pairing rules and all structure-based rules

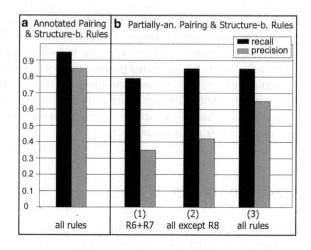

The second set of experiments addresses the significance of rules R8–R10 that exploit process knowledge. It provides the results of partially-annotated-pairing and structure-based rules applied to non-annotated elements. Figure 2.5(b) shows combinations obtained by these rules in three different scenarios: (1) shows the results obtained with rule R6 (*linguistic*) and rule R7 (*tokenOntology*) as the only pairing rules, (2) is based on all partially-annotated-pairing rules except rule R8 (*elimination*) and in the last one (3) all partially-annotated-pairing rules are applied. Comparing recall and precision results of (1) and (2), there is only a small impact of rule R9 and rule R10. Due to our precondition of qualified element names and lexicon definitions, rules R9 and R10 promise an improvement only in few cases where the elements are ambiguous and, thus, have been incorrectly matched before.

In (3), the precision value rises due to the application of rule R8. Wrong combinations with elements in human task variables, e.g., their human task titles, are deleted from the result set. The rules R6 and R7 reveal some problems, since they only find tokens with clear separation hints in the name like underscore or capitalization leading to a still low precision rate. Some other wrong combinations originate from tokens that appear very often in the variables of the rental domain, e.g., the token *car*. This leads to wrong combinations of elements containing this token, e.g., *CarInsuranceID* and *CarSaleID*. A workaround would be to declare *car* and other frequent words as stop word. In some cases, the path rule failed to find structural matches because in flat hierarchies as in operational data models, e.g. of type relational, there are only two possible levels in the path (table and columns).

Comparing the results in Fig. 2.5(a) and (b3) with the results of well-known rules R6 and R7 in Fig. 2.5(b1) shows a big gap in precision. That verifies our claim that the new rules raise precision of the combination. They focus on semantic annotations (Fig. 2.5(a)) as well as on process-specific issues (*elimination, data flow, correlation* in Fig. 2.5(b3)) that have not been taken into account by well-known rules.

Fig. 2.6 Evaluation of the precision of calculated similarity values. (**a**) Annotated pairing & structure-based rules. (**b**) Partially-annot. pairing & structure-based rules

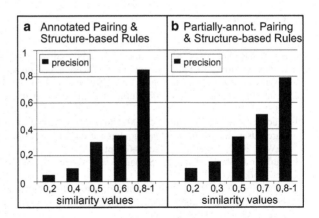

Faulty calculated similarity values also take effects on precision and recall. The tool finds true combinations in fact, but might exclude them in some cases again due to a low, but wrongly calculated similarity value. Thus, we evaluated the whole result set of all combinations with respect to their precision. Figure 2.6a calculates the precision for each similarity group for all combinations that were found by annotated pairing rules. Figure 2.6b illustrates the same calculations for the partially-annotated pairing rules. In both tables, the precision results for combinations the tool found with a similarity value below 0.7 are very low. In contrast most combinations found with similarity value above 0.7 are correct combinations (high precision). This is why we set the threshold to 0.7 during the experiments. Amongst others, the correct setting of the threshold depends on the complexity of the rules. Further experiments and analysis revealed that in other settings, e.g., if the combinations are basically derived by the *dataFlow* rule using complex assignment activities, the similarity threshold should be adjusted to a lower value.

Conclusion

We have shown a promising approach to combine business process variables with operational schemas. It adds another level of combination on top of well-known schema matching approaches by considering the impact of business process features. Based on a prototype and a case study, we have evaluated that our approach derives significant combination results that previous approaches have not found. In future work, we will extend our combination framework with respect to input models and well-known matching rules.

References

1. Agrawal R et al (1998) Mining process models from workflow logs. In: Schek H-J, Saltor F, Ramos I, Alonso G (eds) 6th international conference on extending database technology, advances in database technology – EDBT'98, Valencia, 23–27 Mar 1998
2. Bernstein PA, Haas LM (2008) Information integration in the enterprise. Commun ACM 51(9):72–79
3. Bruckner RM, List B, Schiefer J (2002) Striving towards near real-time data integration for data warehouses. In: 4th international conference on data warehousing and knowledge discovery, DaWaK 2002, Aix-en-Provence, 4–6 Sept 2002
4. Cardoso J, Sheth AP (2006) Semantic web services, processes and applications. Springer, New York
5. Casati F et al (2007) A generic solution for warehousing business process data. In: Koch C et al (eds) Proceedings of the 33rd international conference on very large data bases, University of Vienna, Vienna, 23–27 Sept 2007
6. Castellanos M, Casati F, Dayal U, Shan M-C (2004) A comprehensive and automated approach to intelligent business processes execution analysis. Distrib Parallel Databases 16(3):239–273
7. Corrales JC et al (2008) BeMatch: a platform for matchmaking service behavior models. In: Kemper A et al (eds) 11th international conference on extending database technology EDBT 2008, Nantes, 25–29 Mar 2008
8. Do H, Melnik S, Rahm E (2003) Comparison of schema matching evaluations. In: Web, web-services, and database systems. Springer, Berlin/Heidelberg/New York
9. Do H, Rahm E (2002) COMA – a system for flexible combination of schema matching approaches. In: Proceedings of 28th international conference on very large data bases VLDB 2002, Hong Kong, 20–23 Aug 2002
10. Doan A et al (2004) Ontology matching: a machine learning approach. In: Handbook on ontologies (International Handbook on Information Systems). Springer, Berlin/Heidelberg
11. Dong X et al (2004) Similarity search for web services. In: Nascimento MA et al (eds) (e)Proceedings of the thirtieth international conference on very large data bases, Toronto, 31 Aug–3 Sept 2004
12. Hepp M et al (2005) Semantic business process management: a vision towards using semantic web services for business process management. In: Lau FCM, Lei H, Meng X, Wang M (eds) 2005 IEEE international conference on e-business engineering, ICEBE 2005, Beijing, 18–21 Oct 2005
13. Madhavan J, Bernstein PA, Rahm E (2001) Generic schema matching with Cupid. Technical report, Microsoft Research
14. Radeschütz S, Mitschang B (2008) An annotation approach for the matching of process variables and operational business data models. In: Harris FC Jr (ed) Proceedings of the ISCA 21st international conference on computer applications in industry and engineering, CAINE 2008, Honolulu, 12–14 Nov 2008
15. Radeschütz S et al (2010) BIAEditor – matching process and operational data for a business impact analysis. In: Manolescu I et al (eds) 13th international conference on extending database technology EDBT 2010, Lausanne, 22–26 Mar 2010
16. Radeschütz S, Vrhovnik M, Schwarz H, Mitschang B (2011) Exploiting the symbiotic aspects of process and operational data for optimizing business processes. In: Proceedings of the IEEE international conference on information reuse and integration, IRI 2011, Las Vegas, 3–5 Aug 2011. IEEE Systems, Man, and Cybernetics Society
17. Rahm E, Bernstein PA (2001) A survey of approaches to automatic schema matching. VLDB J 10(4):334–350
18. Rubin V et al (2007) Process mining framework for software processes. In: Wang Q, Pfahl D, Raffo DM (eds) International conference on software process, software process dynamics and agility ICSP 2007, Minneapolis, 19–20 May 2007

19. Sayal M, Casati F, Dayal U, Shan M-C (2002) Business process cockpit. In: Proceedings of 28th international conference on very large data bases VLDB 2002, Hong Kong, 20–23 Aug 2002
20. Schiefer J, Jeng J-J, Bruckner RM (2003) Real-time workflow audit data integration into data warehouse systems. In: Ciborra CU et al (eds) Proceedings of the 11th European conference on information systems, ECIS 2003, Naples, 16–21 June 2003
21. van der Aalst WMP (2001) Re-engineering knock-out processes. Decis Support Syst 30(4):451–468
22. van der Aalst WMP (2011) Process mining: discovery, conformance and enhancement of business processes. Springer, Berlin/Heidelberg/New York
23. Vrhovnik M et al (2007) An approach to optimize data processing in business processes. In: Koch C et al (eds) Proceedings of the 33rd international conference on very large data bases, University of Vienna, Vienna, 23–27 Sept 2007
24. W3C (2007) Semantic annotations for WSDL and XML schema. Available: http://www.w3.org/TR/sawsdl/
25. Weerawarana S et al (2005) Web services platform architecture. Prentice Hall, Upper Saddle River
26. zur Muehlen M (2004) Workflow-based process controlling. Logos, Berlin
27. zur Muehlen M, Shapiro R (2009) Business process analytics. In: Handbook on business process management, vol 2. Springer, Berlin

Chapter 3
Efficient Range Query Processing on Complicated Uncertain Data

Andrew Knight, Qi Yu, and Manjeet Rege

Abstract Uncertain data has emerged as a key data type in many applications. New and efficient query processing techniques need to be developed due to the inherent complexity of this new type of data. In this paper, we investigate a special type of query, range queries, on uncertain data. We propose a threshold interval indexing structure that aims to balance different time consuming factors to achieve an optimal overall query performance. We also present a more efficient version of our structure which loads its primary tree into memory for faster processing. Experimental results are presented to justify the efficiency of the proposed query processing technique.

Introduction

The term *uncertain data* defines data collected with an inherent and distinctly quantifiable level of uncertainty [2]. Whereas values for *certain data* are given as exact constants, values for uncertain data are instead given by probability measures, most notably by probability distribution functions (PDFs) [1, 10, 11, 25, 27]. Uncertain data has been increasingly generated from a great variety of applications such as:

- Scientific measurements include margins of error due to limited instruments [2].
- Sensor networks are imprecise due to hardware limits [2].
- GPS is only accurate to within a few meters [11].
- Uncertainty in mobile object tracking can magnify errors in predictive queries [2, 34].
- Forecasting weather or economic data is based heavily upon statistics and probabilities [3, 25, 30].
- Aggregated demographic data only represent summaries, not actual data [4].

A. Knight (✉) · Q. Yu · M. Rege
Rochester Institute of Technology, One Lomb Memorial Drive, Rochester, NY 14623-5603, USA
e-mail: andy.knig@gmail.com; qyu@it.rit.edu; mr@cs.rit.edu

T. Özyer et al. (eds.), *Information Reuse and Integration in Academia and Industry*,
DOI 10.1007/978-3-7091-1538-1_3, © Springer-Verlag Wien 2013

- Privacy-preserving data mining often introduces jitter to protect individuals [2].
- Lost information creates incompleteness in data [25].

In contrast to certain data whose values are exact constants, uncertain data take values that are described by probability measures, most notably probability distribution functions (PDFs). Due to the inherent complexity of uncertain data, new techniques need to be developed in order to efficiently process queries against this new type of data. A set of novel indexing structures have been developed to accelerate query processing. Representative ones include threshold index [10, 26], the U-tree [30], and 2D mapping techniques [1, 10]. Most of these approaches assume that disk I/Os are the dominating factor that determines the overall query performance. Thus, the indexing structures are usually designed to optimize the number of disk I/Os. However, uncertain data is inherently more complicated than certain data. Computing a range query on uncertain data usually involves complicated computations, which incur high CPU cost. This makes disk I/Os no longer the solely dominating factor that determines the overall query performance. Therefore, new indexing strategies need to be developed to optimize the overall performance of range queries on uncertain data.

Uncertain continuous data is usually modeled by PDFs. Some PDFs, like the uniform PDF, may be very simple to calculate. However, many widely used PDFs involve complicated computations, such as multimodal probability models for cluster analysis [33] or computer simulations of cell signaling dynamics for biology research [21]. Computing a complicated PDF may involve high computational cost. Numerical approaches, such as Monte Carlo integration, have been exploited to improve the performance [30]. Riemann sum, however, provides a better strategy for one-dimensional cases. Even though Riemann sums can be faster than Monte Carlo integrations, they still incur high computational cost. Especially when a high computation accuracy is required, probability calculations may take even longer than disk I/Os. Therefore, the number of probability calculations must also be considered if the distribution of the uncertain data is complicated. In this case, the indexing strategy needs to balance between disk I/Os and the CPU cost to achieve an optimal overall query performance.

In this paper, we present a novel indexing strategy focusing on one-dimensional uncertain continuous data, called *threshold interval indexing*. It addresses the limitations of existing indexing structures on uncertain data, particularly for handling complicated PDFs, by treating uncertain objects as intervals and thereby leveraging interval tree techniques. The proposed indexing structure is also inspired by the optimized interval techniques from [7] to build a dynamic primary tree and store objects in nodes at different levels depending on the objects' sizes. The notion of using an interval tree to index uncertain data was suggested by Cheng et al. in [10] but disregarded in favor of an R-tree with extra probability limits called x-bounds. We assert that x-bounds can just as easily be applied to interval trees to index uncertain data with special benefits. We also propose a *memory-loaded threshold interval index*, which loads the primary tree into memory for faster processing.

The rest of the paper is organized as follows. Section "Background and Motivation" gives the problem statement and provides an overview of previous research. Section "Processing Range Queries on Uncertain Data" presents the threshold interval index. Section "Memory-Loaded Threshold Interval Indexing" introduces the memory-loaded version of the threshold interval index. Section "Experimental Results" gives experimental results of our two indexes versus the probability threshold index. Section "Conclusion" concludes the paper by offering direction for future research.

Background and Motivation

Existing indexes are inadequate for handling complicated uncertain continuous data. This section will give the problem statement, describe existing indexing strategies along with shortcomings, and provide an overview of related work.

Problem Statement

Given a database table T, a *query interval* $[a, b]$ for an uncertain attribute e of an object u_i, and a *threshold probability* τ, a *range query* returns all uncertain objects u_i from T for which $Pr(u_i.e \in [a, b]) \geq \tau$.

Theoretically, an uncertain object could have more than one uncertain attribute. However, for this paper, we focus on indexing objects based on only one uncertain attribute.

With no index, a query must calculate a probability for each object to determine if the object falls within the query interval. Naturally, an efficient index prunes many uncertain objects from a search to avoid unnecessary probability calculations, which, given the complexity of the PDFs, could save a lot of time.

External Interval Tree Index

Interval trees [12] are not specifically designed for handling uncertain data, but one-dimensional uncertain objects may be treated as intervals by using their PDF endpoints. Arge et al. [6] propose two optimal external interval tree indexes. Both indexes use a primary tree for layout and secondary structures to store the objects at each node. The first index's primary tree is a balanced tree over a set of fixed endpoints with a branching factor of $\sqrt{B}$ as the base tree, where B is the block size. The second index replaces the static interval tree with a *weight-balanced B-tree* [6] storing interval endpoints to achieve dynamic interval management. Note that its primary tree does *not* store the intervals, it only stores endpoints to control tree spread. In both indexes, each internal node v represents an interval I_v containing all of its child nodes' endpoints. Each interval I_v is divided into subintervals called *slabs* by the endpoint boundaries on v's immediate child nodes. When using this tree to index a set of interval objects I, an interval $i \in I$ is stored at the lowest node v in the tree such that i is not split across slab boundaries. Each node v stores these intervals in secondary structures for each slab boundary: B-trees normally or in an underflow structure if the number of segments is less than $B/2$ [6, 17]. These lists hold all intervals that cross the boundary on the left side, on the right side, and as a multislab. *Stabbing queries* are used to return results.

Since the endpoints in the first index are fixed, it can become unbalanced and therefore inefficient due to spread and skew in the input interval set. The second index, although much more complicated, adapts well to skew and to new inputs. However, the downfall of both interval indexes, as mentioned in [10], is that if many uncertainty intervals overlap with the query interval's endpoints, then few objects are pruned from the search, and a lot of time is wasted in calculating probabilities. Furthermore, although this external index is theoretically optimal, it is not always practical [23].

Probability Threshold Index

The *probability threshold index* (PTI) [10] allows range queries to prune more branches from searching than interval indexes allow. The PTI uses a one-dimensional R-tree as a base tree. Only leaves store uncertain objects. Each internal node has a *minimum bounding rectangle* (MBR) that encloses the narrowest boundaries $[L, R]$ for all child PDFs. Tighter bounds, called *x-bounds*, are also calculated for each node. X-bounds are the pair of boundaries (L_x, R_x) such that the probability an object attribute's value exists in $[L, L_x]$ or $[R_x, R]$ is equal to x [10]. Thus, when performing a range query for objects in $[a, b]$ with probability threshold τ, if, for a certain node, $\tau \geq x$ and $[a, b]$ does not overlap L_x or R_x at its right or left ends, then the node and its children may be pruned from the search.

The PTI has many advantages. It is an elegant solution, and it is fairly easy to implement. The tree is dynamic as well. All boundaries are calculated when objects are added. Multiple x-bounds can be stored in each node, so queries can choose the most appropriate bounds for its threshold. Required storage space for internal nodes is relatively small. Note that the U-tree is very much like a multi-dimensional PTI with additional pruning techniques [30].

The PTI is not without weaknesses, however. The primary weakness pointed out by Cheng et al. is that differences in interval sizes will skew the balance of the tree [10]. Methods involving *variance-based clustering* are provided in [10] to solve this problem; however, they only work for PDFs that are *variance monotonic*. Furthermore, Cheng et al. do not provide an optimal rectangle layout strategy for the PTI's base tree, the R-tree. The best strategy for any R-tree is to make MBRs as disjoint as possible. When MBRs overlap too much, extra disk I/Os and probability

Fig. 3.1 MBRs can easily become skewed. The *dotted rectangle* shows how the bottom MBR must expand to accommodate the uncertain object denoted by the *dotted line*. These two MBRs now severely overlap

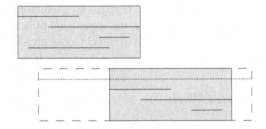

calculations must be performed because fewer nodes can be pruned. Adding new objects, especially objects of vastly different interval lengths, exacerbate overlap, as shown in Fig. 3.1. Simply put, sloppy R-trees are inefficient, but optimal R-trees are very difficult to maintain. Strategies such as segment indexes and the SR-tree [18] address different interval lengths, and interval indexes handle skew very well.

When rectangles overlap, not all objects which fall completely within the query interval can be immediately accepted. Since MBRs might overlap, every node must be checked. There is no exclusivity between node intervals. Nodes may not be stored in any order if their intervals are stretched. Objects might appear in the overlapping portions of nodes, too. These compounding factors force probability calculations on all objects in each unpruned node. This wastes lots of time, especially when the query interval is much larger in size than most uncertainty intervals.

2D Mapping Indexes

Cheng et al. first suggested 2D mapping techniques as an alternative to the PTI for uniform PDFs [10]. Agarwal et al. then expanded 2D mapping techniques to histogram PDFs [1]. Histogram PDFs can easily be transformed into linear piecewise cumulative distribution functions (CDFs). A CDF F can then be transformed into a linear piecewise threshold function g, for which $g(x)$ gives the minimum value y such that $F(y) - F(x) \geq \tau$ for a preset probability threshold τ. Threshold functions are calculated for each uncertain object and turned into a set of line segments. A range query for an interval $[a, b]$ graphs the point (a, b) and returns all objects whose line segment threshold functions are below it.

The structures of the indexes presented in [1] manipulate the line segments. The half-plane range reporting technique partitions the line segments into sets of layers. Queries visit each layer in order until a layer surpasses the query interval. Fractional cascading improves visit time. The segment tree, interval tree, and hybrid tree use the same notions presented in [6] about interval management and slabs to form optimized index structures.

2D mapping indexes are efficient for uniform and histogram PDFs, but they are inapplicable for more general PDFs. Furthermore, each index is rigidly based upon one threshold value; separate indexes must be constructed for additional thresholds.

This is starkly different from the PTI, which can manage several threshold values in one structure. However, the application of interval tree techniques presented in [1] is a novel enhancement over techniques presented in [6].

Related Work

Ranking Queries

A few different types of ranking queries have been proposed for uncertain data, which use the probabilistic database model. U-Top$k$ queries return the list of k tuples with the highest probability of being ranked as the top k [25, 29, 32]. To efficiently perform a U-Top$k$ query, a search of possible states is performed, in which the search is extended only for the tuples of highest probability. A U-kRanks query return the tuple with the highest probability of being ranked at each position. This implies that the same tuple could appear in more than one position [25, 29, 32]. When evaluating a U-kRanks query, only the most probable state for each rank so far needs to be stored. Independent tuples also exhibit the optimal substructure property, meaning a dynamic programming solution is possible. The probabilistic threshold top-k (PT-k) query returns all tuples which have a probability greater than some threshold probability for being ranked in the top k positions [15, 15, 25]. This captures tuples which might be missed by a U-Top$k$ or U-kRanks query. To evaluate, the dominant set property is leveraged, which states that whether or not a tuple is in the result set of the query depends on how many other tuples are ranked higher. Generation rule compressions and pruning improve query time. Sampling methods and Poisson approximation methods can improve efficiency in exchange for accuracy [15].

Joins

A join between tables with uncertain data returns a cross product in which each paired tuple is associated with a probability $p \geq 0$. A *probabilistic join query* (PJQ) between two tables returns all pairs of tuples with a non-zero probability of meeting the join condition. Likewise, a *probabilistic threshold join query* (PTJQ) only returns tuples whose probability is greater than some threshold probability τ. A *confidence-based top-k join query* (PTop$k$JQ) returns the k tuples with the highest probability resulting from the join. It is possible to apply various existing join methods in addition to pruning techniques to optimize query time [11, 20]. Three primary techniques for joining uncertain continuous data are presented in [11]. Joins on discrete data operate differently. For the *similarity join query*, [19, 20], each uncertain object is turned into a vector of its possible attributes. These vectors are then clustered into groups using the k-means clustering algorithm, and each group is approximated by calculating its minimum bounding hyper-rectangle.

Skyline Searches

Skyline analysis of a data set searches for the "best" objects by weighing tradeoffs between attributes. The most desirable objects constitute the *skyline*. Performing skyline searches on uncertain data can also be useful [24]. Pei et al. give the example of data representing NBA players' statistics. Reverse skyline searches can also be applied to uncertain data [22]. A reverse skyline obtains a dynamic skyline based on query parameters [13]. In a sense, it can find lowers layers of skylines instead of just the top layer. Reverse skylines are useful, particularly with uncertain data, when verifying faulty equipment or abnormal data [22]. A monochromatic probabilistic reverse skyline queries find reverse skylines over one data set, and bichromatic queries find reverse skylines between two data sets. Pruning can be performed spatially and probabilistically for both approaches. Offline pre-computation of pruning spaces can optimize queries further.

Indexing Categorical Data

Categorical (discrete) data has a finite data domain $D = \{d_1..d_n\}$. Each uncertain attribute within an object is called an *uncertain discrete attribute* (UDA) u. A UDA's value might be any value in the data domain. Therefore, it is represented by a vector of probabilities $u.P = \langle p_1..p_n \rangle$ such that $Pr(u = d_i) = u.p_i$. The probability that two UDAs are equal is given by the dot product of their probability vectors. Effective indexing strategies make equality queries and ranking queries more efficient [26, 27]. Two strategies are proposed by Singh et al. [27]. The first is the *probabilistic inverted index*, and the second strategy is the *probabilistic distribution R-tree* (PDR-tree). Testing shows that there is no universal winner between the two strategies [27].

High Dimensionality

The strategies discussed for continuous and categorical uncertain data focus on indexing one dimension. Sometimes, however, it makes more sense to think of uncertainty in more than one dimension. For example, spacial data, like for GPS or for location-based services [31], has a region of uncertainty, not just values along one line. The U-tree [30] is a natural extension of the probability threshold index [10]. Instead of using an R-tree as the base, the U-tree uses an R*-tree, which is a multidimensional R-tree that optimizes its structure by minimizing area, margin, overlap, and distance of minimum bounding rectangles [9]. Instead of using just MBRs, the U-tree uses *probabilistically constrained regions* (PCRs) to tighten regions, much like x-bounds for the probability threshold index, based on probability threshold values, and can be used both to prune and to validate results without further PDF calculation. A major problem with multidimensional data is the *sparsity problem*: distances between pairs of points tend to be too similar to garner quality information using standard distance functions [4]. Aggarwal et al. propose an expected distance function which uses a contrast ratio between means and standard deviations for a fraction of the uncertain objects [4].

Moving Objects

Indexing moving objects has been well researched [16,34]. An example of indexing moving objects would be for a city bus route schedule: busses drive along the streets, and they can be tracked to give real-time feedback on their arrival times. For certain moving data, a robust indexing structure is the B^x-tree [16]. Adding uncertainty to the data model for moving objects allows for more accurate models [34].

Processing Range Queries on Uncertain Data

We now present the proposed range query process technique for uncertain data. The cornerstone is the *threshold interval index* (TII). The TII is in essence a combination of a dynamic external interval tree and the x-bounds structure used by PTI. This structure presents two key advantages. The first advantage is that the structure intrinsically and dynamically maintains balance all the time. The second advantage is that the interval-based structure makes all uncertain objects which fall entirely within the query interval easy to find and, therefore, possible to add to the results set without further calculation. The PTI does not allow this because its MBRs might overlap. Furthermore, adding x-bound avoids the interval index's problem for when many uncertainty intervals overlap the query interval.

TII Structure

The TII has a primary tree to manage interval endpoints. It also has secondary structures at internal nodes of the primary tree to store objects. When an object is added to the index, the endpoints of its uncertainty interval are added to the primary tree. Then, the object itself is added to the secondary structures of the appropriate tree node. Each object is also assigned a unique id if it does not already have one. X-bounds are stored for each internal node.

Primary Tree

The primary tree is a *weight-balanced B-tree* with branching parameter $r > 4$ and leaf parameter $k > 0$. The *weight* of a node is the number of items (in this case, endpoints) below it. All leaves are on level 0. All endpoints are stored at the leaves,

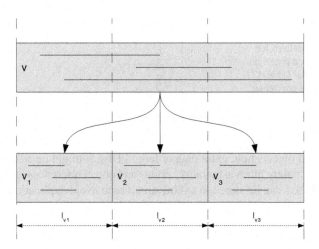

Fig. 3.2 A node v with three child nodes. The *dotted lines* denote slab boundaries. Note how objects are only stored within intervals which can completely contain them

and internal nodes hold copied values of endpoints. The weight-balanced B-tree provides an effective way to dynamically manage intervals and spread. Arge et al. describe this tree in detail, including time bounds, in [7].

Secondary Structures

Each internal node v represents an interval I_v, which spans all interval endpoints represented by children of v. Thus, the c children of v (for $\frac{1}{4}r \le c \le 4r$) naturally partition I_v into subintervals called *slabs* [7]. Each slab is denoted by I_{v_i} (for $1 \le i \le c$), and a contiguous region of slabs, such as $I_{v_2} I_{v_3} I_{v_4}$, is called a *multislab* [7]. All slab boundaries within I_v are stored in v. Note that I_{v_i} is the interval for the child node v_i.

An uncertain object is stored at v if its uncertainty interval falls entirely within I_v but overlaps one or more boundaries of any child node's I_{v_i}. (A leaf stores uncertain objects whose PDF endpoints are contained completely within the leaf's interval endpoints.) Each object is stored at exactly one node in the tree, as shown in Fig. 3.2. Let U_v denote the set of uncertain objects stored in v. In the external dynamic interval index, these objects are stored in secondary structures called *slab lists* [7], partitioned by the slab boundaries. However, only two secondary structures are needed per node for the TII because range queries (described later in this section) work slightly differently than stabbing queries. The *left endpoint list* stores all uncertain objects in increasing order of their uncertainty intervals' left endpoints. The *right endpoint list* stores all uncertain objects in increasing order of their uncertainty intervals' right endpoints. This is drastically simpler than the optimal external interval tree, which requires a secondary structure for each multislab [7].

Fig. 3.3 A node with
x-bounds and objects.
X-bounds are calculated for
each node based on uncertain
objects' PDFs. The *left* and
right 0.25-bounds are tighter
than the MBR

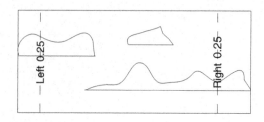

If the uncertain objects hold extra data or large PDFs, it might be advantageous to
store only uncertainty interval boundary points and object references in the two lists.
The actual objects can be stored in a third structure to avoid duplication.

Applying X-Bounds

X-bounds were introduced as part of the probability threshold index [10] and can
easily be applied to the TII.

Definition 1. An *x-bound* is a pair of values (L_x, R_x) for a continuous PDF $f(s)$
with uncertainty domain $[L, R]$ such that

$$x = \int_L^{L_x} f(s)ds = \int_{R_x}^R f(s)ds \tag{3.1}$$

L_x is the *left x-bound*, and R_x is the *right x-bound*. Since the domain of $f(s)$
is $[L, R]$, L_x and R_x are unique. Note that x is a probability value, meaning $0 \leq x \leq 1$. For example, if $x = 0.25$, then there is a 25 % chance that the object's
value appears in the interval $[L, L_{0.25}]$. Furthermore, there would be a 25 % chance
it appears in $[R_{0.25}, R]$ and a 50 % chance it appears in $[L_{0.25}, R_{0.25}]$. Note also that
if $x > 0.5$, then $R_x < L_x$.

The notion of x-bounds can be applied to tree nodes as well as to PDFs, as
seen in Fig. 3.3. The left x-bound for a node is the minimum left x-bound of all
child nodes and objects, and the right x-bound is the maximum right x-bound of
all child nodes and objects. Specifically, for a node v, left and right x-bounds are
calculated for I_v. A child node's x-bounds must be considered when calculating
v's x-bounds: a child node might have tighter x-bounds than any of the uncertain
objects stored at v. The interval I_v accounts for all uncertain objects stored at v and
in any child nodes of v, and so should the x-bounds. The x-bounds for v's slabs
are given by the x-bounds on v's child nodes. All of v's x-bounds are stored in v's
parent. In this way, the interval I_v is analogous to a minimum bounding rectangle
in an R-tree, and intervals are tightened by x-bounds in the same way as MBRs are
tightened in the PTI [10]. X-bounds for more than one probability x can be stored
as well.

Fig. 3.4 A left stab is denoted by the *thick black line*. The *light gray* nodes are visited by the stab. The *white* nodes are not visited. The *dark gray* node is pruned based on x-bounds

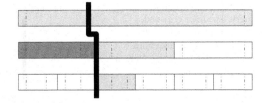

Range Query Evaluation

Evaluating range queries for objects in $[a, b]$ with a threshold τ on the TII is like evaluating stabbing queries on a regular interval tree. Two *stabs* are executed for each endpoint of the query interval: a left stab and a right stab. The nature of the query forces these stabs to be performed slightly differently from how they are described in [7]. Once the stabs are made, a series of *grabs* can be performed for all objects in between. This is called the *stab 'n grab search*.

The Left Stab

The *left stab* is the most complicated part of the stab 'n grab search. The search starts at the root node and continues down one path through child nodes until it hits the leaf containing the closest x-bound to a within its boundaries. This leaf is called the *left boundary leaf*. X-bounds are used to prune this search. If a node's right x-bound is less than a or if a node's left x-bound is greater than b, then the node can be pruned, because the probability that any of its objects falls within the query interval must be less than the query's threshold. Objects are checked at nodes along the stab to see if they belong to the result set (Fig. 3.4).

Before moving to the next child node, the uncertain objects stored in secondary structures at the current node must be investigated, because their uncertainty intervals may overlap the query interval. If they overlap the query interval, then they might be valid query results. Between the secondary structures, only the right endpoint list is needed. A quick binary search can be performed to find which objects fall within the query interval. Any object whose right endpoint is less than a can be disregarded. Any object whose both endpoints are within the query interval is added to the result set automatically. Otherwise, a probability calculation must be performed using the object's PDF to determine if it meets the threshold probability. The same strategy applies for the left boundary leaf. All valid objects are added to the result set.

The Right Stab

The *right stab* is analogous to the left stab, except it searches with b instead of a. The leaf found at the bottom of the stab is called the *right boundary leaf*. X-bound

Fig. 3.5 A stab 'n grab query. The *light gray* nodes are visited during the stabs, and the *dark gray* nodes are visited during the grabs. Note how grabbed nodes fall completely within the query interval

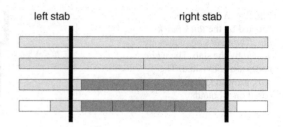

pruning is performed for the rightmost child nodes, not the leftmost. The process for searching the secondary structures is the same as in the left stab, except "left" and "right" are switched wherever mentioned. Furthermore, nodes visited during the left stab can be skipped during the right stab, because the process for investigating uncertain objects accounts for both endpoints of the uncertainty interval. This is why references to visited nodes are stored during the left stab.

The Grabs

The two stabs find the two boundary leaves and some uncertain objects in the result set. The remaining objects to investigate reside in the nodes between the two boundary leaves. Thankfully, all objects in between can be added to the result set without any probability calculations. Remember, intervals for nodes on the same level do not overlap, so all objects stored at nodes between the boundary leaves must fall entirely within the query. The most effective way to grab all of these uncertain objects is to perform a post-order tree traversal starting at the left boundary leaf and ending at the right boundary leaf, skipping each node that has already been visited. No extra searching needs to be done on the secondary structures. Figure 3.5 illustrates a full stab 'n grab query.

Time Bounds

A range query can be answered within the following time bounds using the stab 'n grab search:

Theorem 1. *Let I be a TII storing N uncertain objects, whose primary tree has branching parameter r and leaf parameter k. Assume any calculation on an uncertain object's PDF takes $O(d)$ time. A range query Q with query interval $[a, b]$ and threshold τ can return all T uncertain objects stored in I which fall within the query interval with probability $p \geq \tau$ in $O(kd \, log_r(N/k) + T/k)$ time.*

Proof. The height of the primary tree is $O(\log_r(N/k))$ [7]. If the number of child nodes of any internal node is $O(a)$, then the total number of nodes in the tree is $O(\sum_{i=0}^{\log_r(N/k)} r^i) = O(r^{\log_r(N/k)}) = O(N/k)$. Since the N uncertain objects are distributed relatively uniformly over the tree, each node stores $O(N/(N/k)) = O(k)$ objects. A stab, either right or left, visits $O(\log_r(N/k))$ nodes from root to boundary leaf and must visit all objects stored at a node in the worst case, calculating probabilities for each. Hence, the stabs are performed in $O(kd \log_r(N/k))$ time. The grabs are performed in $O(T/k)$ time, because extra checking at each node in between the leaf boundaries is unnecessary. All nodes visited by the grabs are guaranteed to be valid results, so T is used instead of N for the time bound. Therefore, two stabs and all grabs can be performed in a combined time of $O(kd \log_r(N/k) + T/k)$.   □

Externalization

The TII can easily be externalized by setting k and r for the primary tree appropriately, albeit differently than how described in [7]. Let B be the block size; specifically, the number of data units which can be stored in a block. For the primary tree, an uncertain object is represented only by its uncertainty interval endpoints, each of which is one unit of data. Each child node needs two units for endpoints, one unit for its block pointer, and two units for each set of x-bounds, meaning each node requires $3 + 2n$ units, where n is the number of x-bounds stored for the tree. The number of children per node still ranges from $\frac{1}{4}r$ to $4r$. Thus, $k = \frac{1}{2}B$ and $r = \frac{1}{4(3+2n)}B$.

Theorem 2. *The external TII can be stored using $O(N/B)$ blocks. Range queries can be answered using $O(\log_B N + T/B)$ disk I/Os and $O(B \log_B N)$ probability calculations, and updates can be performed using $O(\log_B N)$ disk I/Os and $O(1)$ probability calculations.*

Proof. Substitute $r = \frac{1}{4(3+2n)}B$ and $k = \frac{1}{2}B$. The bounds from [7] still remain for disk I/Os.   □

Memory-Loaded Threshold Interval Indexing

Although the TII aptly balances the data, the primary tree uses a lot of storage space. For every object, the primary tree must also store two endpoints. This can severely inflate the number of blocks when many objects are indexed externally. In this section, we introduce the *memory-loaded threshold interval index* (MTII) as an alternative external TII to reduce the number of disk I/Os during range queries. Since the primary tree is significantly smaller, all nodes can be preloaded into memory before the query runs to improve runtime.

In the TII, every uncertain object's endpoints are stored in the leaves. However, in the MTII, only those endpoints which form the slab boundaries, e.g., the minimum

Fig. 3.6 Size comparison for
10,000 objects and 1 X-bound

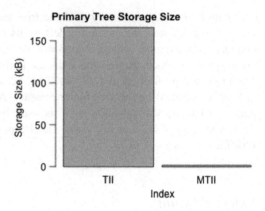

and maximum values for each leaf's interval, must be stored. This means that a leaf stores only two endpoints instead of k endpoints. An internal node stores its own slab boundaries and pointers to child nodes. It does not need to store the slab boundaries or x-bounds for its child nodes.

For the primary tree, let $r = 2$ and let $k = \frac{1}{2}B$. There is no reason to change the leaf parameter k from the value suggested in [6], since k controls the spread of objects at the bottom level of the tree. The branching parameter should be set to $r = 2$ to make the primary tree a binary tree. Since the whole primary tree will reside in memory, increased fanout is unnecessary.

Storing the primary tree is trickier for the MTII, since one block will hold more than one nodes. For each node, a node id, left slab boundary, and right slab boundary must be stored, which requires only three units of data. Blocks store tree nodes in a top-down, breadth-first fashion: start at the root, and store each successive level of the tree left, ordering nodes least to greatest for their intervals. The ordering and slab boundaries will inherently denote parent-child relationships. For example, a root node may have the interval [0, 1,000]. Its two children might have [0, 400] and [400, 1,000]. When reading the nodes the jump from a right endpoint of 1,000 to a left endpoint of 0 denotes a new level in the tree. Since the root contains all nodes between 0 and 1,000, the 2 nodes read after the root must be its children. Figure 3.6 illustrates the drastic reduction in storage size between the TII and the MTII.

Uncertain objects are stored in the same way as for the TII, using secondary structures: the left and right endpoint lists are stored externally in blocks. X-bounds for each primary tree node are stored in a copy tree. For each x-bound x value, another primary tree structure is created as mentioned above, only instead of storing slab boundaries, it stores x-bound pairs as if they were slab boundaries. This x-bound tree is stored the same way as the primary tree. Multiple x-bound trees can be created, one for each x value. This way, a query can load the appropriate x-bound tree and not waste disk I/Os on unnecessary x-bound values. A query will only read blocks for the primary tree and one x-bound tree.

Range queries using the MTII are executed similarly as for the TII. First, the primary tree and appropriate x-bound tree must be preloaded. Note that these structures may remain in memory if multiple queries will be executed. Then the stab 'n grab search is performed, just like for the TII.

Update methods are simpler for the MTII. Inserting an object is the same: find the appropriate node based on intervals and store the object in the secondary structures. The primary tree is not updated because extra endpoints are not stored in the nodes. Once the secondary structures are too large, meaning they use more than one or two blocks of data, then the node can be split using standard binary tree procedures. Intervals and x-bounds must also be updated. Deletion follows similar guidelines as for the TII.

Experimental Results

This section presents an evaluation of our experimental results. We use the probability threshold index as a benchmark against which to test both the standard and memory-loaded threshold interval indexes.

Test Model

The purpose for testing these three indexes is to compare their range query performance. Performance is measured by three primary metrics:

- Number of disk I/Os
- Number of probability calculations
- Runtime (in milliseconds)

Six different performance tests are run. Each test builds the indexes from a common data set and runs range queries on each index. Descriptions are given in Table 3.1. Datasets are generated synthetically. Uncertain objects contain two attributes: an id and a PDF. The PDF interval is determined randomly based on test parameters, given in Table 3.2. X-bounds are calculated for the probability values $\{0.1, 0.3, 0.5, 0.7, 0.9\}$ on each index. The block size is 4,096 bytes.

Each test is run with two types of PDFs. Just like for previous tests against the PTI, one PDF used is a uniform PDF [10]. The second PDF is a multimodal Gaussian distribution, which is significantly more complicated. Each PDF can be stored by left and right endpoints and can be stretched to the appropriate interval length. All probability calculations are performed by using Riemann sums. Thousand rectangles are used for each Riemann sum to keep the average error margin around 0.1 %.

Range queries must also be generated. For each test, 100 queries are generated. Each query interval is random within a given domain. Each query is run against each index, and results for all queries are tabulated aggregately. Except for the Threshold test, which varies τ, the probability threshold used is $\tau = 0.3$.

Table 3.1 Performance tests

Test	Description
Same	Object uncertainty intervals have the same length
Different	Object uncertainty intervals have different length
Dense	Many objects overlap
Sparse	Objects are spaced out
Threshold	Same as Different, but varies probability threshold
Ratio	Varies query interval length versus object interval length

Table 3.2 Test Parameters

Parameter	Same	Different	Dense	Sparse	Ratio
Num objects	10,000	10,000	10,000	10,000	10,000
Min object value	0	0	0	0	0
Max object value	10,000	10,000	1,000	1,000,000	10,000
Min PDF length	100	50	1	1	10
Max PDF length	100	500	100	10	10

Unfortunately, no optimal minimum bounding rectangle (MBR) strategy is proposed for the PTI [10]. Our PTI sorts all objects by their left endpoints and partitions them into leaves for bulk loading. This would most likely represent a "perfect" PTI. However, a more practical PTI goes through insertions and deletions, which will stretch MBRs. For our tests, we separate ten objects from the dataset and insert them into random leaves during bulk loading. This more "practical" PTI is used for comparison testing against the TII and the MTII. Remember, since the TII and MTII are interval trees, they do not experience the same skew problems as the PTI.

Effect of Object Spread

The Same, Different, Dense, and Sparse tests all test the spread of uncertain objects. Figure 3.7 gives results for these tests. It is clear that object spread and size significantly affects performance. All indexes have worse performance for objects of different lengths and for densely clustered objects. What is interesting is the difference in performance metrics. The PTI uses fewer disk I/Os than both the TII and the MTII. Although for objects of the same size the MTII and the PTI are comparable for uniform PDFs, the TII and MTII generally use about 1.5–2 times as many disk I/Os. The PTI is far surpassed, however, in regards to the number of probability calculations. Threshold indexes typically use only half to a third of the number of calculations as the PTI. This number is most staggering for sparse indexes: the TII and MTII make relatively no calculations. Overall, the total runtime favors threshold indexes for complicated probability functions, particularly the MTII.

The trends between uniform and multimodal PDFs are generally the same for disk I/Os and probability calculations. This is not too surprising, because PDF shape

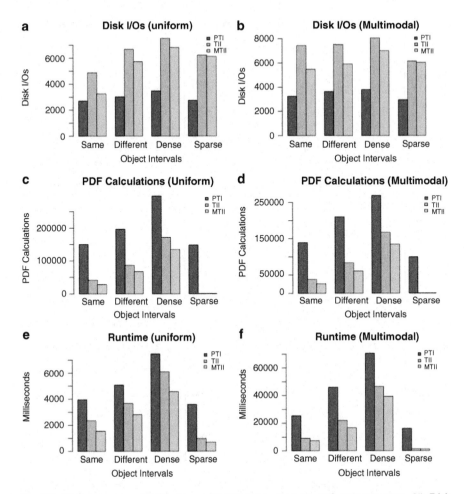

Fig. 3.7 Performance results for Same, Different, Dense, and Sparse tests. (**a**) Disk I/Os for uniform PDFs. (**b**) Disk I/Os for multimodal PDFs. (**c**) Uniform PDF calculations. (**d**) Multimodal PDF calculations. (**e**) Runtime for uniform PDFs. (**f**) Runtime for multimodal PDFs

has only a small affect on index structure. The major difference is in total runtime, as seen in Fig. 3.7e, f. Since the multimodal PDF is more complicated, calculations take longer. Thus, the margin by which the TII and MTII outperform the PTI is much larger for multimodal PDFs than for uniform PDFs.

Effect of Probability Threshold

The Threshold test uses the same test parameters as the Different test, but it runs the query set on multiple probability thresholds. Figure 3.8 gives the

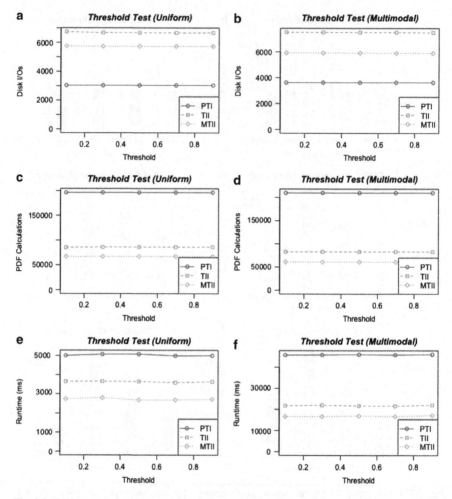

Fig. 3.8 Performance results for the `Threshold` test. (**a**) Disk I/Os for uniform PDFs. (**b**) Disk I/Os for multimodal PDFs. (**c**) Uniform PDF calculations. (**d**) Multimodal PDF calculations. (**e**) Runtime for uniform PDFs. (**f**) Runtime for multimodal PDFs

results. Consistently, probability threshold does not have much effect on any of the indicators of performance, for either PDF.

Effect of Query Interval Size

The `Ratio` test investigates the effect of query size relative to the objects' interval sizes. It runs random queries with a fixed query interval length for different ratios of query interval length to object interval length. For example, a ratio value of 3

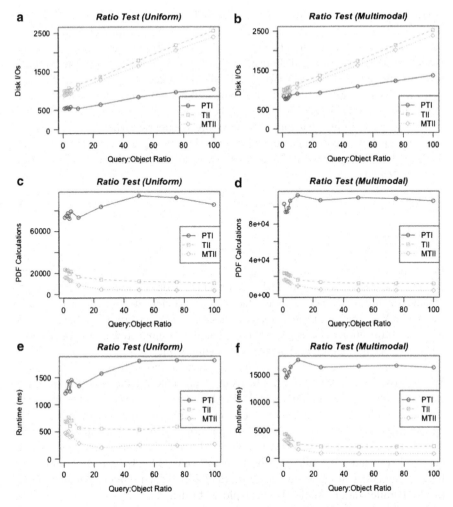

Fig. 3.9 Performance results for the Ratio test. (**a**) Disk I/Os for uniform PDFs. (**b**) Disk I/Os for multimodal PDFs. (**c**) Uniform PDF calculations. (**d**) Multimodal PDF calculations. (**e**) Runtime for uniform PDFs. (**f**) Runtime for multimodal PDFs

means that the query interval length is 3 times as large as the object interval length. Each object has a constant interval length of 10 to make ratios consistent. Indexes are built only once, and 100 queries are constructed for each ratio value.

Figure 3.9 gives the results for the Ratio test. Results are consistent with the other tests' results. It is interesting to note what happens as the query interval ratio is increased. Naturally, the number of disk I/Os for each index increases linearly, since more objects are fetched for a larger query interval. However, the trend for probability calculations diverge between the PTI and the TII and MTII. For the PTI, the number of calculations appears somewhat parabolic: it generally increases until the ratio value is approximately 50 for uniform PDFs and 10 for multimodal PDFs, after which the number decreases. For the TII and MTII, the number of probability calculations decreases asymptotically towards a very low constant value. This value is about 10,000 for the TII and about 3,000 for the MTII for both PDFs. The runtimes level off after a ratio value of 10 for threshold indexes and about 50 for the PTI with uniform PDFs and about 30 for the PTI with multimodal PDFs. For each index and PDF, runtime always levels off.

These results imply that threshold indexing is superior when query sizes are large in respect to the average object size. This benefit is greatest when query sizes are about ten times as large as object sizes. It also shows again that the MTII is more efficient than the TII.

Conclusion

In this paper, we present threshold interval indexing, a new strategy for indexing complicated uncertain continuous data of one dimension. We present two structures: a standard threshold interval index and a more efficient memory-loaded variant. The key advantage of threshold interval indexing over existing strategies, such as the probability threshold index, is that it handles complicated PDFs much more efficiently because it handles balance better with its intervals.

There are many more opportunities for further research on uncertain data. Specifically, future research should focus more on exploring the effects of different types of PDFs on uncertain indexes. PDFs should not be overlooked, because they are inseparable from what makes the data uncertain. Perhaps certain rectangle management strategies could improve the performance of the PTI, such as the priority R-tree [8] or the segment R-tree [18]. Although our paper focuses on range queries, these indexes could also be used for joins [11, 14]. It is also important for uncertain data strategies to be incorporated into database management systems [5, 28]. Parallelization should also be explored further.

References

1. Agarwal PK, Cheng SW, Tao Y, Yi K (2009) Indexing uncertain data. In: Symposium on principles of database systems (PODS), Providence, pp 137–146
2. Aggarwal CC (2009a) An introduction to uncertain data algorithms and applications. In: Managing and mining uncertain data. Springer, New York, pp 2–8
3. Aggarwal CC (2009b) On clustering algorithms for uncertain data. In: Managing and mining uncertain data. Springer, New York, pp 389–406
4. Aggarwal CC, Yu PS (2008) On indexing high dimensional data with uncertainty. In: IEEE international conference on data engineering (ICDE), Cancun
5. Agrawal P, Benjelloun O, Sarma AD, Hayworth C, Nabar S, Sugihara T, Widom J (2006) Trio: a system for data, uncertainty, and lineage. In: Proceedings of the international conference on very large data bases (VLDB), Seoul, pp 1151–1154. Demonstration Description

6. Arge L, Vitter JS (1996) Optimal dynamic interval management in external memory. In: Proceedings of the IEEE symposium on foundations of computer science (FOCS), Burlington, pp 560–569. Extended abstract

7. Arge L, Vitter JS (2003) Optimal external memory interval management. SIAM J Comput 32(6):1488–1508

8. Arge L, de Berg M, Haverkort HJ, Yi K (2004) The priority r-tree: a practically efficient and worst-case optimal r-tree. In: SIGMOD conference, Paris, pp 347–358

9. Beckmann N, Kriegel HP, Schneider R, Seeger B (1990) The r*-tree: an efficient and robust access method for points and rectangles. In: SIGMOD conference, Atlantic City, pp 322–331

10. Cheng R, Xia Y, Prabhakar S, Shah R, Vitter JS (2004) Efficient indexing methods for probabilistic threshold queries over uncertain data. In: Proceedings of the international conference on very large data bases (VLDB), Toronto, pp 876–887

11. Cheng R, Xia Y, Prabhakar S, Shah R, Vitter JS (2006) Efficient join processing over uncertain data. In: Proceedings of the 15th ACM international conference on information and knowledge management, Arlington, pp 738–747

12. Cormen TH, Leiserson CE, Rivest RL, Stein C (2001) Introduction to algorithms, 2nd edn. Massachusetts Institute of Technology, Cambridge

13. Dellis E, Seeger B (2007) Efficient computation of reverse skyline queries. In: Proceedings of the international conference on very large data bases (VLDB), Vienna, pp 291–302

14. Enderle J, Hampel M, Seidl T (2004) Joining interval data in relational databases. In: SIGMOD conference, Paris, pp 683–694

15. Hua M, Pei J, Zhang W, Lin X (2008) Ranking queries on uncertain data: a probabilistic threshold approach. In: SIGMOD conference, Vancouver, pp 673–686

16. Jensen CS, Lin D, Ooi BC (2004) Query and update efficient b+–tree based indexing of moving objects. In: Proceedings of the international conference on very large data bases (VLDB), Toronto, pp 768–779

17. Kanellakis PC, Ramaswamy S, Vengroff DE, Vitter JS (1993) Indexing for data models with constraints and classes. In: Symposium on principles of database systems (PODS), Washington, DC

18. Kolovson CP, Stonebraker M (1991) Segment indexes: dynamic indexing techniques for multi-dimensional interval data. In: SIGMOD conference, Denver, pp 138–147

19. Kriegel HP, Kunath P, Pfeifle M, Renz M (2006) Probabilistic similarity join on uncertain data. In: Proceedings of the 11th international conference on database systems for advanced applications (DASFAA), Singapore, pp 295–309

20. Kriegel HP, Bernecker T, Renz M, Zuefle A (2009) Probabilistic join queries in uncertain databases. Managing and mining uncertain data. Springer, New York, pp 257–298

21. Lan Y, Papoian GA (2007) Evolution of complex probability distributions in enzyme cascades. J Theor Biol 248:537–545

22. Lian X, Chen L (2008) Monochromatic and bichromatic reverse skyline search over uncertain databases. In: SIGMOD conference, Vancouver

23. Manolopoulos Y, Theodoridis Y, Tsotras VJ (2000) Access methods for intervals, chap 4. In: Advanced database indexing. Kluwer, Boston

24. Pei J, Jiang B, Lin X, Yuan Y (2007) Probabilistic skylines on uncertain data. In: Proceedings of the international conference on very large data bases (VLDB), Vienna

25. Pei J, Hua M, Tao Y, Lin X (2008) Query answering techniques on uncertain and probabilistic data. In: SIGMOD conference, Vancouver, pp 1357–1364. Tutorial summary

26. Prabhakar S, Shah R, Singh S (2009) Indexing uncertain data. In: Managing and mining uncertain data. Springer, New York, pp 299–325

27. Singh S, Mayfield C, Prabhakar S, Shah R, Hambrusch S (2007) Indexing uncertain categorical data. In: IEEE international conference on data engineering (ICDE), Istanbul, pp 616–625

28. Singh S, Mayfield C, Mittal S, Prabhakar S, Hambrusch S, Shah R (2008) Orion 2.0: native support for uncertain data. In: SIGMOD conference, Vancouver, pp 1239–1242. Demonstration Description

29. Soliman MA, Chang KC-C, Ihab F. Ilyas (2007) Top-k query processing in uncertain databases. In: IEEE international conference on data engineering (ICDE), Istanbul
30. Tao Y, Cheng R, Xiao X, Ngai WK, Kao B, Prabhakar S (2005) Indexing multi-dimensional uncertain data with arbitrary probability density functions. In: Proceedings of the international conference on very large data bases (VLDB), Trondheim
31. Wolfson O, Sistla AP, Chamberlain S, Yesha Y (1999) Updating and querying databases that track mobile units. Distrib Parallel Databases (Special issue on Mob Data Manage Appl) 7(3):257–387
32. Yi K, Li F, Kollios G, Srivastava D (2008) Efficient processing of top-k queries in uncertain databases. In: IEEE international conference on data engineering (ICDE), Cancun
33. Yu J, Yang MS, Hao P (2009) A novel multimodal probability model for cluster analysis. In: RSKT '09: proceedings of the 4th international conference on rough sets and knowledge technology. Springer, Berlin/Heidelberg, pp 397–404. doi:http://dx.doi.org/10.1007/978-3-642-02962-2_50
34. Zhang M, Chen S, Jensen CS, Ooi BC, Zhang Z (2009) Effectively indexing uncertain moving objects for predictive queries. In: Proceedings of the international conference on very large data bases (VLDB), Lyon

Chapter 4
Invariant Object Representation Based on Inverse Pyramidal Decomposition and Modified Mellin-Fourier Transform

R. Kountchev, S. Rubin, M. Milanova, and R. Kountcheva

Abstract In this work is presented one new method for invariant object representation based on the Inverse Pyramidal Decomposition (IPD) and modified Mellin-Fourier Transform (MFT). The so prepared object representation is invariant against 2D rotation, scaling, and translation (RST). The representation is additionally made invariant to significant contrast and illumination changes. The method is aimed at content-based object retrieval in large databases. The experimental results obtained using the software implementation of the method proved its efficiency. The method is suitable for various applications, such as detection of children sexual abuse in multimedia files, search of handwritten and printed documents, 3D objects, represented by multi-view 2D images, etc.

R. Kountchev (✉)
Department of Radio Communications, Technical University of Sofia, Bul. Kl. Ohridsky 8, Sofia, 1000, Bulgaria
e-mail: rkountch@tu-sofia.bg

S. Rubin
Space and Naval Warfare Systems Center San Diego (SSC-PAC), San Diego, CA, USA
e-mail: stuart.rubin@navy.mil

M. Milanova
Computer Science Department, UALR, 2801 South University Avenue, Little Rock, AR 72204, USA
e-mail: mgmilanova@ualr.edu

R. Kountcheva
T&K Engineering, Mladost 3, Pob.12, Sofia, 1712, Bulgaria
e-mail: kountcheva_r@yahoo.com

T. Özyer et al. (eds.), *Information Reuse and Integration in Academia and Industry*, DOI 10.1007/978-3-7091-1538-1_4, © Springer-Verlag Wien 2013

Introduction

One of the most important tasks, which the creators of contemporary computer visual systems have to solve, is related to objects description, which ensures their exact and reliable classification. Objects description should satisfy contradictory requirements [1, 2]: to be invariable to object rotation, translation and scaling; lighting (respectively – contrast) changes; noises in the image; low intra-class and high inter-class dispersion; maximum compactness of the description and low computational complexity of the operations performed.

The objects descriptions could be divided into two basic groups: local and global. The first group represents the local features of the objects, related to the structure of the visible part of their surface (salient points, contours, edges, texture, etc.) [3, 4]. These descriptions are not resistant enough against noises and have high dimensionality and computational complexity. The second group comprises characteristics, which represent the general qualities of the visible surface, related for example, to object's geometrical parameters (invariable moments), coefficients of the contour lines' Fourier decomposition, global brightness histograms, coefficients of the generalized Hough transform, coefficients of the Mellin-Fourier transform, etc. [5–8]. The advantages of these descriptions are their insensibility to noises and the big compactness, but their computational complexity is relatively high.

The basic methods for invariant object representation with respect to 2D rigid transforms (combinations of rotation, scaling, and translation, RST) are given in significant number of scientific publications. Accordingly, 2D objects in the still grayscale image are depicted by descriptors of two basic kinds: "shape boundary" and "region". To the first kind (shape boundary) are assigned the chain codes, Fourier descriptors; Generalized Hough Transform and Active Shape Model [7]. The skeleton of a shape can be derived by the Medial Axis Transform. To the second kind (region) are assigned some geometric characteristics, such as for example: area, perimeter, compactness, dispersion, eccentricity, etc., zero- and first-order statistical moments, centre of gravity, normalized central moments, seven rotation-invariant moments, Zernike polynomial rotation- and scale-invariant, affine transform invariant in respect to position, rotation and different scales along the coordinate axes, co-occurrence texture descriptor, etc.

The histogram descriptor is proved to be robust to changes of object's rotation, scale, and partial changes in the viewing direction. The structural information however is lost in the histogram. To solve this problem, the combination of Discrete Wavelet Transform (DWT) or Discrete Fourier Transform (DFT) with the feature extraction method is proposed. For the extraction of the rotation-scale-translation (RST) – invariant features are developed descriptors, based on the log-polar transform (LPT) used to convert rotation and scaling into translation [8] and on the 2D Mellin-Fourier Transform (2D-MFT) [9]. As it is known, the modules of the spectrum coefficients, obtained using the 2D-MFT, are invariant with respect to the RST-transforms of the 2D objects in the image. The basic problem for the creation of the RST-invariant descriptors, in this case is the large number of spectrum coefficients, which have to be calculated [10, 11]. With regard to the necessity to reduce their number, and respectively – the time needed for the calculation without decreasing the objects description accuracy, should be solved significant number of problems, regarding the choice of the most informative MFT coefficients and the way of creating the corresponding vector descriptor.

In this work is offered new algorithm for global description of pre-segmented objects in a halftone image. This algorithm differs from the known algorithms in the same group: it requires lower number of computations when compared to the famous MFT and permits multi-layer access which enhances the search by content in indexed image databases. The new algorithm is based on the methods of the inverse pyramid decomposition [12] and of the truncated modified discrete MFT [13, 14], which are combined.

This work is arranged as follows: in section "Invariant Object Representation with Pyramid of Coefficients Based on the Truncated Modified Mellin-Fourier Transform" is described the method for invariant object representation based on pyramid of coefficients, calculated using the truncated Mellin-Furier transform; in section "Search by Content of Closest Objects in Image Databases" is given the new approach for search-by-content of closest object in image database; in section "Fast Search of Closest Vector in the Image Database" – the fast search of closest vector in the image database, in section "Experimental Results" are shown some experimental results, and in section "Conclusions" are given the Conclusions.

Invariant Object Representation with Pyramid of Coefficients Based on the Truncated Modified Mellin-Fourier Transform

The algorithm for 2D object representation is aimed at the preparation of the vector description of the segmented object, framed by a square window.

The description should be invariant to 2D rotation (R), scaling (S), translation (T) and contrast (C) changes. As a basis for the RSTC description is used the discrete 2D Modified MFT (2D-MMFT). As it is known, the MFT comprises DFT, Log-pol transform (LPT) and DFT again. In order to provide multi-layer search-by-content in the image database, the 2D-MMFT coefficients are arranged in a pyramid, called Inverse Pyramid Decomposition (IPD).

The algorithm, presented below, is aimed at digital halftone images, and comprises the following stages:

For the initial (lowest) IPD level:

Step 1.   The pixels B(k,l) of the original halftone image of size M × N are transformed into bi-polar:

$$L(k, l) = B(k, l) - (B_{max} + 1)/2 \qquad (4.1)$$

for $k = 0, 1, \ldots, M-1$ and $l = 0, 1, .., N-1$, where $B_{max} = 255$ is the maximum value in the pixel quantization scale.

Step 2.   The image is processed with 2D Discrete Fourier Transform (2D-DFT). The Fourier matrix is of size $n \times n (n = 2^m)$. The value of n defines the size of the window, used to select the object image. For the invariant object representation are used the complex 2D-DFT coefficients, calculated in accordance with the relation:

$$F(a, b) = \sum_{k=0}^{n-1} \sum_{l=0}^{n-1} L(k, l) \exp\{-j[(2\pi/n)(ka + lb)]\} \qquad (4.2)$$

for $a = 0, 1, .., n - 1$ and $b = 0, 1, .., n - 1$.

The transform comprises two consecutive operations: one-dimensional transform of the pixels L(k,l), first – for the rows and after that – for the columns of the object image. Since

$$\exp\{-j[2\pi(lb/n)]\} = \cos[2\pi(lb/n)] - j \sin[2\pi(lb/n)]$$

and

$$\exp\{-j[2\pi(ka/n)]\} = \cos[2\pi(ka/n)] - j \sin[2\pi(ka/n)],$$

the 2D-DFT is performed as two consecutive one-dimensional DFTs:

- For the fixed values of $k = 0, 1, .., n-1$ and using the 1D-Fast Fourier Transform (1D-FFT) are calculated the intermediate spectrum coefficients:

$$F(k, b) = \sum_{l=0}^{n-1} L(k, l) \exp\{-j[2\pi(lb/n)]\} =$$
$$= \sum_{l=0}^{n-1} L(k, l) \cos[2\pi(lb/n)] - j \sum_{l=0}^{N-1} L(k, l) \sin[2\pi(lb/n)] \qquad (4.3)$$

- For $b = 0, 1, \ldots, n - 1$ and using the 1D-FFT again, are calculated the final Fourier coefficients:

$$F(a, b) = \sum_{k=0}^{n-1} F(k, b) \exp\{-j[2\pi(ka/n)]\} = \sum_{k=0}^{n-1} F(k, b) \cos[2\pi(ka/n)] -$$
$$-j \sum_{k=0}^{n-1} F(k, b) \sin[2\pi(ka/n)] = A_F(a, b) - jB_F(a, b)$$
$$(4.4)$$

where $A_F(a, b)$ and $B_F(a, b)$ are the real and the imaginary components of F(a, b) correspondingly.

Step 3.   The Fourier coefficients are then centered in accordance with the relation:

$$F_0(a, b) = F\left(a - \tfrac{n}{2}, b - \tfrac{n}{2}\right) \text{ for a, b} = 0, 1, .., \text{ n} - 1. \qquad (4.5)$$

Step 4.   For the next operations some of the Fourier coefficients are retained in accordance with the rule:

$$F_{OR}(a, b) = \begin{cases} F_0(a, b), if(a, b) \in retained\ region; \\ 0 \qquad - \qquad in\ all\ other\ cases. \end{cases} \qquad (4.6)$$

The retained coefficients' area is a square with a side H $\leq$ n, which envelopes the centre (0,0) of the spectrum plane (H – even number). For H < n, and $a, b = -(H/2), -(H/2) + 1, \ldots, -1, 0, 1, \ldots, (H/2) - 1$, this square contains low-frequency coefficients only.

Step 5.   The modules and phases of coefficients $F_{OR}(a, b) = D_{F_{OR}}(a, b)e^{j\varphi_{F_{OR}}(a,b)}$ are calculated:

$$D_{F_{OR}}(a, b) = \sqrt{[A_{F_{OR}}(a, b)]^2 + [B_{F_{OR}}(a, b)]^2} \qquad (4.7)$$

$$\varphi_{F_{OR}}(a, b) = arctg[B_{F_{OR}}(a, b)/A_{F_{OR}}(a, b)] \qquad (4.8)$$

Step 6.   The modules $D_{F_{OR}}(a, b)$ of the Fourier coefficients $F_{OR}(a, b)$ are normalized in accordance with the relation:

$$D(a, b) = p\ \ln D_{F_{OR}}(a, b) \qquad (4.9)$$

where p = 64 is the normalization coefficient.

Step 7.   The coefficients D(a, b) are processed with Log-Polar Transform (LPT). The centre (0,0) of the polar coordinate system (ρ, θ) coincides with the centre of the image of the Fourier coefficients' modules D(a, b) (in the rectangular coordinate system). The transformation of coefficients D(a, b) from the rectangular (a, b) into the polar (ρ, θ) coordinate system is performed changing the variables in accordance with the relations:

$$\rho = \log \sqrt{a^2 + b^2}, \quad \theta = arctg(b/a) \qquad (4.10)$$

The coordinate change from rectangular into polar is quite clear in the continuous domain, but in the discrete domain the values of ρ and θ should be discrete as well.

Since a and b can only have discrete values in the range $a, b = -(H/2), \ldots, -1, 0, 1, \ldots, (H/2) - 1$, some of the coefficients $D(\rho, \theta)$ will be missing. At the end of the transform, the missing coefficients $D(\rho_i, \theta_i)$ are interpolated using the closest neighbors D(a, b) in the rectangular coordinate system (a, b) in horizontal or vertical direction (zero-order interpolation).

The number of discrete circles in the polar system with radius ρ_i is equal to the number of the discrete angles θ_i for i =, 2, .., H. The size (in rectangular coordinates) of the side of the square H inscribed in the LPT matrix is calculated so, that to ensure maximum part of the coefficients to be transferred without change.

Fig. 4.1 Geometric relations
between r and H

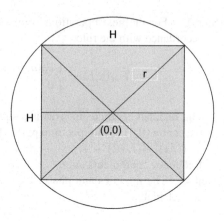

For this, the LP transform is modified in accordance with Fig. 4.1, calculating the
radius of the circumscribed circle in correspondence to the relation:

$$r = (\sqrt{2}/2)H \tag{4.11}$$

The smallest step $\Delta\rho$ between two concentric circles (the most inside) is
calculated as follows:

$$\Delta\rho = r^{(1/H)}. \tag{4.12}$$

The square, with side H, which defines the retained coefficients' area.

As a result, for the discrete radius ρ_i and angle θ_i for each circle are obtained the
relations:

$$\rho_i = (\Delta\rho)^i = r^{i/H} \text{ for } i = 1, 2, .., H, \tag{4.13}$$

$$\theta_i = (2\pi/H)i \text{ for } i = (-H/2), .., 0, .., (-H/2) - 1. \tag{4.14}$$

Thus, instead of the logarithmic relation used in the famous LP transform to set the
values of the magnitude bins (radiuses), in Step 7 here is used the operation "rising
on a power". The so modified LP transform we called *Exponential Polar Transform*
(EPT).

After the EPT and the interpolation of the $D(a, b)$ coefficients is obtained
one new, second matrix, which contains the coefficients $D(x,y)$ for x, y =
$0, 1, 2, .., H - 1$.

Step 8.   The second 2D-DFT is performed for the matrix with coefficients $D(x,y)$,
in accordance with the relation:

$$S(a, b) = \frac{1}{H^2} \sum_{x=0}^{H-1} \sum_{y=0}^{H-1} D_1(x, y) \exp\{-j[(2\pi/H)(xa + yb)]\} \tag{4.15}$$

for $a = 0, ..., H - 1$ and $b = 0, ..H - 1$.

The second 2D-DFT is performed in correspondence with Eqs. 4.3 and 4.4, applying consecutively the 1D-DFT on the rows of the matrix [D] first, and then – on the columns of the intermediate matrix obtained.

Step 9.   The modules of the complex coefficients S(a, b) are then calculated:

$$D_S(a, b) = \sqrt{[A_S(a,b)]^2 + [B_S(a,b)]^2} \qquad (4.16)$$

where $A_S(a, b)$ and $B_S(a, b)$ are the real and the imaginary component of S(a, b) correspondingly.

With this operation the Modified MFT is finished.

The processing then continues in the next step with one more operation, aimed at achieving the invariance against contrast changes. In result is obtained the RSTC invariant object representation.

Step 10.   The modules $D_S(a, b)$ of the Fourier coefficients S(a, b) are normalized:

$$D_{S_0}(a, b) = B_{max}(D_S(a,b)/D_{S\,max}(a,b)), \qquad (4.17)$$

where $D_{S\,max}(a, b)$ is the maximum coefficient in the matrix $[D_S(a,b)]$.

Step 11.   The vector for the RSTC-invariant object representation is based on the use of coefficients $D_{S_0}(a, b)$ of highest energy in the amplitude spectrum 2D-MFT of size H × H. One example test image (Caltech database "Faces" [15]) and its corresponding 2D-MFT spectrum obtained with the software implementation of the method are shown correspondingly on Fig. 4.2a and b. For the extraction of the retained coefficients is used the mask, shown on Fig. 4.2c (the part, colored in yellow, corresponds to the area of the complex-conjugated coefficients,). The shape of the mask approximates the area, where the energy of the mean 2D-MFT spectrum is concentrated.

The parameter α of the mask defines the number of retained coefficients in correspondence with the relation:

$$R = 2\alpha^2 + H - 2\alpha = 2\alpha(\alpha - 1) + H \qquad (4.18)$$

The components v_m for m = 1, 2, .., R of the corresponding RSTC-invariant vector: $\mathbf{V}_0 = [v_{01}, v_{02}, .., v_{0R}]^T$ are defined by coefficients $D_{S_{0R}}(a, b)$, arranged as one-dimensional massif after lexicographic tracking of the 2D-MFT spectrum in the mask area, colored in blue.

The vector $\mathbf{V}_0$ is the RST-invariant description of the processed image for the initial (zero) IPD level. The block diagram of the algorithm for vector calculation in a square window of size n × n is shown on Fig. 4.3.

For the calculation of the vector $\mathbf{V}_1$ for the next IPD level (one) of the processed image is performed inverse Modified Mellin-Fourier transform for the coefficients $D_S(a, b)$. In result is obtained the approximation $\hat{L}(k, l)$ of the processed image. For this is performed the following:

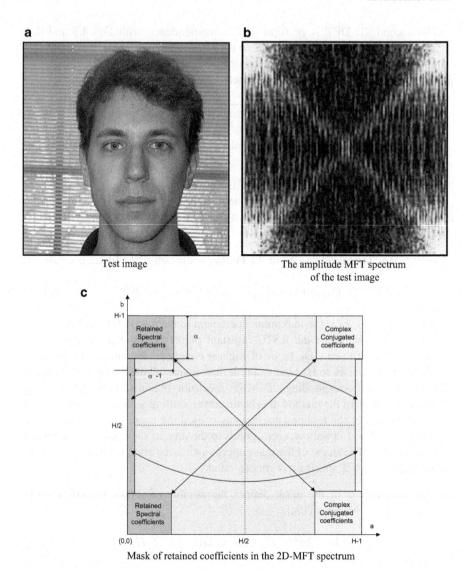

a Test image

b The amplitude MFT spectrum of the test image

c Mask of retained coefficients in the 2D-MFT spectrum

Fig. 4.2 The mask of the retained coefficients in the amplitude 2D-MFT spectrum of the test image

Step 1.   The denormalized coefficients are calculated:

$$D'_S(a,b) = [D_{S_0}(a,b)D_S(a,b)_{\max}]/B_{\max}. \qquad (4.19)$$

Step 2.   The complex coefficients are then calculated:

$$S'(a,b) = D'_S(a,b)e^{-j\varphi_S(a,b)} \qquad (4.20)$$

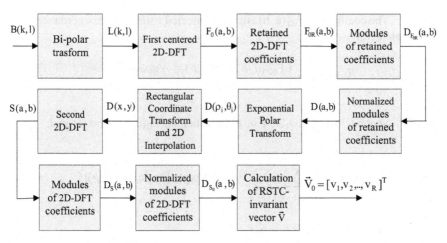

Fig. 4.3 Block diagram of the algorithm for calculation of the R-dimensional RSTC-invariant vector for object description in a *square* window of size n × n, through direct MMFT

Step 3. The so calculated coefficients are processed with inverse 2D-DFT:

$$D'(x, y) = \sum_{a=0}^{H-1} \sum_{b=0}^{H-1} S'(a, b) \cdot \exp\left\{ j \left[\frac{2\pi}{H} (xa + yb) \right] \right\} \qquad (4.21)$$

for x, y = 0, 1, 2, .., H − 1.

Step 4. Then coefficients $D'(x, y)$ are processed with inverse EPT, after replacing the variables (x,y) by (a,b) correspondingly:

$$\begin{aligned} a_i(\rho_i, \theta_i) &= [x(\rho_i, \theta_i)] \cos[y(\rho_i, \theta_i)], \\ b_i(\rho_i, \theta_i) &= [x(\rho_i, \theta_i)] \sin[y(\rho_i, \theta_i)]. \end{aligned} \qquad (4.22)$$

In result are obtained the values of coefficients $D'(a_i, b_i)$, from which after interpolation are restored the missing coefficients in the rectangular coordinate system (a, b). For this is used zero interpolation (each of the missing coefficients $D'(a, b)$ is replaced by the closest one from the group of the existing coefficients in horizontal or vertical direction in the system (a_i, b_i)).

Step 5. The values of the interpolated coefficients $D'(a, b)$ are denormalized in correspondence with the relation:

$$\hat{D}_{F_{0R}}(a, b) = \exp[D'(a, b)/p]. \qquad (4.23)$$

Step 6. The retained complex coefficients are calculated:

$$\hat{F}_{0R}(a, b) = \hat{D}_{F_{0R}}(a, b) e^{-j\varphi_{F_{0R}}(a,b)} \qquad (4.24)$$

<u>Step 7.</u>   The coefficients $\hat{F}_{OR}(a, b)$ are supplemented with zeros in accordance with the rule below:

$$\hat{F}_0(a, b) = \begin{cases} \hat{F}_{OR}(a, b), & if (a, b) \in \textit{retained region;} \\ 0 & - & \textit{in all other cases.} \end{cases} \quad (4.25)$$

<u>Step 8.</u>   Second, inverse 2D-DFT on the coefficients $\hat{F}_0(a, b)$ is performed:

$$\hat{L}(k, l) = \sum_{a=-\frac{n}{2}}^{\frac{n}{2}-1} \sum_{b=-\frac{n}{2}}^{\frac{n}{2}-1} \hat{F}_0(a, b) \exp\{j[2\pi/n(ka + lb)]\} \quad (4.26)$$

for $k = 0, 1, .., n - 1$ and $l = 0, 1, .., n - 1$.

As a result is obtained the approximated image with pixels $\hat{L}(k, l)$ in the frame of the window of size n × n, which contains the object.

For the First IPD level is performed the following:

- The difference image $E_0(k, l)$ is calculated:

$$E_0(k, l) = L(k, l) - \hat{L}(k, l) \text{ for k}, l \in \left(-\frac{n}{2}, \ldots 0 \ldots, \frac{n}{2} - 1\right). \quad (4.27)$$

- The so obtained difference image is divided into four equal sub-images and each is after that processed with the already described direct Mellin-Fourier transform, following steps 2–8. The only difference is that in this case each sub-image is a square of size n/2.
- In a way, similar with Step 11, are calculated the corresponding RSTC vectors for the next (second) IPD level. The length of the vectors is four times smaller. The so calculated vectors are used to compose the general vector for the processed pyramid level – correspondingly V_1 – whose length is equal with that of the vector V_0, calculated for the zero pyramid level.

With this, the building of the two-level pyramid decomposition is finished. As a result are obtained the vectors V_0 and V_1, which are after that used for the search of the closest object in the image database (DB). Each image in the DB is represented by vectors, calculated in similar way for each of the pyramid levels, following the algorithm, presented above. For each IPD level is calculated a corresponding vector, which carries the information about the fine details, which represent the form of the object in the image.

The algorithm for calculation of RSTC-invariant vectors, presented above, could be generalized for IPD of m $=$ lg$_2$n levels. The block diagram of IPD-MMFT for p $= 0, 1, .., $ m $- 1$ is shown on Fig. 4.4. In each consecutive decomposition level is obtained the corresponding vector V_p, which presents information for more and more small details, which represent the form of the object in the image L,

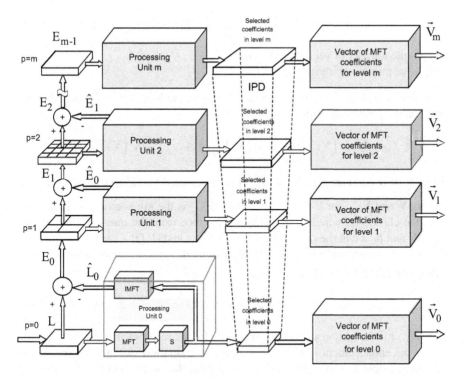

Fig. 4.4 Block diagram of the algorithm for calculation of the RST-invariant vectors $\mathbf{V}_0, \mathbf{V}_1, .., \mathbf{V}_m$, using IPD-MMFT of m levels

of size $n \times n$. It is supposed, that the object is cropped from a larger image after corresponding preprocessing based on segmentation by color, form, etc.

Search by Content of Closest Objects in Image Databases

The search of closest objects in image databases (DB) for the image request is based on the detection of the minimum squared Euclidean distance (EUD) d between their RSTC vectors. For two R-dimensional vectors $\mathbf{V}_i$ and $\mathbf{V}_j$ this distance is defined by the relation:

$$d_E(\mathbf{V}_i, \mathbf{V}_j) = \sum_{m=0}^{R-1} [v_i(m) - v_j(m)]^2, \qquad (4.28)$$

where $v_i(m), v_j(m)$ are the mth components of vectors $\mathbf{V}_i, \mathbf{V}_j$ for $i \neq j$.

The decision for the image request classification, represented by the R-dimensional RSTC-vector $\mathbf{V}$ is taken on the basis of the image classes in the DB and their RSTC-invariant vectors:

$$\mathbf{V}_{\alpha_\beta}^\beta \in C_\beta \text{ for } \alpha_\beta = 1, 2, \ldots, P_\beta \text{ and } \beta = 1, 2, \ldots, Q; \tag{4.29}$$

P_β – the number of vectors in the DB;
Q – the number of image classes.

After that, a classification rule is applied, based on the K-nearest neighbors (k-NN) and "majority vote" algorithms [5]:

$$\mathbf{V} \in C_{\beta_0}, \; if \; d_1\left(\mathbf{V}, \mathbf{V}_{\alpha_{\beta_1}}^{\beta_1}\right) \le d_2\left(\mathbf{V}, \mathbf{V}_{\alpha_{\beta_2}}^{\beta_2}\right) \le \ldots \le d_K\left(\mathbf{V}, \mathbf{V}_{\alpha_{\beta_K}}^{\beta_K}\right) \tag{4.30}$$

where K is an odd number; $d_k\left(\mathbf{V}, \mathbf{V}_{\alpha_{\beta_k}}^{\beta_k}\right)$ is the squared Euclidian distance between vectors $\mathbf{V}$ and $\mathbf{V}_{\alpha_{\beta_k}}^{\beta_k}$ for k = 1, 2, ..., K; $\mathbf{V}_{\alpha_{\beta_k}}^{\beta_k}$ is the kth vector with index α_{β_k} from the class C_{β_k}, which is at minimum distance from the query $\mathbf{V}$ (the indices α_{β_k}, β_k and β_0 are in the ranges: $[1, P_{\beta_k}]$ – for α_{β_k}, and $[1, Q]$ – for β_k and β_0). The class C_{β_0} of the vector $\mathbf{V}$ in Eq. 4.30 is defined by the most frequent value β_0 of the indices β_k of the vectors $\mathbf{V}_{\alpha_{\beta_k}}^{\beta_k}$:

$$\beta_0 = \max\{h(\beta k)\} \text{ for } \beta_k = 1, 2, .., Q \text{ and } k = 1, 2, .., K. \tag{4.31}$$

Here $h(\beta_k)$ is the histogram of the indices β_k, for the relations in Eq. 4.31.

For the enhancement of the object search, the smallest distance for the image request is calculated to a group of images, using the vectors defined for the zero level of the corresponding couple of pyramid decompositions. After that the smallest distance is calculated in the so selected group only, using the vectors for the next (first) pyramid level of the corresponding pyramids, etc.

Fast Search of Closest Vector in the Image Database

In order to perform the search of closest vector $\mathbf{V}_j$ (j = 1, 2, .., J) to the vector request $\mathbf{V}$ in the database (DB) with $J = Q \sum_{\beta=1}^{Q} P_\beta$ vectors could be used the approach in [16], based on the EUD between R-dimensional vectors:

$$d_E(\mathbf{V}, \mathbf{V}_j) = \sum_{m=0}^{R-1} [v(m) - v_j(m)]^2 = \|\mathbf{V}\|^2 + \|\mathbf{V}_j\|^2 - 2 \sum_{m=0}^{R-1} v(m) \times v_j(m), \tag{4.32}$$

where $\|\mathbf{V}\|^2 = \sum_{m=0}^{R-1} [v(m)]^2$, $\|\mathbf{V}_j\|^2 = \sum_{m=0}^{R-1} [v_j(m)]^2$.

The modules of vectors $\mathbf{V}$ and $\mathbf{V}_j$ in the equation above are not related to $d_E(\mathbf{V}, \mathbf{V}_j)$, but their scalar product is related as follows:

$$f(j) = \sum_{m=0}^{R-1} v(m) \times v_j(m). \tag{4.33}$$

The vectors $\mathbf{V}_j$ (j $= 1, 2, .., $ J) are calculated in advance for the images used as a training set for each image class and are stored as additional information (metadata) in the DB. In case, that the function f(j) has a maximum for some value of the variable j $=$ j$_0$, the corresponding distance $d_E(\mathbf{V}, \mathbf{V}_{j_0})$ is minimum. For the exact detection of j$_0$ is accepted the value, for which j$_0 =$ min. The closest vector $\mathbf{V}_{j_0}$ in the DB to the vector request $\mathbf{V}$ could be defined in accordance with the rule:

$$d_E(\mathbf{V}, \mathbf{V}_{j_0}) = \text{min, if } \left| \sum_{m=0}^{R-1} v(m) \times v_{j_0}(m) \right| = \text{max for } j_0 = 1, 2, .., J. \quad (4.34)$$

Additional acceleration for the calculations in Eq. 4.34 is achieved, when the following suggestions are taken into account:

• In case, that $v(m) \geq 0$ and $v_j(m) \geq 0$ the following relation is satisfied:

$$\sum_{m=0}^{R-1} v(m) \times v_j(m) < v_{\max} \sum_{m=0}^{R-1} v_j(m), \quad (4.35)$$

where:

$$v_{\max} = \max\{v(m)\} \text{ for m} = 0, 1, .., R - 1. \quad (4.36)$$

Then, for the so-called "modified" squared Euclidean distance $D_E(\mathbf{V}_i, \mathbf{V}_j)$ (MEUD) follows:

$$D_E(\mathbf{V}, \mathbf{V}_j) = \|\mathbf{V}\|^2 + \|\mathbf{V}_j\|^2 - 2v_{\max} \sum_{m=0}^{R-1} v_j(m) \leq d_E(\mathbf{V}, \mathbf{V}_j). \quad (4.37)$$

Then Eq. 4.34 could be transformed as follows:

$$d_E(\mathbf{V}, \mathbf{V}_{j_0}) = \text{min, if } \left[v_{\max} \sum_{m=0}^{R-1} v_{j_0}(m) \right] = \text{max for } j_0 = 1, 2, .., J. \quad (4.38)$$

• In case, that the components $v(m)$ and $v_j(m)$ have positive and negative values, they should be transformed in such a way, that to have positive values only:

$$v'(m) = v(m) + \min\{v(m), v_j(m)\}, \quad (4.39)$$

$$v_j = v_j + \min\{v(m), v_j(m)\} \text{ for m} = 1, 2, .., R - 1. \quad (4.40)$$

In this case, for the modified distance $D_E(\mathbf{V}, \mathbf{V}_j)$ is obtained:

$$D_E(\mathbf{V}, \mathbf{V}_j) = \|\mathbf{V}\|^2 + \|\mathbf{V}_j\|^2 - 2v'_{max} \sum_{m=0}^{R-1} v'_j(m) \leq d_E(\mathbf{V}, \mathbf{V}_j), \qquad (4.41)$$

and the rule, represented by Eq. 4.38 is changed accordingly:

$$d_E(\mathbf{V}, \mathbf{V}_{j_0}) = \min, \quad if \quad \left[v'_{max} \sum_{m=0}^{n-1} v'_{j_0}(m) \right] = \max \quad for \ j_0 = 1, 2, .., J. \qquad (4.42)$$

where $v'_{max} = \max\{v'(m)\}$ for $m = 0, 1, .., R-1$

The rule for the classification of the vector $\mathbf{V}$ (Eq. 4.30), based on the K-NN and MEUD is transformed as follows:

$$\mathbf{V} \in C_{\beta_0}, \quad if \quad S_1\left(\mathbf{V}, \mathbf{V}_{\alpha\beta_1}^{\beta_1}\right) \geq S_2\left(\mathbf{V}, \mathbf{V}_{\alpha\beta_2}^{\beta_2}\right) \geq .... \geq S_K\left(\mathbf{V}, \mathbf{V}_{\alpha\beta_K}^{\beta_K}\right), \qquad (4.43)$$

where

$$\beta_0 = \max\{h(\beta_k)\} \text{ for } \beta_k = 1, 2, .., Q \text{ and } k = 1, 2, .., K; \qquad (4.44)$$

$$S_k\left(\mathbf{V}, \mathbf{V}_{\alpha\beta_k}^{\beta_k}\right) = \left[v'_{max} \sum_{m=0}^{R-1} v'^{\beta_k}_{\alpha\beta_k}(m) \right] \qquad (4.45)$$

Comparing Eqs. 4.30, 4.32, and 4.33 with Eqs. 4.43, 4.44, and 4.45 respectively follows, that the use of the similarity criterion $S_k\left(\mathbf{V}, \mathbf{V}_{\alpha\beta_k}^{\beta_k}\right)$ instead of $d_k\left(\mathbf{V}, \mathbf{V}_{\alpha\beta_k}^{\beta_k}\right)$ does not influence the classification results for the vector $\mathbf{V}$, but the number of multiplications is reduced ($n \times J$) times, with retained number of sums. Besides, the corresponding sum $\sum_{m=0}^{R-1} v'^{\beta_k}_{\alpha\beta_k}(m)$ for each vector $\mathbf{V}_{\alpha\beta_k}^{\beta_k}$ could be defined in advance and saved in the DB metadata. In result, the computational complexity is significantly reduced and the classification of the vector-request $\mathbf{V}$-enhanced.

In order to improve the similarity arrangement for the first K-nearest vectors to the vector-request, in Eq. 4.43 is possible to use the criterion "Cosine similarity" (CSim) [10, 17], instead of $S_k(.)$. In correspondence to this criterion, the nearness between the two vectors, $\mathbf{V}$ and $\mathbf{V}_j$ could be evaluated using the relation:

$$CSim(\mathbf{V}, \mathbf{V}_j) = \frac{\sum_{m=0}^{R-1} v'(m) \times v'_j(m)}{\left[\sqrt{\sum_{m=0}^{R-1} [v'(m)]^2} \right] \times \left[\sqrt{\sum_{m=0}^{R-1} [v'_j(m)]^2} \right]} \qquad (4.46)$$

In order to avoid "square root" operations, Eq. 4.46 could be transformed as Squared Cosine Similarity (SCSim) = $(CSim)^2$. Further reduction of the needed calculations is achieved using the Modified Squared Cosine Similarity (MSCSim), defined as follows:

$$MSCSim(\mathbf{V}, \mathbf{V}_j) = \frac{\left[v'_{max} \times \sum_{m=0}^{R-1} v'_j(m) \right]^2}{\left[\sum_{m=0}^{R-1} [v'(m)]^2 \right] \times \left[\sum_{m=0}^{R-1} [v'_j(m)]^2 \right]} \qquad (4.47)$$

Then, in Eq. 4.43 the term $S_k(.)$ is substituted by MSCSim(.). In result, the number of multiplications, needed for the calculation of MSCSim is reduced n times, and the search of the closest vector in a DB, containing J vectors, to the vector request, is enhanced (n.J) times. The efficiency of the presented approach for enhanced search of closest vector grows up with the increasing of the number of vectors in the DB.

Experimental Results

For the experiments was used the software implementation of the method in C + +, Windows environment. Significant part of the experiments aimed to prove the efficiency of the Modified Mellin-Fourier Transform. For the experiments was used the well-known test image "Lena", 256 × 256 pixels, 8 bpp. The experiments were performed for various values of the main parameters: the side of the subscribed circle, the number of discrete radiuses, etc.

On Fig. 4.5a is shown the experimental image "Lena", on which are indicated the points, which participate in the EPT (the black points are not retained and the image is restored after corresponding interpolation). On Fig. 4.5b is shown the discretization grid of LPT, and on Fig. 4.5c – the points, which participate in the LPT (the used points here are marked as black). This experiment confirms the efficiency of the new approach, because in the well-known LPT the retained central part of the processed image is smaller.

Some of the experimental results performed with the same test image "Lena", are given below on Figs. 4.6 and 4.7.

The next part of the experiments was aimed at the content-based object retrieval. For this were used three specially developed image databases of the Technical University of Sofia: the first contained 180 faces of adult people, the second – 200 faces of adult people and children and the third – more than 200 scanned documents. Most of the faces in the databases are cropped from larger images. These photos were taken in various lighting conditions with many shadows, different views, etc. Very good results were obtained for search of similar faces in the databases. In the test database of adults, were included the images "Lena", rotated in 90° and 270° and scaled up cropped part of the same original test image.

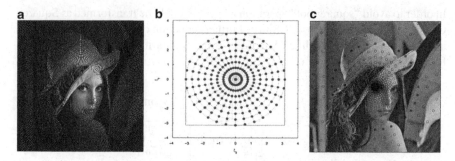

Fig. 4.5 Experimental images which indicate the points, retained after EPT and LPT. (**a**) Points retained by EPT. (**b**) Discretization grid of LPT. (**c**) Points retained by LPT

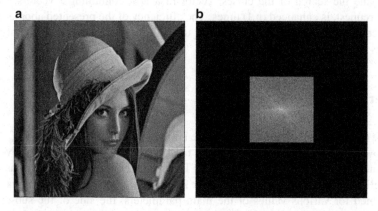

Fig. 4.6 Original test image and the result after DFT when the window of selected coefficients is of size H = 96. (**a**) Original image "Lena". (**b**) After first DFT

The image request (one of the cropped images from the test image "Lena") was the upper-left one in Fig. 4.8. The experiments proved the method efficiency. The results obtained confirm the RST-invariance of the method representation: the first five images are of the test image "Lena" – the first two are scaled up and cropped; the next three are the original, and the same image rotated on 180° and 90° correspondingly.

The experiments aimed at the detection of children sexual abuse in multimedia files need additional pre-processing. For this, color image segmentation was first performed, in order to detect naked parts of human bodies and then these parts were extracted from the images and defined as individual objects. After that the object search in the corresponding database was initiated. Special attention was paid to ability for children and adults faces recognition. The experiments confirm that this recognition is successful enough.

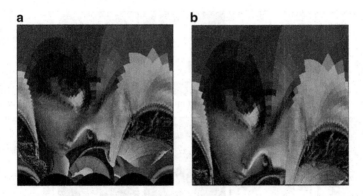

Fig. 4.7 Results after EPT for two values of the window of selected coefficients. (**a**) The test image after EPT, for H = 96. (**b**) The test image after EPT, for H = 64

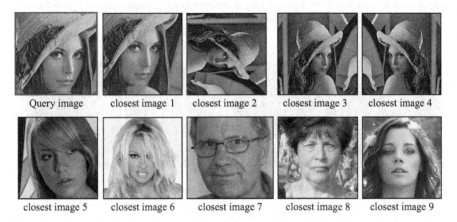

Fig. 4.8 The first K = 9 closest images from a database of 180 faces

On Fig. 4.9 are shown some of the results obtained for search of child's face in a mixed database, containing 200 faces of children and adults. Each image in the database was classified as belonging to one of these two classes. The experiments were performed under following conditions: $B_{max} = 255$, K = 11 and H = 128. In accordance with Eq. 4.18 the size R = 888 of RSTC vector is calculated for $\alpha = 20$.

The images on Fig. 4.9 are the closest to the image request (upper-left) in the test database. The experiment confirmed the method reliability when the searched face is of same person: the images 1, 2, and 4 in the first row are of the same child as the image request. The situation is same with images 6, 7, and 10 in spite of the fact that in the database comprised photos of more than 40 children. The error in this search result is one face only – the image 8. In some cases is possible to get large number of wrong images in the selection. In order to solve possible uncertainties, the final decision is taken in correspondence with Eq. 4.28 – i.e., with longer vector.

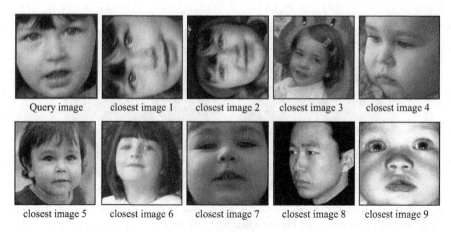

Query image	closest image 1	closest image 2	closest image 3	closest image 4
closest image 5	closest image 6	closest image 7	closest image 8	closest image 9

Fig. 4.9 Results for first $K = 9$ closest images obtained to image request (*upper left*) in a mixed image database of 200 faces (children and adults)

Fig. 4.10 Various 3D objects (**a**) Glass; (**b**) Mug; (**c**) Cup; (**d**) Egg

Significant attention was paid for the detection of 3D objects, represented by several multi-view 2D images. For this, was used the special database of the Technical University of Sofia, containing more than 200 multi-view 2D images of various 3D objects. All images were of size 256 × 256 pixels; 24 bpp. Each object was represented by four views, placed at equal distances in a sector of 20°. Another set of four images was taken from positions, placed at 5° up. For illustration, here is used a small database of four objects (Fig. 4.10), represented by 30 images. Each object had four views. More views (4.8) were used in the database for the object "Cup" only. Each image represented the object in different scale.

The experiments proved that the 3D object recognition is reliable in a view angle of 20°. On Fig. 4.11 are shown the results obtained for one of the test images. The image request ("Mug") is at the upper left corner of Fig. 4.11, and after it on the same row follow the closest images detected in the database (the names of the images are in accordance with their number in the database). The remaining closest images are arranged in the next two rows.

The graphic representation of the distances, calculated for the corresponding vectors of the objects represented by the 2D images in the database, is shown on

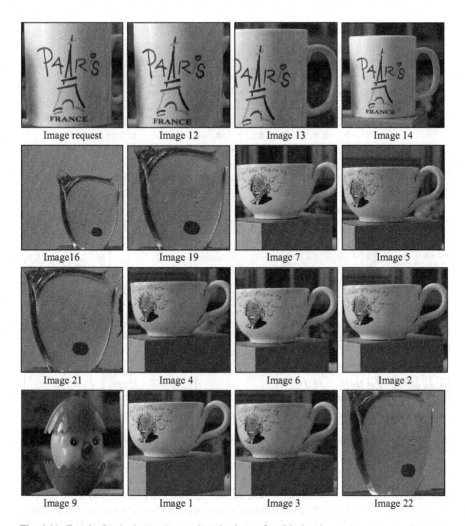

Fig. 4.11 Results for the image request in a database of multi-view images

Fig. 4.12. It is easy to notice, that the first closest images (No. 1–3, corresponding to images 12–14 from Fig. 4.11) are of the same object. Besides, they are the only images of this object in the test database. The vectors of next closest images are at much larger distance, which proves their belonging to another object. This example was used for illustration purposes only. In real application tasks, special decision rules should be set, developed in accordance with the objects features.

Another group of experiments was aimed at the analysis of scanned documents. The database of scanned documents, comprised images of scanned texts, and signatures ($Q = 2$). The database contained more than 100 samples ($P > 100$) of each class; texts comprised examples of Latin and Cyrillic alphabets, printed

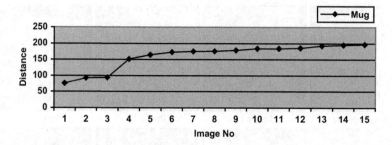

Fig. 4.12 Distances between the vector of the image request and the vectors of closest objects in the database

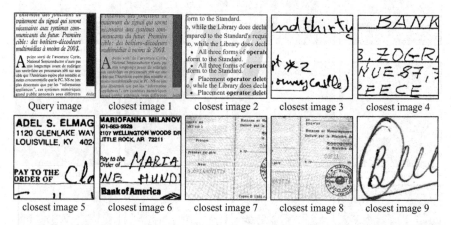

Fig. 4.13 Results obtained for image request in a database with 100 scanned texts documents for $H = 96$ and $K = 94$

and handwritten texts. All images were of size 256×256 pixels, grayscale (8 bpp, $n = 256$); $B_{max} = 255$. The experiments were performed for two versions of vector generation: *1st version*: the size of the retained coefficients square (H) equal to 96; *2nd version*: the size of the retained coefficients square (H) equal to 128. In Figs. 4.13 and 4.14 are shown results obtained for one of the test images (the image request is the upper left one) and the closest $K = 11$ images. In most cases (90 %) the information provided for H = 96 was enough for the right classification, but for some test images we had small number of mistakes. In Fig. 4.13 is given the result for version 1. There are three mistakes, i.e. the last three images (signatures) were classified as text, instead as belonging to the class of signatures. As it is seen in Fig. 4.14, the use of version 2 (H = 128) ensured the right decision (there are no mistakes at all). One of the images in the DB (the second in Figs. 4.13 and 4.14) was the same as the image request, but with changed contrast. In both experiments it was qualified as closest, which proves the method invariance to contrast changes.

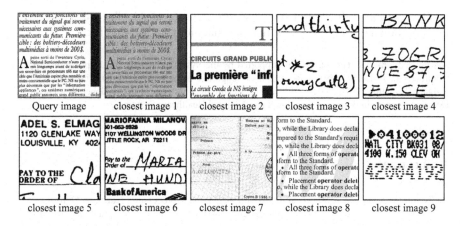

Fig. 4.14 Results obtained for image request in a database with 100 scanned texts documents for $H = 128$ and $K = 9$

Conclusions

In this paper is presented a method for invariant object representation with Modified MFT based on the IPD. The main differences from the famous MFT are: (a) the first DFT is performed for limited number of coefficients only. In result is obtained an approximated image representation, suitable for the object representation; (b) instead of the Log-Pol Transform, here was used the Exponential-Polar Transform (EPT), in accordance with the description in Step 7 of the algorithm. As a result, the part of the participating points from the matrix of the Fourier coefficients' modules is larger (i.e. bigger central part of the image participates in the EPT and correspondingly – in the object description). The number of coefficients, used for the object representation is additionally limited in accordance with the vector length selection. Besides, the new transform is invariant to contrast changes because of the normalization performed in Step 10.

In result, the MMFT described above has the following advantages over the MFT:

- The number of transform coefficients used for the object representation is significantly reduced and from this naturally follows the lower computational complexity of the method, which permits real-time applications.
- The choice of coefficients, used for the vector calculation offers wide possibilities by setting large number of parameters, each of relatively wide range, which permits the method use in various applications: content- and context-based object retrieval in image databases, face recognition, etc.
- A new, simplified algorithm for fast search of closest vector in large image databases is developed.
- The method permits to detect similarity of 3D objects, represented by multiple 2D views, in a view angle of 200. Additional experiments show that the view angle could be wider for 3D objects of high symmetry.

The new approach, presented in this work, permits reliable object detection and identification in various positions, lighting conditions and view points.

Acknowledgements This paper was supported by the System Research and Application (SRA) Contract No. 0619069. This work was also supported in part by the Joint Research Project Bulgaria-Romania (2010–2012): "Electronic Health Records for the Next Generation Medical Decision Support in Bulgarian and Romanian National Healthcare Systems".

References

1. Nixon M, Aguado A (2002) Feature extraction and image processing. Newness, Oxford
2. Costa L, Cesar R (2001) Shape analysis and classification: theory and practice. CRC, LLC, Boca Raton
3. Lowe D (2005) Distinctive image features from scale-invariant keypoints. Int J Comput Vis 60(2):91–110
4. Carneiro G, Jepson A (2004) Flexible spatial models for grouping local image features. CVPR 2:747–754
5. Theodoridis S, Koutroumbas K (2009) Pattern recognition, 4th edn. Academic, Amsterdam/Boston/Heidelberg/London/New York/Oxford/Paris/San Diego/San Francosko/Singapore/Sidney/Tokyo
6. Schmid C, Dorko G, Lazebnik S, Mikolajczyk K, Ponce J (2005) Pattern recognition with local invariant features. In: Chen CH, Wang PS-P (eds) Handbook of pattern recognition and computer vision. World Scientific, Singapore/Hackensack, pp. 71–92
7. Cootes T, Taylor C, Cooper D (1995) Active shape models-their training and application. CVIU 61(1):38–59
8. Lu Z, Li D, Burkhardt H (2006) Image retrieval based on RST-invariant features. IJCSNS 6(2A):169–174
9. Reddy B, Chatterji B (1996) An FFT-based technique for translation, rotation, and scale-invariant image registration. IEEE Trans Image Process 5(8):1266–1271
10. Javidi B (ed) (2002) Image recognition and classification: algorithms, systems and applications. Marcel Dekker, New York
11. Derrode S, Ghorbel F (2001) Robust and efficient Fourier-Mellin transform approximations for gray-level image reconstruction and complete invariant description. Comput Vis Image Underst 83(1/1):57–78. Elsevier
12. Kountchev R, Rubin S, Milanova M, Todorov Vl, Kountcheva R (2009) Non-linear image representation based on IDP with NN. WSEAS Trans Signal Process 9(5):315–325
13. Kountchev R, Todorov Vl, Kountcheva R (2010) RSCT-invariant object representation with modified Mellin-Fourier transform. WSEAS Trans Signal Process 6(4):196–207
14. Kountchev R, Rubin S, Milanova M, Kountcheva R (2011) Invariant object description with inverse pyramid based on the truncated modified discrete Mellin-Fourier transform. In: The 2011 IEEE international conference on information reuse and integration (IEEE IRI'11), Las Vegas, pp 360–365
15. Caltech database "Faces". http://www.vision.caltech.edu/Image_Datasets/faces/. Accessed 26 June 2013
16. Wu K, Lin J (2000) Fast VQ encoding by an efficient kick-out condition. IEEE Trans Circuits Syst Video Technol 10(1):59–62
17. Qian G, Sural S, Gu Y, Pramanik S (2004) Similarity between euclidean and cosine angle distance for nearest neighbor queries. In: Proceedings of the 2004 ACM symposium on applied computing, Nicosia, pp 1232–1237

Chapter 5
Model Checking State Machines Using Object Diagrams

Thouraya Bouabana-Tebibel

Abstract UML behavioral diagrams are often formalized by transformation into a state-transition language that sets on a rigorously defined semantics. The state-transition models are afterwards model-checked to prove the correctness of the models construction as well as their faithfulness with the user requirements. The model-checking is performed on a reachability graph, generated from the behavioral models, whose size depends on the models structure and their initial marking. The purpose of this paper is twofold. We first propose an approach to initialize formal models at any time of the system life cycle using UML diagrams. The formal models are Object Petri nets, OPNs for short, derived from UML state machines. The OPNs marking is mainly deduced from the sequence diagrams. Secondly, we propose an approach to specify the association ends on the OPNs in order to allow their validation by means of OCL invariants. A case study is given to illustrate the approach throughout the paper.

Introduction

Formalisms integration is a key concept in software engineering. It enhances the development process quality and ensures its reliability. Often, when complex systems need to be studied with regard to various aspects, it doesn't make it easy to find a unique formalism supporting all the aspect constructs and their related semantics. One used technique is to integrate two or more formalisms to accurately specify each aspect. The provided specification is thus constructed by integration, in a complementary way. It must satisfy completeness and consistency properties. It also must rely on a well defined semantics allowing a formal verification. On

T. Bouabana-Tebibel (✉)
Laboratoire de Communication dans les Systèmes Informatiques - LCSI, Ecole nationale
Supérieure d'Informatique - ESI, Algiers, Algeria
e-mail: ttebibel@ini.dz

T. Özyer et al. (eds.), *Information Reuse and Integration in Academia and Industry*,
DOI 10.1007/978-3-7091-1538-1_5, © Springer-Verlag Wien 2013

the other hand, for formalization and verification purposes, informal specifications are often transformed into specifications whose formalism is chosen according to the numerous verification mechanisms it supports. We talk here about formalisms integration per derivation.

The purpose of this paper is to verify UML [27] modeling by deriving the constructed diagrams into OPNs [21]. In UML, data initialization is provided by means of object diagrams specifying the object identity, its attribute values as well as its state at the time of initialization. Objects state can be omitted when, by default, all data are given for the initial state of the system life cycle. However, in software engineering, some systems are sometimes studied beginning from a state that is different from their initial state. Indeed, when a system already exits, and designers only project to update, restructure or extend some of its functionalities, just a part of its life cycle needs to be revised or added. In these cases, some of the system objects will move from their initial state whereas others have already moved through their life cycle and so are located on states that are different from the initial one at the moment of the analysis. The object life cycle may be described by means of a state machine, in case of UML modeling, or by an object Petri net (OPN) if a formal specification is provided. In the latter case, allowing an OPN marking at the places translating the appropriate time, not necessarily the initial one, will better describe the real-world system without need to rework the unchanged object models. Just the initial marking of those OPNs has to be reset when new and revised object models are constructed and then connected to the existing OPNs. The OPNs modular architecture appears to be especially convenient for this kind of deployment. It makes it easy to execute new systems considering changes only on the OPNs marking. Another advantage behind starting a system behavior at a time different from the initial one is to reduce the accessibility graph size which will be truncated of all the states space preceding the new system starting. Reduction of the accessibility graph size prevents a combinatory explosion of its states.

The key idea of the present contribution focuses on the relevance of the association ends, specified on the class and object diagrams, regarding the information they provide to deal with a model analysis. We will show how this information can be used in the validation process to check the models correctness. So, we firstly propose to mark the OPNs, derived from state machines, at a specific point in time, with objects extracted from the object diagram. The association ends specified on the object diagram will also provide the OPNs with marks representing objects with specific roles at a given time of the system lifecycle. The marks are composed of object identities and attribute values. The initial marking approach proposed in this work provides the possibility of lunching the model checking at different states of the system life cycle without need to revise the OPNs.

The other results we propose regarding the association ends concern the way they will be specified on the OPNs in order to allow the checking of OCL invariants transformed into temporal logics. This specification is derived from link actions described on the state machine. In fact, as long as OCL navigation expressions are not used, the association end specification onto the object life cycle is not required.

Otherwise, this specification provides after transformation into OPNs a formal basis for the validation of the OCL invariants.

The remainder of the paper begins with a brief presentation of the state machines formalization work we published in [8]. We show in section "Background" the novelty and relevance of this work by comparison with related works. In sections "Association End Specification" and "Initialization Approach" the proposed approach is presented and the techniques on which it rests are developed. This approach is validated in section "Validation of the Approach". We conclude with some observations on the obtained results and recommendations for future research directions.

Related Works

Many works [10, 17, 19, 22, 23, 29, 30] proposed a denotational semantics to the notation by projecting it in a rigorously defined semantic domain. Some studies have already addressed the formalization of UML behavioral diagrams by translation into OPNs semantics domain. The most known are those of Baresi. He proposed in [4] a textual and graphical formalization of some UML behavioral specifications using OPNs. He afterwards reinforced his proposal in [3] by defining translation recommendations. He only achieved the formulation of formal conversion rules for syntactic models in [5]. The drawback of this work is the constraint of writing the UML models in a canonical language called LEMMA. More recently, he formalized in [6] some constructs of the interaction overview diagram using a temporal logic called TRIO. The proposed semantics was implemented in the Zot tool to prove some user-defined properties. Contrary to our approach, the properties are written in a generic manner abstracting the object values.

Bokhari and Poehlman offer in [7] to transform UML state machines in OPNs in order to analyze them. The model validation resulting from the derivation is performed on the model checker DesignCPN. No details are however given about the initialization of the model that deals with identified objects. Similarly, Hsiung et al. presented in [20] an approach for the formalization of statecharts with colored Petri nets. For this purpose, they use sequence diagrams to initialize their models and OCL constraints transformed into temporal logic to validate them. But the model initialization starts from time zero. Other authors, as Harel, establish a strong relationship between state machines and sequence diagrams. In [18] Harel et al. describe a methodology for synthesizing statechart models from scenario-based requirements. The requirements are given in the language of live sequence charts (LSCs), and may be played in directly from the GUI. The resulting statecharts are of the object-oriented variant, as adopted in the UML. Besides its theoretical interest, this work also has practical implications, since finding good synthesis algorithms could bring about a major improvement in the reliable development of complex systems.

In [16] the basic structure of UML sequence diagrams is first analyzed and then their formal description using OPNs is given. For reuse, the formal description of reusable interactions is studied. Next, the authors put forward the mapping algorithm of UML sequence diagrams into OPNs, which ensures the accuracy, integrity and simplicity of the results by four steps, including abstraction, merging, synchronization and reduction. This approach provides a good foundation for automatic verification except that the only considered starting time is the beginning of the system life cycle.

Fish and Störrle offer in [13] a number of principles applicable to visual languages characterized by imprecise semantics in order to analyze and discuss their quality. Based on this approach, they identify many sources of potential errors in UML diagrams and propose solutions to these deficiencies.

New approaches of the UML formalization techniques are graph transformation [19] and more recently, grammar graphs [24]. These techniques give more precision to the UML diagrams semantics without the use of formal languages. Holscher et al. propose in [19] to integrate UML diagrams, namely use case, class, object and statechart diagrams, into a graph transformation system. They afterwards provide rules to change the system states. To construct the first state, they were faced with the issue of retrieving the appropriate state of each modeled object. To achieve this purpose, they constrain the modeler to specify for each object on the object diagram its current state. The approach we propose removes this constraint by only using the association ends specification. In [24], a graph grammar is automatically derived from a state machine to summarize the hierarchy of the states. Based on the graph grammar, the execution of a set of non-conflict state transitions is interpreted by a sequence of graph transformations.

More recent works tackle the formalization of the interaction overview diagram which integrates sequence diagrams, thus providing some data to the behavioral models. But none focuses on the use of valuated objects to mark the targeted formalisms. Andrade et al. formalize in [1,2] the interaction overview and sequence diagrams by means of Time Petri Nets to analyze and verify embedded real-time systems with energy constraints. The approach resorts to the use of annotations provided by the MARTE UML profile for verifying qualitative properties as time and energy savings. To improve the formalization, the transformation needs to be automated and the models hierarchically structured. In [22] the interaction overview diagram semantics is formalized by the stochastic process algebra PEPA where the sequence diagrams are abstracted by colored tokens. This work is completed in [11] to analyze the modeling. But contrary to ours, the analysis is restricted to generic models.

Regarding the association ends, no works tackle their integration within state machines. We can explain this arguing that the UML/OCL association is rarely used to formally validate the UML models. When done, it is limited to OCL invariants handling only attribute expressions [32] or OCL pre and postconditions [14, 15]. Generally, the formalized UML models are rather coupled with formalisms for the expression of system properties.

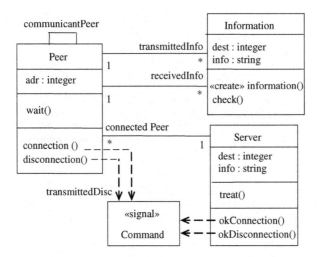

Fig. 5.1 Peer to peer class diagram

The work we are presenting in this paper brings a new contribution in the field of UML formalization. It extends the approach that we proposed in [9] by focusing on the relationship between sequence diagrams and state machines. It also proposes an approach to specify the association ends on the OPNs in order to deal later with the models validation.

Background

We present in this section the main results obtained after transformation of state machines into OPNs. This approach was developed in [8].

Case Study

To illustrate the transformation mechanisms and those proposed in this paper, we take a case study on a brokered peer to peer system. The main activity of this system is the information exchange between the peers after they have been identified by the server. Identification is established after a connection request confirmed by the server. Once connected, peers interact by exchanging information. Figure 5.1 shows the class diagram of the application, illustrating the various system objects and their actions.

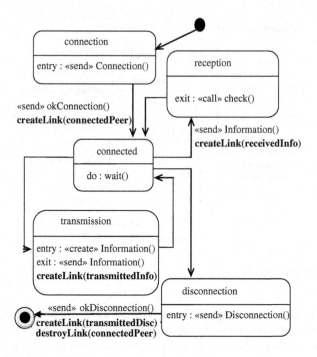

Fig. 5.2 State machine of a peer

Transforming State Machines to OPNs

A state machine [27], noted SM in the following, formally describes the behavior of objects of a given class, through states, when they receive or generate events. The generated events appear either on transitions or at the input or exit of states. They are noted *evt*. The received events appear on transitions. They are noted trg. Fig. 5.2 shows the state machine of a peer.

In the OPN approach, classes are represented by subnets that can be instantiated as many times as needed to describe, in a nominative manner, the objects dynamics. This instantiation is done using tokens, written in the form of n-tuples, to model class instances. According to the object-oriented concepts, the subnet encapsulates the attributes and class methods. The attributes are expressed as components of the n-tuple. As for the methods, they are specified in a flow of places, transitions and functions describing the object life cycle. Places are categorized into simple and super places. The simple places are those defined for ordinary Petri nets [21]. They include single tokens. The super places generate these tokens. Transitions are also of two types: simple and super. A simple transition models a single action. The super transition represents an internal processing described by a set of actions. Transitions can be guarded.

Fig. 5.3 Transformation of
SM constructors into OPNs

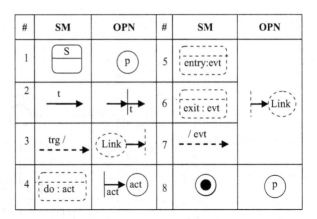

Fig. 5.4 OPNs
interconnection architecture

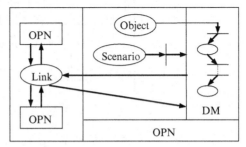

Due to UML and OPNs suitability for the object-oriented modelling, we proposed in [8] to specify the semantics of state machines by means of OPNs. The mapping results are represented in Fig. 5.3.

Thus, each SM is derived into an object subnet called Dynamic Model or DM, see Fig. 5.4. To construct the DM, each SM state is converted to a Petri net place and each SM transition is converted to a Petri net transition related to input and output arcs. As for do activity, it is translated to a pair of transition-place connected by arcs, see Fig. 5.3. Only active objects have a behavioral model, a SM for instance. Passive objects are exchanged messages. They haven't their own behavior.

Petri nets initial marking is of two types: static and dynamic. The static marking provides the class instances and their attribute values. These instances are extracted from the object diagram to initialize the *Object* place with tokens of *object* type. The dynamic marking provides the exchanged messages among the interactive objects. These messages are extracted from the sequence diagram to initialize the *Scenario* place with tokens of *event* type.

The *DM* associated to the places *Object* and *Scenario* constitutes an Object Petri net Model that we call *OPN*. To connect the different *OPNs*, we use the *Link* place through which all the exchanged messages should pass.

Figure 5.5 shows the peer OPN derived from its state machine. The bold places *connectedPeer*, *transmittedInfo*, *receivedInfo* and *transmittedDisc* represent association ends.

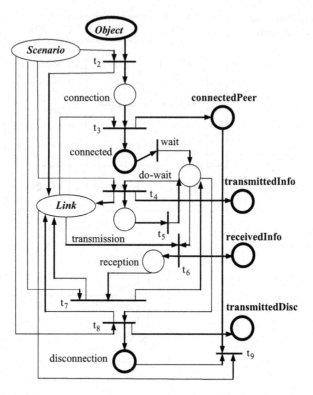

Fig. 5.5 OPN of a peer

Association End Specification

The used approach to validate OPN models is based on their consistency with the system properties transcribed in temporal logic. However, the formulation of system properties in temporal logic can be a hard task for the UML designer unfamiliar with this class of formalism. To spare him this task, we propose that he expresses the properties in a familiar language and we take care of transforming the properties in temporal logic. OCL, Object Constraint Language [26], seems to be the appropriate formalism. It is a part of the UML notation allowing the expression of constraints on models while conserving their readability.

OCL is mainly based on the use of operations on collections for specifying object invariants. Since these collections correspond to association ends, the latter must appear on Petri net specification so that the translated LTL and CTL properties (whose expression is essentially made of these constructs) can be verified. This requires the integration of the association ends onto the state machines in order to get, after their transformation, the equivalent Petri net constructs. This object flow modeling is realized by means of the link actions. But the latter are generally omitted in the behavioural diagrams. Indeed, when constructing his diagrams, the designer does not necessarily think of modeling these concepts which are rather specific to the link and association end updates. For example, for connecting a peer to the server, the connection request and connection confirmation actions are naturally and systematically modeled by the designer, but the addition of the connected peer to the association end is usually omitted from the modeling, see Figs. 5.2 and 5.5. That is why we recommend to the designer to specify the link actions on the state machine so that the OCL invariants can be verified.

UML action semantics was defined in [25] for model execution and transformation. It is a practical framework for formal descriptions. For this work, we are particularly interested in the create link, and destroy link actions. The create link action permits the addition of a new end object in the association end. The destroy link action removes an end object from the association end. These actions will be represented on the state machine as constraints of the form linkAction(associationEnd), following the event which provokes the association end update.

In Fig. 5.2, once the peer is connected (by reception of "send" okConnection) or disconnected (by reception of "send" okDisconnection), it adds or removes itself from the association end connectedPeer, using respectively, createLink(connectedPeer) or destroyLink(connectedPeer). It adds a sent or received information with createLink(transmittedInfo) or create-Link(receivedInfo), respectively.

The link actions may concern an active or passive end object. The active objects interact exchanging passive objects. For example, in the peer to peer application, the *Server* and *Peer* objects are active while the *Information* object is passive.

The object-oriented approach, on which both UML and Petri nets rely, is based on modularity and encapsulation principles. To deal with modularity, a given association end should appear and be manipulated in only one state machine. In Petri nets, the association end is modeled by a place of *role* type. This place holds the name of the association end and belongs to the *DM* translating the state machine.

Furthermore, an association end regrouping active objects must be updated within the state machine of the class of these objects, in order to comply with the encapsulation concept. Indeed, since the end object is saved in the role place with its attributes, these attributes must be accessible when adding the object to or removing it from the association end. The exchanged objects are usually manipulated by the active objects and are not specified by dynamic models. So, the association end representing them could be updated in the state machine of the class that is at the opposite end. For exchanged objects, the encapsulation constraint is lifted given that the exchanged object's attributes are transmitted within the message and so, accessible by the active objects.

The create link action is semantically equivalent to a Petri net arc going from the transition with the association end update towards the place specifying the association end. The destroy link action is semantically equivalent to an arc from the association end place to the transition corresponding to the link action, see Fig. 5.6.

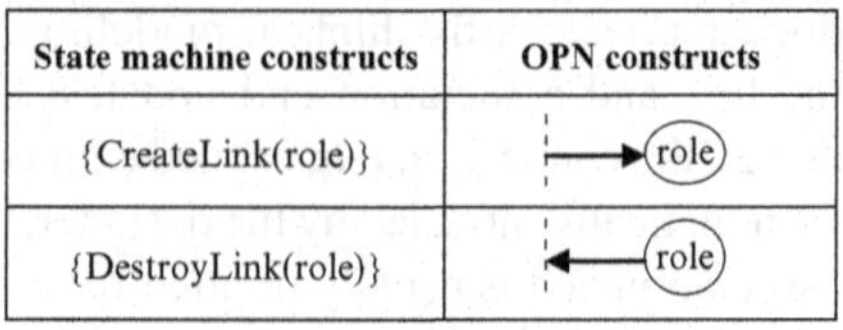

Fig. 5.6 Transformation
of the link actions into OPNs

State machine constructs	OPN constructs
{CreateLink(role)}	
{DestroyLink(role)}	

Initialization Approach

The verification of OPNs models, derived from state machines, requires the initialization of the specification. Most of the research works [12, 29, 31] undertake this validation with an initial marking made of anonymous objects. Such marking is appropriate when one has to evaluate particularly the objects dynamics characteristic. When the interactivity feature is taken into account, the verification with anonymous objects proves to be insufficient because it inhibits many aspects of the communication. Indeed, running the verification by considering a single object as class representative may remove any meaning to inter-classes communication, especially when anonymity is on the exchanged messages.

To remedy this, we initialize the marking of OPNs models by considering objects identified by names and attribute values. Thus, the object is identified by the 2-tuple <obj, attrib> where obj is its identity and attrib, its attribute values. When getting a role through an association end, it is identified by the 3-tuple <assoc, obj, attrib> where *assoc* designates the identity of the object to which it is associated. The initialization is deduced from object and sequence diagrams.

Object and Sequence Diagrams

The object diagram [27], also called instances diagram, shows the structural links between class instances at a given time. It thus constitutes the system structural state at one a precise moment. It is composed of objects, symbolized by rectangles with two compartments. The first compartment contains the instance name concatenated to the one of the class as follows: object:Class. The state of the object may be specified in brackets. It corresponds to the object state on the state machine diagram at a given time. In the second compartment, the attributes of the object are initialized with values. The associations between objects show the links between these objects at a given time, see Fig. 5.7.

Sequence diagrams are a very attractive visual notation, widely used for modeling specific behaviors, related to the system dynamics. These behaviors are also called scenarios. They describe interactions by providing the sequence of messages exchanged between objects. Each participant in the interaction (or object) is represented by a vertical lifeline and is identified by a name appended to the one of the class as follows: object:Class. Call, send, create and destruct messages are

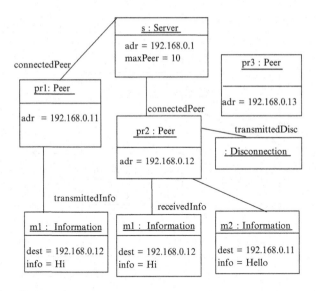

Fig. 5.7 Object diagram of a peer

respectively specified with attribute values of called operation, exchanged objects, created objects or destroyed objects as follows: "call" operation(attrib), <<send>> object: Class(attrib), <<create>> Class(attrib) or <<destroy>> Class(attrib) where $attrib = attribute_1, \ldots, attribute_n$. These messages are generated by a source object in direction of a target object. The local operations are modeled by loop arrows on the object lifeline, see Fig. 5.8.

Distribution of the Objects on the OPN

To allow an OPN simulation starting from any state of the model lifecycle, the objects (tokens) can't be put into the OPN Object place. They must be appropriately distributed into the OPN places. These places correspond to the states of the state machine from which the OPN derives. The marking of the OPN by means of objects and association ends is given by the procedure MarkObject(OD, SD, SM).

Procedure MarkObject(OD, SD, SM)

- Let OD be the object diagram, SD the sequence diagram and SM the state machine modeling the behavior of an object class ;
- For each active object obj on the OD:

    - Get the first action to be executed on the corresponding lifeline ; let act this action ;
    - Fetch, on the SM modeling the object behavior, the state(s) including act ;

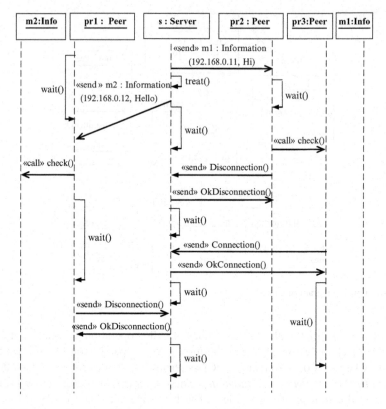

Fig. 5.8 Sequence diagram of the peer to peer system at time t

- Let s be the appropriate state ; if more than one state are found this decision is made by the designer ;
- Create a token ¡obj, attrib¿ where attrib represents the object attribute values specified on the OD ;
- Let p be the OPN place derived from the corresponding state s on the SM ;
- Put the token in the place p ;

• For each association end representing an active object specified on the OD, let asc be this association end :

- For each link specified on the OD such that *link = asc* :

- Create a token <assoc, obj, attrib>, assoc is the class to which the object obj is associated and attrib represents the object attribute values specified on the OD ;
- Let be rol an OPN place representing an association end asc ;
- Put the token in the place rol.

To illustrate this concept, we propose the object diagram of Fig. 5.7 where the server s is already connected to pr1 and pr2 peers. The peer pr3 is not yet connected. The peer pr1 is in a connected state after it has sent the message m1. The peer pr2 has received the message m1, answered it by the message m2 and then placed itself in a disconnection state.

After *MarkObject(OD,SD,SM)* has been executed, the marking of the OPN derived from the Peer state machine is given in the bold places of Fig. 5.5, as follows :

Place *Object : pr3 : Peer*, 192.168.0.13
Place *connected : < pr1 : Peer*, 192.168.0.11 >
Place *disconnection: < pr2 : Peer*, 192.168.0.12 >
Place *connectedPeer: < pr1 : Peer*, 192.168.0.11 > +
< pr2 : Peer, 192.168.0.12 >

We observe that the place *Object*, which usually contains the initial marking regarding objects when the used time is zero, only contains, in this case, the object pr3. We explain this arguing that pr3 has none action on its lifeline. It also presents none link on the object diagram. So it is at time zero of its life cycle. The places *connected* and *disconnected* are initialized with tokens representing objects at a time, of their life cycle, which is different from zero. As for the place *peerConnected*, it represents an association end and is initialized according to the used link on the object diagram, namely two links.

Validation of the Approach

To test the proposed approach, we built a tool whose components work as follows. We first developed a graphic interface to construct the used UML diagrams, namely state machines, object and sequence diagrams. We afterwards implemented a translator which derives OPNs from state machines. The derived OPNs were proved to be well constructed and faithful to the client requirements by means of the model checker PROD [28].

Verification by model checking as treated in PROD is based on the state space generation and the verification of safety and liveness system properties on this space. The properties may be basic, about the correctness of the model construction or specific written by the modeler to ensure the faithfulness of the system modeling. For each of these approaches, given a property, a positive or negative reply is obtained. If the property is not satisfied, it generates a trace showing a case where it is not verified.

The basic properties are verified according to two ways: the on-the-fly tester approach and the reachability graph inspection approach. The on-the-fly tester approach detects deadlock, livelock and reject states. As for the reachability inspection approach, it permits the verification of some other properties such as quasiliveness, boundedness or reinitializability. To validate the system faithfulness with the client requirements, specific properties are written by the designer in OCL, automatically translated into Linear Temporal Logic (LTL) and then, verified by PROD. Three of these properties are expressed below in a paraphrased (textual) form and then, specified as OCL invariants and translated into LTL properties. To make easier the comprehension of the properties, refer to the class diagram of the peer to peer application (Fig. 5.1).

Property 1

The number of connected peers is limited to maxPeer.

Property 1 expression in OCL

context s:Server inv : $s.connectedPeersize <= s.maxPeer$

Property 1 expression in PROD

For each server s and for each place of its DM^* write the property: # verify henceforth $(card(connectedPeer : field[0] == s_{server}) <= (placeDM * Server : field[2]))$

where:

- Field[0] designates the first component (assoc) of the *connectedPeer* tokens,
- Field[2] designates the third component ($attrib_2 = maxPeer$) of the tokens of the server DM^*.

Property 2 Only connected peers can transmit messages.

Property 2 expression in OCL

Context *s:Server* inv : $s.connectedPeer \rightarrow excludes(pr1 : Peer)$ implies $pr1.transmittedMessage \rightarrow$ isEmpty()

Property 2 expression in PROD

verify henceforth $(connectedPeer : (field[0] == s_{server}\&\& field[1] == pr1_{Peer}) == empty$ implies $(transmittedMessage: field[0] == pr1_{Peer}) == empty)$

where :

- *Connectedpeer*: $field[0] == s_{server}\&\&field[1] == pr1_{Peer}$ designate the first and second components of the connectedPeer tokens,
- *Transmittedmessage*: $field[0] == pr1_{Peer}$ designates the 1st component of the *transmittedMessage* tokens.

Property 3 While a peer pr2 is connected, it receives all the information transmitted from a peer pr1.

Property 3 expression in OCL context *s:Server* inv : $s.connectedPeer \rightarrow$ includes(pr2 : Peer) and $pr1.transmittedInfo \rightarrow$ includes(m1 : Information) implies will $pr2.receivedInfo \rightarrow$ includes(m1 : Information)

Property 3 expression in PROD # verify henceforth $((connectedPeer: (field[0] == s_{server}\&\&field[1] == pr2_{Peer})! = empty)\&\&(transmittedInfo : (field[0] == pr1_{Peer}\&\&field[1] == m1_{Information})! = empty)$ implies eventually $(receivedInfo : (field[0] == pr2_{Peer}\&\&field[1] == m1_{Information})! = empty));$

where:

- *Connectedpeer*: $field[0] == s_{server}\&\&field[1] == pr2_{Peer}$ designate the 1st and 2nd components of the *connectedPeer* tokens,

- *Transmittedinfo* : *field*$[0] == pr1_{Peer}$&&*field*$[1] == m1_{Information}$ designate the 1st and 2nd components of the *Transmittedinfo* tokens.
- *Receivedinfo* : *field*$[0] == pr2_{Peer}$&&*field*$[1] == m1_{Information}$ designate the 1st and 2nd components of the *Receivedinfo* tokens.

Once the OPNs generated and then verified at the starting time of the system life cycle, we used object and sequence diagrams defined at specific times, different from time zero, to initialize them. This was performed using the implemented algorithm MarkObject(OD, SD, SM). The obtained markings reveal to be conformed to the object and sequence models.

Conclusion and Perspective

Many research results are published on the formalization of the UML but none so far on the initialization of the derived formal models, starting from UML diagrams set at times different from time zero. This paper proposes an approach to validate models, derived from state machines, at any time of the system life cycle. The initialization of these models is obtained from object and sequence diagrams. To locate the marks on the OPNs, the key idea focuses on the relationship between the sequence and state diagrams.

We also proposed an approach to express the association ends on the OPNs. The relevance of such an approach is to exploit all OCL capabilities to formally validate the system properties. These capabilities concern most of the OCL expressions. The only constraint of the proposed solution concerns the obligation for the user to specify the link actions on the state machine. However, this constraint is minimal compared to that of limiting OCL expressions or specifying using formal languages like temporal logics.

An interesting perspective to this work is to perform OPNs model initialization without resorting to the use of the first actions of the lifelines to locate the object states. The use of the association ends, modeled on object diagrams, is a promising research direction.

References

1. Andrade E, Macie0l P, Callou G, Nogueira B (2008) Mapping UML interaction overview diagram to time petri net for analysis and verification of embedded real-time systems with energy constraints. CIMCA 2008, Vienna
2. Andrade E, Maciel P, Callou G, Nogueira B, Araüjo C (2009) Mapping UML sequence diagram to time petri net for requirement validation of embedded real-time systems with energy constraints. SAC'2009, Hawaii, pp 377–381
3. Baresi L (2002) Some premilinary hints on formalizing UML with object petri nets. The 6th world conference on integrated design and process technology, Pasadena

4. Baresi L, Pezzè M (2001) On formalizing UML with high-level Petri Nets. Concurrent Object-Oriented Programming and Petri Nets, Advances in Petri Nets Series. LNCS. Springer, pp 276–304
5. Baresi L, Pezzè M (2005) Formal interpreters for diagram notations. ACM Trans Softw Eng Methodol 14(1):42–84
6. Baresi L, Morzenti A, Motta A, Rossi M (2011) From interaction overview diagrams to temporal logic. MODELS'10 Oslo LNCS 6637:90–104
7. Bokhari A, Poehlman WPS (2006) Translation of UML models to object coloured petri nets with a view to analysis. SEKE 2006, San Francisco, pp 568–571
8. Bouabana-Tebibel T (2007) Object dynamics formalization using object flows within UML state machines. Enterp Model Inf Syst Archit 2(1):26–39
9. Bouabana-Tebibel T (2011) Language integration for model formalization. The 12th 2011 IEEE international conference on information reuse and integration, Las Vegas
10. Bouabana-Tebibel T, Belmesk M (2007) An object-oriented approach to formally analyze the UML 2.0 activity partitions. Inf Softw Technol 49(9–10):999–1016
11. Bowles J, Andrews S, Kloul L (2010) Synthesising PEPA nets from IODs for performance analysis. WOSP/SIPEW '10, San Jose
12. Delatour J, De Lamotte F (2003) ArgoPN: A CASE tool merging UML and petri nets. The 1st international workshop on validation and verification of software for enterprise information systems, Angers
13. Fish A, Störrle H (2007) Visual qualities of the unified modeling language: deficiencies and improvements. IEEE symposium on visual languages and human-centric computing, Coeur d'Alène pp 41–49
14. Flake S (2003) UML-based specification of state-oriented real-time properties. PhD thesis, Faculty of Computer Science, Electrical Engineering and Mathematics, Paderborn University, Germany
15. Flake S, Mueller W (2004) Past- and future-oriented temporal time-bounded properties with OCL. 2nd international conferance on software engineering and formal methods, Beijing. ©IEEE Computer Society, pp 154–163
16. Guangyu Li, Yao S (2009) Research on mapping algorithm of UML sequence diagrams to object petri nets. WRI Glob Congr Intell Syst 4:285–289
17. Harel D, Maoz S (2006) Assert and negate revisited: modal semantics for UML sequence diagrams. 5th international workshop on scenarios and state machines: models, algorithms, and tools. ACM, New York, pp 13–20
18. Harel D, Kugler H, Pnueli A (2005) Synthesis revisited: generating statechart models from scenario-based requirements. In: Formal methods in software and system modeling. LNCS, vol 3393. Springer, pp 309–324
19. Holscher K, Ziemann P, Gogolla M (2006) On translating UML models into graph trans-formation systems. J Vis Lang Comput 17:78–105
20. Hsiung P-A, Lin S-W, Tseng C-H, Lee T-Y, Fu J-M, See W-B (2004) VERTAF: an application framework for the design and verification of embedded real-time software. IEEE Trans Softw Eng 30(10):656–674
21. Jensen K (1998) An introduction to the practical use of coloured petri nets. Lectures on Petri Nets II: Applications. LNCS, vol 1492. Springer, pp 237–292
22. Kloul L, Filipe KJ (2005) From intraction overview diagrams to PEPA nets. The work-shop on PASTA. Edinburgh
23. Knapp A, Wuttke J (2007) Model checking of UML 2.0 interactions. LNCS, vol 4364. Springer, pp 42–51
24. Kong K, Zhan K, Dong J, Xu D (2009) Specifying behavioral semantics of UML diagrams through graph transformations. J Syst Softw 82:292–306
25. Object Management Group (2001) The UML action semantics
26. Object Management Group (2003) UML 2.0 OCL specification
27. Object Management Group (2011) UML 2.4.1 superstructure specification

28. PROD 3.4 (2004) An advanced tool for efficient reachability analysis. Laboratory for Theoretical Computer Science, Helsinki University of Technology. Espoo
29. Saldana JA, Shatz SM, Hu Z (2001) Formalization of object behavior and interactions from UML models. Int J Softw Eng Knowl Eng 11(6):643–673
30. Staines TS (2008) Intuitive mapping of UML 2 activity diagrams into fundamental modeling concept petri net diagrams and colored petri nets. 15th IEEE inttenational conferance and workshop on the engineering of computer based systems, Belfast. IEEE Xplore, pp 191–200
31. Störrle H, Hausmann JH (2005) Towards a formal semantics of UML 2.0 activities. Softw Eng 64:117–128
32. Truong N, Souquiéres J (2004) Validation des propriétés d'un scénario UML/OCL à partir de sa dérivation en B. Approches Formelles dans l'Assitance au Développement de Logiciels, France

Chapter 6
Measuring Stability of Feature Selection Techniques on Real-World Software Datasets

Huanjing Wang, Taghi M. Khoshgoftaar, and Randall Wald

Abstract In the practice of software quality estimation, superfluous software metrics often exist in data repositories. In other words, not all collected software metrics are useful or make equal contributions to software defect prediction. Selecting a subset of features that are most relevant to the class attribute is necessary and may result in better prediction. This process is called feature selection. However, the addition or removal of instances can alter the subsets chosen by a feature selection technique, rendering the previously-selected feature sets invalid. Thus, the robustness (e.g., stability) of feature selection techniques must be studied to examine the sensitivity of these techniques to changes in their input data (the addition or removal of instances). In this study, we test the stability of 18 feature selection techniques as the magnitude of change to the datasets and the size of the selected feature subsets are varied. All experiments were conducted on 16 datasets from 3 real-world software projects. The experimental results demonstrate that Gain Ratio shows the least stability while two different versions of ReliefF show the most stability, followed by the PRC- and AUC-based threshold-based feature selection techniques. Results also show that making smaller changes to the datasets has less impact on the stability of feature ranking techniques applied to those datasets.

H. Wang (✉)
Western Kentucky University, Bowling Green, KY 42101, USA
e-mail: huanjing.wang@wku.edu

T.M. Khoshgoftaar · R. Wald
Florida Atlantic University, Boca Raton, FL 33431, USA
e-mail: taghi@cse.fau.edu; rdwald@gmail.com

T. Özyer et al. (eds.), *Information Reuse and Integration in Academia and Industry*,
DOI 10.1007/978-3-7091-1538-1_6, © Springer-Verlag Wien 2013

Introduction

For most software systems, superfluous software metrics are often collected. The quality of data (metrics) is an important issue in the data mining and software engineering field. When building software defect prediction models using all available software metrics, the defect prediction ability may be affected since some metrics may be redundant or irrelevant to defect prediction results. Therefore in software defect prediction problems, the identification and selection of relevant metrics from a metric dataset is very important. The identification and selection process is called feature (metric) selection. Feature selection is a critical component in data mining or machine learning preprocessing. Numerous feature selection methods have been proposed in the data mining and software engineering domains. One common way to evaluate a feature selection method is the performance of a chosen classifier trained with the selected features. The classification performance demonstrates the effectiveness of the feature selection technique used to identify the most relevant metrics. Another way to evaluate a feature selection technique is robustness (stability), which has received less attention in the past. Stability is an important aspect of feature selection techniques because by choosing the most stable feature rankers, software practitioners can be confident that the selected features represent actual properties of the underlying data, and aren't subject to random change based on minor fluctuations in the data. Few studies exist on the stability of feature selection algorithms.

In this study, we assess the stability performance of 18 different feature selection techniques, including chi-squared (CS), information gain (IG), gain ratio (GR), 2 types of ReliefF (RF and RFW), symmetrical uncertainty (SU), 11 threshold-based feature selection techniques (TBFS), and signal-to-noise (S2N). The stability of a technique is evaluated by measuring the changes between the subset chosen using the full dataset and that chosen from modified datasets with instances removed. The experimental results showed that GR and SU performed significantly worst among the 18 techniques and RF performed best. Also, the fewer instances deleted from (or equivalently, added to) a dataset, the more stable feature ranking will be on that data.

The main contribution of the present work is that we consider the stability of feature selection techniques by comparing the selected features before and after some instances are deleted from a dataset (or equivalently, before and after some instances are added), rather than directly comparing separate subsamples of the original dataset. This is an important distinction because in many real-world situations, software practitioners want to know whether adding additional instances to their dataset will change the results of feature selection. The experiments discussed in this study contain the answer. We have found that if software practitioners want to build models on one set of data using feature selection and then continue to use that set of features as new instances are added to the dataset, ReliefF and the AUC- and PRC-based TBFS methods will be the best choices for feature selection.

In addition, we consider a wide range of feature selection techniques to ensure that our comparison is as thorough as possible.

The reminder of the chapter is organized as follows: section "Related Work" provides an overview of related work, while section "Filter-Based Feature Ranking Techniques" presents 18 feature selection techniques. Section "Experimental Design" describes the datasets and experimental design. Section "Results and Analysis" presents the experimental results and analysis. Finally, we conclude the chapter in section "Conclusions and Future Work" and provide suggestions for future work.

Related Work

The main goal of feature selection is to select a subset of features that excludes features which are irrelevant (not useful for predicting the class) or redundant (contain information already found in other features). Feature selection techniques can be broadly classified as *feature ranking* and *feature subset selection*. Feature ranking sorts the attributes according to their individual predictive power, while feature subset selection finds subsets of attributes that collectively have good predictive power. Feature selection techniques can also be categorized as *filters*, *wrappers*, or *embedded* methods. Filters are algorithms in which a feature subset is selected without involving any learning algorithm. Wrappers are algorithms that use feedback from a learning algorithm to determine which feature(s) to include in building a classification model. Embedded methods do not perform explicit feature selection like filters and wrappers; instead, feature selection is incorporated within a learning algorithm.

Guyon and Elisseeff [14] outlined key approaches used for attribute selection, including feature construction, feature ranking, multivariate feature selection, efficient search methods, and feature validity assessment methods. Liu and Yu [23] provided a comprehensive survey of feature selection algorithms and presented an integrated approach to intelligent feature selection. Hall and Holmes [15] investigated six attribute selection techniques that produce ranked lists of attributes and applied them to several datasets from the UCI machine learning repository. Forman [11] investigated multiple filter-based feature ranking techniques.

Although feature selection has been widely applied in many application domains for many years, its application in the software quality and reliability engineering domain is limited. Chen et al. [7] have studied the applications of wrapper-based feature selection in the context of software cost/effort estimation. They conclude that the reduced dataset improved the estimation. Rodríguez et al. [28] applied attribute selection with three filter models and two wrapper models to five software engineering datasets using the WEKA [33] tool. All techniques were feature subset selection and not ranking techniques. It was stated that the wrapper model was better than the filter model; however, that came at a very high computational cost. Gao et al. [13] considered a hybrid approach, using filter-based ranking techniques to first reduce the size of the feature space and then a filter-based subset evaluation technique to choose the final feature set. They found that this hybrid approach greatly improved the speed of the modeling process while producing results similar to using the subset evaluation technique alone.

The stability of a feature selection method is normally defined as the degree of agreement between its outputs to randomly selected subsets of the same input data [22, 24]. Recent work in this area mainly focuses on consistency of the outputs by measuring the variations between subsets of features obtained from different subsamples of the original training dataset. Saeys et al. [29] used the Spearman rank correlation coefficient. Abeel et al. [1] studied the process for selecting biomarkers from microarray data and presented a general framework for stability analysis of such feature selection techniques. Lustgarten et al. [25] devised a new stability measure called Adjusted Stability Measure (ASM) that can be applied to classifier based feature selecting methods. Kalousis et al. [16] used different measures of correlation to measure the stability of the feature ranker. Note that the present work (unlike the works here cited) considers stability in terms of the difference in feature subset selected before and after instances are removed from the dataset, rather than comparing multiple reduced subsamples to each other; our approach permits us to more closely simulate the use case of determining which feature subsets will remain appropriate even after new instances are added to a dataset.

To assess robustness of feature selection techniques, past works have used different similarity measures, such as Hamming distance [8], correlation coefficient [16], consistency index [22], and entropy [21]. Among these four similarity measures, consistency index is the only one which takes into consideration bias due to chance. Because of this, in our work the consistency index was used as stability measure. The term consistency index was defined by Kuncheva et al. [22]. The consistency index is a measure of similarity between two different feature subsets. They devised this measure as a way to choose the best set of features for an experiment. If stability was high, then the features chosen in rank order by stability that has the minimum local error were chosen as the feature subset. If stability was low, the best individual subset would be used. In the present work, the consistency index is not used for this purpose, but instead is the metric used to evaluate whether a given ranker is stable even in the face of additions or deletions of instances from the dataset.

Filter-Based Feature Ranking Techniques

In this study, we focus on filter-based feature ranking techniques and applied these feature ranking techniques to software engineering datasets. Filter-based feature ranking techniques rank features independently without involving any learning algorithm. Feature ranking consists of scoring each feature according to a particular method, then selecting features based on their scores. This chapter uses 18 feature ranking techniques, which can be placed into 3 categories: 6 commonly used feature ranking techniques, 11 threshold-based feature selection techniques (TBFS) that

Table 6.1 List of 18 filter-based feature selection techniques

Abbreviation	Name
CS	χ^2 statistic
GR	Gain ratio
IG	Information gain
RF	ReliefF
RFW	ReliefF—weight by distance
SU	Symmetric uncertainty
FM	F-measure
OR	Odds ratio
PO	Power
PR	Probability ratio
GI	Gini index
MI	Mutual information
KS	Kolmogorov-Smirnov statistic
Dev	Deviance
GM	Geometric mean
AUC	Area under the ROC curve
PRC	Area under the precision-recall curve
S2N	Signal-to-noise

were developed by our research team, and a new filter technique called Signal-to-Noise (S2N). Table 6.1 contains all of the feature selection techniques used and their abbreviations.

Commonly Used Feature Ranking Techniques

The commonly used feature ranking techniques include chi-squared [33], information gain [15, 33], gain ratio [33], two types of ReliefF [19], and symmetrical uncertainty [15, 33]. All of these feature selection methods are available within the WEKA machine learning software suite [33]. Since these methods are widely known, we provide only a brief summary; the interested reader should consult with the included references for further details.

The chi-square (CS) [6] test is used to examine if there is 'no association' between two attributes, i.e., whether the two variables are independent. CS is more likely to find significance to the extent that (1) the relationship is strong, (2) the sample size is large, and/or (3) the number of values of the two associated features is large.

Information gain, gain ratio, and symmetrical uncertainty are measures based on the concept of entropy, which is based on information theory. Information gain (IG) [27] is the information provided about the target class attribute Y, given the value of independent attribute X. Information gain measures the decrease of the weighted average impurity of the partitions based on attribute X, compared with the impurity of the complete set of data. A drawback of IG is that it tends to prefer attributes with a larger number of possible values; that is, if one attribute has a larger number of values, it will appear to gain more information than those with fewer values, even if it is actually no more informative. One strategy to counter this problem is to use the gain ratio (GR), which penalizes multiple-valued attributes. Symmetrical uncertainty (SU) [15] is another way to overcome the problem of IG's bias toward attributes with more values, doing so by dividing IG by the sum of the entropies of X and Y. These techniques (CS, IG, GR, and SU) utilize the method of Fayyad and Irani [10] to discretize continuous attributes, and all four methods are bivariate, considering the relationship between each attribute and the class, excluding the other independent variables.

Relief is an instance-based feature ranking technique which measures how much the feature's value changes when comparing an instance to its nearest same-class and different-class neighbors [18]. ReliefF is an extension of the Relief algorithm that can handle noise and multi-class datasets. When the 'weightByDistance' (weight nearest neighbors by their distance) parameter is set as default (false), the algorithm is referred to as RF; when the parameter is set to true, the algorithm is referred to as RFW.

Threshold-Based Feature Ranking Techniques

Eleven threshold-based feature selection techniques (TBFS) were recently proposed by our research group [31] and have been implemented within WEKA [33]. The procedure is shown in Algorithm 1. First, each attribute's values are normalized between 0 and 1 by mapping F^j to $\hat{F}^j$. The normalized values are treated as posterior probabilities. Each independent attribute is then paired individually with the class attribute and the reduced 2 attribute dataset is evaluated using 11 different performance metrics based on this set of "posterior probabilities." In standard binary classification, the predicted class is assigned using the default decision threshold of 0.5. The default decision threshold is often not optimal, especially when the class is imbalanced. Therefore, we propose the use of performance metrics that can be calculated at various points in the distribution of $\hat{F}^j$. At each threshold position, we classify values above the threshold as positive, and below as negative. Then we go in the opposite direction, and consider values above as negative, and below as positive. Whatever direction produces the more optimal performance metric values is used.

The true positive (*TPR*), true negative (*TNR*), false positive (*FPR*), and false negative (*FNR*) rates can be calculated at each threshold $t \in [0, 1]$ relative to the normalized attribute $\hat{F}^j$. The threshold-based attribute ranking techniques we propose utilize these rates as described below.

– *F-measure (FM)*: is a single value metric derived from the F-measure that originated from the field of information retrieval [33]. The maximum F-measure is

---

Algorithm 1: Threshold-based feature selection algorithm

---

input :
1. Dataset D with features F^j, $j = 1, \ldots, m$;
2. Each instance $x \in D$ is assigned to one of two classes $c(x) \in \{fp, nfp\}$;
3. The value of attribute F^j for instance x is denoted $F^j(x)$;
4. Metric $\omega \in \{FM, OR, PO, PR, GI, MI, KS, Dev, GM, AUC, PRC\}$;
5. A predefined threshold: number (or percentage) of the features to be selected.
output:
Selected feature subsets.

for F^j, $j = 1, \ldots, m$ **do**

  Normalize $F^j \mapsto \hat{F}^j = \frac{F^j - \min(F^j)}{\max(F^j) - \min(F^j)}$;

  Calculate metric ω using attribute $\hat{F}^j$ and class attribute at various decision thresholds in the distribution of $\hat{F}^j$, considering both cases where $\hat{F}^j > threshold$ indicates a positive instance and where it indicates a negative instance. The optimal ω is used, $\omega(\hat{F}^j)$.

Create feature ranking $\mathbb{R}$ using $\omega(\hat{F}^j) \forall j$.
Select features according to feature ranking $\mathbb{R}$ and a predefined threshold.

---

obtained when varying the decision threshold value between 0 and 1. The formula for the F-measure maximized over all thresholds is:

$$\text{F-measure} = \max_{t \in [0,1]} \frac{(1 + \beta^2) \times PRE(t) \times TPR(t)}{\beta^2 \times PRE(t) + TPR(t)}$$

PRE(t), the precision, is defined as the number of true positives divided by the total number of instances classified as positive (e.g., true positives plus false positives). β is a parameter that can be changed by the user to place more weight on either the true positive rate or precision. We decided to use a value of 1 for β.

– *Odds Ratio (OR)*: is the ratio of the product of correct (*TPR* times *TNR*) to incorrect (*FPR* times *FNR*) predictions [11]. The maximum value is taken when varying the decision threshold value between 0 and 1.

– *Power (PO)*: is a measure that avoids common false positive cases while giving stronger preference for positive cases [11]. Power is defined as:

$$PO = \max_{t \in [0,1]} \left((TNR(t))^k - (FNR(t))^k \right)$$

where $k = 5$.

– *Probability Ratio (PR)*: is the sample estimate probability of the feature given the positive class divided by the sample estimate probability of the feature given the negative class [11]. PR is the maximum value of the ratio when varying the decision threshold value between 0 and 1. The ratio is defined as:

$$PR = \max_{t \in [0,1]} \frac{TPR(t)}{FPR(t)}$$

- *Gini Index (GI)*: measures the impurity of a dataset [4]. GI for the attribute is then the minimum Gini index at all decision thresholds $t \in [0, 1]$. The equation for the Gini index is:

$$GI = \min_{t \in [0,1]} [2PRE(t)(1 - PRE(t)) + 2NPV(t)(1 - NPV(t))]$$

where $NPV(t)$ is the negative predictive value, or the percentage of instances predicted to be negative that are actually negative at threshold t. Since lower values here mean lower chances of misclassification, lower is better, and so the minimum Gini index score is the chosen score for the attribute [5].

- *Mutual Information (MI)*: measures the mutual dependence of the two random variables [26]. High mutual information indicates a large reduction in uncertainty, and zero mutual information between two random variables means the variables are independent. The actual definition of mutual information is "the amount by which the knowledge provided by the feature vector decreases the uncertainty about the class" [2]. The equation for mutual information is:

$$MI = \max_{t \in [0,1]} \sum_{\hat{c}^t \in \{P,N\}} \sum_{c \in \{P,N\}} p(\hat{c}^t, c) \log \frac{p(\hat{c}^t, c)}{p(\hat{c}^t)p(c)}$$

where c represents the actual class of the instance and $\hat{c}^t$ is the predicted class of the instance [2].

- *Kolmogorov-Smirnov (KS)*: utilizes the Kolmogorov-Smirnov statistic to measure the maximum difference between the empirical distribution functions of the attribute values of instances in each class [17]. It is effectively the maximum difference between the curves generated by the true positive and false positive rates as the decision threshold changes between 0 and 1. The formula for KS is [30]:

$$KS = \max_{t \in [0,1]} |TPR(t) - FPR(t)|$$

- *Deviance (Dev)*: is the residual sum of squares based on a threshold t [30]. That is, it measures the sum of the squared errors from the mean class given a partitioning of the space based on the threshold t and then the minimum value is chosen.

- *Geometric Mean (GM)*: is a single-value performance measure which is calculated by finding the maximum geometric mean of *TPR* and *TNR* as the decision threshold is varied between 0 and 1 [30].

- *Area Under ROC (Receiver Operating Characteristic) Curve* (AUC): has been widely used to measure classification model performance [9]. The ROC curve is used to characterize the trade-off between true positive rate and false positive rate. In this study, ROC curves are generated by varying the decision threshold t used to transform the normalized attribute values into a predicted class.

- *Area Under the Precision-Recall Curve* (PRC): is a single-value measure that originated from the area of information retrieval. The area under the PRC ranges from 0 to 1. The closer the area is to one, the stronger the predictive power of the attribute [30]. The PRC diagram depicts the trade off between recall and precision.

Signal-to-Noise

Signal-to-noise is a measure used in electrical engineering to quantify how much a signal has been corrupted by noise. It is defined as the ratio of signal's power to the noise's power corrupting the signal. The signal-to-noise (S2N) can also be used as feature ranking method [35]. For a binary class problem (such as *fp*, *nfp*), the S2N is defined as:

$$S2N = (\mu_{fp} - \mu_{nfp})/(\sigma_{fp} + \sigma_{nfp})$$

where μ_{fp} and μ_{nfp} are the mean values of that particular attribute in all of the instances which belong to a specific class, either *fp* or *nfp* (the positive and negative classes). σ_{fp} and σ_{nfp} are the standard deviations of that particular attribute as it relates to the class. If one attribute's expression in one class is quite different from its expression in the other, and there is little variation within the two classes, then the attribute is predictive. Therefore S2N favors attributes where the range of the expression vector is large, but where most of that variation is due to the class distribution. S2N is rarely used as a feature ranking technique.

Experimental Design

To test the stability of different feature selection techniques under different circumstances, we performed a case study on 16 different software metric datasets, using 18 feature selection techniques, 4 different levels of change to the datasets, and 9 different numbers of chosen features. Discussion and results from this case study are presented below.

Datasets

Experiments conducted in this study used software metrics and fault data collected from real-world software projects, including a very large telecommunications software system (denoted as LLTS) [12], the Eclipse project [36], and NASA software project KC1 [20]. These are all binary class datasets. That is, each instance is assigned one of two class labels: fault-prone (*fp*) and not fault-prone (*nfp*).

The software measurement dataset of LLTS contains data from four consecutive releases, which are labeled as SP1, SP2, SP3, and SP4. This dataset includes 42 software metrics, including 24 product metrics, 14 process metrics, and 4 execution metrics [12]. The dependent variable is the class of the program module: fault-prone (*fp*) or not fault-prone (*nfp*). A program module with one or more faults is considered *fp*, and *nfp* otherwise.

From the PROMISE data repository [36], we also obtained the Eclipse defect counts and complexity metrics dataset. In particular, we use the metrics and defects data at the software package level. The original data for the Eclipse packages consists of three releases denoted 2.0, 2.1, and 3.0 respectively. We transform the original data by: (1) removing all non-numeric attributes, including the package names, and (2) converting the post-release defects attribute to a binary class attribute: fault-prone (*fp*) and not fault-prone (*nfp*). Membership in each class is determined by a post-release defects threshold t, which separates *fp* from *nfp* packages by classifying packages with t or more post-release defects as *fp* and the remaining as *nfp*. In our study, we use $t \epsilon \{10, 5, 3\}$ for release 2.0 and 3.0, while we use $t \epsilon \{5, 4, 2\}$ for release 2.1. These values are selected in order to have datasets with different levels of class imbalance. All 9 derived datasets contain 208 independent attributes. Releases 2.0, 2.1, and 3.0 contain 377, 434, and 661 instances respectively.

The original NASA project, KC1 [20], includes 145 instances containing 94 independent attributes each. After removing 32 Halstead derived measures, we have 62 attributes left. We used three different thresholds to define defective instances, thereby obtaining three structures of the preprocessed KC1 dataset. The thresholds are 20, 10, and 5, indicating that instances with numbers of defects greater than or equal to 20, 10, or 5 belong to the *fp* class. The three datasets are named KC1-20, KC1-10, and KC1-5.

The 16 original datasets used in the work reflect software projects of different sizes with different proportions of *fp* and *nfp* modules. Table 6.2 lists the characteristics of the 16 datasets utilized in this work.

Dataset Perturbation (Changing)

For this study, we consider stability on changes to the datasets (perturbations) at the instance level. Consider a dataset with m instances: a smaller dataset can be generated by keeping a fraction, c, of instances and randomly removing $1 - c$ of instances from the original data, where c is greater than 0 and less than 1. We removed from each class instead of just from the dataset as a whole in order to maintain the original level of class balance/imbalance for each dataset. For a given c, this process can be performed x times. This will create x new datasets, each having $c \times m$ instances, where each of these new datasets is unique (since each was built by

Table 6.2 Software datasets characteristics

	Data	#metrics	#modules	% fp	% nfp
LLTS	SP1	42	3,649	6.28	93.72
	SP2	42	3,981	4.75	95.25
	SP3	42	3,541	1.33	98.67
	SP4	42	3,978	2.31	97.69
Eclipse	Eclipse2.0-10	208	377	6.1	93.9
	Eclipse2.0-5	208	377	13.79	86.21
	Eclipse2.0-3	208	377	26.79	73.21
	Eclipse2.1-5	208	434	7.83	92.17
	Eclipse2.1-4	208	434	11.52	88.48
	Eclipse2.1-2	208	434	28.8	71.2
	Eclipse3.0-10	208	661	6.2	93.8
	Eclipse3.0-5	208	661	14.83	85.17
	Eclipse3.0-3	208	661	23.75	76.25
KC1	KC1-20	62	145	6.90	93.10
	KC1-10	62	145	14.48	85.52
	KC1-5	62	145	24.83	75.17

randomly removing $(1 - c) \times m$ instances from the original dataset). In this study, x was set to 30 and c was set to 0.95, 0.9, 0.8, or 0.67, thereby obtaining 30 datasets for each original dataset and choice of c.

Feature Selection

First the features are ranked according to their relevance to the class using 18 different feature selection techniques separately. The rankings are applied to each combination of dataset and level of perturbation. Therefore, (16 original datasets $\times$ 18 rankers) + (16 datasets $\times$ 4 levels of perturbation $\times$ 30 repetitions $\times$ 18 rankers) = 34,848 different rankings were generated. The next step is to select a subset consisting of the most relevant ones. In this study, nine subsets are chosen for each dataset. The number of features that is retained in each subset for each dataset are 2, 3, 4, 5, 6, 7, 8, 9, and 10. These numbers are deemed reasonable after some preliminary experimentation conducted on the corresponding datasets [32].

Stability Measure

In order to measure stability, we decided to use consistency index [22] because it takes into consideration bias due to chance. First, we assume the original dataset has n features. Let T_i and T_j be subsets of features, where $|T_i| = |T_j| = k$. The consistency index [22] is obtained as follows:

$$I_C\left(T_i, T_j\right) = \frac{dn - k^2}{k\left(n - k\right)},\qquad(6.1)$$

where d is the cardinality of the intersection between subsets T_i and T_j, and $-1 < I_C\left(T_i, T_j\right) \leq +1$. The greater the consistency index, the more similar the subsets are. When we apply the consistency index to the original dataset and one of the derivative datasets we can use the resultant consistency measurement as a measurement of stability for the feature ranker.

Results and Analysis

Experiments are conducted with 18 filter-based feature ranking techniques on 16 software engineering metrics datasets. Their effects on stability are examined in terms of choice of filters, number of features used, and degree or perturbation.

Most and Least Stable Filters

Given a dataset, a ranker, number of features selected, and a perturbation level c, the average stability can be computed (30 I_C values are computed, 1 for each pair of original dataset and 1 of 30 repetitions of perturbation (see section "Stability Measure")). Therefore the average stability across 16 datasets can be computed. Tables 6.3–6.6 summarize the results of the robustness analysis of each ranker, with each table holding perturbation level constant and showing the results for all feature rankers and number of selected features separately, averaged across all 16 datasets. Each cell shows the average I_C value for the 30 repetitions of each of the 16 datasets using the specified perturbation level, with the feature ranker and number of features based on the exact row and column where the cell is located. The top value for each level of features is in boldface. These tables show the following observations:

- Among the 18 rankers, GR shows the least stability, on average, while RF shows the most stability when 2–5 features are selected and PRC has the most stability when more than 6 features are selected.
- The size of the feature subset can influence the stability of a feature ranking technique. For most rankers, stability is improved by an increased number of features in the selected subset.

Table 6.3 Average stability across all 16 datasets, 67 %

	Number of features used								
	2	3	4	5	6	7	8	9	10
CS	0.5669	0.5230	0.5273	0.5294	0.5575	0.5687	0.5865	0.6021	0.6183
GR	0.3001	0.3358	0.3561	0.3539	0.3673	0.3778	0.3848	0.4043	0.4157
IG	0.5743	0.5582	0.5555	0.5431	0.5544	0.5637	0.5724	0.5863	0.6051
RF	**0.7905**	**0.7661**	**0.7342**	**0.7275**	0.7138	0.7034	0.7008	0.7094	0.7043
RFW	0.7324	0.6935	0.7014	0.7160	0.7359	0.7212	0.7212	0.7155	0.7191
SU	0.4059	0.4138	0.4217	0.4313	0.4450	0.4518	0.4769	0.4849	0.5024
FM	0.6349	0.5984	0.6039	0.6036	0.6165	0.6326	0.6548	0.6710	0.6869
OR	0.4164	0.3906	0.4313	0.4582	0.4554	0.4683	0.4981	0.5213	0.5325
PO	0.6271	0.5959	0.5910	0.6104	0.6386	0.6508	0.6691	0.6817	0.6924
PR	0.4075	0.4307	0.4307	0.4463	0.4774	0.5047	0.5257	0.5436	0.5646
GI	0.4227	0.4472	0.4446	0.4698	0.4899	0.5156	0.5377	0.5668	0.5821
MI	0.6114	0.5926	0.5860	0.5890	0.5942	0.6103	0.6236	0.6474	0.6568
KS	0.5895	0.5894	0.5850	0.6016	0.6091	0.6222	0.6329	0.6520	0.6648
Dev	0.6056	0.5662	0.5803	0.5876	0.6077	0.6246	0.6464	0.6593	0.6785
GM	0.5909	0.5772	0.5797	0.5863	0.6074	0.6153	0.6328	0.6480	0.6676
AUC	0.6590	0.6584	0.6843	0.6940	0.7109	0.7348	0.7483	0.7643	0.7749
PRC	0.6915	0.6664	0.7132	0.7200	**0.7392**	**0.7482**	**0.7682**	**0.7842**	**0.7940**
S2N	0.6944	0.6571	0.6391	0.6350	0.6237	0.6250	0.6277	0.6381	0.6429

Table 6.4 Average stability across all 16 datasets, 80 %

	Number of features used								
	2	3	4	5	6	7	8	9	10
CS	0.6323	0.6199	0.6017	0.6039	0.6394	0.6610	0.6723	0.6791	0.6909
GR	0.4305	0.4512	0.4560	0.4535	0.4587	0.4639	0.4830	0.5085	0.5238
IG	0.6632	0.6379	0.6528	0.6352	0.6443	0.6483	0.6497	0.6642	0.6777
RF	**0.8520**	**0.8466**	**0.8282**	**0.8179**	0.7991	0.7844	0.7839	0.7971	0.7907
RFW	0.8184	0.7925	0.7937	0.8045	**0.8176**	0.7986	0.7980	0.7926	0.7952
SU	0.4875	0.5078	0.5186	0.5152	0.5266	0.5388	0.5640	0.5700	0.5842
FM	0.7172	0.6945	0.7094	0.7040	0.7055	0.7097	0.7275	0.7487	0.7600
OR	0.5142	0.5013	0.5488	0.5804	0.5855	0.5965	0.6124	0.6339	0.6474
PO	0.7211	0.6863	0.6850	0.7019	0.7276	0.7310	0.7497	0.7620	0.7632
PR	0.5424	0.5443	0.5658	0.5897	0.6229	0.6451	0.6645	0.6801	0.6870
GI	0.5650	0.5574	0.5677	0.5998	0.6162	0.6429	0.6533	0.6769	0.6859
MI	0.6907	0.6677	0.6845	0.6769	0.6896	0.7003	0.7087	0.7245	0.7325
KS	0.6761	0.6803	0.6782	0.6935	0.7103	0.7119	0.7282	0.7386	0.7501
Dev	0.6934	0.6579	0.6798	0.7000	0.7102	0.7190	0.7299	0.7346	0.7488
GM	0.6731	0.6683	0.6789	0.6847	0.7045	0.7073	0.7289	0.7372	0.7511
AUC	0.7527	0.7422	0.7782	0.7740	0.7829	0.8067	0.8121	0.8297	0.8343
PRC	0.7673	0.7439	0.8039	0.7983	0.7977	**0.8190**	**0.8370**	**0.8488**	**0.8591**
S2N	0.7819	0.7628	0.7314	0.7269	0.7127	0.7152	0.7214	0.7372	0.7497

Table 6.5 Average stability across all 16 datasets, 90 %

	Number of features used								
	2	3	4	5	6	7	8	9	10
CS	0.7221	0.7070	0.7051	0.6973	0.7259	0.7417	0.7503	0.7612	0.7727
GR	0.5699	0.5689	0.5813	0.5788	0.5857	0.5927	0.6120	0.6335	0.6461
IG	0.7347	0.7143	0.7294	0.7174	0.7224	0.7280	0.7331	0.7469	0.7622
RF	**0.8977**	**0.9125**	**0.9025**	**0.8941**	0.8745	0.8668	0.8631	0.8688	0.8627
RFW	0.8768	0.8728	0.8903	0.8826	**0.8852**	0.8716	0.8768	0.8679	0.8676
SU	0.5965	0.6209	0.6269	0.6427	0.6430	0.6409	0.6672	0.6766	0.6898
FM	0.8247	0.7811	0.7923	0.7878	0.7949	0.7949	0.8163	0.8310	0.8383
OR	0.6511	0.6429	0.7016	0.7249	0.7176	0.7327	0.7371	0.7532	0.7618
PO	0.7961	0.7582	0.7706	0.7906	0.8067	0.8090	0.8254	0.8432	0.8496
PR	0.6791	0.6877	0.6914	0.7002	0.7390	0.7581	0.7725	0.7831	0.7940
GI	0.6996	0.7037	0.7123	0.7254	0.7506	0.7737	0.7796	0.7946	0.8008
MI	0.7732	0.7673	0.7904	0.7743	0.7875	0.7981	0.7929	0.8000	0.7964
KS	0.7762	0.7887	0.7854	0.7818	0.7998	0.8100	0.8255	0.8290	0.8312
Dev	0.7905	0.7471	0.7648	0.7768	0.7943	0.8004	0.8092	0.8180	0.8260
GM	0.7723	0.7861	0.7823	0.7882	0.8089	0.8052	0.8203	0.8327	0.8340
AUC	0.8268	0.7896	0.8531	0.8506	0.8504	0.8595	0.8646	0.8755	0.8795
PRC	0.8452	0.8290	0.8842	0.8696	0.8655	**0.8768**	**0.8896**	**0.8949**	**0.8999**
S2N	0.8636	0.8444	0.8341	0.8324	0.8112	0.8143	0.8248	0.8323	0.8471

Table 6.6 Average stability across all 16 datasets, 95 %

	Number of features used								
	2	3	4	5	6	7	8	9	
CS	0.7681	0.7715	0.7870	0.7729	0.7949	0.8127	0.8162	0.8285	0.8269
GR	0.6779	0.6758	0.6976	0.6922	0.6872	0.6937	0.7120	0.7344	0.7431
IG	0.8082	0.7895	0.7840	0.7816	0.7821	0.7878	0.7952	0.8056	0.8165
RF	**0.9285**	**0.9427**	**0.9400**	**0.9330**	0.9107	0.9039	0.9025	0.9094	0.9054
RFW	0.9128	0.9207	0.9269	0.9275	**0.9258**	0.9080	0.9185	0.9045	0.9067
SU	0.6691	0.7142	0.7200	0.7346	0.7263	0.7306	0.7485	0.7569	0.7641
FM	0.8685	0.8242	0.8438	0.8408	0.8483	0.8433	0.8695	0.8792	0.8821
OR	0.7415	0.7328	0.8022	0.8255	0.8072	0.8041	0.8032	0.8191	0.8310
PO	0.8615	0.8335	0.8462	0.8498	0.8644	0.8661	0.8786	0.8803	0.8866
PR	0.7628	0.7519	0.7664	0.7724	0.8176	0.8265	0.8345	0.8437	0.8531
GI	0.7873	0.7863	0.7991	0.8124	0.8407	0.8541	0.8519	0.8623	0.8667
MI	0.8253	0.8247	0.8520	0.8395	0.8451	0.8572	0.8455	0.8504	0.8436
KS	0.8357	0.8361	0.8587	0.8494	0.8599	0.8671	0.8835	0.8836	0.8847
Dev	0.8448	0.7945	0.8190	0.8456	0.8573	0.8549	0.8609	0.8651	0.8709
GM	0.8285	0.8508	0.8436	0.8537	0.8583	0.8594	0.8775	0.8889	0.8866
AUC	0.8820	0.8453	0.9018	0.8927	0.8928	0.9051	0.9038	0.9103	0.9124
PRC	0.8958	0.8754	0.9175	0.9153	0.8988	**0.9107**	**0.9202**	**0.9242**	**0.9271**
S2N	0.9084	0.8826	0.8867	0.8714	0.8528	0.8626	0.8691	0.8812	0.8889

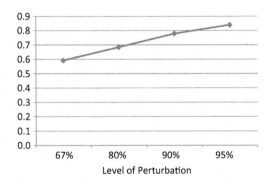

Fig. 6.1 Degree of perturbation impact on stability

Table 6.7 Analysis of variance

Source	Sum Sq.	d.f.	Mean Sq.	F	p-value
A	267	17	15.7056	524.92	0
Error	2,326.03	77,742	0.0299		
Total	2,593.02	77,759			

Degree of Perturbation Impact on Stability

Figure 6.1 shows the effect of the degree of dataset perturbation on the stability of feature ranking techniques across all 16 datasets and 9 feature subsets. From this figure, we can observe that the more instances retained in a dataset (e.g., the fewer instances deleted from the original dataset), the more stable the feature ranking on that dataset will be.

ANOVA Analysis

We performed an ANalysis Of VAriance (ANOVA) F test [3] to statistically examine the robustness (e.g., stability) of feature selection techniques. An n-way ANOVA can be used to determine if the means in a set of data differ when grouped by multiple factors. If they do differ, one can determine which factors or combinations of factors are associated with the difference. The ANOVA model we built includes 1 factor: Factor A, in which 18 rankers were considered. In this ANOVA test, the results from all 16 datasets with 95 % perturbation level were taken into account together. The ANOVA results are presented in Table 6.7. The *p* value of Factor A is 0, which indicates there was a significant difference between the average stability values of the 18 rankers.

We further conducted multiple pairwise comparison tests for the main factor to identify which pair(s) of means significantly differ from each other. The multiple

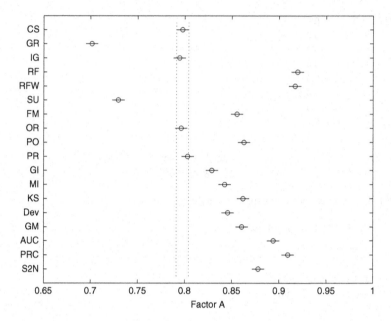

Fig. 6.2 Multiple comparisons

comparison test results are shown in Fig. 6.2. The figure presents each group mean with a symbol (∘) and the 95 % confidence interval with a line around the symbol. Two means are significantly different if their intervals are disjoint, and are not significantly different if their intervals overlap. Matlab was used to perform the ANOVA and multiple comparisons presented in this work, and the assumptions for constructing ANOVA models were validated. The results show the following facts: For factor A, GR and SU performed significantly worst among the 18 rankers and RF and RFW performed best, followed by PRC and AUC.

Threats to Validity

There are two types of threats to validity which are frequency considered in empirical software engineering [34]. Threats to internal validity pertain to unanticipated factors which may affect the experimental results, while threats to external validity are concerns which arise from generalizing the results to a wider setting and what limits must be considered in this generalization.

The case study presented here is an empirical software engineering effort, and in order to satisfy the software engineering community must therefore meet the following requirements [34]: (1) developed by a team, and not by a single programmer; (2) be a large, industry-sized project, and not a toy problem; (3) developed by professionals, not by students; and (4) developed in an government/industry setting, and not in a university laboratory. All of these criteria are met by the software systems that are used in our case study: they were developed by professionals in large software development organizations using established software development processes and management practices. All software systems were developed to address real-world problems.

Threats to internal validity are unaccounted for influences on the experiments that may affect case study results. Poor fault proneness estimates can be caused by a wide variety of factors, including measurement errors while collecting and recording software metrics, modeling errors due to the unskilled use of software applications, errors in model-selection during the modeling process, and the presence of outliers and noise in the training dataset. Measurement errors are inherent to the data collection effort. In our comparative study, a common model-building and model-evaluation approach is used for all feature selection techniques and classifiers considered. Moreover, the experiments and statistical analysis was performed by only one skilled person in order to keep modeling errors to a minimum.

Other threats to internal validity would relate to the software system used perform our analysis. For example, errors in preparing and running the experiments would naturally have an impact on experimental results. To ensure these did not impact this work, we used the WEKA machine learning environment, which has been thoroughly tested by our group and others. The six standard filters used in this paper are available in the publicly-available distribution of WEKA; the 11 different versions of TBFS and signal-to-noise were implemented by our research group and have been tested extensively to ensure that no errors were made. Post-processing of the results was extensively evaluated, and assumptions for ANOVA modeling were validated.

Threats to external validity are aspects of the experiment which limit how much of the case study can be generalized. All results in this work are based upon the metrics and defect data obtained from 16 datasets generated from 3 software projects. It must be granted that the same analysis might produce different results for another software system or learner. However, this is a potential threat in all empirical software engineering research. Thus, we focus on the process of comparing the different feature selection techniques. Therefore, our comparative analysis may be applied to another software system. Even if the results themselves do not generalize, the approach does. In addition, since all our experiments employ ten runs of five-fold cross-validation and statistical tests for significance, our findings are grounded in using sound methods.

In summary, we contend that there are no significant threats to either internal or external validity that would compromise our empirical results.

Conclusions and Future Work

The procedure of feature ranking is to score each feature according to a particular method, allowing the selection of the best set of features. Feature (software metric) selection plays an important role in the software engineering domain.

Typically, the robustness or stability of a feature selection algorithm is found by creating many reduced datasets (by deleting instances from the original dataset) and comparing these reduced datasets to each other. In this study, rather than comparing these reduced datasets to each other, each is compared solely to the original dataset which it came from. Those techniques whose outputs are insensitive to different perturbations in the input data are said to be robust, and they are preferred over those that produce inconsistent outputs.

In this study we conducted robustness (or stability) analysis on 18 feature selection techniques. Sixteen datasets from three real-world software projects were used, with different levels of class imbalance. Experimental results show that GR and SU performed significantly worst among the 18 rankers and RF and RFW performed best, followed by PRC and AUC. Results also showed that the number of instances deleted from the dataset affects the stability of the feature ranking techniques. These results are supported by ANOVA and Tukey's Honestly Significance Different tests. The fewer instances removed from (or equivalently, added to) a given dataset, the less the selected features will change when compared to the original dataset (or the smaller dataset), and thus the feature ranking performed on this dataset will be more stable.

Future work will involve conducting additional empirical studies with data from other software projects and application domains. Additional experiments with other feature selection techniques can also be conducted.

References

1. Abeel T, Helleputte T, Van de Peer Y, Dupont P, Saeys Y (2010) Robust biomarker identification for cancer diagnosis with ensemble feature selection methods. Bioinformatics 26(3):392–398
2. Battiti R (1994) Using mutual information for selecting features in supervised neural net learning. IEEE Trans Neural Netw 5(4):537–550
3. Berenson ML, Goldstein M, Levine D (1983) Intermediate statistical methods and applications: a computer package approach, 2nd edn. Prentice-Hall, Englewood Cliffs
4. Breiman L, Friedman J, Olshen R, Stone C (1984) Classification and regression trees Chapman and Hall/CRC, Boca Raton
5. Breiman L, Friedman J, Olshen R, Stone C (1993) Classification and regression trees. Chapman and Hall, New York
6. Cameron AC, Trivedi PK (1998) Regression analysis of count data. Cambridge University Press, New York
7. Chen Z, Menzies T, Port D, Boehm D (2005) Finding the right data for software cost modeling. Softw IEEE 22(6):38–46
8. Dunne K, Cunningham P, Azuaje F (2002) Solutions to instability problems with sequential wrapper-based approaches to feature selection. Technical report TCD-CD-2002-28, Department of Computer Science, Trinity College, Dublin
9. Fawcett T (2006) An introduction to ROC analysis. Pattern Recognit Lett 27(8):861–874
10. Fayyad UM, Irani KB (1992) On the handling of continuous-valued attributes in decision tree generation. Mach Learn 8:87–102
11. Forman G (2003) An extensive empirical study of feature selection metrics for text classification. J Mach Learn Res 3:1289–1305

12. Gao K, Khoshgoftaar TM, Wang H (2009)   An empirical investigation of filter attribute selection techniques for software quality classification.   In: Proceedings of the 10th IEEE international conference on information reuse and integration, Las Vegas, 10–12 Aug 2009, pp 272–277
13. Gao K, Khoshgoftaar TM, Wang H, Seliya N (2011)   Choosing software metrics for defect prediction: an investigation on feature selection techniques.   Softw Pract Experience 41(5):579–606
14. Guyon I, Elisseeff A (2003) An introduction to variable and feature selection. J Mach Learn Res 3:1157–1182
15. Hall MA, Holmes G (2003) Benchmarking attribute selection techniques for discrete class data mining. IEEE Trans Knowl Data Eng 15(6):1437–1447
16. Kalousis A, Prados J, Hilario M (2006) Stability of feature selection algorithms: a study on high-dimensional spaces. Knowl Inf Syst 12(1):95–116
17. Khoshgoftaar TM, Seliya N (2003) Fault-prediction modeling for software quality estimation: comparing commonly used techniques. Empir Softw Eng J 8(3):255–283
18. Kira K, Rendell LA (1992) A practical approach to feature selection. In: Proceedings of 9th international workshop on machine learning. Morgan Kaufmann, Aberdeen, Scotland, UK pp 249–256
19. Kononenko I (1994) Estimating attributes: analysis and extensions of RELIEF. In: European conference on machine learning. Springer, Catania, Italy, pp 171–182
20. Koru AG, Zhang D, El Emam K, Liu H (2009) An investigation into the functional form of the size-defect relationship for software modules. IEEE Trans Softw Eng 35(2):293–304
21. Křížek P, Kittler J, Hlaváč V (2007) Improving stability of feature selection methods. In: Proceedings of the 12th international conference on computer analysis of images and patterns, CAIP'07. Springer, Vienna, Austria, pp 929–936
22. Kuncheva LI (2007) A stability index for feature selection. In: Proceedings of the 25th conference on proceedings of the 25th IASTED international multi-conference: artificial intelligence and applications. ACTA, Innsbruck, Austria, pp 390–395
23. Liu H, Yu L (2005) Toward integrating feature selection algorithms for classification and clustering. IEEE Trans Knowl Data Eng 17(4):491–502
24. Loscalzo S, Yu L, Ding C (2009) Consensus group stable feature selection. In: KDD '09: proceedings of the 15th ACM SIGKDD international conference on knowledge discovery and data mining, New York, pp 567–576
25. Lustgarten JL, Gopalakrishnan V, Visweswaran S (2009) Measuring stability of feature selection in biomedical datasets. In: AMIA 2009 symposium proceedings, San Francisco, USA, pp 406–410
26. Peng H, Long F, Ding C (2005) Feature selection based on mutual information: criteria of max-dependency, max-relevance, and min-redundancy. IEEE Trans Pattern Anal Mach Intell, 27(8):1226–1238
27. Quinlan JR (1986) Induction of decision trees. Mach Learn 1(1):81–106
28. Rodriguez D, Ruiz R, Cuadrado-Gallego J, Aguilar-Ruiz J (2007) Detecting fault modules applying feature selection to classifiers. In: Proceedings of 8th IEEE international conference on information reuse and integration, Las Vegas, 13–15 Aug 2007, pp 667–672
29. Saeys Y, Abeel T, Peer Y (2008) Robust feature selection using ensemble feature selection techniques. In: ECML PKDD '08: proceedings of the European conference on machine learning and knowledge discovery in databases – Part II. Springer, Antwerp, Belgium, pp 313–325
30. Seliya N, Khoshgoftaar TM, Van Hulse J (2009) A study on the relationships of classifier performance metrics. In: Proceedings of the 21st IEEE international conference on tools with artifical intelligence (ICTAI'09). IEEE Computer Society, Newark, pp 59–66
31. Wang H, Khoshgoftaar TM, Van Hulse J (2010) A comparative study of threshold-based feature selection techniques. In: 2010 IEEE international conference on granular computing (GrC), Silicon Valley, USA, Aug 2010, pp 499–504

32. Wang H, Khoshgoftaar TM, Seliya N (2011) How many software metrics should be selected for defect prediction? In: Proceedings of the twenty-fourth international Florida artificial intelligence research society conference, Palm Beach, USA, pp 69–74
33. Witten IH, Frank E (2005) Data mining: practical machine learning tools and techniques, 2nd edn. Morgan Kaufmann, Boston
34. Wohlin C, Runeson P, Host M, Ohlsson MC, Regnell B, Wesslen A (2000) Experimentation in software engineering: an introduction. Kluwer international series in software engineering. Kluwer, Boston
35. Yang C-H, Huang C-C, Wu K-C, Chang H-Y (2008) A novel ga-taguchi-based feature selection method. In: IDEAL '08: proceedings of the 9th international conference on intelligent data engineering and automated learning, Berlin/Heidelberg, pp 112–119
36. Zimmermann T, Premraj R, Zeller A (2007) Predicting defects for eclipse. In: ICSEW '07: proceedings of the 29th international conference on software engineering workshops, IEEE Computer Society, Washington, DC, p 76

Chapter 7
Analysis and Design: Towards Large-Scale Reuse and Integration of Web User Interface Components

Hao Han, Peng Gao, Yinxing Xue, Chuanqi Tao, and Keizo Oyama

Abstract With the trend for Web information/functionality integration, application integration at the presentation and logic layers is becoming a popular issue. In the absence of open Web service application programming interfaces, the integration of conventional Web applications is usually based on the reuse of user interface (UI) components, which partially represent the interactive functionalities of applications.

In this paper, we describe some common problems of the current Web-UI-component-based reuse and integration and propose a solution: a security-enhanced "component retrieval and integration description" method. We also discuss the related technologies such as testing, maintenance and copyright. Our purpose is to construct a reliable large-scale reuse and integration system for Web applications.

H. Han (✉)
Kanagawa University, Kanagawa, Japan
e-mail: han@kanagawa-u.ac.jp

P. Gao
Tokyo Institute of Technology, Tokyo, Japan
e-mail: gao@tt.cs.titech.ac.jp

Y. Xue
National University of Singapore, Singapore
e-mail: yinxing@comp.nus.edu.sg

C. Tao
Southeast University, Nanjing, Jiangsu, China
e-mail: taochuanqi@seu.edu.cn

K. Oyama
National Institute of Informatics, Tokyo, Japan

The Graduate University for Advanced Studies (SOKENDAI), Tokyo, Japan
e-mail: oyama@nii.ac.jp

T. Özyer et al. (eds.), *Information Reuse and Integration in Academia and Industry,*
DOI 10.1007/978-3-7091-1538-1_7, © Springer-Verlag Wien 2013

Introduction

More and more information/data is available on the World Wide Web as a result of the development of the Internet, but it is not always in forms that support end-users' needs. Mashup implies easy and fast integration of information to enable users to view diverse Web content in an integrated manner. However, there is no uniform interface used to access the data, computations (application logic) and user interfaces provided by different kinds of Web content. Although there are widely popular and successful Web services such as the Google Maps API [15], most existing websites unfortunately do not provide Web services. Web applications are still the main information distribution methods. Compared with Web services and Web feeds, it is difficult to integrate Web applications with other Web content because open APIs are not provided. For example, the famous global news site CNN[1] provides an online news search function at the site side for general users. However, this news search function cannot be integrated into other systems because CNN has not opened its search function as a Web service. Similarly, BBC Country Profiles[2] does not provide the Web service APIs, so it is difficult for developers to integrate it with other Web services.

Beyond the limitation of open APIs, the integration of Web application content and functionalities at the presentation and logic layers based on the reuse of UI components is becoming an important issue. Here, the Web application functionality indicates part of a Web application/page, and it works as a mechanism for dynamically generating content in response to an end-user request. These functionalities are usually achieved by server-side logic processing or client-side scripting, as shown in Fig. 7.1, and the end-users use the UI components (e.g., the drop-down list in the form in Fig. 7.2 or text input field in Fig. 7.3) to complete the request/response message exchange. Some approaches and systems have been proposed for integrating general Web applications by reusing UI components or emulating the functionality (and content extraction).

However, all of these current technologies and approaches face some common problems such as UI component retrieval in a large-scale Web resource. They are usually limited to a small-scale Web resource, such as frequently used Web applications and websites, or only applicable to some specific domains considering the possible security or copyright issues. The developed mashup applications are weak and have a short lifespan because there are no corresponding systematic testing and maintenance methods.

Moreover, with the development of Rich Internet Application (RIA) technologies, more and more Web content is being generated dynamically by client-side scripts or plug-ins. Originally, the Web browser's role was just to render and display static content. But now to support interacting components (data and code) from

---

[1]http://www.cnn.com

[2]http://news.bbc.co.uk/2/hi/country_profiles/

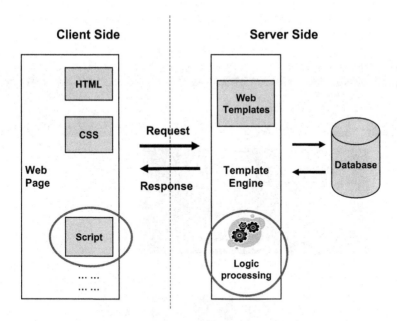

Fig. 7.1 Functionality of Web application

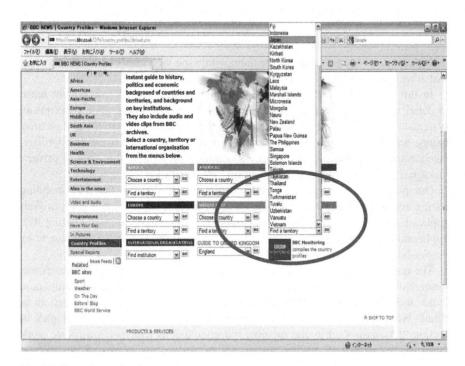

Fig. 7.2 Example: option list

Fig. 7.3 Example: text input field

multiple parties together and execute them within the Web user's browser, it is clear that at least we need certain security mechanism to be enforced.

In this paper, we describe the main problems with current component reuse in detail and propose our solutions: component retrieval, integration description, systematic testing, and maintenance. We also state the current reliability and security issues, and present our solutions, which involve leveraging some standardized mechanisms, and also present an access control policy (here, the issue of privacy leakage risk of the server-side composition [55] is out of our scope).

Our purpose is to construct a reliable system and develop the corresponding testing and maintenance technologies for large-scale reuse and integration of Web applications. *Our research emphasis is on the reuse and integration of existing Web applications by general Web users at the client side instead of the component or portlet-based development by application developers.*

The rest of this paper is organized as follows. In section "Current Problems and Research", we describe the current problems and research about UI component reuse and integration. In section "Our Solution", we explain our solution in detail. We discuss and evaluate the implementation and related technologies in section "Discussion". Finally, we give our conclusions and mention future work in section "Conclusion".

Current Problems and Research

Most Web mashup technologies are based on the combination of Web services or Web feeds. Yahoo Pipes [51] and Microsoft Popfly [30] are composition tools for the aggregation, manipulation, and mashup of Web services or Web feeds from different websites via a graphical user interface. Mixup [53] is a development and runtime environment for UI integration [10]. It can quickly build complex user interfaces for easy integration by using available Web service APIs. Mashup Feeds [42] and WMSL [38] support integrated Web services as continuous queries. They create new services by connecting Web services by using join, select, and map operations. Like these methods, Google Mashup Editor [16], IBM QEDWiki (IBM Mashup Center) [22], and some other service-based methods [29, 48, 54] are also limited to the combination of existing Web services, Web feeds, or generated Web components.

In this paper, we focus on general Web applications. For the reuse and integration of parts from Web applications that do not have open APIs, the partial Web page clipping method is widely used. The user clips a selected part of a Web page, and pastes it into a personal Web page. Internet Scrapbook [26] is a tool that allows users to interactively extract components of multiple Web pages by clipping, and it assembles them into a single personal Web page. However, the extracted information is part of a static HTML (HyperText Markup Language) document and the users cannot change the layout of the extracted parts. C3W [13] provides an interface for automating data flows. It enables users to clip elements from Web pages to wrap an application and connect wrapped applications using spreadsheet-like formulas and it also enables them to clone the interface elements so that several sets of parameters and results may be handled in parallel. However, it does not appear to be easy for the C3W method to make the interaction between different Web applications (like Safari Web Clip Widgets [6]) and this method also requires a C3W-only Web browser. Extracting data from multiple Web pages by end-user programming [18] is more suitable for generating mashup applications at the client side. Marmite [49], implemented as a Firefox plug-in using JavaScript and XUL, uses a basic screen-scraping operator to extract content from Web pages and integrate it with other data sources. The operator uses a simple XPath pattern matcher, and the data is processed in a manner similar to Unix pipes. Intel MashMaker [12] is a tool for editing, querying, manipulating and visualizing continuously updated semi-structured data. It allows users to create their own mashups on the basis of data and queries produced by other users and by remote sites. However, these methods need professional Web programming ability [9] or have other limitations (e.g., these methods need components produced by portlets [25] or Web Services for Remote Portlets (WSRP) [47]) and they face the following common problems like Mashroom [44] and Dapper [11].

- *"How to find the most suitable UI component from large-scale Web resources?"*. Users currently need to find functionalities from websites by using search engines

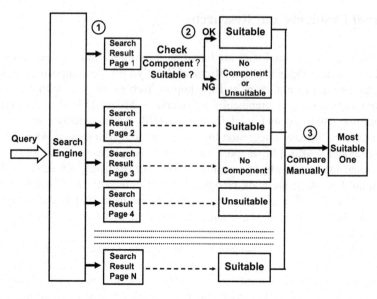

Fig. 7.4 Conventional Web functionality/component retrieval method

(e.g., Google,[3] Bing[4]) or by using a library of predefined UI components, which is also manually constructed and limited to a small scale. As shown in Fig. 7.4, if they use search engines, users must check the search results through the following steps.

1. The user sends the query request (keywords) to the search engine and gets the response page, which contains a list of Uniform Resource Locators (URLs) linked to search result pages.
2. The user checks each result page to determine whether the page contains the suitable Web functionality (UI component) or not (i.e., unsuitable component or no component).
3. The user compares the suitable components and selects one as the most suitable component (for further reuse and integration).

The conventional Web functionality retrieval method is inefficient (even ineffective) because current general Web search engines mainly use a content-oriented search mechanism and information about functionality is beyond the analysis range. Moreover, the search result ranking method of these non-functionality-oriented search engines cannot satisfy the requirements of our functionality retrieval and leads to time-consuming manual checking and comparison.

---

[3]http://www.google.com/
[4]http://www.bing.com/

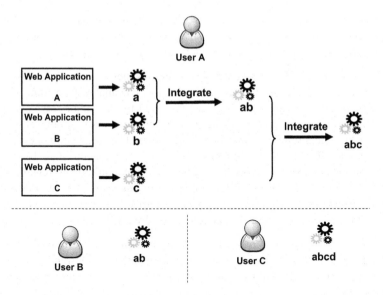

Fig. 7.5 Users need to share and reuse developed parts

In our past experiments and implementations, we had to spend more than 1 h finding and selecting each suitable component on average.

- *"How to share and reuse the developed parts of a mashup application with other users/developers?"*. Users can currently select and integrate desired parts (functionality or content) from different applications to develop the mashup applications. However, it is still difficult to share parts of a developed mashup application if they do not know detailed information about the parts such as the interface or parameters. For example, as shown in Fig. 7.5, User A integrates *a* and *b* from Web applications A and B, respectively, and generates *ab*; then, *c* of Web application C is integrated and finally *abc* is generated. However, if User B wants to reuse *ab*, or if User C wants to integrate *abc* with other content such as *d* of Web application D, they must know the detailed internal structures and interface of *abc*. It is difficult for general users to share the developed parts for further reuse easily because there is not a uniform interface or structure for different Web resources and for mashup development.

- *"How to enhance the new integrated software in a stable and seamless composition of UI components from heterogeneous sources?"*. Unlike in the case of general Web-service-based Web applications, many UI components (one kind of service) searched by our approach are not registered in online service repositories. Thus, these UI components may be more unstable than ones in a service repository. The more unstable they are, the higher the probability of service evolution is. Overall, these UI components may evolve in terms of their interfaces or functionality from time to time, or they may even vanish or collapse. Apart from evolutions imposed on UI components, access by different users means that various behaviors can be expected from the same UI components. Specifically, to achieve the goal of stable and seamless composition of the UI components, we need to resolve problems related to two aspects:

- Availability of UI components: No matter how these services were discovered initially, some of them may later become unavailable from time to time. Compared with the public services provided by the major service vendors, UI components are more vulnerable to the changes arising from websites. We need to find a solution that prevents the sudden loss of UI components.
- Adaptability of UI components: These UI components may be used in multiple contexts by users who may have varying requirements regarding their functionality [28]. These differences in requirements for UI components may not be known in advance, but may instead arise from new users when such a service based on certain UI components is already in use.

- "*How to achieve flexible integration of various Web applications?*". The most widely used mode of integrating Web applications is currently "emulating a request submission functionality and getting the response page and then extracting partial information from the response page for further reuse and integration". It is the simplest mode and may fail to treat the following possible situations.

  - Between the page for submitting a request and the page containing the target partial information, there is more than one page transition.
  - For a request, there is more than one possible response. For example, the string comparison is often used in the emulation of optionlist-based page transitions, and the number of corresponding options is not always one.
  - Errors or exceptions are generated and thrown during the implementation of mashup applications.

  To further achieve flexible integration of UI components, a tradeoff analysis of the service granularity is required. The service granularity generally refers to the size of a service. In our approach, it means how big a new service integrated from several UI components should be. The fact that services should be large-sized or coarse-grained is often postulated as a fundamental design principle of applications based on SOA [17]. Some studies on this topic have been conducted [27, 36]. Acquiring a balance between granularity and maintenance efforts will facilitate the sharing and reuse of the developed new service with other users/developers.
- "*How to interoperate components from different origins reliably and securely?*". Currently, Web developers routinely use sophisticated scripting languages and other active client-side technologies to provide users with powerful and fascinating experiences that approximate the performance of desktop applications. However, all extracted UI components execute their functionality directly on the client-side platform, which is usually a Web browser and most Web browsers look like monolithic architectures to mashups at the operating-system level.

- From the standpoint of reliability, allocating all functionalities in the same address space and offering weak isolation between them will allow the functionalities to interfere with each other in undesirable ways.
- From a security viewpoint, all components run in a single protected domain, allowing malicious code to exploit unpatched vulnerabilities to compromise the entire mashup.

Concerning the application level, the Web browser provides only a single principal trust model based on the Same-Origin Policy (SOP) [24] as a base security mechanism to regulate cross-origin interaction among different web content [3]. The specifications of SOP state that content of one origin can access only other content from its own origin: access to resources of other origins is forbidden. This causes either component-component separation with controlled interaction or component-server communication to be impossible. However, the nature of the information/functionality integration and reuse involves interoperation between content of multiple parties' to provide extra-value. Consequently, a contradiction arises: when components of different origins are incorporated, there is either no trust or full trust. Therefore, in a lot of cases, the composers are forced to abandon security in order to get greater functionality, which incurs high security risks because the confidentially and integrity of a component from one site could be completely controlled by components from a malicious site.

On the basis of our analysis of the abovementioned questions, we assert that the current approaches cannot achieve the various types of complicated integration systematically. In our past research, we also developed solutions based on the end-user programming method [18] or non-programming description system DEEP [20] and WIKE [19]. However, those systems were also unable to solve the abovementioned problems well.

Our Solution

To achieve the integration of large-scale Web resources through component reuse, it is necessary to construct a UI component retrieval system and propose a description approach to describing the integration process. Here, we propose our solution, which is being developed to solve the current problems including retrieval, description, reliability and security, maintenance, and access control.

Component Retrieval

The component-oriented search mechanism is used in the UI component retrieval system. As shown in Fig. 7.6, the Web functionality search engine designed for component retrieval works as follows.

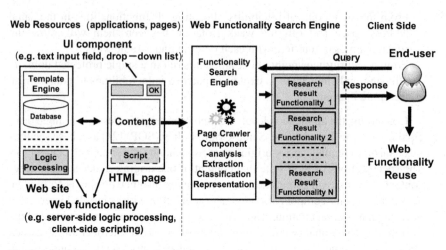

Fig. 7.6 Web functionality search engine

1. A crawler is used to collect Web pages. For each page, the following related information is extracted to judge whether the page contains Web functionalities.

   - Page

     - URL
     - Title
     - Meta data names and values

   - Form

     - ID (ID attribute)
     - Name (name attribute)
     - Method (HTTP method used to submit form)
     - Action (Server-side form handler)
     - Event (e.g., defined events trigger JavaScript functions)
     - Other related information (e.g., hidden values inside the form)
     - Path (XPath containing the tag names and ID values of ancestor tags)

   - Component (See Table 7.1)

     - Type (tag name)
     - Name (name attribute)
     - ID (ID attribute)
     - Value (e.g. current content of text input field)
     - Alt (alternative text for user agents not rendering the normal content)
     - Title (advisory title)
     - Event (e.g., defined events trigger JavaScript functions)
     - Other related information (e.g., text immediately preceding the text input field, text contained within the option element)
     - Structure (e.g., a single text input field, a list of links)

Table 7.1 Information extraction from component (○: extracted, ×: not extracted)

Component	Type	Name	ID	Value	Alt	Title	Event	Other
Input text	○	○	○	○	○	○	○	Previous sibling text
Input password	○	○	○	×	×	○	×	×
Input checkbox	○	○	○	×	×	○	○	Next sibling text
Input radio	○	○	○	×	×	○	○	Next sibling text
Input file	○	○	○	×	×	○	×	Previous sibling text acceptable file type
Input submit	○	○	○	×	×	○	○	×
Input button	○	○	○	×	×	○	○	×
Input image	○	○	○	×	○	○	○	×
Button	○	○	○	○	×	×	○	×
Select option	○	○	○	×	×	○	×	Optionlist text
Applet	○	○	○	×	×	○	×	Class file
Object	○	○	○	×	×	○	×	Code type and URI

2. The extracted information is split into a word list using whitespace, punctuation mark and numeric character as the delimiter. We remove articles, prepositions, and conjunctions from this word list. Finally, these words are analyzed and classified to generate the recognition pattern of each Web functionality and the index information is then created for component retrieval.

Here, the component type is the type of request-input element, such as InputBox (text input field), OptionList (drop-down option list in the selection box), and LinkList (anchor list), in the page where the end user's request was submitted. The users search for the components by giving the component type and other search keywords.

Description and Emulation

After the desired components have been found, they are described in an annotation method for the integration. Here, we define the uniform format shown in Fig. 7.7 for the following basic entities, which describe reuse and integration based on the page transition (*Fig. 7.12 in section "Discussion" gives examples*).

- Flow: a flow represents the data flow or work flow of an integration. It works like the main function of an executive program and receives parameters from users as the request.
- Page: a page is a basic information container in a Web application. It contains the desired partial information such as the component or content, which is extracted in the manner designated by the users.
- Component: a component is used to emulate the functionality and get the response (page) according to the request.
- Collection: a collection contains polymorphic algorithms that operate on collections such as sort, reverse, and swap.

Fig. 7.7 Format of entity

```
<Entity>
    <name></name>
    <comment></comment>
    <input>
        <source></source>
        <element>
            <name></name>
            <path></path>
            <property></property>
            <type></type>
            <matcher></matcher>
        </element>
    </input>
    <output>
        <element>
            <name></name>
        </element>
    </output>
    <exception>
        <message></message>
    </exception>
</Entity>
```

- Checker: a checker is used to check whether the extracted data is valid.
- Convertor: a convertor is used to convert the data into another format.
- Pattern: a pattern is used for comparing strings, searching strings, extracting substrings, and performing other string-based operations as a selective option.

The format contains five main parts: name, comment, input, output and exception. These items reflect the end-user operations (e.g., users find the text input field, input the keywords, submit the request, and search for the target content in the response page) and give the description of the target Web content type/property.

- Name: a name is a simple description of the entity and comments contain the keywords, which reflect the entity's specifications.
- Input:
  - Source: the source of the input is the URL, link, or object output from other entities.
  - Path: a path is used to locate a piece of target content. The value of path is the XPath expression of the target part in the HTML document of the Web page. In the tree structure of an HTML document, each path represents a root node of a subtree and each subtree represents part of a Web page. The response Web pages usually have the same layout or similar layouts if the requests are sent to the same request-submit function. During the node search, if a node cannot be found by a path, similar paths will be used to search for the node. Two paths are similar to each other if they have the same forms, ignoring the difference in node order among sibling nodes when the difference in node order is within a given deviation range.
  - Property: property means text or an image, link, object, or component. Text is a character string in a Web page such as an article. Image is one instance of a graph. Link is a reference in a hypertext document to another document

or resource. Object is one instance of a video or other multimedia file. Component is the type of request-input element.

- Type: type contains single, list, or table. Single means a part without similar parts such as the title of an article. List means a list of parts with similar path values such as result list in the search result page. Table means a group of parts arranged in two-dimensional rows and columns such as the result records in a Google Image Search result page.
- Matcher: a matcher performs matching operations on a string by interpreting a pattern entity.

• Output: output gives the names of output elements and the exception defines the error message generated when an exception occurs.

Compared with the Web services, it is not as easy to access and integrate Web applications because they are designed for browsing by users rather than for parsing by a computer program. The Web pages of Web applications, usually in the HTML or XHTML formats, are used to display the data in a formatted way, not to share the structured data across different information systems. Without an interface like Simple Object Access Protocol (SOAP) [40] or Representational State Transfer (REST) [37], we have to use extraction and emulation technologies to interact with Web applications. Extraction is used to reach the target content and extract it from Web pages. Emulation is used to achieve the processes of sending a request and receiving the response. For request submission, there are the POST and GET methods, and some websites use encrypted code or randomly generated code. In order to get the response Web pages from Web applications of all kinds automatically, we use HtmlUnit[5] to emulate the submission operation instead of using a URL templating mechanism. The emulation is based on the event trigger, as shown in the following examples.

• In the case of InputBox (enter the query keywords into a form-input field from the keyboard and click the submit button by using a mouse or trackpad to send the query), the text input field is found according to the path and the query keywords are input. Then the submit button's click event is triggered to send the request and get the response Web page.
• In the case of LinkList (clicking a link in the link list on a Web page to go to the target Web page), the text contained inside each link tag along the path is compared with the keyword by matcher until a matching one is found. The link's click event is then triggered to get the target Web page.
• In the case of OptionList (click an option in the drop-down list of the selectbox in a Web page to view a new Web page), the text of each option within path is compared with keyword by matcher until a matching one is found. Then the select event of option is triggered to get the target Web page.

---

[5]http://htmlunit.sourceforge.net/

Maintainability of Integrated Application

The essence of our approach is to broaden the scope of reusable UI components and further distill useful ones from the massive amount of Web resources. With the advantage of more reuse opportunities, however, our approach compromises in the maintainability of the new integrated applications.

First, the availability and stability of these UI components are an important issue that we must address. In our approach, many Web resources, such as some static Web pages that are officially not qualified to be "so-called" services, will be considered as potential candidates for extraction targets. Compared with Web applications based on Web services, these services are usually all provided by third-party service providers. For example, an system based on Google Office Service [14] and Amazon Storage Service [1] is usually stable because the leading IT companies have a team of engineers maintain their service. But what if office services and storage services were based on UI components from unknown websites, rather than from those major service vendors? Thus, these components are subjected to evolution, and they are more unpredictable. To overcome this problem, we propose to empower the mashup application in looking up the backup UI components in case of an emergency such as some existing components being unavailable or suddenly changed. For example, in our own implemented news release system, we usually extract the desired news from CNN[6] or the BBC[7] according to some tags or keywords. If CNN and BBC were to be unavailable for a while, our mashup application would detect the sudden loss of the corresponding UI components and immediately substitute new ones from the New York Times[8] or ABC News[9] for the lost ones. We propose to design a ranking algorithm to rate components when multiple UI components with the same or similar functionality are available. The rating strategy can be based on service recommendations based on users' client-side performance [43].

Second, the maintenance of such an integrated application is bound to be complicated when the desired UI components are gathered together to implement a new application. Instead of being treated as a single independent service, our new integrated application logically has external coupling with many other websites from which the internal UI components are extracted. As a recent empirical study [34] pointed out, intra-service coupling (in our case, intra-service coupling refers to the coupling between UI components) can potentially have a smaller effect on maintainability (i.e. analyzability, changeability, stability, and testability) than indirect and direct extra-service coupling (in our case, intra-service coupling refers to the coupling between a UI component and other components from other website).

---

[6] http://www.cnn.com

[7] http://www.bbc.co.uk

[8] http://www.nytimes.com/

[9] http://abcnews.go.com/

Overall, our integrated application has high cohesion and also a certain degree of external coupling. As an aspect of security reasons, the UI component isolation principle (see details in section "Reliability and Security") is advocated in our design. It is this principle that makes the UI components (intra-service) have high cohesion and low coupling. However, the drawback is that with more isolated UI components from more external websites, the external coupling between our integrated application and the other websites will correspondingly increase. In our solution, a case-by-case tradeoff analysis between external coupling and finer-grained isolation of components for the different integrated applications will be beneficial to the maintenance.

Third, we are concerned with the adaptability of the UI components in our approach. A multi-tenant architecture allows many tenants (users) to share the same application (or service) instance [28]. Supporting service variability in the scope of a one-fits-all service creates extra challenges. The existing approaches allow users to adapt workflows via configuration options with only weak provisions for service adaptability [32, 39]. The high variability of multi-tenant services usually translates into higher maintenance costs. Relaxing the single-instance requirement, Model-Driven Development has been applied to produce custom services in the ERP domain [41]. Our approach to service variability may contribute to multi-tenant services (dynamic reconfiguration), and the situation where custom instances of a service are generated for users. The Software Product Line (SPL) approach to reuse [5] exploits commonalities and variability in a domain to improve productivity of developing and maintaining many similar yet different applications. The variability management techniques used in SPL [35, 52] are relevant to handling service variability [31], which is exactly the direction we plan to explore in the further studies.

To sum up, if the problems with the availability and stability of these UI components are overcome, mashup applications will be enhanced to prevent the sudden loss of their UI components and to rate the candidate UI components. To achieve a balanced design between external coupling and finer-grained isolation of components, we will use some metrics [34] to calculate the external coupling and reduce it to a manageable degree. Finally, we will also customize and encapsulate the internal UI components to satisfy the diverse requirements of customers by applying SPL techniques.

Reliability and Security

The trend of RIA technologies is accelerating the development of rich client solutions. For example, many websites use DHTML (Dynamic HTML) or Document Object Model (DOM) scripting to create interactive Web pages. They contain HTML, client-side scripts (such as JavaScript), DOM, etc. The scripts change variables (including elements outside the target parts such as hidden values) in a programmed manner in an HTML document, and affect the look and function of static content. The trend shows that there has been a dramatic increase in the number of active programs over the past few years, and these applications are larger and more complex than before. When arbitrarily mixed on the client side, such active content will lead to problems with reliability and security. For example, if a bug crashes one functionality, it may crash all the others being executed within the browser; if a functionality has an SQL injection vulnerability, it has the potential to leak private data of other functionalities. In this situation, to integrate and reuse components reliably and securely within our approach, we give four specific requirements.

- UI Component Isolation: UI components from different origins should be isolated from others by sandboxing. The mechanism should be in the system layer, which can prevent memory leaks.
- Script Separation: A functionality that contains script code needs to be separated from other functionalities. Even when scripts are from the same origin, the DOM tree and scripts must not be modifiable in an unauthorized manner by other functionalities.
- Functionality Interaction: Each functionality should have the ability to interact with other functionalities and the integrator. The restriction is that an entity that contains critical information should not be read or rewritten by others without authorization. Another aspect is that functionalities should be able to perform cross-domain communication. Then a functionality can communicate not only with others from its own origin but also with those from other origins in a controlled manner.
- Usage Control: The author of reusable components should be able to decide whether or not the specific functionality can be accessed by other components, which can bring merits about the copyright and risk declaration.

On the basis of the requirements presented above we firstly leverage the multiple processes of the operating system (OS) to isolate cross-origin components to resolve the reliability problems for UI-component-based mashup applications. And we present a security policy for separating JavaScript code from the same origin. Then concerning practicality and extensibility, it is meaningful to leverage existing standardized technologies to solve the functionality-interoperating and cross-origin communication issues in the application layer. Finally, we present a functionality access interface in order to enforce the usage control on components.

The solutions are illustrated with the scenario in Fig. 7.8: functionality N_1 from website N, which refer to scripts X_{ai} from origin X, is integrated into the integrator page A, which also contains functionality A_1 from website A. As a result, the integrator contains two parts: functionality A_1 and functionality N_1, which are from different origins. Each functionality may contain both static (HTML) content and active (Script) content.

- The iframe [23] separates one inclusion of site N (N1.html) from site A with no interaction under the SOP restriction. The architecture of our solution for component isolation makes each UI-component-based mashup application into

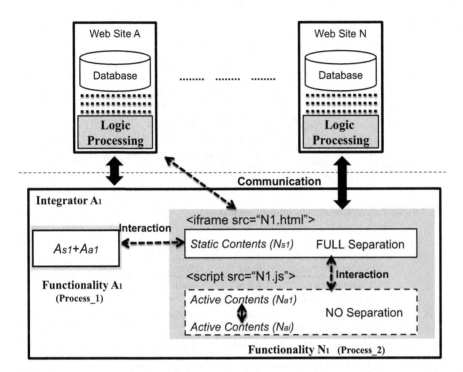

Fig. 7.8 Example of interoperation model (An *arrowed dashed line* implies that interaction or communication is restricted by the SOP)

a separate OS process. UI components from different origins $(A, B, \ldots, N)$ are isolated from each other in different processes (shadowed region on the client side). For the included page A and each functionality that the mashup contains, a new rendering process will be created; it draws HTML pages and runs JavaScript code. The included page is rendered by one process while UI components from different origins are rendered by different processes. The process creation policy is that for each UI component in a mashup, if a process for that origin has not already been created, then a new rendering process is launched.

- The component isolation targets UI components from different origins. However, as shown in Fig. 7.9, we still need to consider an appropriate security mechanism for separating JavaScripts from same origin because third-party JavaScript references are commonly used in Web applications/pages, such as X_{ai} in Fig. 7.8, which might be malicious. If access to the JavaScript context is fully allowed, then code in a malicious user's JavaScript references could override the original functions and other objects with malicious ones. In that case, when a trusted script calls the "original" function, the malicious code will be executed. To handle this case, we propose an access control policy, as shown in Table 7.2, for the JavaScripts from the same origin within a process where the *read* operation is to read the value or property of an object; the *write* operation is to create a new

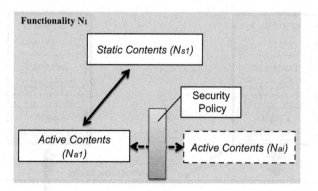

Fig. 7.9 Separation of JavaScripts from the same origin

Table 7.2 Access control policy for JavaScript objects

Access direction	Read	Write	Execute
Origin trust to destination trust	Allow	Allow	Allow
Origin trust to destination distrust	Audit	Allow	Allow
Origin distrust to destination trust	Disallow	Disallow	Audit

object, assign a value to an existing object, or define or redefine a function object; the *execute* operation is to invoke a JavaScript function.

- The iframe tag separates one inclusion of site N (N1.html) from site A and even from its own scripts with no interaction under the SOP restriction. The postMessage [21] is a popular browser API extension that provides principal interaction between frames and iframes. It provides the postMessage( ) operation on a DOM window and iframes object. Combining the postMessage with iframes, which offers restricted interaction and separation, is an efficient method. The XMLHttpRequest object of JavaScript is not allowed to make cross-origin requests. If component N_1 needs to communicate with integrator A_1's remote Web server, Cross-Origin Resource Sharing (CORS) [8] is an efficient and widely supported extension of HTTP to provide cross-origin requests. It allows the remote Web server to indicate whether or not a functionality of another origin has the rights to access its resources.

- As shown in Fig. 7.10, our framework has an interface for inserting a new item called "access" into the format of entity. The access tag that assigns permissions to the UI components in an application and specifies an usage policy to protect its resources. It uses the "public" or "private" attribute to declare the *copyrightType*, which indicates whether the entity can be accessed by the normal public flow or only used privately in order to protect the copyright of a special component. Moreover, it can specify the applications/pages of which origin can

```
<access>
    <name></name>
    <comment></comment>
    <copyrightType></copyrightType>
    <permissionOrigin></permissionOrigin>
    <permissionDestination></permissionDestination>
    <accessLevel></accessLevel>
</access>
```

Fig. 7.10 Access item

have access by means of the *permissionOrigin* and *permissionDestionation* tags. Furthermore, given the type of UI component, such as InputBox or OptionList, the access item uses *accessLevel* tag, which contains "normal", "dangerous", "specific" attribute, to indicate the system's security level, which should be brought to the composer's notice, and the tag should grant permission to a functionality requesting it.

- Normal: Low risk access level. The functionality has only a fixed value or it does not access any other functionalities. For example, the OptionList and LinkList belong to this level.
- Dangerous: High risk access level. The functionality has the ability to receive input or has the right to access private data (e.g., SQL Injection). For example, the InputBox belongs to this level.
- Specific: An access level specified manually by the composer. This option is used for certain special situations and should be set with great care, as any possible composition could be done without regulation.

Discussion

We consider different performance measures to evaluate our approach and to discuss related topics in actual integration.

Retrieval and Description

The construction of the functionality/component search engine solves the component retrieval problem described in section "Current Problems and Research", and the uniform format of the basic entities provides a solution to the problems of flexible description and integration, as shown in the following example.

As shown in Fig. 7.11, we describe the function of country information search by the entities. We search for the select-option at the top page of BBC Country

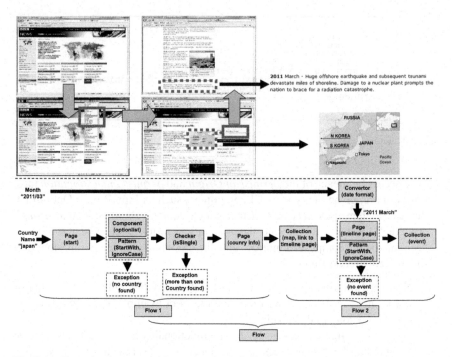

Fig. 7.11 Example of page transition and entity definition

Profiles[10] and submit the request to get the target country page. We extract the map of the country and the URL of the timeline page from the country page. We search for key events using the given month and extract them from the timeline page. The definitions of Page (Start) and Component (optionlist) are given in Fig. 7.12 as examples. We use Firebug[11] to get the XPath of the target part via the Graphical User Interface (GUI) and avoid manual analysis of the HTML document. The entities are combined with each other, and finally the whole flow is generated. The matcher, pattern, and checker are used to keep the correct process, and exception messages are generated if errors occur. Moreover, the convertor and collection create the event searching function by extracting the corresponding information from a simple static Web page. As a part of the *Flow*, the *Flow 1* or *Flow 2* can be reused by other users, who do not need to know the detailed internal structures of these sub flows because their formats are the same.

We achieve component-based reuse and integration of Web content with component retrieval and entity description. Similarly, Web Service Definition Language (WSDL) [46] and Web Application Description Language (WADL) [45] are used to describe a series of Web services in detail such as abstract types, abstract interfaces,

---

[10]http://news.bbc.co.uk/2/hi/country_profiles/

[11]http://getfirebug.com/

```
<Entity:Page>
    <name>BBC_Country_Profiles_Page</name>
    <comment>BBC, country profile, search</comment>
    <input>
        <source>URL:http://news.bbc.co.uk/2/hi/country_profiles/default.stm</source>
        <element>
            <name>CountrySelection</name>
            <path>/html/body/div/div/div[2]/table/tbody/tr/td[2]</path>
            <property>Component:OptionList</property>
            <type>Table</type>
            <matcher></matcher>
        </element>
    </input>
    <output>
        <element>
            <name>Component:CountrySelection</name>
        </element>
    </output>
    <exception>
        <message></message>
    </exception>
</Entity:Page>

<Entity:Component>
    <name>Country_Name_Selector</name>
    <comment>BBC, country profile, search, optionlist</comment>
    <input>
        <source>Page:BBC_Country_Profiles_Page/Component:CountrySelection</source>
        <element>
            <name>CountryName</name>
            <path></path>
            <property>String</property>
            <type>Single</type>
            <matcher>Pattern:{StartWith,IgnoreCase}
            </matcher>
        </element>
    </input>
    <output>
        <element>
            <name>Page:CountryInfo</name>
        </element>
    </output>
    <exception>
        <message>no country found</message>
    </exception>
</Entity:Component>
```

Fig. 7.12 Start page and optionlist components

and concrete binding. We could not believe that all the tasks could be completed in a fully automated way by handing WSDL or WADL files to WSDL2Java or WADL2Java [2]. Compared with the WSDL and WADL, our entities can use a shorter and simpler description format and are applicable to the description of general Web applications. It is easier to read, write, reuse, and update any part of a mashup Web application than to use end-user programming methods. Our annotation approach makes it possible for users with no or little programming experience to implement Web content integration from various Web applications. Any content from any kind of Web applications can be handled.

Layout Personalization

Different content extracted from different websites has its own different layout, such as size, font, color and other view styles. Except the components and the objects generated by client-side scripts, both the Web service response and the partial information extracted from Web applications are in XML format. During the integration, we need a personalizable template processor to transform XML data into HTML or XHTML documents. Our approach provides an XSL Transformation (XSLT) [50] library, which contains the following two types of XSLT files.

- We created an XSLT file (automatch.xslt), which automatically transforms the XML format into HTML format by using the type/property. It is applicable to the basic types including text, images, links and objects. For example, it uses the <img> tag to embed an image and set the extracted URL as the attribute value of "src". The transformed result is a simple list/table of Web content, and the optional attributes (font, size and etc.) are left unset. This file is a recommended default template for the transformation of extracted results.
- We designed a number of XSLT files to create XSLT library, and users can select suitable XSLT files for the target Web content. These XSLT files are applicable to often-used structures of partial information of Web applications (list, table, etc.) after some manual modifications.

Users can select our predefined XSLT files as the stylesheet transformations or modify them to get customized visual effects. Moreover, the fully original XSLT files created by users are valid in our approach.

Reliable and Secure Composition

Currently, the only browser that supports multiple-processes is Google Chrome.[12] However, our experimental results show that it still cannot deal with the UI-component-based mashups. For instance, in the case of the example shown in Fig. 7.11, which we introduced above, all application content including the select-option and the country page are executing together; here, where a reliability problem can occur if one functionality that is CPU-bound can prevent the CPU from interacting with the other functionalities. In our proposed architecture, each process runs in a separating address space. Therefore, crashes caused by one origin will not affect the content of other origins. The OS has a process scheduling mechanism, so expensive computations and the freezing of function calls from one origin will not starve the system of resources from other origins. The OS also supports the killing of any process that becomes unresponsive because of memory leakage.

---

[12]http://www.google.com/chrome/

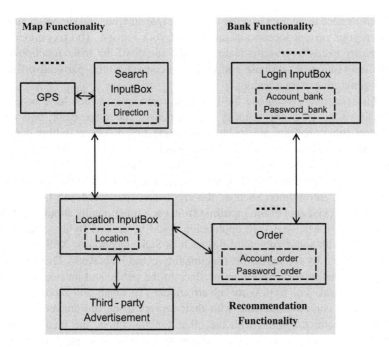

Fig. 7.13 Example of a travel mashup application

In terms of performance, processes are efficient because the time overhead for process startup and work is lower compared with page rendering and JavaScript execution times. The memory overhead is higher than in the conventional method because an HTML rendering engine must be loaded in many processes. Regarding backwards compatibility, because our approach places pages from different origins in different processes, it can support effective isolation without breaking the current architecture of Web pages, it does not bring communication boundaries among pages through the shared memory.

The aim of the example shown in Fig. 7.11 which contains almost all static content from one origin, is to address the workflow of our approach. However, we still emphasize that the reliably and security issues cannot be ignored because the active content such as the JavaScript code is widely used within attractive and complex Web applications and pages. To perceive the security requirement more directly, we start our discussion from the practical scenario shown in Fig. 7.13: you (a Web user) composite a travel mashup application into your smart phone by reusing and integrating several functionalities from existing popular Web applications. The travel application extracts a component of a map application with Global Positioning System (GPS) location and transportation query functionality, an online payment functionality from the credit card authentication component of your bank, and a functionality from a tourism agency component for getting tour or shopping recommendations. The functionalities from the map and recommendation applications need to interact in order to provide relevant tour and shopping guidance based on your current location at the time of your request. The recommendation functionality needs to communicate with the server of the bank functionality to make a reservation or purchase and may also contain a third-party advertisement part for generating extra revenue.

In this scenario, we can use the following techniques, which have been introduced above, to meet the security requirements: The map, bank, and recommendation functionalities are isolated as single OS processes within the same functionalities and interoperation of static content and active content is enabled through the combination of the iframe and the postMessage; however, we propose to use object access control to ensure that the third-party advertisements cannot request private information such as the credit card password and GPS location history. The *accessLevel* of the InputBox from each functionality should be defined as "dangerous" because a Web application could be created by a malicious user intentionally with some vulnerabilities such as SQL injection or XSS attack (user privacy accessed by the malicious functionality could be leaked). The recommendation functionality will expose an interface to the public and its interface can be used by the bank and third-party advertisement. The map and recommendation functionalities can communicate with their servers using the conventional XHR method. For communication with the other functionalities, the recommendation functionality can use CORS to make the remote server allow requests coming from other origins.

Integration Testing

When developing a Web-UI-component-based mashup application, we test each UI component individually. Clearly, components may have been developed separately, written in diverse programming language, and executed in different Web platforms. Therefore, integration testing is necessary to ensure that communication between components is correct. Some interaction-related faults are likely to be overlooked during unit-level testing. These faults can be classified into programming-related faults, which are inter-component faults, and non-programming-related faults, which are interoperability faults.

Conventional integration testing of component-based applications is based on the function decomposition, which includes the big-bang, top-down, bottom-up, and sandwich approach. Function decomposition approaches, which do not consider the internal structure of the individual components, are based on the specification of the system.

Owing to the heterogeneity and implementation transparency of Web-UI-component-based applications, we propose a model-based approach to integration testing. The core model here is the Component Interaction Graph (CIG), and the testing method is UML-based state testing. Here, CIG addresses the relationships that include message-communication, usage, etc. CIG can be defined to model interactions between UI components by depicting interaction scenario. CIG can be used to develop a family of test adequacy criteria, such as all nodes and all links coverage. In a component-based application, a component may interact with other components directly through an invocation of the interfaces exposed by those components, an exception, or a user action that triggers an event. A component may also interact with other components indirectly through a sequence of events. Interface and event testing ensure that every interaction between two UI components is exercised. UML provides high-level information for the internal behavior of components, which can be processed efficiently and used effectively during testing. In UML, collaboration diagrams and sequence diagrams are used to represent interactions between different objects in a component. A state diagram can be used to characterize the internal behaviors of objects in a component. Object Constraint Language (OCL) can be used to formally specify the behavior and constraints of a UI component. UML collaboration diagrams and sequence diagrams focus on interactions among various objects within a use case (say a component for simplicity here). If a UI component covers multiple use cases, we need to develop a consolidated collaboration diagram. If a use case includes more than one component, we need to develop a subset of the collaboration diagram. In UML sequence diagrams, interactions are ordered by time, while in collaboration diagrams, the same information is presented with the interactions ordered by the numeric message sequence.

With collaboration diagrams, we can obtain all possible sequences that could be invoked to model how interfaces and events interact with each other. The behavior of a Web UI component can be modeled more precisely by combining the collaboration diagram with statechart diagrams. By using the statechart diagram, we can further refine the interactions between interfaces and events. Given a statechart diagram, context-dependence relationships include not only all possible sequences in a collaboration diagram, but all possible combinations of the sequences that are shown in the statechart diagram as well.

Service Granularity

Insofar our approach has not achieved automatic and flexible composition of the intra-services (the UI components) based on the optimization of service granularity for better sharing and reuse. At the current stage of our prototype, we are focusing on addressing the maintenance and security issues discussed in section "Our Solution". Since the optimization of service granularity is such an advanced issue, it should be considered mainly after the desired UI components have been extracted from external websites and integrated by the mashup application as the intra-services.

Service granularity has never been stated as a purely technical issue [4,17,27,36]. More specifically, Haesen et al. proposed that the decision about service granularity should be made according to the following types of granularity [17]:

- Functionality granularity referring to the size and scope of functions offered by a service. In our integrated application, if two UI components are often used together, we can wrap these two components as one bigger service and further share and reuse this service with other applications. For example, in a travel mashup application, the users want to use the GPS location components provided by Google Maps to find the path to a destination; meanwhile, users are also concerned about the weather situation at the destination and the traffic situation on the way to the destination. Thus, we integrate the UI components for GPS search from Google, the weather enquiry from Yahoo, and the traffic situation enquiry from some real-time traffic monitoring system. These UI components are encapsulated as a bigger service from this viewpoint of functionality granularity.
- Data granularity reflecting the amount of data that is exchanged. In our application, if two UI components have their own data dependency from external websites, it will be difficult to compose these two components as a bigger one. Nevertheless, in the travel mashup application, the UI components from a bank website require login and authentication, and the UI components from an on-line hotel reservation website also require registration and login. Consequently, it is inconvenient to compose these two components, as they have their own authorization operations. Actually, the data granularities are attributed to the coupling, cohesion, and statelessness [33] of the intra-services.
- Business value granularity of a service indicating to what extent the service provides added business value. This aspect actually does not affect the design of the service granularity in our solution. Business value granularity is about attaining cost effectiveness from the business viewpoint. To maximize the profits from these services, the service vendors will provide a coarse-grained service to general customers and a finer-grained service to some special customers. As our application is to build open and reusable services from existing UI components, the business motivation may not be our major concern.

Kulkarni et al. [27] also argued that a tradeoff decision should take into consideration non-functional requirements, particularly performance issue. Except performance, Steghuis [4] reported that designers must make tradeoffs about service granularity in and between the following areas: flexibility in business processes and reusability. Thus, service granularity is actually relevant to every aspect of the system. Further exploration on this topic is included in our plans for future work.

Copyright

We have to face up to the problem of copyright in information reuse and integration. Copyright is the right of the owner to reproduce or permit someone else to reproduce copyrighted works. Websites usually own the copyright of content that they publish, so we need permission from the websites before we can reuse it.

Many websites or services give a clear declaration about the copyright. Public domain, such as the works of Shakespeare and Beethoven, means publicly available and covered by "No rights reserved". The most common type of copyright is "All rights reserved". In this case, if we use an image on our website that we did not create ourselves, we must get permission from the owner. It is also common for the text, HTML, and Script elements of a Web page to be taken and reused. If we have not obtained permission, we have violated the owner's copyright. Between these two copyright policies, there is a more flexible copyright model: "Some rights reserved". Wikipedia is provided under the terms of the Creative Commons [7] public license, which is devoted to expanding the range of creative works available for others to build upon legally and share.

Open Web service APIs are provided by some websites. The websites usually give a detailed policy of copyright for users. Information reuse based on open APIs has to obey the copyright policy defined by websites. Compared with open APIs, general Web applications do not provide clear end-user-programming-oriented interfaces. The legal and practical reuse of content extracted from Web applications cannot be left out of the consideration.

Here, we classify the content of Web applications into two categories as follows.

- No rights reserved content. Copyright does not protect facts, ideas, systems, or methods of operation. For example, facts like the population or national flag of a country may be freely reused without permission. Moreover, there are some special permissions. For example, reuse of the titles (not body) of Web news articles, book introduction headlines, and other brief descriptions is permitted without copyright. Furthermore, some social services/applications, such as the micro-blog Twitter, permit general Web users to share and reuse their content.
- All rights reserved content. Typically, most of the intellectually created content is protected by copyright. For example, photographs, Web news/blog content, and map information. For content of these types, reuse is forbidden without copyright permission. So, we need to declare the copyright information if we want to reuse the content. If others use our description and definition of component-based reuse, the declaration (*copyrightType*) should and must be inherited.

Conclusion

In this paper, we described current problems of Web-UI-component-based large-scale Web application reuse and integration and presented a UI component retrieval system that achieves quick and effective component searching. We also proposed a description method to define the basic entities in application reuse and integration. Moreover, we analyzed the contradictions between the conventional security mechanism SOP and the nature of mashup interoperation. We then presented our security requirements and solutions. Finally, we presented a systematic maintenance method and discussed personalization, testing, and copyright. Our retrieval and description system enables typical Web users to construct mashup Web applications easily and quickly.

As future work, we plan to conduct a more comprehensive analysis of current problems and modify our approach as follows.

- We will combine and develop various techniques/tools and propose a friendly GUI for users to generate the entity description file more easily and completely automatically.
- We will explore more flexible ways of integration and construct an open community for sharing various mashup components. The technologies of the Semantic Web and RDF will be used to centralize various Web applications, Web services, and other Web content.
- We will propose a quantitative and qualitative analysis as the evaluation standard for components (e.g., speed, stability and reuse range).
- We will develop a fine-grained access mechanism that can trace the information flow in the functionalities.
- We will propose a more stable extraction method to solve the problems of frequently changing content formats.

Acknowledgements This work was supported by a Grant-in-Aid for Scientific Research A (No.22240007) from the Japan Society for the Promotion of Science (JSPS).

References

1. Amazon Web Services. http://aws.amazon.com/. Accessed on 2011
2. Axis. http://ws.apache.org/axis/java/. Accessed on 2011
3. Barth A, Jackson C, Reis C (2008) Security architecture of the chromium browser. Stanford technical report
4. Claudia S (2006) Service granularity in SOA-projects: a trade-off analysis. Master's thesis, Electrical Engineering, Mathematics and Computer Science, University of Twente
5. Clements P, Northrop L (2002) Software product lines: practices and patterns. Addison-Wesley, Boston
6. Creating Web Clip Widgets. http://www.apple.com/pro/tips/webclip.html. Accessed on 2011
7. Creative Commons. http://creativecommons.org/. Accessed on 2011
8. Cross-Origin Resource Sharing. http://www.w3.org/TR/cors/. Accessed on 2011
9. Daniel F, Matera M (2009) Turning Web applications into mashup components: issues, models, and solutions. In: The proceedings of the 9th international conference on web engineering, San Sebastián, pp 45–60
10. Daniel F, Yu J, Benatallah B, Casati F, Matera M, Saint-Paul R (2007) Understanding UI integration: a survey of problems, technologies, and opportunities. Internet Comput 11(3):59–66
11. Dapper. http://www.dapper.net. Accessed on 2011
12. Ennals R, Garofalakis M (2007) MashMaker: mashups for the masses. In: The proceedings of the 33th SIGMOD international conference on management of data, Beijing, pp 1116–1118
13. Fujima J, Lunzer A, Hornbaek K, Tanaka Y (2004) C3W: clipping, connecting and cloning for the Web. In: The proceedings of the 13th international world wide web conference, Manhattan, pp 444–445

14. Google Docs. http://docs.google.com/. Accessed on 2011
15. Google Maps API. http://code.google.com/apis/maps/. Accessed on 2011
16. Google Mashup Editor. http://editor.googlemashups.com. Accessed on 2011
17. Haesen R, Snoeck M, Lemahieu W, Poelmans S (2008) On the definition of service granularity and its architectural impact. In: The proceedings of the 20th international conference on advanced information systems engineering, Montpellier
18. Han H, Tokuda T (2008) A method for integration of Web applications based on information extraction. In: The proceedings of the 8th international conference on web engineering, Yorktown Heights, pp 189–195
19. Han H, Tokuda T (2008) WIKE: a Web information/knowledge extraction system for Web service generation. In: The proceedings of the 8th international conference on web engineering, Yorktown Heights, pp 354–357
20. Han H, Guo J, Tokuda T (2010) Deep mashup: a description-based framework for lightweight integration of Web contents. In: The proceedings of the 19th international conference on world wide web, Raleigh, pp 1109–1110
21. Hickson I, Hyatt D Html 5 working draft – cross-document messaging. http://www.w3.org/TR/html5/comms.html. Accessed on 2011
22. IBM Mashup Center. http://www-01.ibm.com/software/info/mashup-center/. Accessed on 2011
23. iframe. http://www.w3.org/TR/html4/present/frames.html. Accessed on 2011
24. Jackson C, Bortz A, Boneh D, Mitchell JC (2006) Protecting browser state from Web privacy attacks. In: The proceedings of the 15th international conference on world wide web, Edinburgh, pp 737–744
25. Java Portlet. http://www.jcp.org/en/jsr/detail?id=286. Accessed on 2011
26. Koseki Y, Sugiura A (1998) Internet scrapbook: automating Web browsing tasks by demonstration. In: The proceedings of the 11th annual symposium on user interface software and technology, San Francisco, pp 9–18
27. Kulkarni N, Dwivedi V (2008) The role of service granularity in a successful SOA realization a case study. In: The proceedings of the 2008 IEEE congress on services, Honolulu
28. Kwok T, Nguyen T, Lam L (2008) A software as a service with multi-tenancy support for an electronic contract management application. In: The proceedings of the 2008 IEEE international conference on services computing, Honolulu
29. Maximilien EM, Wilkinson H, Desai N, Tai S (2007) A domain-specific language for Web APIs and services mashups. In: The proceedings of the 5th international conference on service-oriented computing, Vienna, pp 13–26
30. Microsoft Popfly. http://www.popfly.com. Accessed on 2011
31. Mietzner R, Metzger A, Leymann F, Pohl K (2009) Variability modeling to support customization and deployment of multi-tenant-aware software as a service applications. In: The proceedings of the 2009 ICSE workshop on principles of engineering service oriented systems, Vancouver, pp 18–25
32. Nitu (2009) Configurability in SaaS (software as a service) applications. In: The proceedings of the 2nd India software engineering conference, Pune
33. Papazoglou MP, van den Heuvel W-J (2006) Service-oriented design and development methodology. Int J Web Eng Technol 2(4):412–442
34. Perepletchikov M, Ryan C (2011) A controlled experiment for evaluating the impact of coupling on the maintainability of service-oriented software. IEEE Trans Softw Eng 37(4):449–465
35. Pettersson U, Jarzabek S (2005) Industrial experience with building a Web portal product line using a lightweight, reactive approach. In: The proceedings of the 10th European software engineering conference held jointly with 13th ACM SIGSOFT international symposium on foundations of software engineering, Lisbon, pp 326–335
36. Reldin P, Sundling P (2007) Explaining SOA service granularity: how IT-strategy shapes services. Master's thesis, Department of Management and Engineering Industrial Economics, Institute of Technology, Linkoping University

37. Representational State Transfer. http://www.ics.uci.edu/~fielding/pubs/dissertation/rest_arch_style.htm. Accessed on 2011
38. Sabbouh M, Higginson J, Semy S, Gagne D (2007) Web mashup scripting language. In: The proceedings of the 16th international conference on world wide web, Banff, pp 1035–1036
39. Sengupta B, Roychoudhury A (2011) Engineering multi-tenant software-as-a-service systems. In: The proceedings of the 3rd international workshop on principles of engineering service-oriented systems, Waikiki, Honolulu, Hawaii
40. Simple Object Access Protocol. http://www.w3.org/TR/soap/. Accessed on 2011
41. Stollberg M, Muth M (2009) Service customization by variability modeling. In: The proceedings of the 2009 international conference on service-oriented computing, Stockholm
42. Tatemura J, Sawires A, Po O, Chen S, Candan KS, Agrawal D, Goveas M (2007) Mashup feeds: continuous queries over Web services. In: The proceedings of the 33th SIGMOD international conference on management of data, Beijing, pp 1128–1130
43. Thio N, Karunasekera S (2007) Web service recommendation based on client-side performance estimation. In: The proceedings of the 18th Australian software engineering conference, Melbourne, pp 81–89
44. Wang G, Yang S, Han Y (2009) Mashroom: end-user mashup programming using nested tables. In: The proceedings of the 18th international conference on world wide web, Madrid, pp 861–870
45. Web Application Description Language. https://wadl.dev.java.net/. Accessed on 2011
46. Web Service Definition Language. http://www.w3.org/TR/wsdl. Accessed on 2011
47. Web Services for Remote Portlets. http://www.oasis-open.org/committees/wsrp/. Accessed on 2011
48. Wohlstadter E, Li P, Cannon B (2009) Web service mashup middleware with partitioning of XML pipelines. In: The proceedings of 7th international conference on web services, Los Angeles, pp 91–98
49. Wong J, Hong JI (2007) Making mashups with marmite: towards end-user programming for the Web. In: The proceedings of the SIGCHI conference on human factors in computing systems, San Jose, pp 1435–1444
50. XSL Transformations. http://www.w3.org/TR/xslt20/. Accessed on 2011
51. Yahoo Pipes. http://pipes.yahoo.com/pipes/. Accessed on 2011
52. Ye P, Peng X, Xue Y, Jarzabek S (2009) A case study of variation mechanism in an industrial product line. In: The proceedings of the 11th international conference on software reuse: formal foundations of reuse and domain engineering, Falls Church, pp 126–136
53. Yu J, Benatallah B, Saint-Paul R, Casati F, Daniel F, Matera M (2007) A framework for rapid integration of presentation components. In: The proceedings of the 16th international conference on world wide web, Banff, pp 923–932
54. Zhao Q, Huang G, Huang J, Liu X, Mei H (2008) A Web-based mashup environment for on-the-fly service composition. In: The proceedings of 4th international symposium on service-oriented system engineering, Jhongli, pp 32–37
55. Zibuschka J, Herbert M, Rossnagel H (2010) Towards privacy-enhancing identity management in mashup-providing platforms. In: The proceedings of the 24th annual IFIP WG 11.3 working conference on data and applications security and privacy, Rome, pp 273–286

Chapter 8
Which Ranking for Effective Keyword Search Query over RDF Graphs?

Roberto De Virgilio

Abstract Ranking solutions is an important issue in Information Retrieval because it greatly influences the quality of results. In this context, keyword based search approaches use to consider solutions sorting as least step of the overall process. Ranking and building solutions are completely separate steps running autonomously. This may penalize the retrieving information process because it binds to order all found matching elements including (possible) irrelevant information. In this chapter we present a theoretical study of YAANII, a novel technique to keyword based search over semantic data. The approach presents a joint use of scoring functions and solution building algorithms to get the best results. We demonstrate how effectiveness of the answers depends not so much on the quality of the scoring metrics but on the way such criteria are involved. Finally we show how YAANII overcames other systems in terms of efficiency and effectiveness.

Introduction

Nowadays availability of data is constantly increasing [2]. Nevertheless one principal difficulty users have to face is to find and retrieve the information they are looking for. To precisely access data, a user should know how data is organized in the source, and how to write a query in the language required by the source. For this reason keywords search based systems are increasingly capturing the attention of researchers. In this context many approaches [5, 10] implement IR strategies on top of traditional systems, like DBMSs: the goal is to free users from knowing the details of the query language or of the structure (schema) of the data. Usually, a generic approach identifies two main steps. Firstly it retrieves the parts of the data structure matching the keywords of interest and discovers a connection between

R. De Virgilio (✉)
Dipartimento di Informatica e Automazione, Università Roma Tre, Rome, Italy
e-mail: dvr@dia.uniroma3.it

T. Özyer et al. (eds.), *Information Reuse and Integration in Academia and Industry*,
DOI 10.1007/978-3-7091-1538-1_8, © Springer-Verlag Wien 2013

such identified parts. Second step is to rank candidate solutions, generated on top of found connections, through a scoring function [3, 13–15]. In case Top-k solutions are computed after all candidate ones have been generated. In this framework the sort of results is only the final stage and orthogonal in the overall process. This means to simplify the problem solving separately two sub-tasks but increasing the complexity of both. Moreover the evaluation of results mainly focuses on finding the answers more exhaustive. Nevertheless the goodness of the search results is highly dependent on both the return of all referenced documents and the proper ranking of them according to the relevance. For this reason the problems of search and sort the results are strongly linked. To this aim, in [1] we provided YAANII, a novel keyword based search technique that leverages a joint use of scoring functions and solution building algorithms. As we will demonstrate in section "Complexity of Keyword Search", our technique allows us to reduce relevantly the computational complexity of the overall process. The contribution of this chapter is a theoretical study on using an incremental IR ranking process when building solutions for the keyword search on RDF graphs. This study regards both computational efficiency and satisfaction of user information need. In particular to assess the effectiveness of our approach we use Exhaustivity and Specificity [7, 11] instead of Precision and Recall measures. Exhaustivity and Specificity provide more sophisticated instruments to answers assessment in order to avoid flattening evaluation and dataset dependance. We will illustrate how effectiveness of the answers depends not so much on the quality of the metrics used to score the results but on the way such scoring criteria are involved. Therefore an efficient and effective way to rank answers enforces the overall process. We will illustrate a case study to compare YAANII with two recent and innovative approaches to keywords search on graph structures: BLINKS [3] and SearchWebDB [15]. We focus on them for two reasons: (i) they are two important representatives of two different paradigms for keyword search, (ii) they are computationally efficient in PTIME class complexity. The chapter is organized as follows: section "State of the Art" illustrates in detail the state of the art approaches. Section "Complexity of Keyword Search" discusses the complexity of keyword search query processing. Section "Ranking of Solutions" analyzes the ranking of solutions to show the desired characteristics. Sections "A Comparative Study" and "Experimental Results" provide a case study and experimental results to support the considerations made in the previous section. Finally section "Conclusions and Future Works" sketches conclusions and future work.

State of the Art

In this section we give in-depth details of the three approaches we study in this chapter.

BLINKS. BLINKS [3] provides a *Bi-Level INdexing Keyword Search* approach for data graph. It starts partitioning the entire data graph in many sub-graphs called *blocks*. Nodes in common between different blocks are called *portals*. The *Bi-Level Index* consists of the top-level *block index* and one *intra-block index*. The former maps information about nodes and keywords within the block, the latter indexes information inside the block exploiting a *single-level index* for the whole data graph. The *single-level index* is supported by a set of *keyword-node lists* (L_{KN}), which keeps track of the nodes that can reach a given node matching a keyword, and by a *node-keyword map* (M_{NK}), an hash table that stores the shortest distance between pairs of nodes and keyword matching nodes. Moreover BLINKS provides backward expansion to expand from a keyword matching node to other nodes using inverse edges, and forward expansion (i.e through the D_{NP} and M_{NK}) to infer if a path from a node u to a keyword matching node within the block is sub-optimal (i.e. the path is optimal for the solution having u as root). Given a query $Q = \{k_1, k_2, \ldots, k_n\}$ and a directed graph G, in BLINKS a solution, with respect to Q, is a substructure of G, as $T = < r, (n_1, n_2, \ldots, n_m) >$ where r (i.e. a node in G) is the *root* of the answer and $n_1, \ldots, n_m$ are nodes (i.e. of G) matching a keyword of Q such that for each i there exists a directed path in G from r to n_i. Through the index discussed previously, such solutions are generated and at the end ordered with respect to a scoring function, as follows

$$S(T) = f(\overline{S}_r(r) + \sum_{i=1}^{m} \overline{S}_n(n_i, w_i) + \sum_{i=1}^{m} \overline{S}_p(r, n_i))$$

$\overline{S}_r(r)$ evaluates the contribution of the root r, $\overline{S}_n$ is the contribute of a node n_i and $\overline{S}_p(r, n_i)$ denotes the shortest-path distance from r to n_i. This function considers both graph structure and content, and exploits several measures developed by database and IR communities.

SearchWebDB. SearchWebDB [15] presents alternative techniques to solve the problem. The initial data graph is reduced to a *summary graph* that contains only some kind of nodes and edges. Authors' intuition is that only nodes representing classes need to be stored in the working memory, independently from the query request. This is because nodes representing entities and containing values are ending elements for the graph, i.e. they are not connecting elements. Once the algorithm runs with a query, the summary graph is augmented with nodes and edges by which we can reach the keyword matching elements. The resulting graph is called *augmented summary graph*. The algorithm returns *conjunctive queries*, corresponding to sub-graphs of the augmented summary graph, from which the user can perform more precise selections. The final selection is submitted again and it is computed using the database engine with an element-to-query mapping. As in BLINKS, SearchWebDB considers a solution as a set of paths p_i from a root to a node n matching a keyword. Similar to BLINKS, once the solution were generated, they have to be ordered with respect to a score. The authors provide three different kinds of scoring functions (i.e. $C1$, $C2$ and $C3$) based on different evaluation granularities. In this study we consider only the $C3$ scoring function for two reasons: (i) it is the one which gets better results, and (ii) it is the function more similar to the scoring functions used in the other approaches. $C3 = \sum_{p_i \in P} \sum_{n \in p_i} \frac{c(n)}{s_m(n)}$: it takes into account the *popularity* score $c(n)$ and the *matching* score $s_m(n)$ of the elements in the graph. Also in this case, the scoring function evaluates both graph structure and content.

Yaanii. YAANII [1] is based on a clustering approach. A cluster is a partition over paths in the graph starting from a *root* and ending into a node matching a keyword. We mean root as a node without incoming edges and we call such paths *informative paths*. At each path a *template* corresponds, i.e. the ordered list of labels on the edges in the path. Each template defines a cluster and consequently all the paths with the corresponding template belongs to it. If a path *pt* is subsumed by a path *pt'*, present in a cluster, *pt* is discarded. As for the other approaches, in YAANII a solution is a set of paths (i.e. in our case a set of informative paths). Differently from the state-of-the-art techniques, an interesting characteristic of YAANII is that it ranks solutions while it builds them. Our approach leverages on the clusters to assembly a solution. Each solution merges the highest-scoring paths from the several clusters. YAANII scores informative paths, clusters and solutions. Each structure is evaluated with respect to a query $Q = (k_1, k_2, \ldots, k_n)$, and considering both structural information and content information with the following pattern formula:

$$R(e, Q) = \sum_{k \in Q} weight(k, Q) \cdot weight(k, e)$$

$$weight(k, e) = \frac{weight_{ct}(k, e)}{weight_{str}(k, e)}$$

where $weight(k, Q)$ is the weight associated to each keyword k with respect to the query Q and $weight(k, e)$ is the weight associated to each keyword k with respect to the structure e (i.e. an informative path, a cluster or a solution). $weight(k, e)$ evaluates the combination between structural information (i.e. $weight_{st}(k, e)$) and content information (i.e. $weight_{ct}(k, e)$). The intuition is that the score of a structure e with respect to a keyword k is the weight of the content information in e normalized by the structural information of e.

In the following we present the computational complexity study of the approach, highlighting a comparative study with actual PTIME state-of-the-art solutions. The comparative study focuses on a theoretical analysis of different frameworks to define complexity ranges, which they correspond to, in the polynomial time class. We characterize such systems in terms of general measures, which give a general description of the behavior of these frameworks according to different aspects that are more general and informative than mere benchmark tests on a few test cases.

Complexity of Keyword Search

Formally, the problem we are trying to solve may be defined as follows. Given a directed graph $G = (V, E)$, where each node (resource) $v \in V$ and each edge (property) $e \in E$ present a label (i.e. the URI of the resource, the name of the property), a query Q composed of a set of keywords $q_1, \ldots, q_m$, we find the answers $S_1, \ldots, S_k$ to Q where S_i is a subgraph of G.

Following this scenario, we study the complexity of the approaches presented above. Such complexity is evaluated in terms of the number of basic operations to compute in the worst case. Due to space constraints, we do not report the algorithms of the approaches but during the analysis we make exact reference to the lines of corresponding pseudo-codes in the respective works [1, 3, 15].

Let us introduce the notation we use:

- N: number of solutions.
- $|Q|$: length of Q (i.e. number of keywords $q_i \in Q$).
- $|G|$: number of nodes in the graph G.

BLINKS

In this section we show that the complexity of BLINKS is $O(\text{BLINKS}) \in O(|G|^2 \times |Q|^2)$. With respect to the previous notation, we have to introduce the following terms:

- K: number of matching elements in BLINKS.
- B: number of blocks in the BLINKS partition.
- P: number of portals p_i.
- R: number of roots in the graph G.
- $|A|$: number of current determined solutions
- $|RC|$: number of candidates to be solution

The search algorithm of BLINKS (i.e. searchBLINKS) calls a main procedure visitNode that is supported by the functions sumDist and sumLBDist. For a node u, just visited but not yet determined as the root of a solution, these functions are used, respectively, to calculate the distance and the lower bound distances from u to individual keywords. Therefore:

$$\texttt{sumDist}(u) = \sum_{i=0}^{|Q|} Dist_i(u) \in O(|Q|)$$

$$\texttt{sumLBDist}(u) = \sum_{i=0}^{|Q|} LBDist_i(u) \in O(|Q|)$$

About visitNode we can say
lines[21–27]: $O(|Q|)$ because it computes two hash table accesses and one update $\forall q_i \in Q$.
lines[28–29]: $O(\texttt{sumLBDist}) \in O(|Q|)$.
lines[30–31]: $O(1)$.
lines[32–34]: $O(\texttt{sumDist}) \in O(|Q|)$.

Since those lines are in an `if-then-else` instruction, we have $O(\texttt{visitNode}) \in$
$O(|Q| + |Q|) = O(|Q|)$.

For $lines[2–5]$ we have $O(|Q| \times B)$ because in $lines[2–5]$ the algorithm creates
$|Q|$ queues and for each of them it inserts $O(B)$ times a cursor in it. But if one
considers that there is only one queue insertion for each matching element, then we
have $O(|Q| + K)$. Since $|Q| \leq K$, then we conclude $O(K)$ in $lines[2–5]$.

In $lines[6–17]$ we need to distinguish between portals p_i and normal nodes u_i.

- Nodes p_i:
  $line[10] : O(\texttt{visitNode}) \in O(|Q|)$.
  $lines[11–14]: O(B)$.
  $line[16] : O(|RC| - |A|) \times O(sumLBDlist)$.

  Since $O(|RC|) \in O(|G|)$, $O(|A|) \in O(N)$, $O(\texttt{sumLBDlist}) \in O(|Q|)$, and
  $|G| \gg N$, then in $line[16]$ we have $O(|G| \times |Q|)$.
  We remind the so-called Lemma 1 of BLINKS: "*the number of cursors opened
  by searchBLINKS for each query keyword is O(P), where P is the number of
  portals in the partitioning of the data graph*". Hence, considering $line[11]$ and
  Lemma 1, iterations on $lines[6–17]$ are at most $|Q| \times P$, i.e. a portal p_i cannot
  be traversed more than once for each keyword q_i.

- Nodes u_i:
  $line[10]: O(\texttt{visitNode}) \in O(|Q|)$.
  $line[11–14]: O(1)$ because $LPB(u) = \emptyset$ in the worst case.
  $line[16]: O(|G| \times |Q|)$ as showed above.

  Iterations on these nodes occur $(|G| \times |Q|) - (|Q| \times P)$, because the total number
  of iterations is less than the number of iterations for the portals.

To sum up, the global complexity results as follows:

$lines[2–5]: O(K)$
$lines[6–17]: O((|Q| \times P) \times (|Q| + B + (|G| \times |Q|)))$, for the iterations on portals p_i
$lines[6–17]: O((|G| \times |Q| - |Q| \times P) \times (|G| \times |Q|))$, for the iterations on nodes u_i

Considering that $|G| > 1, |G| \geq B, |Q| \geq 1$ we have:

$lines[6–17]: O((|Q| \times P) \times O(|G| \times |Q|))$, for the iterations on portals p_i
$lines[6–17]: O((|G| \times |Q| - |Q| \times P) \times O(|G| \times |Q|))$, for the iterations on nodes u_i

Furthermore, because $K \leq |G|$:

$$O(\text{BLINKS}) \in O(K + |G|^2 \times |Q|^2 - |Q|^2 \times |G| \times P + |Q|^2 \times |G| \times P)$$

$$\in O(|G|^2 \times |Q|^2).$$

The complexity result we obtain for BLINKS is aligned with the experimental results authors present in [3]. There is no dependence on the number of keyword matching elements. However BLINKS shows longer response time for queries with more keywords. This is a strong proof since $|Q|$ is much smaller than K. Moreover the computing time is not affected by the block size of the partitioning. Authors state that query response times longer than 90 s are trunked. This means that in some case the algorithm down-performs the average behavior. We believe that the problem relies in aiming at finding the exact matching sub-graph which tend easily to fall in the worst case scenario. In fact if there is no matching keyword node for at least one keyword the algorithm cannot return an answer due to the condition in *line*[16], and neither prune the search in *line*[28]. It just can return for the condition into the while instruction that means exploring all the search space.

SearchWebDB

The complexity of SearchWebDB should consider the augmentation of the summary graph (AUGMENTATION) and the Top-N query computation (SEARCH). We have to introduce the following terms:

- k_i: number of elements matching the keyword q_i.
- K: number of matching elements.
- S: number of augmented summary graph nodes.

We show that such complexity is $(O(\text{AUGMENTATION}) + O(\text{SEARCH})) \in O(|G| \times K^2)$. In this approach, we should consider S as the number of nodes in the exploration, i.e. the number of augmented summary graph nodes we use for top-N query retrieval. Moreover, because we are analyzing the worst case, we consider $O(S) \in O(|G|)$.

$O(\text{AUGMENTATION}) \in O(K)$ because we have to insert K elements to generate the summary graph.

The procedure SEARCH is supported by the function TOP-N for the query computation. Referring to this function, we say

- In *lines*[1–7] TOP-N possibly completes a sub-graph by merging the paths from the given connecting element and to some keyword element. In the algorithm a path can be computed efficiently due to the presence of a cursor that keeps track of his parent cursor, which, recursively, defines a path up to some element matching a keyword. For each node K cursors can be generated at most. Then we have $O(K)$.
- In *lines*[11–16], we have $O(N)$, where we can ignore function *maptoQuery* having constant complexity.

Since *lines*[11–16] are executed only if the top-N solutions are found (i.e. only once in the execution), we do not include the complexity of this block in the study. Therefore $O(\text{TOP} - \text{N}) \in O(K)$.

Going back to the procedure SEARCH, in *lines*[1–6] we have $O(|Q| \times max\{k_1, k_2, \ldots, k_{|Q|}\})$ because $\forall q_i \in Q$ the algorithm computes k_i basic inserts. However a cursor is inserted for each matching element, then the complexity in *lines*[1–6] is $O(K)$. Analyzing *lines*[7–27], in the worst case the condition of *line*[10] fails at all iterations. This makes ineffective the heuristic *minCostCursor* at *line*[8], implying that all the cursors generated by the algorithm have to be extracted later from their respective queues. This means that iterations in *lines*[7–27] will be computed once for each generated cursor, where the total number of generated cursors is $|G| \times K$ (since *lines*[1–6] generated K cursors). Therefore in *lines*[7–27] we have $O(|G| \times K) \times O(TOP - N) \in O(|G| \times K^2)$.

If we consider $K \geq 1$, the global complexity of the algorithm is:

$$O(\texttt{SearchWebDB}) \in O(\texttt{AUGMENTATION}) + O(\texttt{SEARCH})$$

$$\in O(K) + O(|G| \times K^2) \in O(K + |G| \times K^2)$$

$$\in O(|G| \times K^2)$$

As for BLINKS, complexity of SearchWebDB is aligned with the experiments presented in [15]. The complexity of SearchWebDB is independent from the query length. However authors noticed better performance when the number of keyword is large and it can correspond averagely to a large K. Additionally authors say that there is a linear dependence on N that we did not demonstrate because we analyzed the worst case which did not take into account pruning conditions. In fact we considered $|G|$ instead of S, which is supposed to be much smaller than $|G|$. On the other hand, we noticed that query processing time increases when $|Q|$ changes for a given $N > 3$. In particular in top-20 cases the query processing time does not increase linearly in the query length, but is (almost) quadratic.

Yaanii

In this section we discuss the complexity of YAANII. We introduce the following terms

- C: number of clusters $c_i \in$ CL.
- T: number of paths $p_i \in$ PT.

We show that $O(\text{YAANII}) \in O(C \times T)$. This result is the sum of complexities in three sub-phases of the on-line computation: $O(\texttt{QUERYSUBMISSION}) + O(\texttt{CLUSTERING}) + O(\texttt{BUILDING})$. Since there is direct access to each keyword through the index, $O(\texttt{QUERYSUBMISSION}) \in O(|Q|)$.

With respect to [1] we improved the clustering phase as shown in the Algorithm 1.

Algorithm 1: Clustering of informative paths

Input : An List PT of informative paths, a query Q
Output: A Priority Queue CL of clusters

1   CL' ← CreateSet() ;
2   PT' ← subsumedDelete(PT);
3   **while** PT' *is not empty* **do**
4   PT' - {*pt*};
5   **if** $\exists Cl_i \in$ CL' $: pt \approx t_{Cl_i}$ **then**
6   Enqueue (*pt*, Score (*pt*,Q), Cl_i);
7   UpdateScore (Cl_i);
8   **else**
9   Cl_i ← CreateCluster (*pt*);
10   Enqueue (*pt*, Score (*pt*,Q), Cl_i);
11   CL' ∪ {Cl_i};

12   CL ← OrderClusters (CL');
13   **return** CL;

In *lines*[5–7] the algorithm checks if there exists a cluster Cl_i matching the path template. Hence we have $O(C)$. In *lines*[8–11] we have $O(1)$. In *lines*[3–11] the iteration is computed for each path (i.e T times). As a consequence, the complexity in *lines*[3–11] is $T \times O(C) \in O(T \times C)$. In *line*[12] we obtain $O(C \times log_2 C)$ to order the queue. Finally $O(\text{CLUSTERING}) \in O(T \times C) + O(C \times \log_2 C)$. Knowing that $C, T > 1$ and $T > C$ then $O(\text{CLUSTERING}) \in O(T \times C)$.

Referring to BUILDING, we have

lines[4–6]: $O(1)$.
line[8]: $O(T)$.
lines[12–15]: $O(T)$
lines[16–17]: $O(T)$
lines[18–21]: $O(1)$

In *lines*[9–22] we consider the complexity of *lines*[12–15] and the maximum complexity between executions in *lines*[16–17] and *lines*[18–21]. Since we have C iterations, in *lines*[9–22] we have $C \times (O(T) + O(T))$. Notice that in *lines*[12–15] and *lines*[16–17] we iterate all the paths at most. Hence we have $O(T)$ and $O(T)$, and, consequently, in *lines*[9–22] the complexity is $O(T) + O(T) \in O(T)$. In *lines*[24–26] we have $O(C)$ because we just iterate on the visited cluster list. Since $\forall Cl : \exists pt \in PT \Rightarrow T \geq C$, final complexity becomes

$$O(\text{BUILDING}) \in N \times (O(1) + O(T) + O(T) + O(C))$$

$$\in N \times O(T) \in O(N \times T)$$

Table 8.1 Comparison with relations

Case	BLINKS	SearchWebDB	YAANII
1. $T = R \times K$	$O(|Q|^2 \times |G|^2)$	$O(K^2 \times |G|)$	$O(R \times K \times C)$
2. $T = K$	$O(|Q|^2 \times |G|^2)$	$O(K^2 \times |G|)$	$O(K \times C)$
3. $C = K$	$O(|Q|^2 \times |G|^2)$	$O(K^2 \times |G|)$	$O(T \times K)$
4. $K^2 = |Q|^2, T = R \times K$	$O(K^2 \times |G|^2)$	$O(K^2 \times |G|)$	$O(R \times K \times C)$
5. $T = K, C = K, |Q| = K$	$O(|G|^2 \times K^2)$	$O(|G| \times K^2)$	$O(K^2)$
6. $T = \frac{|G|}{K}, |Q| = K, C = K$	$O(|Q|^2 \times |G|^2)$	$O(|Q|^2 \times |G|)$	$O(K \times \frac{|G|}{K}) = O(|G|)$

We can conclude that the overall complexity of YAANII is $O(\text{QUERY SUBMISSION}) + O(\text{CLUSTERING}) + O(\text{BUILDING}) \in O(|Q|) + O(T \times C) + O(N \times T) \in max\{O(T \times C), O(N \times T)\}$. Given that most of times $C > N$, we result the final complexity:

$$O(\text{YAANII}) \in O(C \times T).$$

Comparison

We now compare the results obtained in the previous section. Recall that:

$$O(\text{BLINKS}) \in O(|Q|^2 \times |G|^2)$$

$$O(\text{SearchWebDB}) \in O(|G| \times K^2)$$

$$O(\text{YAANII}) \in O(C \times T)$$

Comparison can be performed in two ways: (i) by expressing relations between the terms of all complexities, or (ii) by a pairwise comparison. We present both manners.

Comparison with Relations : in this case we have to define some *relations* between the different terms used in each study. In Table 8.1 we show such relations between the terms we used in our study and provide the resulting complexities. We now explain each single relation taking into account that we combined them in some case.

- $T = R \times K$: it means that we can reach a keyword matching node from all the roots with different paths. It is an average/worst case for YAANII because we can have more than one path starting from a given root to a keyword matching node but even no paths connecting a root to a keyword matching node.
- $T = K$: it means that each path contains a different keyword matching node. It is a good case for YAANII since usually there are more paths sharing the same keyword.

- $C = K$: it means that we have a different cluster for each keyword matching element. In this case we are dependent on data graph structure even if usually $C < K$.
- $K^2 = |Q|^2, |Q| = K$: they mean that we have one keyword matching element for each keyword q_i. SearchWebDB take advantages against BLINKS with these relations since usually $|Q| < K$.
- $T = \frac{|G|}{K}$: it means that all the nodes in the data graph are involved in a path and one node cannot belong to more than one path. This is a very extreme case.

Using these relations we produce six different cases, as shown in Table 8.1. In particular the cases (5) and (6) result from the combination of the previous ones. Such cases clearly show the complexity ranges of each approach. Using an approximation measure d of complexity we can say:

- $O(\text{BLINKS}) \in [O(d^3), O(d^4)]$
- $O(\text{SearchWebDB}) \in [O(d^2), O(d^3)]$
- $O(\text{YAANII}) \in [O(d), O(d^2)]$

This is a relevant result. All the presented algorithms are promising representative of an efficient solution for keyword based search in PTIME class complexity. However we demonstrated how YAANII is more efficient with respect to the others, presenting a quadratic complexity as upper-bound.

Pairwise Comparison: we demonstrate that:

$$O(\text{BLINKS}) > O(\text{SearchWebDB}) > O(\text{YAANII})$$

By comparing the complexity result from previous sections, for the algorithms we have:
BLINKS vs SearchWebDB:

$$\frac{O(|G| \times K^2)}{O(|Q|^2 \times |G|^2)} = \frac{O(K \times K)}{O(|Q| \times |Q| \times |G|)}$$

In a very extreme case we have that each node of the graph matches the query (i.e. all keywords). Therefore:

$$O(K \times K) \approx O(|Q| \times |Q| \times |G|)$$

From this result, we infer that in a real case:

$$O(K^2) \ll O(|Q|^2 \times |G|) \implies O(\text{BLINKS}) > O(\text{SearchWebDB})$$

SearchWebDB vs YAANII:

In this case we consider again S instead of $|G|$ to be more effective. Therefore we use $O(C \times T)$ and $O(S \times K^2)$. We separately compare $O(T)$ against $O(S \times K)$ and $O(C)$ against $O(K)$. First of all we can say $C \leq K$ because in the worst case each matching keyword element corresponds to a path having a different template (i.e. a different cluster). Furthermore we can consider $O(C) \in O(K)$ that allows to focus the comparison on $O(T)$ against $O(S \times K)$. In fact, $C < T$ and $K < K \times S^2$. In an extreme case we have that for each node v_c of the summary graph (sg) and for each matching element v_k we have an informative path pt such that pt starts with v_c (i.e. the root of the path) and ends in v_k (i.e. the last node of the path), where there doesn't exist an informative path pt', ending into v_k (we denote with $last(pt')$), that subsumes pt (i.e. $pt \lhd pt'$). In other words

$$\forall v_c \in sg, \forall v_k$$

$$\exists pt \in \text{PT} : pt = v_c - \ldots - v_k$$

$$\text{and } \nexists pt' \in \text{PT} : pt \lhd pt', last(pt') = v_k$$

In this case we have

$$\frac{O(T)}{O(S \times K)} = 1$$

Hence, we infer that in a real case:

$$O(T) \ll O(S \times K) \implies O(\texttt{SearchWebDB}) > O(\text{YAANII})$$

BLINKS vs YAANII:
From the previous results

$$O(\texttt{SearchWebDB}) > O(\text{YAANII}) \text{ and } O(\text{BLINKS}) > O(\texttt{SearchWebDB})$$

Hence we deduce $O(\text{BLINKS}) > O(\text{YAANII})$.
Given the above results, we can make the following call:

$$O(\text{BLINKS}) > O(\texttt{SearchWebDB}) > O(\text{YAANII})$$

Ranking of Solutions

In this section we show how much the ranking of the approaches discussed above affects the efficiency and effectiveness of solution exploration. In particular we demonstrate that the effectiveness of the final result is depending on how (and when) the ranking is used, rather than on the quality of the metric itself.

Efficiency of Ranking. In the previous section we described the computational complexity of the frameworks cited in the Introduction. The final result we have obtained is that YAANII shows the lowest computational cost among the approaches considered. In this section we would follow a similar study with respect to the ranking of each technique, considering its contribute in terms of complexity in the overall process. We need to define the following notation: (i) $|Q|$: the number of keywords in the query Q, (ii) N: the number of output solutions, (iii) $|G|$: the number of nodes in the data graph G and, (iv) K: the number of the elements matching a keyword. The impact in the global computational time of the scoring functions will be referred as *SCORING*.

The search algorithm of BLINKS calls a main procedure visitNode that is supported by the functions sumDist and sumLBDist. For a node u, just visited but not yet determined as the root of a solution, these functions are used, respectively, to calculate the distance and the lower bound distances from u to individual keywords. The scoring function of BLINKS is implemented in sumDist defined as

$$\text{sumDist}(u) = \sum_{i=0}^{|Q|} Dist_i(u) \in O(|Q|)$$

As we can notice it just sums the distances from a root u to the nearest nodes matching a keyword (i.e. one for each keyword $q_i \in Q$). Even if in the paper the authors focus on the term $\sum_{i=1}^{m} \overline{S}_p(r, n_i)$ (partially computed off-line), at each iteration of sumDist we have the complexity $O(|Q|)$. Since sumDist is executed each time that visitNode is called, that is $|G| \times |Q|$ times, we can conclude that

$$SCORING(\text{BLINKS}) \in O(|G| \times |Q|^2).$$

In SearchWebDB, only $s_m(n)$ has to be computed on-line since it depends on the keywords of the query. In this framework the score $C3$ is evaluated within the TOP-N function when we need to know the score of the newest candidate solution, if any. The cost of $s_m(n)$ is $O(s_m(n)) \in O(|Q|)$ because it has to compare the informative content of a node n with all the keywords $q_i \in Q$. Since $s_m(n)$ is called once for each TOP-N execution we have the complexity of the scoring is $O(s_m(n)) \times$ #(TOP-N *executions*). TOP-N is called at each iteration of the algorithm, and since the iterations are at most $|G| \times K$ we can conclude

$$SCORING(\text{SearchWebDB}) \in O(|Q| \times |G| \times K)$$

Our framework presents three sub-phases in the on-line computation of the solutions: QUERY SUBMISSION, CLUSTERING and BUILDING. Since the score of a cluster is the highest score recurring in contained paths, we have to analyze only the scoring about informative paths and solutions during such computation. We will consider them separately. The scoring of an informative path is evaluated during the QUERY SUBMISSION step. Since the paths are indexed, scoring the paths is $O(|Q|)$: we have one access to the index for each keyword $q_i \in Q$. We do not score paths during the clustering and during the main iteration in the BUILDING. The scoring of a solution is evaluated only in the BUILDING. It is used to evaluate if an informative path deserves to be inserted in the current solution S_i. Once the score of S_i is computed we don't need to calculate it anymore and it can be inserted within the set of the final solutions S in the right priority order. Let us provide the complexities of $weight_{ct}(k, e)$ and $weight_{st}(k, e)$ for a solution as follows. $weight_{ct}$ computes elementary math operations and $weight_{str}(k, S)$ is iterated for each keyword of the query. Definitively scoring a solution is $O(1) \times O(|Q|) \in O(|Q|)$. Given T the number of informative paths retrieved by the index, the scoring function is evaluated at most T times for each iteration. Since the iterations are in number of N we have:

$$SCORING(\text{YAANII}) \in O(|Q|) \times N \times T \in O(|Q| \times N \times T)$$

Let's recall a result of section "Complexity of Keyword Search". Using an approximation measure d, we demonstrated the following:

$$O(\text{BLINKS}) \in [O(d^3), O(d^4)], O(\text{SearchWebDB}) \in [O(d^2), O(d^3)]$$
$$O(\text{YAANII}) \in [O(d), O(d^2)].$$

The complexities of the corresponding scoring functions perfectly reflect the complexities of the main processes. Therefore the efficiency of the approach is depending on the scoring and in particular on how (and when) it is used in the generation of solutions. In BLINKS and SearchWebDB the complexity is depending on $|G|$ while in YAANII on T. This is due to apply the ranking respectively at the end or in the meanwhile of the computation of a solution.

Effectiveness of Ranking. Usually the effectiveness of results is evaluated in terms of precision (more often) and recall, and typically they are considered separately. An optimal solution should contain the most relevant information to the user in terms of relevant linked elements [4, 6, 8, 9, 12, 16]. In particular the solution has to aim to the *core* answer without giving irrelevant information. In this context the use of precision and recall can lead to a flat evaluation of results to reach the *completeness*. Some more sophisticated measures have been proposed [7, 11] to standardize the assessment. These measures introduce the concepts of *Exhaustivity*, *Specificity* and *Overlap*. Exhaustivity is the extent to which the result component discusses the topic of request. It measures the relevance of a solution in terms of the number of keywords contained in the result. Specificity is the extent to which the result component focuses the topic of request. It measures the number of matching elements contained in the result, which are relevant to the user. Overlap is the extent to which the result component is already showed in previous results with high score. Consequently, the best solution would balance Exhaustivity and Specificity limiting Overlap. Referring to such measures, we will show important properties of YAANII against BLINKS and SearchWebDB. In all frameworks a solution is a set of paths even if they are retrieved in different ways. Given PT' the set of paths retrieved by

YAANII, *PT″* and *PT‴* respectively the paths explored by `SearchWebDB` and `BLINKS` we can say

$$PT' \subseteq PT'' \text{ and } PT' \subseteq PT'''$$

While `SearchWebDB` and `BLINKS` consider all paths matching a keyword, YAANII can exclude some path *pt* even if it matches the query due to the presence of a path *pt′* that subsumes *pt*. Moreover all the approaches share a common criteria: paths with the highest score correspond to the most relevant information to retrieve. Therefore if we apply the same criteria but in different stages of the exploration of a solution, the result will be affected by the different behavior. In `BLINKS` and `SearchWebDB` the paths of a solution are directly computed by the nodes matching a keyword. In YAANII the clustering aims to group paths with similar templates. In other words, in different clusters there are not only different kinds of paths but probably also paths matching different keywords of the query. `BLINKS` and `SearchWebDB` try to maximize the number of matching element into a solution. The former leads to enrich a solution with an high level of detail, the latter provides query templates with different levels of detail whereby the user has to make a choice. In an automatic process (i.e. without human participation) `SearchWebDB` presents a behavior similar to `BLINKS`. Differently, YAANII tries to provide solutions with the most relevant linked elements through a *core* level of detail. If a more detail matches the query (i.e. the detail is relevant to the user), it will result in a separate solution. Then we conclude the following: (i) YAANII can build a solution even if it does not match some of the keywords. This capability supports the user unaware with both the domain of interest and information unavailability; (ii) `BLINKS` mainly privileges the Exhaustivity while `SearchWebDB` the Specificity. YAANII satisfies Specificity providing first of all the core answer and reaches the Exhaustivity by returning additive details in the next results; and (iii) YAANII cannot build overlapped solutions despite of `SearchWebDB` and `BLINKS`.

In the next section we provide a case study to bear out the considerations presented in this section.

A Comparative Study

Let's consider an ontology of reference, as shown in Fig. 8.1. It describes the concept of *Conference* where it is possible to *publish* a *Paper*. A *Conference* has a *name* while a *Paper* presents a *title*. A *Person* can be the *author* of a *Paper* published in a *Conference* or the em reviewer in a *Program Committee*. Each *Person* presents a *fullname*. In Fig. 8.2 it is depicted an instance corresponding to the ontology. We used the short names *URI1, URI2, URI3, URI4* as URIs to simplify the notation.

Now we define two queries: $Q_1 = \{$`Atzeni, CAISE, author`$\}$ and $Q_2 = \{$`CAISE, Atzeni, author`$\}$. Both the queries contain the same keywords but

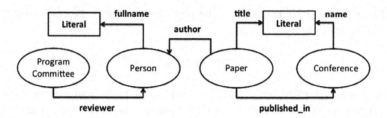

Fig. 8.1 An ontology of reference

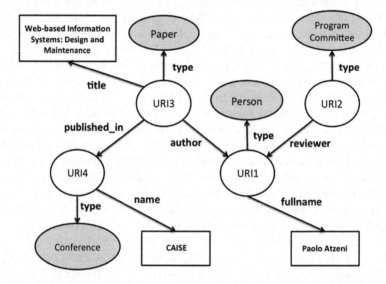

Fig. 8.2 The corresponding case study

submitted in different orders. This means that the keywords will have different weights (i.e. relevance) in Q_1 and Q_2. We assume a decreasing weight with respect to the presentation order. Therefore Q_1 = {Atzeni [1], CAISE [0.7], author [0.49]} and Q_2 = {CAISE [1], Atzeni [0.7], author [0.49]}. It means that in the first query Q_1 the user is interested to know information about Paolo Atzeni in the conference CAISE where he is author (in case). In the second query Q_2, the user would know information about the conference CAISE where there is Paolo Atzeni that is author (in case).

We would study the behavior of BLINKS, SearchWebDB and Yaanii in this context. BLINKS starts to compute the partitioning of the data graph depicted in Fig. 8.2. The partitioning results the set of blocks shown in Fig. 8.3. We obtain three blocks **b1**, **b2** and **b3** connected between them by the portals $v1$ and $v10$. On top of this partition, BLINKS builds the bi-level indexing described in Fig. 8.4.

b1
v7
v6
Paper
Web-based Information Systems: Design and Maintenance
type
title
URI 3
Published_in
v1
v2
URI 4
name
type
v4
v5
Conference
CAISE
b2
Program Committee
v9
v8
v1
Person
type
UR13
URI 2
v10
type
author
reviewer
URI 1
v3
fullname
v11
Paolo Atzeni
b3
URI 2
v10
b1 out-portal: {v1}
b2 out-portal: {v10}
b2 in-portal: {v1}
b3 in-portal: {v10}

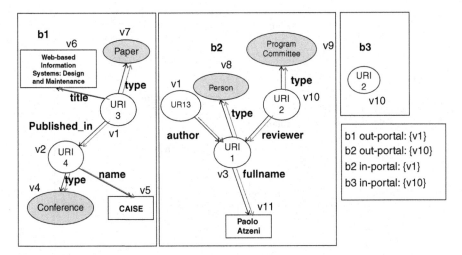

Fig. 8.3 BLINKS partitioning

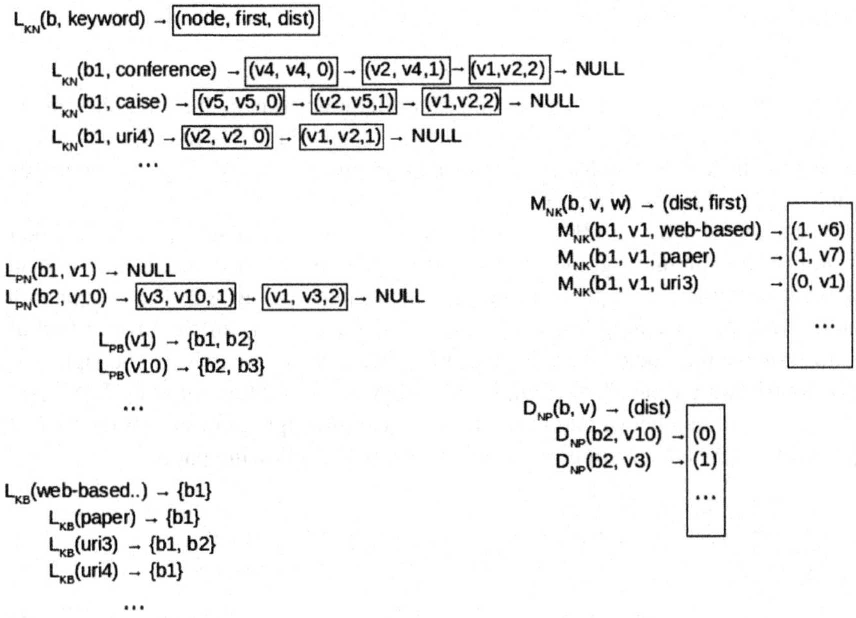

L_KN(b, keyword) → (node, first, dist)
L_KN(b1, conference) → (v4, v4, 0) → (v2, v4,1) → (v1,v2,2) → NULL
L_KN(b1, caise) → (v5, v5, 0) → (v2, v5,1) → (v1,v2,2) → NULL
L_KN(b1, uri4) → (v2, v2, 0) → (v1, v2,1) → NULL
...
M_NK(b, v, w) → (dist, first)
M_NK(b1, v1, web-based) → (1, v6)
M_NK(b1, v1, paper) → (1, v7)
M_NK(b1, v1, uri3) → (0, v1)
...
L_PN(b1, v1) → NULL
L_PN(b2, v10) → (v3, v10, 1) → (v1, v3,2) → NULL
L_PB(v1) → {b1, b2}
L_PB(v10) → {b2, b3}
...
D_NP(b, v) → (dist)
D_NP(b2, v10) → (0)
D_NP(b2, v3) → (1)
...
L_KB(web-based..) → {b1}
L_KB(paper) → {b1}
L_KB(uri3) → {b1, b2}
L_KB(uri4) → {b1}
...

Fig. 8.4 Bi-level INdex

We submit the query Q_1. Figure 8.5 provides the solutions generated by BLINKS. The computation starts exploring the graph from the nodes $v5$ and $v11$ and the goes on backward for six iterations. At the end of the sixth iteration a first solution S_1 having the root in v_1 is generated. The score of this solution is 4. Going

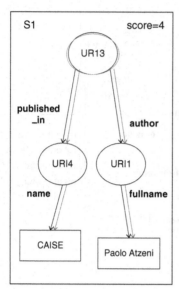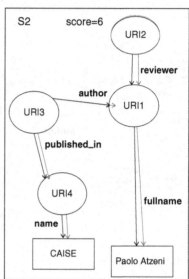

Fig. 8.5 BLINKS solutions

back to the search algorithm, after other four iterations (i.e. at the tenth one) and by crossing the out-portal v_1 a second solution S_2 rooted in $v10$ is found. The score of S_2 is 6. Following the same procedure, also submitting the query Q_2 we obtain the same set of solutions S_1 and S_2.

Let's consider SearchWebDB and the query Q_1. The first step is the augmentation of the summary graph once a query is submitted. In the left side, Fig. 8.6 depicts the summary graph resulting from the instance of Fig. 8.2. The computation starts from the matching keyword nodes $v5$, $v6$ and $v7$. Then we have to find all paths connecting nodes to $v5$, $v6$ and $v7$ by a backward search. In the right side Fig. 8.6 shows the resulting augmented summary graph. Let consider $N = 3$ as the maximum number of output solutions. Executing eight iterations of the TOP-N procedure, we obtain a solution S_1 composed by the following paths

```
Author-Paper
CAISE-name-Conference-published_in-Paper
Paolo Atzeni-fullname-Person-author-Paper
```

The root of S_1 is the node $v1$ (i.e. *Paper*). Following the iterations, at the 12th the algorithm provides a second solution S_2 by merging the following paths:

```
Author-Paper-published_in-Conference
CAISE-name-Conference
Paolo Atzeni-fullname-Person-author-Paper-Conference
```

The root of S_2 is the node $v3$ (i.e. *Conference*). At the 13th iteration SearchWebDB returns the third solution S_3 by merging the following paths:

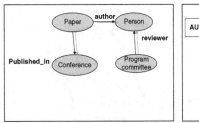

Fig. 8.6 (Augmented) summary graph

```
Author-Paper-author-Person
Paolo Atzeni-fullname-Person
CAISE-published_in-Paper-author-Person
```

The root of S_3 is $v2$ (i.e. *Person*). The computation goes on finding lower scored solutions until a branching of the search space is done. Now these solutions are mapped to conjunctive queries to be submitted to the user. The choice of the user will be computed in a DBMS to result the final solutions. In this case all three conjunctive queries would have to return the same result, that is the subgraph S_1 of BLINKS, shown in Fig. 8.6. Also for the query Q_2 we have the same behavior (i.e. result).

Let's refer now to Yaanii. In the graph of Fig. 8.2 there are two roots that are nodes with labels URI3 and URI2. For both Q_1 and Q_2, Yaanii will compute the following informative paths

```
pt1 : [URI3-published_in-URI4-name-CAISE]
pt2 : [URI3-author-URI1-fullname-Paolo Atzeni]
pt3 : [URI2-reviewer-URI1-fullname-Paolo Atzeni]
pt4 : [URI3-author-URI1]
```

Since pt4 is subsumed by pt2, pt4 will be discarded. Therefore we have three clusters CL1, CL2 and CL3 containing respectively pt1, pt2 and pt3. With respect to Q_1, Yaanii assigns the following scores: pt1 [1,31], pt2 [4,55] and pt3 [1,83]. In this way we have the following ranking between clusters: [CL2, CL3, CL1]. Since Paolo Atzeni is the keyword more relevant and pt2 matches two keywords (including Paolo Atzeni), pt2 is the most important path, following pt3 and pt1. In Fig. 8.7 there is the resulting solution $S1'$ (that is the unique solution).

Yaanii starts from the cluster CL2 extracting the path pt2 that represents the core of $S1'$. Then we go to CL3 extracting pt3 and we try to include it into $S1'$. In this case the structural weight of the solution introduce a new root, so it complicates the topology of the solution. However pt3 contains a keyword with high relevance (that is Paolo Atzeni) and for this reason it will be included in $S1'$. At the end we have pt1 that could complicate (less) the topology of $S1'$ but bringing a new keyword (that is CAISE) it can be included in the solution. The resulting $S1'$

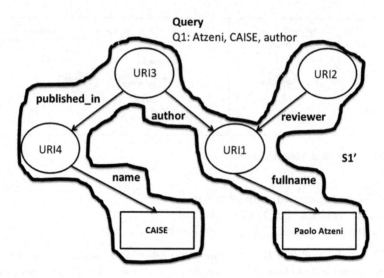

Fig. 8.7 Yaanii solution to Q_1

presents information of Paolo Atzeni that is both author and reviewer in the CAISE conference. If we consider the query Q_2, we have to evaluate again the score of pt1, pt2 and pt3. The result is pt1 [1,88], pt2 [3,85] and pt3 [1,23]. In this case we rank the clusters as follows: [CL2, CL1, CL3]. This is due to the more relevance of the keyword CAISE with respect to Paolo Atzeni. In Fig. 8.8 we show the resulting solutions $S1$ and $S2$ matching Q_2. In this case Yaanii starts from CL2, extracts pt2 and include it into the core solution $S1$. Then it extracts pt1. Since pt1 matches the keyword more relevant (i.e. CAISE) and does not complicate (too much the topology of $S1$, it can be included in $S1$. Since pt3 would introduce a new root (i.e a more complex topology) and matches a keyword less relevant (i.e. Paolo Atzeni), it can not included in $S1$ and it will represent a new solution $S2$.

Comparison. Summing up, this case study highlights the different behavior between the traditional ranking of BLINKS and SearchWebDB and the novel strategy of Yaanii. In detail, BLINKS privileges the exhaustivity of results. With respect to Q_1, the solution S1 is incomplete while S2 matches perfectly the query submitted. In this situation we have an impressive overlap: S1 is subsumed by S2. Whereas with respect to Q_2 the solution S1 matches Q_2 while S2 presents information not so relevant to the user. Also in this case the overlap is decisive. SearchWebDB privileges the specificity of results. For both Q_1 and Q_2 the result is the solution S1 provided by BLINKS. Referring to Q_2, the solution S1 is incomplete because the answer doesn't contain information about Paolo Atzeni as reviewer. In this case the exhaustivity of result is not completely satisfied. Referring to Q_2 the solution matches perfectly the user query. In both cases SearchWebDB doesn't present overlap. An interesting result is that BLINKS

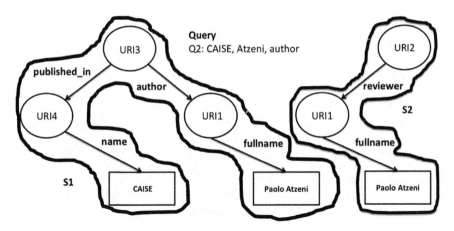

Fig. 8.8 Yaanii solutions to Q_2

and SearchWebDB return the same answer to both queries. This is due to the fact that they apply the ranking after the generation of the set of possible solutions. In this way the linked components of a solution are independent of the keywords weight until the solution is completely generated. Differently from that systems, Yaanii points to balance exhaustivity and specificity. It provides different answers to Q_1 and Q_2. In the first case our system returns a complete answer where Paolo Atzeni is both reviewer and author in the conference CAISE. In this case the result satisfies both exhaustivity and specificity. In the other case Yaanii provides two solutions S1 and S2. The first solution S1 represents the core answer (i.e. Paolo Atzeni is author in the conference CAISE), satisfying the specificity. The second solution S2 completes the previous result S1 (i.e. Paolo Atzeni is also a reviewer), satisfying the exhaustivity.

Experimental Results

In this section we provide experiments to asses our thesis. We evaluated the performance of BLINKS, SearchWebDB and YAANII. Since it has been commonly used for keyword search evaluation, we employ the public available DBLP (i.e. in RDF) monthly updated dataset, about computer science publications. We exploit the benchmark proposed in [1]. It implements eight test queries. Differently by the query test set used by BLINKS and SearchWebDB, including keywords matching only resources (nodes) in the graph, this test set refers to both resources and properties in the dataset. In the three frameworks we executed the queries over the entire DBLP dataset to obtain the Top-10 answers.

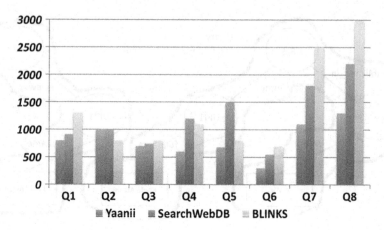

Fig. 8.9 Performance evaluation

Efficiency Evaluation. In order to study the efficiency, we performed the queries on the same DBLP data set and we measured both the time needed for query computation and the time needed for query processing. In particular we used the 1,000 BFS graph indexing [3] for BLINKS. In Fig. 8.9 we show the final results. The vertical axis presents the average query processing time (i.e. in ms) and the horizontal axis the queries. YAANII outperforms relevantly the other systems. In particular YAANII exploits the increasing size of a query (i.e. number of keywords) to speed-up the ranking evaluation. Instead, the increasing size of a query makes complex the graph exploration step of SearchWebDB. Since BLINKS considers only the labels on the nodes, such systems evaluated only the keywords matching resources (e.g. 'paolo atzeni', 'torlone') while skipped the keywords matching properties.

Effectiveness Evaluation. To guarantee the effectiveness, we have asked colleagues to submit keyword queries to the system and evaluate the results. In particular (30) people from several departments of Computer Science faculties of different International Universities participated. To evaluate the effectiveness of the generated answers we used a standard IR metric called *Reciprocal Rank* (RR) defined as RR $= 1/r$, where r is the rank of the most relevant answer. Then we evaluated the average of the RR (MRR) scores obtained from the thirty participants. Figure 8.10 shows the results. YAANII obtained the best MRR (i.e. the value 1) in all queries. The first resulting solution was always the most relevant. SearchWebDB is comparable only in such queries where keywords matching a resource (i.e. a node) are selective while queries with keywords matching a huge amount of properties influences relevantly the rank of the answers. BLINKS presents low MRR values due to not consider the labels on the properties in the query processing.

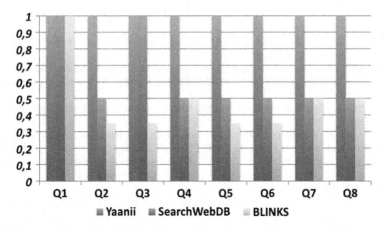

Fig. 8.10 Effectiveness evaluation

Conclusions and Future Works

We have precisely described the computational complexity of three representative approaches to keyword based search over graph structures. We have identified reference measures that allow comparison of computational complexity. Our results show that YAANII shows the lowest computational cost among the approaches considered, which is an indication of the potentiality behind the intuition in YAANII. The more desirable relevance is in term of Exhaustivity and Specificity among the approaches considered. A lower complexity means that the approach is less susceptible to variations of the keyword search setting and can leverage on the scoring function to define completeness answers without irrelevant information. From a theoretical point of view, future directions focus on improving both the search algorithm of YAANII to reach a linear time complexity and the scoring function by using a more sophisticated keyword weight algorithm.

References

1. De Virgilio R, Cappellari P, Miscione M (2009) Cluster-based exploration for effective keyword search over semantic datasets. In: ER 2009, Gramado
2. De Virgilio R, Giunchiglia F, Tanca L (eds) (2010) Semantic web information management: a model-based perspective. Springer, Berlin/Heidelberg
3. He H, Wang H, Yang J, Yu PS (2007) Blinks: ranked keyword searches on graphs. In: SIG-MOD, Beijing
4. Hristidis V, Gravano L, Papakonstantinou Y (2003) Efficient IR-style keyword search over relational databases. In: VLDB, Berlin
5. Kacholia V, Pandit S, Chakrabarti S, Sudarshan S, Desai R, Karambelkar H (2005) Bidirectional expansion for keyword search on graph databases. In: VLDB, Trondheim

6. Kazai G, Lalmas M (2005) INEX 2005 evaluation measures. In: INEX Workshop on Element Retrieval Methodology, pp 16–29
7. Kazai G, Lalmas M, de Vries A (2004) The overlap problem in content-oriented XML retrieval evaluation. In: SIGIR, Sheffield
8. Knuth DE (1997) The art Of computer programming, vol 1, 3rd edn. Addison-Wesley, Boston
9. Lalmas M, Tombros A (2007) INEX 2002–2006: understanding XML retrieval evaluation. In: DELOS, Pisa
10. Liu F, Yu CT, Meng W, Chowdhury A (2006) Effective keyword search in relational databases. In: SIGMOD, Chicago
11. Piwowarski B, Dupret G (2006) Evaluation in (XML) information retrieval: expected precision-recall with user modelling (EPRUM). In: SIGIR, Seattle
12. Radev DR, Qi H, Wu H, Fan W (2002) Evaluating web-based question answering systems. In: Proceedings of the 3rd international conference on language resources and evaluation (LREC'02), Las Palmas
13. Singhal A (2001) Modern information retrieval: a brief overview. IEEE Data Eng Bull 24: 35–43
14. Singhal A, Buckley C, Mitra M (1996) Pivoted document length normalization. In: SIGIR, Zurich
15. Tran T, Wang H, Rudolph S, Cimiano P (2009) Top-k exploration of query graph candidates for efficient keyword search on rdf. In: ICDE, Shanghai
16. Voorhees EM (1999) The TREC-8 question answering track report. In: Proceedings of the 8th text retrieval conference (TREC-8), Maryland

Chapter 9
ReadFast: Structural Information Retrieval from Biomedical Big Text by Natural Language Processing

Michael Gubanov, Linda Shapiro, and Anna Pyayt

Abstract While the problem to find needed information on the Web is being solved by the major search engines, access to the information in Big text, large-scale text datasets, and documents (Biomedical literature, e-books, conference proceedings, etc.) is still very rudimentary (Lin and Cohen (2010) A very fast method for clustering big text datasets. In: ECAI, Lisbon). Thus, keyword-search is often the only way to find the needle in the haystack. There is abundance of relevant research results in the Semantic Web research community that offers more robust access interfaces compared to keyword-search. Here we describe a new information retrieval engine that offers advanced user experience combining keyword-search with navigation over an automatically inferred hierarchical document index. The internal representation of the browsing index as a collection of UFOs (Gubanov et al. (2009) Ibm ufo repository. In: VLDB, Lyon; Gubanov et al. (2011) Learning unified famous objects (ufo) to bootstrap information integration. In: IEEE IRI, Las Vegas) yields more relevant search results and improves user experience.

Introduction

While the problem to find needed information on the Web is being quite successfully solved by the major search engines, access to the information in Big text, large-scale text datasets, and documents (Biomedical literature, e-books, conference proceedings, etc.) is still very rudimentary [38]. Currently, keyword-search

M. Gubanov (✉) · L. Shapiro
University of Washington, Seattle, WA, USA
e-mail: mgubanov@uw.edu; shapiro@uw.edu

A. Pyayt
Stanford University, Stanford, CA, USA
e-mail: pyayt@stanford.edu

T. Özyer et al. (eds.), *Information Reuse and Integration in Academia and Industry*,
DOI 10.1007/978-3-7091-1538-1_9, © Springer-Verlag Wien 2013

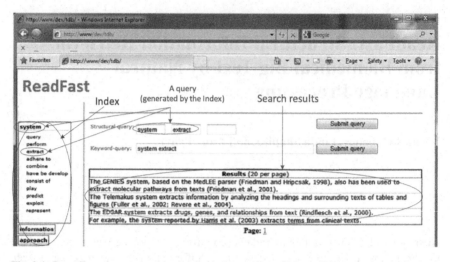

Fig. 9.1 READFAST browser and navigation index constructed for a 600-page reference book on Biomedical Informatics. A user navigates over the terms *system* and *extract* to learn more about recent Biomedical information extraction systems discussed in the book

(exact substring match) is a de-facto standard for search over text documents (e.g. Microsoft Word, Adobe PDF). Although simple and easy to use, keyword-search returns either too few relevant or too many irrelevant search results, and it is difficult to correct due to its inflexibility. For example, consider finding all information extraction systems discussed in a 600-page reference book on Biomedical Informatics using keyword search. One can first try the separate queries *system, extract, information* to get more substring matches and better coverage, but they would return hundreds of mostly irrelevant results; the longer query *information extraction system* and other permutations of these tokens would return one-two relevant matches or none at all. After that, nothing is left but reading or skimming through the entire relevant parts of the book.

Nevertheless, most of the current research on search is devoted to WWW, Web 2.0, and personal resources, and it cannot be directly applied to search over large documents. In contrast searching at Web scale, search on a smaller scale – in a book allows leveraging the context of the book to improve search relevance. This context is defined by the book's area/domain (e.g. medicine, biology, software) and the main concepts of the domain being discussed. It can be represented as a domain/concept index and leveraged to facilitate more advanced structural text search. In fact, several recent venues highlighted structural search over text as an area of growing interest to the information retrieval research community [2, 3, 17, 19, 23–25, 47].

In this paper, we propose a new information retrieval engine that simplifies access to needed information inside large documents and books (in the Biomedical domain). Figure 9.1 illustrates the interface of this system (READFAST (RF)) that was made possible by recent advances in Natural Language Parsing (NLP), Machine

Table 9.1 Populated system UFO in XML

```
<System SO_simf="GENIES system|Telemakus system|EDGAR system|..">
 <Query SO_simf="Query|Ask|Question|Inquire|.." />
 <Perform SO_simf="Perform|Do|Execute|Work|.." />
 <Extract SO_simf="Extract|Get|Obtain|.." />
 ...
</System>
```

Learning, and Data Management. RF automatically analyzes large texts and creates
a hierarchical document summary based on the document's domain and the main
concepts being discussed. The left frame in Fig. 9.1 depicts this index automatically
constructed for a 600-page book on Biomedical Informatics describing different
state-of-the-art software systems. The most important concepts that are discussed
end up on the top of the list. We can see from this index that the book addresses
topics such as *Systems*, *Approaches*, and *Models* without even opening it. By picking
concepts from the index, the user can read only highly relevant document content
compared to what would have been returned by a standard *keyword*-search.

Naturally, one of the key challenges here is *automatic* extraction of this hierarchical index to access the document. In general it is a very hard problem, because
there are many different domains and data representations. Therefore, even the
state-of-the-art information extraction systems, Semantic Web search-engines, and
other solutions usually focus on a specific domain, a subset of objects, extraction
patterns, a specific corpus or another reasonable limitation to make *fully automatic*
extraction feasible.

The second challenge is providing a convenient browsing interface for the
extracted information. Often the extracted objects, their actions or properties are
named differently in the document by nature of natural language expression. It might
be the syntactic difference – two terms being synonyms in the specific context,
for example *provide* and *offer*; a shorter reference to the same object, for example
system for *information extraction system*; or another reason to differently name the
same object in the context of the document. By representing the entities in the index
as UFOs [24, 25] we conceal all these differences under a standard search interface
shown to the user, thus simplifying access to the document. At the same time, each
UFO accumulates all the different names, so it can use them at query time to return
more results to the user. Table 9.1 illustrates a fragment of the *System* entity from the
browsing index from Fig. 9.1 represented internally as a UFO. More UFO examples
are available in [24, 25].

RF automatically extracts the hierarchical index from any English text using
Natural Language Processing and uses it to provide a browser for the document
that can return more relevant document content. Alternatively, a user can get the
same search results by using the search interface on the right in Fig. 9.1. It allows
the concept and its actions to be entered separately. This interface might be more
convenient when the user is already familiar with the book and knows the concepts
she is looking for. At the same time, navigation allows users to get a higher-level
impression of what the book is about and to dive into details only when interested.

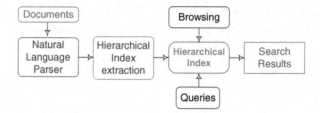

Fig. 9.2 READFAST (RF) architecture. Loading of a document into RF repository starts with NLP parsing and extracting its hierarchical browsing index. Next, a pre-processed document representation is stored in the repository. The user browses and queries the document using the extracted hierarchical index

It is the first hybrid NLP-based navigational engine that is capable of automatically constructing this specific index of concepts/actions for any natural language text. With this tool, users save time by gaining access to all relevant portions of the text without reading substantial parts of it first.

Architecture

Figure 9.2 illustrates the READFAST (RF) architecture. While importing a text document into its repository, RF automatically extracts its hierarchical browsing index using a natural language parser [34] and an `extraction` module on top of it. The information in the RF document repository is accessed by users through the extracted index using a user-friendly interface (Fig. 9.1) that supports both *browsing* and *search*. A brief description of each of the RF components is given in more detail below.

Hierarchical Index: `Entities` in the extracted index are the main objects discussed in the text (i.e. `Pedestrian, Driver, Bicyclist` for the drivers manual) and the `attributes` are their main actions (e.g. *Turn, Signal, Yield*). See the next section for more details.

User interface: RF offers a user-friendly interface (Fig. 9.1) that provides convenient browsing and search over the document. First, the user can click on the left frame (top left corner) to select a document repository (e.g. `MedInf` for the Medical Informatics book) and to see its navigation index. When the user clicks on the entity (e.g. `System`), it expands to reveal its attributes (e.g. `query, perform, extract`). When the user picks the entity or the attribute, RF queries the repository and returns all sentences in the document that have subject (and) predicate in their linguistic normalized root form equal to the entity (and) attribute. Later on, the user can select another entity or submit a manually composed query in the right frame.

Table 9.2 Entities
extracted from Washington
state drivers manual and a
Web server user manuals.
Attributes extracted for
the Washington's Driver
entity

Washington tables

vehicle, **driver**, sign, lane, license, bicyclist, light,
tire, people, drug, manual, pedestrian, person,
rider, alcohol, area, brake, condition, drink, . . .

Apache tables

directive, server, apache, client, request, document,
configuration, header, variable, argument, url,
log, script, command, string, directory, handler,
certificate, browser, . . .

Driver attributes

have, see, pay, share, take, dispose of, fail, find, go,
learn, pass, obey, seem, sit, steer, tend, yield, . . .

Implementation: A UNIX machine with Intel Core 2 Duo 2.8 GHz CPU
and 2 GB memory was used for experiments. READFAST stores and queries the
post-processed document and its index using Galax native-XML data storage.
RF parses the sentences using a state-of-the-art natural language parser [34]. Thanks
to significant progress in natural language processing, most recent NLP parsers are
accurate and fast enough for practical applications. Parsing usually took several
minutes or less depending on the document size. The RF query processor and user
interface are implemented in DHTML and AJAX.

Index Extraction

First, plain text is parsed using a linguistic dependency parser to extract
{subject, predicate, object} triples in the root form from each
sentence [34]. Next, the top subjects by frequency, are defined to be Entities
in the index. Similarly, for each top subject, its main predicates are defined by its
Attributes. Table 9.2 illustrates main entities and attributes extracted from a
drivers manual and a Web server manual.

Often the extracted objects and their actions are named differently in the
document by nature of natural language expression. Thus we represent entities in
the index as UFOs [24, 25] that accumulate all different ways to name objects and
their actions. The system uses them at query time to return more search results.
Table 9.1 illustrates a fragment of *System* entity from the browsing index from
Fig. 9.1 represented internally as a UFO.

Experimental Setup

READFAST takes a large text, automatically infers its index and provides structural
browsing and search capabilities.

For evaluation purposes, all source documents, user queries, extracted indexes, and query answers are stored in a database. MySQL on a 64-bit UNIX machine with Intel i7 2.6 GHz CPU and 8 GB memory was used for this purpose. Several real test corpuses from large to medium size in different domains. Size as well as domain were intentionally varied.

- Software manuals (SFWT) A collection of software manuals, $\approx$ one million terms.
- Novels (NOV) A collection of novels, $\approx$ 400,000 terms.
- Drivers manuals (MAN) A collection of drivers manuals for different U.S. states, $\approx$ 60,000 terms.

Measures: The standard measures: *Recall, Precision, F-measure, TF/IDF* (Term Frequency/Inverse Document Frequency), and *NDCG* (Normalized Discounted Cumulative Gain) were used for evaluation. Given S_1 – a set of results that outputs READFAST and S_2 – a set of answers in the *golden standard*, *Recall, Precision, F-measure* are defined as follows: $R = \|S_1 \cap S_2\|/\|S_2\|$, $P = \|S_1 \cap S_2\|/\|S_1\|$, $F = 2 \times R \times P/(R + P)$.

A standard technique to extract main terms from a document in a collection is TF/IDF [33]. This weight is a statistical measure used to evaluate how important a word (term) is to a document in a collection or corpus. The importance increases proportionally to the number of times a word appears in the document, but is offset by the frequency of the word in the corpus. Variations of the TF/IDF weighting scheme are often used by the Vector Space Model [44] to assign weights to documents' terms and derive overall documents' similarity.

$$w_{ij} = tf_{ij} \times \log(N/df_i),$$

- tf_{ij} – number of occurrences of term i in document j
- df_i – number of documents containing i
- N – total number of documents in a collection

NDCG is a standard IR search relevance measure used to assess how fast a user would find needed information. It was introduced by Järvelin and Kekäläinen [32] and is intensively used in IR benchmarks (e.g. TREC). It is also employed by major search engines to track and improve Web-search ranking quality.

Similarly to the F-measure it is a combined measure of precision and recall. The important difference, however, is that it gauges not only the quality of the answers, but also their relative *order* in the returned result set. Thus, the top result contributes to the overall NDCG score the most, the second one less, the third even less, and so on. Additionally, NDCG rewards highly relevant answers more than marginally relevant ones.

During the evaluation, the answers in a result set for each query are labeled by an independent annotator on a relevance scale from (5) "Perfect" to (2) "Poor".

Table 9.3 Term extractor(TE) and TF/IDF performance. TE outperforms TF/IDF in all domains by both precision and recall

Corpus	P_{TE}	R_{TE}	$P_{TF/IDF}$	$R_{TF/IDF}$
SFWT	0.57	0.8	0.30	0.47
MAN	0.50	0.66	0.40	0.53
NOV	0.62	0.70	0.52	0.57
AVG	0.57	0.72	0.41	0.52

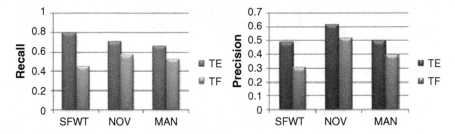

Fig. 9.3 Term extraction (*TE*) recall and precision compared to TF/IDF

NDCG rewards perfect labels the most, good ones less, and poor ones even less. NDCG is computed for each query and averaged over all test queries.

Index Extraction Evaluation

The extraction algorithm takes as input a document and outputs its *index* that can be used for navigation. The most important for navigation are *entities* in this index as they represent the most important document terms (see Fig. 9.1 on the left). READFAST *Term Extractor (TE)* is a part of *index extraction* algorithm, and it is evaluated using *Precision, Recall, and F-measure* information retrieval measures using test sets from several domains. To evaluate *TE* two independent annotators were asked to compose a *gold-standard* test set by manually picking main terms from the test corpus. Then *TE*'s precision, recall, and F-measure were computed based on this *gold standard*.

Results: Table 9.3 demonstrates that *TE* outperforms TF/IDF in all domains. In general accurate term extraction is a very hard problem, because of a term's variety in different domains. We can see that for specialized texts (i.e. SFWT is more specialized than NOV corpus) TF/IDF – a purely statistical measure performs worse than it does for the general purpose texts. By contrast, *TE*'s performance surprisingly remains almost the same regardless of the corpus.

Figures 9.3 and 9.4 sheds more light on *TE*'s and TF/IDF's performance in SFWT domain. Recall is varied over the x-axis by taking top results based on their rank.

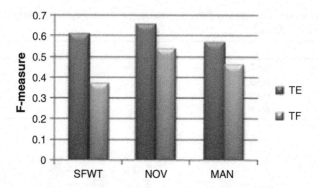

Fig. 9.4 Term extraction (*TE*) f-measure compared to TF/IDF

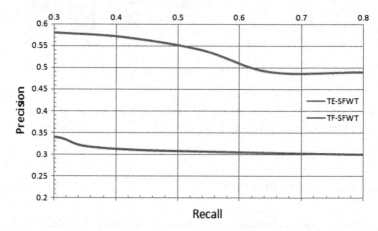

Fig. 9.5 Term extraction (*TE*) performance for SFWT domain. The *TE* significantly outperforms TF/IDF

For example, to calculate *TE* precision for recall = 80 %, the terms that give 80 % recall are pre-selected. Then, precision for these terms is calculated.

It is unlikely that some unsupervised method would have the same performance regardless of the domain, similar to human intelligence. Nevertheless, we can see from these results that a linguistic measure – *TE* by leveraging the sentence structure performs better than a purely statistical method – TF/IDF (Fig. 9.5).

READFAST *Search Relevance Evaluation*

The majority of Web search-engines return a page of ordered links to the Web-pages most relevant to the user's query. Since there are usually too many pages returned to look at, the goal is to rank the web pages according to their relevance to the

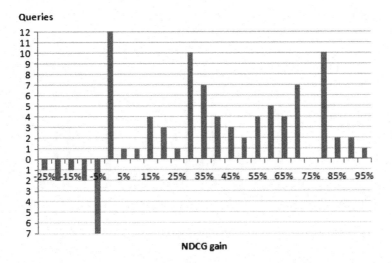

Fig. 9.6 NDCG gain distribution over all queries

user's query and display the most relevant pages on the top. Ideally, the best match comes first, followed by the second best, and so on. Similarly, in large texts users want to read sentences most *relevant* to their query, but not a random sentence just *mentioning* a word from the query.

Because relevance of returned search results is critical for any search engine, it must be measured regularly using a special metric – Normalized Discounted Cumulative Gain (NDCG) [4] and compared with other search-engines' scores. The NDCG score reflects how close is the order of returned search results for a set of queries to the ideal ordering (i.e most relevant result first, less relevant second, etc.).

We conducted a series of experiments to measure READFAST (RF) search-relevance gain over the de-facto standard keyword-search (e.g. Microsoft Word, Adobe Acrobat, Apple Safari, etc.). Search relevance is traditionally evaluated using a manually labeled subset of search corpus on a pre-selected representative static set of queries [4]. We used 100 different queries on a subset of the test corpus manually pre-labeled by an independent annotator in order to calculate NDCG. The test set consisted of 110,000 natural language sentences composed from different domains including fiction, computer science, electronics, cars, etc.

Two independent annotators were given specific pre-defined labeling instructions to guarantee labeling quality of {query, sentence} pairs and alleviate subjectivity. They were asked to assign a label from 2 (poor) to 5 (excellent) to {query, sentence} pairs and only the labels, where the annotators agreed were included in the test set. Both annotators worked independently and did not have access to each other's results. Next, we ran keyword-search and RF search on the test queries and computed NDCG for both sets of returned sentences. The total NDCG gain over computed for all test-set queries was about 30 % which is significant. Finally, Figs. 9.6–9.8 illustrate NDCG gain distribution over all, 1-term, and 2-term test-set

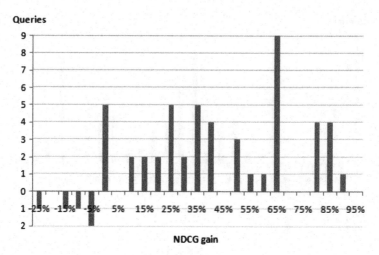

Fig. 9.7 NDCG gain distribution over 1-term queries

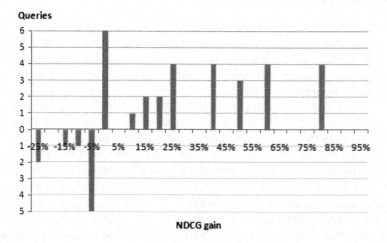

Fig. 9.8 NDCG gain distribution over 2-term queries

queries, respectively. The number of queries is varied over the y-axis (positive in both directions), whereas the RF NDCG gain is varied over the x-axis.

Related Work

Overall, the systems leveraging document structure to improve user search experience can be (roughly) classified into the following groups: Languages for wrapper development, HTML-aware tools, NLP-based tools, Wrapper-induction tools, Modeling-based tools, and Ontology-based tools.

One of the first initiatives to improve search by extracting structure and tagging was the development of languages designed to help assist users in constructing wrappers [7,14,26,30,35]. These languages were proposed as a better option to Perl, Java, and other languages widely used for this task. HTML-aware tools [15,39,43] before extraction parse the HTML document into a DOM-tree. Later on, the tree is used to apply extraction rules that are either designed manually or generated semi-automatically. NLP techniques have been used mainly for named-entity tagging of fixed number of classes or for question-answering of specific question types [8, 11, 22, 46, 47]. Wrapper induction tools generate delimiter-based rules derived from training data [7, 9, 14, 26]. The generated wrappers usually heavily rely on the HTML encoding present in the training data. Modeling-based tools given a target structure (e.g. tuples, lists) try to locate it in Web-pages [1, 37, 42]. These tools differ from the previous group by having a pre-defined set of modeling primitives (tuples, lists, etc.). Ontology-based tools [20, 48] leverage an existing application-specific ontology to locate constants present in the page and construct objects with them.

Trying to generalize wrapper induction (i.e. make less dependent on HTML tagging from training corpus) Brin in [9] introduced an algorithm to extract simple relations from the Web that are similar to a small "training set" of pairs (e.g. $\ll author, title \gg$). The basic idea was to match a given set of tuples against web pages to generate a general pattern that can be further bootstrapped to retrieve more results. In [2] Agichtein extended this idea by using named-entity tagging (e.g. location, organization), weighting and confidence metrics to compose better patterns. Downey et al. in [19] suggested using learned patterns as extractors and discriminators to improve extraction coverage and accuracy.

Banko et al. in [8] described a question-answering system reformulating the specific questions into likely substrings of declarative answers to the question and submitting them to Google. For example, for "Where is the Louvre Museum located" the reformulations will be "+the Louvre Museum +is located", "+the Louvre Museum +is +in", "+the Louvre Museum +is near", etc. Ask.com is, probably, the most widely known commercial question-answering system that also works by reformulating specific questions and matching the resulting phrases against the Web.

Etzioni et al. in [21] extracts hyponym relation from Web pages by using domain independent patterns (cf. Hearst [28]). Crescenzi in [15] tries to generalize wrapper generation by matching dynamically generated HTML pages of data-intensive web sites (e.g. online book stores) and approximating the underlying database schema. Mindnet [49] is, probably, the most general system to automatically construct an approximation of a semantic network [16] that is a graph representing semantic relationship between words.

Semantic desktop search, Deep-Web search, vertical search, Dataspaces, EntityRank, ExDBMS, Libra, [10, 12, 13, 18, 38, 40, 41] attempt to query and index collections of Web and personal data but the extraction techniques are less general. Therefore, their extracted structures and search results differ significantly from READFAST navigational index and search results respectively.

READFAST is more general in that it is neither restricted to a specific wrapper format, HTML DOM-tree structure, HTML/XML tagging conventions, pre-defined classes of named-entities, nor aims to extract a given relation or answer specific types of questions.

There is also prior work on different flavors of graph-oriented text- and RDF-search [6, 8]. SPARQL-like languages are geared more towards graphs than schemas and treat ranking as a second-class citizen. Other methods operate on text nodes in a graph and also do not have an explicit navigational index. In contrast, READFAST offers an index – a higher-level abstraction derived from the lower-level structures that is leveraged to provide a more convenient user experience.

DISCOVER and DBXplorer [5, 29] are the examples of *keyword*-search over a relational database that leverage a graph of foreign-key relationships. More recent work in this direction is focused more on efficiency optimization rather than introducing richer features [27, 45].

Finally, [36] is a survey of web data extraction approaches and tools. Reference [31] is a search-engine that leverages NLP to resolve part-of-speech-, phrasal-, and contextual ambiguity and provide better search experience.

Conclusion

We demonstrated the first hybrid NLP search/navigation engine for Big text, large-scale text datasets and documents that is capable of constructing the document concept/action index on the fly using NLP [38]. Our experiments justify that it provides more relevant search-results compared to document keyword-search for specific classes of queries. Having both navigational and search interfaces adds flexibility depending on the user's familiarity with the document and interest in diving into more details. Finally, in contrast with keyword search and simple reading, ReadFast's two interfaces (navigational and search), balance the time and effort the users might want to put into the search task with their familiarity with the document and interest in the fine details. For first-time users, navigation helps gain higher-level insight into their main concepts from the text without reading too much, while more familiar users can quickly write queries that produce precise and exhaustive results in their specific search tasks.

References

1. Adelberg B (1998) NoDoSE – a tool for semi-automatically extracting structured and semistructured data from text documents. In: SIGMOD record, Seattle
2. Agichtein E, Gravano L (2000) Snowball: extracting relations from large plain-text collections. In: ACM DL, San Antonio
3. Agichtein E, Ipeirotis P, Gravano L (2003) Modeling query-based access to text databases. In: WebDB, San Diego

4. Agichtein E, Brill E, Dumais S (2006) Improving web search ranking by incorporating user behavior information. In: SIGIR, Seattle
5. Agrawal S, Chaudhuri S, Das G (2002) Dbxplorer: a system for keyword-based search over relational databases. In: ICDE, San Jose
6. Anyanwu K, Maduko A, Sheth A (2007) Sparq2l: towards support for subgraph extraction queries in rdf databases. In: WWW, Banff
7. Arocena GO, Mendelzon AO (1998) Weboql: restructuring documents, databases, and webs. In: ICDE, Orlando
8. Banko M, Brill E, Dumais S, Lin J (2002) Askmsr: question answering using the worldwide web. In: EMNLP, Philadelphia
9. Brin S (1998) Extracting patterns and relations from the world wide web. In: EDBT, Valencia
10. Cai Y, Dong XL, Halevy A, Liu JM, Madhavan J (2005) Personal information management with semex. In: SIGMOD, Baltimore
11. Califf ME, Mooney RJ (1998) Relational learning of pattern-match rules for information extraction. In: AAAI, Madison
12. Chakrabarti S (2007) Dynamic personalized pagerank in entity-relation graphs. In: WWW, Banff
13. Cheng T, Yan X, Chang KCC (2007) Entityrank: searching entities directly and holistically. In: VLDB, Vienna
14. Crescenzi V, Mecca G (1998) Grammars have exceptions. J Inf Syst (Special issue on Semistructured Data) 23(9):539–565
15. Crescenzi V, Mecca G, Merialdo P (2001) Roadrunner: towards automatic data extraction from large web sites. In: VLDB, Roma
16. Crestani F (1997) Application of spreading activation techniques in information retrieval. Artif Intell Rev 11:453
17. Diederich J, Balke WT, Thaden U (2007) Demonstrating the semantic growbag: automatically creating topic facets for faceteddblp. In: JCDL, Vancouver
18. Dong X, Halevy A (2007) Indexing dataspaces. In: SIGMOD, Beijing
19. Downey D, Etzioni O, Soderland S, Weld D (2004) Learning text patterns for web information extraction and assessment. In: AAAI, San Jose
20. Embley DW, Campbell DM, Jiang YS, Liddle SW, Ng YK, Quass D, Smith, RD (1999) Conceptual-model-based data extraction from multiple-record web pages. Data Knowl Eng 31:227–251
21. Etzioni O, Cafarella M, Downey D, Kok S, Popescu A, Shaked T, Soderland S, Weld D, Yates A (2004) Web-scale information extraction in knowitall. In: WWW, Manhattan
22. Freitag D (1998) Machine learning for information extraction in informal domains. Ph.D. thesis, Carnegie Mellon University
23. Gubanov M, Shapiro L (2011) Using unified famous objects (ufo) to automate Alzheimer's disease diagnosis. In: IEEE BIBM, Atlanta
24. Gubanov MN, Popa L, Ho H, Pirahesh H, Chang P, Chen L (2009) Ibm ufo repository. In: VLDB, Lyon
25. Gubanov M, Shapiro L, Pyayt A (2011) Learning unified famous objects (ufo) to bootstrap information integration. In: IEEE IRI, Las Vegas
26. Hammer J, McHugh J, Garcia-Molina H (1997) Semistructured data: the TSIMMIS experience. In: Proceedings of the East-European workshop on advances in databases and information systems, St. Petersburg
27. He H, Wang H, Yang J, Yu PS (2007) Blinks: ranked keyword searches on graphs. In: SIGMOD, Beijing
28. Hearst MA (1992) Automatic acquisition of hyponyms from large text corpora. Technical report S2K-92-09
29. Hristidis V, Papakonstantinou Y (2002) Discover: keyword search in relational databases. In: VLDB, Hong Kong
30. Hsu CN, Dung MT (1998) Generating finite-state transducers for semi-structured data extraction from the web. J Inf Syst (Special issue on Semistructured Data) 23(9):521–538

31. http://www.infocious.com
32. Järvelin K, Kekäläinen J (2000) IR evaluation methods for retrieving highly relevant documents. In: SIGIR, Athens
33. Jones KS (1972) A statistical interpretation of term specificity and its application in retrieval. J Doc 60:493–502
34. Klein D, Manning C (2007) Fast exact inference with a factored model for natural language parsing. In: NIPS, Vancouver
35. Kushmerick N (2000) Wrapper induction: efficiency and expressiveness. Artif Intell 118:15–68
36. Laender A, Ribeiro-Neto B, Silva A, Teixeira J (2002) A brief survey of web data extraction tools. In: SIGMOD record, Madison,
37. Laender AHF, Ribeiro-Neto B, da Silva AS (2002) Debye – date extraction by example. Data Knowl Eng 40(2):121–154
38. Lin F, Cohen WW (2010) A very fast method for clustering big text datasets. In: ECAI, Lisbon
39. Liu L, Pu C, Han W (2000) XWRAP: an XML-enabled wrapper construction system for web information sources. In: ICDE, San Diego
40. Madhavan J, Cohen S, Dong X, Halevy A, Jeffery S, Ko D, Yu C (2007) Navigating the seas of structured web data. In: CIDR, Asilomar
41. Nie Z, Ma Y, Shi S, Wen JR, Ma WY (2007) Web object retrieval. In: WWW, Banff
42. Ribeiro-Neto BA, Laender AHF, da Silva AS (1999) Extracting semi-structured data through examples. In: CIKM, Kansas City
43. Sahuguet A, Azavant F (2001) Building intelligent web applications using lightweight wrappers. Data Knowl Eng 36:283–316
44. Salton G, Wong A, Yang C (1975) A vector space model for automatic indexing. Commun ACM 18:613–620
45. Sayyadian M, LeKhac H, Doan A, Gravano L (2007) Efficient keyword search across heterogeneous relational databases. In: ICDE, Istanbul
46. Sekine S (2006) On-demand information extraction. In: COLING/ACL, Sydney
47. Soderland S (1999) Learning information extraction rules for semi-structured and free text. Mach Learn 34:233
48. Udrea O, Getoor L, Miller RJ (2007) Leveraging data and structure in ontology integration. In: SIGMOD, Beijing
49. Vanderwende L, Kacmarcik G, Suzuki H, Menezes A (2005) Mindnet: an automatically-created lexical resource. In: HLT/EMNLP, Vancouver

Chapter 10
Multiple Criteria Decision Support for Software Reuse: An Industrial Case Study

Alejandra Yepez Lopez and Nan Niu

Abstract In practice, many factors must be considered and balanced when making software reuse decisions. However, few empirical studies exist that leverage practical techniques to support decision-making in software reuse. This paper reports a case study that applied SMART (Simple Multi-Attribute Rating Technique) to a company that considered reuse as an option of re-engineering its web site. The company's reuse goal was set to maximize benefits and to minimize costs. We applied SMART in two iterations for the company's software reuse project. The main difference is that the first iteration used the COCOMO (COnstructive COst MOdel) to quantify the cost in the beginning of the software project. In the second iteration, we refined the cost estimation by using the COCOMO II model. This combined approach illustrates the importance of updating and refining the decision support for software reuse. The company was informed the optimal reuse percentage for the project, which was reusing 76–100 % of the existing artifacts and knowledge. Our study not only shows that SMART is a valuable and practical technique that can be readily incorporated into an organization's software reuse program, but also offers concrete insights into applying SMART in an industrial setting.

Introduction

Software reuse is the use of existing artifacts and knowledge in order to produce new software products [8]. The goal of software reuse is to improve software quality and productivity [7, 14, 21, 24], because reuse offers a lot of advantages, such as reduced development time, increased reliability, reduced risk, and enforced standards [14]. One of the major disadvantages of reuse is related to cost. The cost of doing software

A.Y. Lopez (✉) · N. Niu
Department of Computer Science and Engineering, Mississippi State University, Starkville, MS 39762, USA
e-mail: ay68@msstate.edu; niu@cse.msstate.edu

T. Özyer et al. (eds.), *Information Reuse and Integration in Academia and Industry*,
DOI 10.1007/978-3-7091-1538-1_10, © Springer-Verlag Wien 2013

reuse (e.g., codifying reusable assets and retrieving an asset for reuse) is most of the time twice the cost of creating a new software product from scratch [8].

Reusable assets include procedures, knowledge, documentation, architecture, design and code [26]. An asset can be reused to a certain extent given the amount of reusable content, attributes of the asset, and costs. It can be thus inferred that there should be a percentage of reuse that maximizes benefits, minimizes costs, and at the same time balances off other factors. Indeed, the identification of this optimal reuse percentage requires a multiple criteria decision making technique that helps to select the best alternative(s).

SMART (Simple Multi-Attribute Rating Technique) [10] is a pragmatic aid to decision-making and has been applied to cases involving a complex problem where a lot of information needs are to be handled simultaneously. The central idea of SMART consists of decomposing the problem into small parts and analyzing each part individually. This is the main reason that decision-making with SMART has been very helpful given the large amount of alternatives with multiple benefits, costs, and conflicting goals in most of the information systems [13].

Although decision tools have been applied to information systems in general [27], we are aware of no empirical studies that view software reuse as a multi-criteria decision-making problem and leverage practical techniques to support such a decision-making process. To shorten this gap, we applied SMART to a company that considered reuse to be an option of re-engineering its web site. Our goal is to investigate to what extent SMART helps the company to identify the optimal reuse percentage. The contributions of our work lie in the vision of treating software reuse as a multi-criteria decision-making problem, the quantification of reuse-related factors, the instantiation of SMART stages, the iteration of cost estimations, and the derivation of the final reuse decision. This paper also reports our insights and recommendations for the practitioners who consider the application of multi-criteria decision-making techniques for their software reuse programs.

Background

SMART Technique

Most of the decisions in software information systems involve a lot of specific criteria and they can vary depending on the subjective world of the decision maker. However, due to the costs and difficulties associated with creating or updating an information system, most organizations prefer to conduct an objective systematic analysis of multiple benefits and costs before taking any decision [19].

SMART has a series of stages that indicate how the decision maker will behave in a rational way [10, 16, 33]. It is important to clarify some basic concepts. Objective is defined as a parameter that shows the preferred direction of movement, e.g., common objectives can be to minimize costs or maximize benefits [10]. An attribute is used to measure anything related to an objective. Other important concepts are value and utility. For each alternative, there is a numerical score to measure its attractiveness to the decision maker; if the decision involves risk, we will refer to this score as the "utility of the course of action [10]".

There are eight main stages in SMART. The first stage consists of identifying the decision maker(s). The second stage is identifying the alternative courses of action. Stage 3 is to identify the attributes which are relevant to the decision problem, and then for each attribute, assign values to measure the performance of the alternatives of that attribute (stage 4). Stage 5 consists of determining a weight for each attribute; then for each alternative, calculating the weighted average of the values assigned to that alternative (stage 6). In stage 7, a provisional decision is made, and if needed, it is analyzed using sensitivity analysis in the final stage [10, 16].

Description of the Organization

The subject of this study is a research organization based on the health and economic issues of one region in the southeast of the United States with the help of the academic, public service and government sectors. To allow this company to be anonymous, it will be called SRo throughout this paper. SRo requires interdisciplinary contributions from various professions, disciplines and educational organizations in order to accomplish its research programs and practices. SRo is interested in collaborating with researchers to investigate ways of improving its services in general and its software development in particular.

Currently, SRo is using an information system web site that has not fully met its needs. This system is divided in two parts, the first focuses on providing information about the research projects, programs and initiatives, resources, partners and news that is publicly accessible on the Internet. The second part is an internal system, which is used by administrators of SRo in order to update the information about press releases and news shown on the public site. The web site was designed and implemented by a third-party web site development agency, and the cumulative investment in this product was about $10,000. The contract with this agency was terminated since the operation of the system has shown many defects that could not be easily fixed; fixing these bugs originated high costs that were not expected by SRo. For this reason, one programmer has been hired in order to fix the defects with the help of the users and customers of SRo. However, the web site has many design and development issues to be fixed in a short period of time (e.g., within 3 months as originally envisioned by SRo). At this moment, some SRo management and development team have been thinking of reusing some portions of the existing web site instead of creating a completely new web site from scratch.

Applying a multiple criteria decision model (e.g., SMART) is necessary to decide the best project alternative in terms of the amount of reuse needed. For SRo, the alternatives of selection concern the optimal reuse percentage. At the same time, each alternative has several evaluation attributes or criteria. In this study, two evaluation criteria, benefits and costs, will be considered. This is mainly because SRo, especially its management, is interested in these practical concerns.

Description of the Current Web Information System

Internally, the current web site has a common file-based library where all the resources are stored. Each module of the web site is located in a specific folder in the library, and each folder contains all the files associated with that module. There are seven modules including research projects, programs and initiatives, resources, partners, news, press releases and admin. These modules are the sections of the web site and provide relevant information about SRo.

There is also a template folder in the library that contains the common user interface (UI) design that is used to modify the visual effect of each module of the web site. The current UI design is consistent among modules. There is a menu bar on the left, a search field on the top, an "About this web site" button located in a panel on the top of the window, a right side bar with links to research projects, and an image header and footer with information about the organization. There is a common database with 29 tables where information about news and press releases is stored and managed by the administrator through the internal web system.

Methodology

The study done in [14] categorizes reusability efforts into four types. Following that, software reuse in this paper will be based on building new systems from existing reusable components (third type) and building new systems with future reuse in mind (fourth type) since the existing system's components can be considered for reuse. Documentation is not considered as an attribute since there is currently not any available documentation.

SMART 1 & 2: Identify the Decision Maker and Alternatives

The ultimate decision maker is SRo management. The executive decision makers are programmers and customers who present internal and external viewpoints of SRo's web site respectively. It is these executive decision makers that are the focus of our case study.

After consulting with SRo's decision makers, we identify four alternatives according to the ranges of reuse percentage. The first alternative is in the range of 0–5 % of reuse, which means building the web site mostly from scratch. The

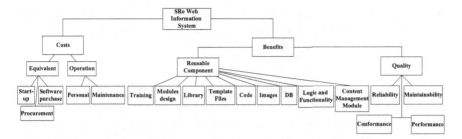

Fig. 10.1 A value tree

second alternative is 6–45 % of reuse; it means that the web site will be built based on a small proportion of reused components from the existing web site. The third alternative is 46–75 %; it consists of reusing most part of the current site. And the last alternative, 76–100 %, indicates reusing almost everything.

Stage 3: Identify the Relevant Attributes

This stage focuses on addressing the attributes that the decision maker considers important for the decision. There is no restriction on the number of attributes to be set [10]. A good practice is to break down each general attribute into more specific attributes by building a value tree [10]. Figure 10.1 shows the final value tree generated after several rounds of analysis of the attributes for each course of action. The costs were calculated based on the development and maintenance time; the unit is based on calendar months. The benefits were generally classified in two ways: reusable components and quality. The attributes are described in detail as follows.

Costs

The costs are divided in equivalent and operation costs. The equivalent corresponds to one-time costs like startup, software purchase and procurement. Startup is related with the costs of the operating system and host, and the cost of communication equipment installation. Software purchase includes the web and programming languages development tools. Procurement corresponds to equipment purchase and installation, and lease costs.

The operation corresponds to continuing costs, which includes the cost of hiring a programmer and project manager in order to reuse the web site. The personal cost also includes the cost for becoming familiar with the components, for catalog the reusable components and research support [24], and for re-engineering of existing work products in order to be reusable in the future [21]. System maintenance is the cost of maintaining the system after the alternative or course of action has been taken. It includes the addition, update or removal of features after the system is launched.

Benefits: Reusable Component

These benefits are the reused components that will generate the web system desired by the customer. *Training* is the process for a user to learn to manage the site. This factor in reuse is indispensable [14]. *Modules design* is the design and code shared by all the modules in a common library [15]. The *library* is the directory where all the source code is located and centralized; it makes reuse more efficient [14]. The *template files* have the content of each component of the web page; for example, header and footer. The *code* is the programming code. It is important to determine if the code is systematically intended in order to count its number of lines and identify the meaning of each module and the variables it uses [15]. *Images* are used to decorate the design view, and can be reused from the current one or be created from scratch. The *database* contains the information about the press releases and news of the web page. *Logic and functionality* are the general functions and logic of the site. It includes the way that modules are interconnected with each other and the function of buttons and links and their implementations. The *content management module* improves the administration of the current site by the user and adds more functionality to it.

Benefits: Quality

This kind of benefits is described in terms of desired quality attributes of the system. *Reliability* is an essential attribute since the users should trust that everything shown in the web site has been check through authority and authentication. Non-pertinent and confidential information shall not be released to the public. *Maintainability* refers that the system shall be easy to modify in the future. *Conformance* indicates that the system must conform to user's requirements and standards. *Performance* implies that the system shall be responsive and reactive to user interactions [21].

Stage 4: Determine a Weight for Each Attribute

Once the attributes of the system are identified, the next stage is calculating the value for each one and assigning values to measure the performance of the different alternatives [10].

Table 10.1 Number of lines of code per alternative of reuse

Sections of site (Number of lines)	% of reuse			
	0–5	6–45	46–75	76–100
Research projects	1,400	1,100	700	300
Programs and initiatives	1,800	1,400	720	400
Resources	400	350	100	50
Partners	2,700	2,200	1,100	500
News	5,500	4,400	3,500	2,450
Press releases	200	150	80	30
Admin	7,000	4,800	3,500	2,100
Template folder	1,000	600	300	170
Total	20,000	15,000	10,000	6,000

Costs Estimation

The costs were estimated using the COCOMO (COnstructive COst MOdel) [2, 11] and are expressed in calendar months [2, 18]. The model was very useful to assess the development time associated with the creation or reuse of the current system in general. It is based on the estimation of the number of lines of code (LOC) and four parameters selected according to the project characteristics. The formula of the COCOMO model predicts the effort and duration of a software project based on variables related to the size of the resulting system and the cost that affects productivity. The model provides an algorithm for estimating the software cost, and uses a basic regression formula with parameters derived from historical data and project characteristics [2, 18].

The basic COCOMO model takes the form of the equations shown in Eqs. (10.1) and (10.2) [2, 11, 18, 30]. In this formula, a_b, b_b, c_b and d_b are parameters, and KLOC is a software metric used to measure the size of a software program and is expressed in term of thousands of lines of code [11, 18, 30]. This model can be applied to our study since the system under our investigation can be categorized as an "organic project", which is characterized by small teams with good experience working in less rigid requirements [11].

$$\text{Effort Applied} = a_b(KLOC)^{b_b} \quad \text{[man-months]} \tag{10.1}$$

$$\text{Development Time} = c_b(\text{Effort Applied})^{d_b} \quad \text{[months]} \tag{10.2}$$

In order to calculate the lines of source code that are delivered, the project was broken down by the seven sections of the website and the template files (stylesheet, JavaScript, flash files, and images). The approach to decompose the structure of a project is essential to a successful estimation [31]. Results from our case study are expressed in Table 10.1. The estimation for the first option, 0–5 % of reuse, was done analyzing the number of lines of the current project. The number of lines for the other options was estimating by all the experts in the projects. During numerous

Table 10.2 Costs per alternative of reuse

	% of reuse			
	0–5	6–45	46–75	76–100
KLOC (Thousand of lines)	20	15	10	6
Development time (months)	12	10	9	7
Maintenance (months)	1	3	5	8
Cost (months)	13	13	14	15

iterations, these estimations were compared and discussed until a final choice was agreed [20, 30].

Referring back to the COCOMO equations, the selected parameters already standardized are $a_b = 2.4$, $b_b = 1.05$, $c_b = 2.5$ and $d_b = 0.38$ [11, 30]. The costs of start-up that includes the cost of operating system and host, the procurement costs (actual equipment purchase and equipment installation cost), and the costs of application software purchase are the same for all the alternatives of this study; for this reason, they are not reflected in the costs associated with it. In addition, the costs of electricity and place (rent of a local place) are not necessary since the programmer could work from home. However, the costs of personnel, including hiring a programmer and project manager, are included. The system maintenance is also included since it varies depending on the level of reuse given to the system. These costs are calculated using the COCOMO equations with prior approval from SRo management. Results of the cost calculation of the alternatives can be found in Table 10.2.

Measure Alternatives on Each Benefit

During this stage, values are derived to measure how well each alternative of reuse performs on each benefit [10, 33]. However, the reuse benefits are usually hard to be represented by quantifiable variables. In this case, the technique applied to measure is a direct rating based on "an internal scale, which allows only intervals between points to be compared" [10]. The alternatives are ranked for each attribute using a scale from 0 as the lowest rank to 100 as the highest. Then the consistency is checked by comparing the raking between the alternatives [10]. Table 10.3 shows the ranking collaboratively achieved by SRo's programmer and customers. In addition, these stakeholders complete a survey about some of the benefits previously explained. The survey helps determine stakeholders' perceptions of each benefit and reactions to the potential change of the benefit. Note that the stakeholders are asked to express their opinions only on relevant benefits, e.g., the internal programming features are relevant only to the programmers. The survey results are analyzed by coding and categorizing the different benefits. Table 10.4 summarizes the results, which provide qualitative evidence for the weights used in Table 10.3.

Table 10.3 Weights of benefits per alternative of reuse

Benefits	Alternatives – % of reuse			
	0–5	6–45	46–75	76–100
Reusable component				
Training	0	60	90	100
Modules design	5	80	90	100
Library	0	70	20	0
Template files	100	90	40	20
Code	30	40	90	100
Images	0	10	70	100
Database	0	20	80	90
Logic and functionality	50	40	60	70
Content management module	100	50	40	30
Quality				
Reliability	60	20	10	30
Maintainability	80	70	60	50
Conformance	50	10	10	50
Performance	90	80	20	10

It is important, at this stage, to leverage the strategy of using the two extremes, 100 and 0, to designate the most preferred benefit and the least preferred one respectively [10]. For example, "Images" reuse under the fourth alternative (76–100 % of reuse) shows the most preferred benefit and is thus assigned a value of 100. On the contrary, the "no reuse" or "creating the images from scratch" alternative (0–5 % of reuse) will not be beneficial since many high-quality images exist already in SRo's system.

Stage 5: Determine Weight of Benefits

At this point, the values for each attribute needs to be combined in order to obtain the overall benefits which each alternative has to offer; "this may reflect how important the attribute is to the decision maker" [10]. The best way to do this is to determine a weight per benefit that shows its importance to the analyst [33]. This technique is called swing weights [10]. It consists of "asking the decision maker to compare a change (or swing) from the least-preferred to the most-preferred value on one attribute to a similar change in another attribute" [10]. The rank of the benefits in our case study is shown in Table 10.5. The first column represents the choices that range from the most-preferred to the least-preferred. The middle column represents original weights. The last column is the result of dividing the weighted benefit by the total and then multiplying by 100. The result is rounded to the nearest whole number.

Table 10.4 Summary of subjective evaluation of the web site

Benefit	Evaluation	Answer	Result
Module design	Conformance with the current overall interface design	Somewhat dissatisfied and neutral	The overall result shows dissatisfaction with the current design but satisfaction with changing it, and it is very dissatisfied with creating it new. The fourth alternative (76–100 % reuse) is mostly preferred, so it was rated 100
	Current "Admin" module's design	Somewhat dissatisfied	
	Design of the modules of the web site	Satisfied	
	Conformance of changing the general interface design	Satisfied	
	Accordance about changing the "Admin" design	Satisfied	
	Compliance of creating a new interface design	Dissatisfied and neutral	
	Idea of creating a new design of the "Admin" module	All responded very dissatisfied	
Images	Current images of the web site	Somewhat satisfied	Mostly somewhat satisfied with images
	Accordance about changing the images	Somewhat satisfied and neutral	
	Conformance of creating new images	Very dissatisfied	
Logic and functionality	Overall logic	Somewhat dissatisfied	Preference of reusing the logic is greater than creating it
	Current quality of the general functionality	Very dissatisfied	
Content mgmt.	Conformance with the idea of creating a new module	Somewhat satisfied	Creating a new module is mostly preferred

Reliability	Current reliability	One responded very dissatisfied; others responded neutral	Alternative one is preferred; the next two decrement; the fourth one is perceived more preferred than the previous two
Conformance	General conformance with the web site	Somewhat dissatisfied and neutral	The first and last alternative has the same preference (somewhat dissatisfied) with changing and creating a new web page
	Conformance with the idea of changing the current site	Somewhat dissatisfied	
	Idea of creating a new web site from scratch	Somewhat dissatisfied	
Performance	Current speed of the web site	Neutral and satisfied	Speed can be improved by creating a new site
Maintenance	Current maintenance tools	Half very dissatisfied and satisfied	It is preferred to create a new module; but there is also preference for reusing it
	Change of the current maintenance tools		

Table 10.5 Normalized weights of benefits

New benefit's organization	Original weight	Normalized weight
Conformance to user	100	17
Logic & functionality	90	15
Performance	80	13
Reliability	65	11
Code	50	8
Modules design	45	7
Template files	40	6
Maintainability	38	6
Library	30	5
Database	27	5
Content management module	25	4
Images	10	2
Training	4	1
Total	602	100

Stage 6: Calculate the Weighted Average of Each Alternative

The weighted average of the values assigned to each alternative is calculated. This means it is possible to find out how well each alternative of reuse performs in overall by combining the value score allocated to the benefits of an alternative with the overall weight's benefit. For each alternative, the procedure is to multiply each normalized weight (Table 10.5) by the benefit's weight for that alternative.

Then, these values are added and divided by 100; this will be the aggregate value for each option.

Stage 7: Data Collection and Analysis

In this study, the data has been collected and analyzed using different qualitative methods such as interviews, observations, artifact analysis, meetings with the customers and project manager of SRo, and surveys filled out by them. The interviews and survey were done to the members of SRo (customers and project manager) and were transcribed in order to analyze the information. The artifact analysis is based on the study of the current web site, its directories, and all the source code files. The meetings were done on-site and by phone with the members of SRo; all of them were also transcribed.

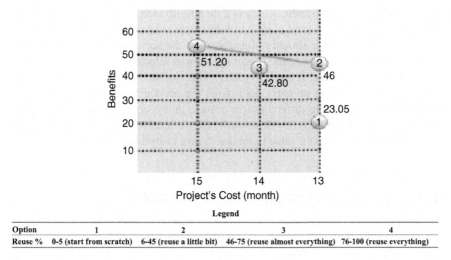

Fig. 10.2   Plot of costs vs. benefits per alternative (using COCOMO)

Results

Provisional Decision and Sensitivity Analysis

After the costs and benefits are calculated, they are compared to inform the decision maker. In order to do this, a chart is drawn in the benefits–costs coordinates. The benefits' aggregate value needs to be plotted against the cost for each alternative [10]. In Fig. 10.2, the higher benefit is located on the top of the Y-axis and the lower cost is located on the right of the X-axis. Thus, the higher an alternative of reuse is on the benefit scale and the further to the right on the cost scale, the more attractive it will be. Since the first and the second option have the same cost, the second option is chosen because it has higher benefit. Option three is not considered since it has fewer benefits and a higher cost than the second option. However, the fourth alternative can be also selected. Thus, the pre-selected alternatives are the second and fourth. They "are said to lie on the efficient frontier" [10]. This frontier is shown in Fig. 10.2 with a cut line.

The plot shown in Fig. 10.2 is informative for the decision maker to select a choice based on the main objective: maximize benefits and minimize costs. Such a selection will depend on the relative weight that this person attaches to [10]. In this case study, the decision has to be made on a common accordance between the programmer and SRo's customers. However, it is possible to be unsure to decide between the two pre-selected options. In this case, another approach can be taken [10]: in Fig. 10.2, a move from the option 2 to 4 will lead to an increase in the value of benefits from 46 to 51.20, an amount of 5.2; however, it will lead to an increase in costs of 2 months. Therefore, each one-point increase in the value of the benefits will cost 0.38 months, which is 2 months divided by 5.2 proportions of the benefits [10]. So, if one extra point worth less than 0.38 months to the customer of SRo, the decision maker should rationally select the second option. After meeting with the SRo's management, the fourth option was selected for costs associated to COCOMO. This means: *reuse everything*. This decision was taken based on the results explained where an extra point from the second to the fourth option will be worthwhile since the differences in costs is not a concern for the customers (0.38 months to be exact). In other words, the customers are willing to pay more than 11 days for each extra value point that "reuse everything" provides.

Refining the Cost Estimation with COCOMO-II

Upon the completion of the first iteration of our study, SRo's management was interested in the accuracy and reliability of the software reuse recommendation resulted from our analysis. This demand became particularly relevant once SRo began to adopt the "reuse everything" strategy. For this reason, we conducted a second iteration of our analysis by using a finer-grained cost model, COCOMO-II [3, 5, 23, 29, 30, 32]. Our objective was to confirm, refute, or update the findings drawn from the first iteration by taking some concrete reuse characteristics into consideration. We also expected the finer-grained study would shed further light on the practical decision support for an organization's software reuse program.

COCOMO-II is a refined cost estimation model that helps to determine the degree to which the number of lines of reused code is equivalent to the number of lines of new code, and serves as an estimation of costs based on that percentage of products built on already existing code [3,23,29,30,32]. The COCOMO-II model has been evaluated in many organizations and proved to be useful in examining and predicting the project costs across different domains [3, 23, 29, 30, 32]. Usually, an accurate estimation of the number of lines of code is difficult to obtain in early stages of the project due to the business and design decisions that have not been made [30]. However, as project data being accumulated (e.g., software size, engineer time, etc.), the management and development teams could fine tune the parameters in the model, which can also be facilitated through automated tool support [9].

In our case study, the application of COCOMO-II was made possible by including various artifacts, such as SRo's customer needs and requirements, rapid prototyping code, reusable component code and documentation, etc. The reuse models, such as the value tree shown in Fig. 10.1, was also helpful to qualitatively determine the effort magnitude required to apply reusable program code from previous projects [30, 32]. In this refined analysis stage, one of the main differences from COCOMO used in the first iteration was the use of scale factors for the modified code [5].

COCOMO-II models software reuse by using a nonlinear equation that involves the estimation of three factors: the proportion of design modified (DM), the percentage of the code modified (CM), and the proportion of effort required to

Table 10.6 Number of equivalent lines of code per alternative of reuse

Sections of site (Number of lines)	% of reuse			
	0–5	6–45	46–75	76–100
Research projects	1,400	1,321	963	446
Programs and initiatives	1,800	1,699	1,237	573
Resources	400	378	275	127
Partners	2,700	2,548	1,856	859
News	5,500	5,191	3,780	1,751
Press releases	200	189	137	64
Admin	7,000	6,606	4,811	2,228
Template folder	1,000	944	687	318
LOC	20,000	18,876	13,746	6,366
KLOC	20	18.9	13.8	6

integrated the reused code (IM) [5, 32]. This calculation is specified in Eq. (10.3). The equivalent code ESLOC is the new number of lines compare to the number of lines of reuse code to be modified. It is calculated following the Eqs. (10.4) and (10.5) [29]. These formulas were used in this study to estimate the adapted lines of code on each section of the web site depending on the level of reuse. For most results, the value was also calculated and computed from the average of percentages associated with different options of reuse: 0, 5, 25, 45, 60, 75, 88, and 100 %. ASLOC is the number of lines of reusable code, which must be modified [29]. The resulting ESLOC was also computed from the average of percentages associated with each option where SU is "Software Understanding", AA is "Assessment and Assimilation" and UNFM is "Unfamiliarity with Software". The values of these factors [30, 32] were extracted following the information provided in [4] for each section of the site and percentage of reuse. Table 10.6 shows the number of lines of code obtained for each option of reuse after calculating the equivalent lines of code.

$$AAF = 0.4DM + 0.3CM + 0.3IM \tag{10.3}$$

$$ESLOC = ASLOC(AA + AAF(1 + 0.02(SU)(UNFM)))/100, \text{ if } AAF <= 50 \tag{10.4}$$

$$ESLOC = ASLOC(AA + AAF + (SU)(UNFM))/100, \text{ if } AAF > 50 \tag{10.5}$$

$$PM_M = A(Size_M)^B \prod_{i=1to17} EM_i, \text{ where} \tag{10.6}$$

$$EM = RELY * DATA * CPLS * RUSE * DOCU * TIME * STOR * PVOL * ACAP * PCAP * PCON * APEX * PLEX * TLEX * TOOL * SITE * SCED$$

$$E = B + 0.01SFj, \text{ where } SFj = PREC * FLEX * RISK * TEAM * PMAT \tag{10.7}$$

Table 10.7 Costs per alternative of reuse

	% of reuse			
	0–5	6–45	46–75	76–100
KLOC (Thousand of lines)	20	18.9	13.8	6
Development time (months)	9.7	9.5	8.6	6.5
Maintenance (months)	2.4	5.8	7.2	8.6
Cost (months)	12.1	15.3	15.8	15.1

The COCOMO-II effort estimation model is calculated in Eq. (10.6) and is expressed as person-months (PM) [5, 12, 17, 23, 29, 30, 32]. A is a constant for calibration (A = 2.94) [5], E is equal to 1 and B is calculated from Eq. (10.7) [5]. Size corresponds to the equivalent thousand of source lines of code (EKSLOC). ΠEM is obtained from product attributes, Platform attributes, Personnel attributes, and Project attributes [23, 32]. Products attributes describe the environment where the code is built. The platform corresponds to the relations between the program and its host. Personnel attributes describe the experience and expertise of the developers of the system. Project attributes correspond to software management facets of the program. Scale factors are features that can increment or decrement the estimation of the economies. These values were selected from parameters shown in tables in [9, 23]. The cost in months of development is shown in Table 10.7, and they are computed using Eq. (10.8) [4].

$$T_{Dev} = cPM^d, \text{where } c = 3.67, d = 0.28 + 0.2[B - 1.01] \text{and} B = 1.1 \qquad (10.8)$$

$$SizeM = (size\ added + size\ modified)MAF, \qquad (10.9)$$

$$where\ MAF = 1 + (su/100 + UNFM)$$

The maintenance costs are related to the assessment of the parts of the system that may cause problems after the development and launch. It will generate high maintenance costs. These are calculated using the same equation shown previously in the COCOMO-II with the exclusion of SCED and RUSE for the calculation of EM [32]. Also, the size corresponds to the size of maintenance computed using Eq. (10.9) [32]. Table 10.7 shows the results in cost of maintenance.

The result of our updated analysis according to COCOMO-II is shown in Fig. 10.3. The preselected options, start from scratch (option 1) and reuse everything (option 4), were the focal points of discussion with SRo's stakeholders. From this updated analysis, a move from the option 1 to 4 would lead to an increase in the value of benefits from 23.05 to 51.20, an amount of 28.15 with a different of 3 months in costs. Each one-point increase in the value of the benefits would cost 0.1 months (3 days), which is 3 months divided by 28 proportions of the benefits. In this case, the fourth option, reuse everything, was confirmed to be an acceptable choice for the costs associated to COCOMO-II.

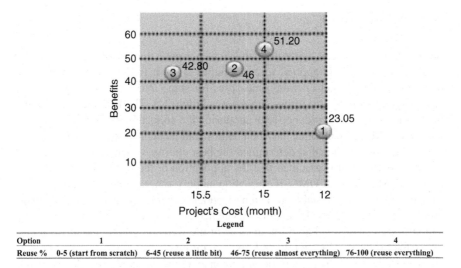

Fig. 10.3 Plot of costs vs. benefits per alternative (using COCOMO-II)

Related Work

In previously studies, SMART has been illustrated to guide measurement system decisions [33]. A multiple criteria decision model and the "Analytic Hierarchy Process" similar to SMART has been also applied as a multi criteria decision model to the selection of information systems projects [13, 27]. In addition, there are studies that has used and showed the importance of SMART as a multi criteria decision analysis in different areas of energy and environmental management and projects [1, 16, 22].

On the other hand, there have been efforts related to the analysis of costs and benefits of development of information systems and their operation [19], and studies based on software costs estimation models to help management decisions [2, 6, 28]. In addition, similar efforts have been focused on determining the costs of information systems based on domain architecture, and others on finding the costs of reuse and its effects on quality, maintainability and productivity [14, 21, 25].

The SRo study reported here shows how to integrate practical decision-making techniques into an organization's software reuse program. To the best of our knowledge, this study is the first to show SMART application as a multiple criteria decision model for software systems used with the goal of calculating the proportion of reuse needed to increase benefits at lower costs.

Threats to Validity

Several factors [34] can affect the validity of our case study. *Construct validity* is challenging when it is applied to case studies since it is used in the process of determining the correct operation measures for some attributes of a study. There are three tactics used to address construct validity [34]. The first tactic is the use of multiple sources of evidence relevant during the collection of data. In our study, the use of SMART technique has been helpful and its application has been used by observing other studies that determined the best alternative where many attributes were present [33]. It is assumed that the application of the SMART technique and the COCOMO and COCOMO-II estimation model has been done in the correct way. The second tactic is to establish a chain of evidence that is also important during the collection of data. The only chain of evidence is the selection of the alternatives and attributes, which is based on analysis of the web site's code and environment where the problem is located. In addition, the rating of each attribute can vary from study to study, since the perception of human assessing is subjective. However, this subjective construct has been the best measure of our case study. The last tactic is to have the draft case study report viewed by the people who provide the information. In this case, the customers and project manager of SRo has participated in our study in a regular basis, which helped address the construct validity.

Regarding *internal validity* [34], a limitation is the researchers' knowledge and experience about SMART, e.g., assigning utilities for each attribute per alternative. Another confounding variable is the interview and survey data. The SRo's personnel could have omitted relevant information about the web site or misunderstood the questions. This threat was mitigated by on-site ethnographic observations at SRo. At the same time, pre-defined qualitative data analysis was done by coding and categorizing the results collected from interviews and surveys.

The results of this study might not be generalized beyond the SRo's organizational conditions and its web-based information system, a threat to *external validity* [34]. However, it is our contention that SMART can be applied to other studies in the same way it was used here, though the experience of the decision maker will differ, as well as the definition of alternatives and assessment of the utilities.

Summary

Software reuse is an important area of software engineering that helps to improve quality and productivity. The decision of how much to reuse is often made by considering multiple criteria. In this paper, we have applied SMART to support a company's reuse decision making. The benefits and costs of software reuse were quantified, and two options were pre-selected for each cost model. For COCOMO-I, the first option was concerned with reuse of a small part (6–45 %) of the knowledge and artifacts; the second, reuse everything. We updated our analysis by using

COCOMO-II to cross-check the cost estimation. The results of the second iteration were in line with those of the first analysis, namely, the option of "reuse everything" was recommended. This effectively increased the organization's confidence of choosing a reuse program suited for its software projects.

From our experience, we feel that SMART is a valuable and practical technique that can be incorporated in an organization's software reuse program. More in-depth empirical studies are needed to address the limitations of our case study. Our future work also includes refining weight estimation with user's feedback and assessing inter-rater consistencies.

References

1. Bakus GJ, Stillwell WG, Latter SM, Wallerstein MC (1982) Decision making: with applications for environmental management. Environ Manage 6(6):493–504
2. Boehm BW (1981) Software engineering economics. Prentice Hall, Englewood Cliffs
3. Boehm BW et al (2000) Software cost estimation with COCOMO II. Prentice Hall, Upper Saddle River
4. COCOMO II Model Definition Manual (1999) ftp://ftp.usc.edu/pub/soft_engineering/COCOMOII/cocomo99.0/modelman.pdf. Accessed 27 Mar 2012
5. COCOMO II Model Definition Model (2000) Center for Software Engineering, University of Southern California. http://csse.usc.edu/csse/research/COCOMOII/cocomo2000.0/CII_modelman2000.0.pdf. Accessed 27 Mar 2012
6. Dillibabu R, Krishnaiah K (2005) Cost estimation of a software product using COCOMO II.2000 model – a case study. Int J Proj Manage 23(4):297–307
7. Frakes W, Pole BT (1994) An empirical study of representation methods for reusable software components. IEEE Trans Softw Eng 20(8):617–630
8. Frakes WB, Terry C (1996) Software reuse: metrics and models. ACM Comput Surv 28(2):415–435
9. Galorath DD, Evans MW (2006) Software sizing, estimation and risk management. Auerbach Publications/Taylor & Francis Group, Boca Raton
10. Goodwin P, Wright G (2004) Decision analysis for management judgment. Wiley, Chichester
11. http://en.wikipedia.org/wiki/COCOMO. Accessed 27 Mar 2012
12. http://www3.hi.is/pub/cs/2002-03/hv1/COCOMO/Help/Model/ModelPartII.html. Accessed 27 Mar 2012
13. Huizingh EKRE, Vrolijk HCJ (1995) Decision support for information systems management: applying analytic hierarchy process. Research report 95B26, The Netherland Universiteitsbibliotheek Groningen, Groningen
14. Incorvaia A, Davis RE (1990) Case studies in software reuse. In: Proceedings of the 14th annual international computer software and applications conference, Chicago, IL, USA, pp 301–306
15. Isoda S (1992) Experience report on software reuse project: its structure, activities, and statistical results. In: Proceedings of the 14th annual international conference on software engineering, Melbourne, Australia, pp 320–326
16. Jones M, Hope, Hughes CR (1990) A multi-attribute value model for the study of UK energy policy. J Oper Res Soc 41(10):919–929
17. Keil P, Paulish DJ, Sangwan RS (2006) Cost estimation for global software development. In: Proceedings of the 5th international workshop on EDSER, Shanghai, China, pp 7–10
18. Kemerer CF (1987) An empirical validation of software cost estimation models. Commun ACM 30(5):416–429

19. King JL, Schrems EL (1978) Cost-benefit analysis in information systems development and operation. ACM Comput Surv 10(1):19–34
20. Leung H, Fan Z (2006) Software cost estimation. Department of Computing, The Hong Kong Polytechnic University. ftp://cs.pitt.edu/chang/handbook/42b.pdf. Accessed 27 Mar 2012
21. Lim WC (1994) Effects of reuse on quality, productivity, and economics. IEEE Softw 11(5):23–30
22. Linkov I, Varghese A, Jamil S, Seager TP, Kiker G, Bridges, T (2004) Multi-criteria decision analysis: a framework for structuring remedial decisions at contaminated site. Comp Risk Assess Environ Decis Making 38(1):15–54
23. Lum K et al (2003) Handbook for software cost estimation. Jet Propulsion Laboratory, Pasadena
24. Noseck H (1994) Cost-benefit analysis for software-reuse – a decision procedure. In: First international Eurospace – Ada-Europe symposium on Ada in Europe. Springer, Copenhagen, Denmark, pp 397–405
25. Rothenberger MA, Nazareth D (2002) A cost benefit model for systematic software reuse. In: 10th European conference on information systems, pp 371–378
26. Rothenberger MA, Dooley KJ, Kulkarni UR, Nada N (2003) Strategies for software reuse: a principal component analysis of reuse practices. IEEE Trans Softw Eng 29(9):825–837
27. Santhanam R, Kyparisis J (1995) A multiple criteria decision model for information system project selection. Comput Oper Res 22(8):807–818
28. Sharma TN (2011) Analysis of software cost estimation using COCOMO II. Int J Sci Eng Res 2(6):1–5
29. Sommerville I (2000) Software engineering. Addison Wesley, Harlow
30. Sommerville I (2004) Software engineering. Addison Wesley, Bosto
31. Stellman A, Greene J (2005) Applied software project management, O'Reilly, Sebastopol
32. USC COCOMO II (2000) Software reference manual. University of Southern California. http://csse.usc.edu/csse/research/COCOMOII/cocomo2000.0/CII_manual2000.0.pdf. Accessed 27 Mar 2012
33. Valiris G, Chytas P (2005) Making decisions using the balanced scorecard and the simple multi-attribute rating technique. Perform Meas Metr 6(3):159–171
34. Yin RK (2003) Case study research: design and methods. Sage, Thousand Oaks

Chapter 11
Using Local Principal Components to Explore Relationships Between Heterogeneous Omics Datasets

Noor Alaydie and Farshad Fotouhi

Abstract In the post-genomic era, high-throughput technologies lead to the generation of large amounts of 'omics' data such as transcriptomics, metabolomics, proteomics or metabolomics, that are measured on the same set of samples. The development of methods that are capable to perform joint analysis of multiple datasets from different technology platforms to unravel the relationships between different biological functional levels becomes crucial. A common way to analyze the relationships between a pair of data sources based on their correlation is canonical correlation analysis (CCA). CCA seeks for linear combinations of all the variables from each dataset which maximize the correlation between them. However, in high dimensional datasets, where the number of variables exceeds the number of experimental units, CCA may not lead to meaningful information. Moreover, when collinearity exists in one or both the datasets, CCA may not be applicable. Here, we present a novel method, (LPC-KR), to extract common features from a pair of data sources using **L**ocal **P**rincipal **C**omponents and **K**endall's **R**anking. The results show that the proposed algorithm outperforms CCA in many scenarios and is more robust to noisy data. Moreover, meaningful results are obtained using the proposed algorithm when the number of variables exceeds the number of experimental units.

Introduction

In the post-genomic era, high-throughput technologies enable the generation of large amounts of 'omics' data which have different characteristics and attributes. Several popular 'omics' platforms have been studied in systems biology such as transcriptomics, which measures mRNA transcript levels; proteomics, which

N. Alaydie (✉) · F. Fotouhi
Department of Computer Science, College of Engineering, Wayne State University, Detroit, MI 48202, USA
e-mail: alaydie@wayne.edu; fotouhi@wayne.edu

T. Özyer et al. (eds.), *Information Reuse and Integration in Academia and Industry*, DOI 10.1007/978-3-7091-1538-1_11, © Springer-Verlag Wien 2013

quantifies protein abundance; metabolomics, which determines abundance of small cellular metabolites; interactomics, which resolves the whole set of molecular interactions in cells; and fluxomics, which establishes dynamic changes of molecules within a cell over time [23]. There has been much interest recently in studying and extracting common features from two sets of quantitative variables observed on the same experimental units [17]. Highlighting significant relationships between two sets of variables is important for many real-world applications [12, 17]. For example, there has been an interest in fusing heterogeneous data such as pixel values in images, assets and liabilities in banks and audio and face images of speakers [10]. There are two standard techniques in multivariate data analysis for extracting correlated features from two sets of variables: Partial Least Squares regression (PLS) [14, 22] and canonical correlation analysis (CCA) [13]. PLS is appropriate when there is a dependency among the two sets of variables. In other words, PLS is suitable when one set of variables can be explained by the other set [8, 12]. On the other hand, CCA is more suitable when the two sets of variables have symmetric role in the analysis, and when the objective is to analyze the correlations between them [9, 12].

CCA, defined by Hotelling [13], is a statistical method that explores the sample correlations between two spaces of different dimensions and structures observed on the same experimental objects [21]. It determines linear correlations between two data sources using cross-covariance matrices [10]. Over the few recent years, CCA has regained attention again and several disciplines have used CCA either as a stand-alone tool or as a step for further analysis methods [6, 7, 17, 18, 21]. More recently, in the context of post-genomic data, there has been a rapid growth in biological data sources containing gene-related information that are observed on the same samples [3, 12]. Such sources include gene expression data, functional annotation data and protein-protein interaction data [2]. The goal in such contexts is to identify and quantify common relationships between two or more data sources, for example, gene expression data and pharmacological activities [12].

However, CCA cannot be applied directly when the number of variables exceeds the number of samples. In fact, applying CCA in such scenarios may not provide meaningful information [12]. Moreover, due to the high dimensionality of biological data, a linear combination of the entire set of variables may lack biological plausibility and interpretability [17]. One of the main disadvantages of CCA is its sensitivity to a small number of samples [21]. Furthermore, in many real-world applications, noise may be acquired with data measures. The solution provided by CCA to noisy data changes dramatically. Ridge-type CCA must be considered when there is a small number of samples [11, 12, 20].

Regularized CCA methods, such as RCCA [11, 12], can also be used when the number of variables is greater than the number of observations. RCCA is considered as an improved version of CCA as it prevents overfitting in the present of insufficient training data.

In summary, CCA searches for the identification of relationships between two or more sets of variables. Regularized-type CCA focuses on analyzing and finding the relationships between datasets in which the number of variables is greater than the number of samples. However, regularized-type CCA do not perform feature selection, it works by adding L2 penalty to the covariance matrices so that the classical CCA can be performed.

We propose a new algorithm, LPC-KR, to find the "within-group" and the "between-groups" correlations based on the subspace principal curves and the Kendall's ranking correlation coefficients. The LPC-KR algorithm can be considered as a two step process. In the first step, linear models are constructed based on the local principal components to find the within-group correlated features from each dataset. In the second step, the ranks provided by the linear models from each within-group correlated features are used to find the correlations between the two datasets. Our hypothesis is that finding associations between groups of correlated features from each dataset (within-group correlated features) leads to meaningful information in many disciplines. We applied LPC-KR algorithm on two 'omics' datasets in which we identified groups of features from each dataset with the highest between-groups correlations.

The chapter is organized as follows: In the next section, we describe the motivation for our algorithm using a synthetic dataset. Then, the proposed algorithm, namely the LPC-KR algorithm, is presented in detail. We present and discuss the results of applying the LPC-KR algorithm on different datasets in the following section. Finally, the "Conclusion" section concludes our discussion and presents directions for future work.

Motivation

In this section, we show the motivation for the proposed algorithm through several experiments. We generated two datasets, X and Y of dimensions $n \times p$ and $n \times q$ respectively, with some correlated features measured on 20 different objects. The first dataset has six variables $(p_1, \ldots, p_6)$ while the second dataset has seven variables $(q_1, \ldots, q_7)$. The variables are represented as columns in the matrices. The variables p_1 and p_3 are collinear, and likewise the variables q_1 and q_3 are collinear. The variables q_1 and q_2 from the second dataset have strong within-group local correlation and the variables q_4 and q_5 also have strong within-group local correlation. The variables p_1 and q_1 have the strongest between-groups correlation while the variables p_3 and q_4 have a weak between-groups correlation. The variables p_5, p_6, q_6 and q_7 are noisy variables.

Four major weakness points for CCA motivated us to develop the new algorithm:

1. Dataset size: CCA may not yield optimal results when the dataset size is small or when there are outliers in the data. In order to demonstrate the behavior of CCA when the dataset size is small, we applied CCA on the datasets excluding the noisy features (i.e., p_5, p_6, q_6 and q_7). The correlated features found by CCA and by the LPC-KR algorithm are listed in Table 11.1. Since the datasets have only few samples and collinearity exists in the datasets, CCA was not able to discover all of the significant correlations. Note that in all the shown results when there

Table 11.1 The correlated features using CCA and the LPC-KR algorithm on synthetic datasets excluding the noisy features

CCA	The LPC-KR algorithm
p_1, p_3, q_1, q_3	p_1, p_3, q_1, q_3 (0.82)
p_4, q_5, q_4	p_1, p_3, q_2, q_3 (0.75)
–	p_4, q_4, q_5 (0.70)
–	p_4, q_2, q_3, q_5 (0.65)
–	q_2, q_3, q_4, q_5 (0.60)

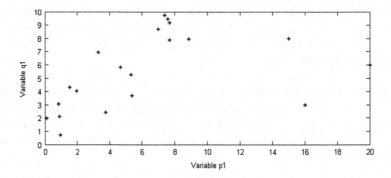

Fig. 11.1 The variables p_1 and q_1 after adding the outliers

is a dash (−), it means that the corresponding method was not able to find the correlated features.

As a second experiment, we added a few outliers to the features and tried to discover the correlated features. In particular, we added outliers to the p_1 and the q_1 variables. Figure 11.1 shows the variables p_1 and q_1 after adding the outliers. Table 11.2 shows the results of adding the outliers. As it is clear, the solution of CCA is changed in a very obvious way when the outliers exist in some features. CCA shows that the variables p_1, q_1 and q_3 have a stronger correlation than the correlation between p_3 and q_2 although that p_1 and p_3 are highly collinear. Moreover, some of the correlations that were found to be significant (p_4, q_5 and q_4), are considered as not correlated features. This means that CCA does not provide a stable solution when the outliers exist in the data. In fact, the LPC-KR algorithm is robust to outliers and works well on low sample problems even if the number of variables (features) is much less than the number of samples.

2. Noisy data: CCA and its variations are sensitive to noise. In many applications (such as the bio-medical application), the available data always contain noise. To show how CCA behaves when the noise is presented in the data, the noisy variables p_5, p_6, q_6 and q_7 are added to the first and the second datasets, respectively. The results are shown in Table 11.3. Using CCA, noisy features show strong correlations either with each other or with other features. As an

Table 11.2 The correlated features using CCA and the LPC-KR algorithm on synthetic datasets with outliers and collinear features	CCA	The LPC-KR algorithm
	p_1, q_1, q_3, p_3, q_2	p_1, p_3, q_1, q_3 (0.74)
	—	p_1, p_3, q_1, q_2 (0.7)
	—	p_1, p_3, q_2, q_3 (0.65)

Table 11.3 The correlated features using CCA and the LPC-KR algorithm on synthetic datasets in the presence of noisy features	CCA	The LPC-KR algorithm
	p_1, q_1, q_3, p_3, q_2	p_1, p_3, q_1, q_3 (0.75)
	p_4, q_5, q_7	q_1, q_2, q_3 (0.72)
	q_5, q_6	p_1, p_3, q_2, q_3 (0.7)
	—	p_1, p_3, q_1, q_2 (0.65)
	—	p_4, q_4, q_5 (0.60)

example, the noisy variable q_7 shows strong correlation with the variable p_4. Since noisy features are meaningless, such correlations are not helpful and do not reveal any useful information.

3. Ranking of the correlated features: Although CCA highlights the significant correlations, it does not provide enough information about the ranking for the correlations obtained in terms of their strength. On the other hand, using our method, each highlighted correlation has a score indicating its strength compared to all other correlations. The numbers shown in Tables 11.1–11.3 represent the scores for the correlated features found by our method. The correlated features can be ranked, based on their scores, to indicate the strength of the correlation. The lower the score, the stronger the correlation.

4. Collinearity: When there is collinearity in one or both of the datasets, the covariance matrices for the datasets that have the collinearity tend to be ill-conditioned and their inverses are unreliable [12]. This leads to an invalid computation of CCA and an unreliable metaspace. Using the LPC-KR algorithm, collinearity is not a concern because the algorithm can identify collinear features as other strong correlations. In Table 11.2, we show the results of CCA applied on a dataset with outliers and collinear features. Using CCA, those collinear features where not the closest ones to each other, which indicates again that the solution provided by CCA, in such situations, is not stable.

In the following discussion, we compare our results with the results obtained by applying RCCA [12] and CCA, when applicable. The results of RCCA are not shown on the synthetic datasets because we have the number of variables less than the number of samples. In fact, when we applied RCCA on our synthetically generated dataset, we obtained similar results as the CCA results. The LPC-KR algorithm finds the *'within-group'* and the *'between-groups'* correlations in an efficient manner. We refer to the correlations between subsets of variables as local correlations. Moreover, our method is robust to outliers and noisy data. When the data is noisy, identifying the within-group correlations and the between-groups correlations is a challenging problem.

The Proposed Algorithm

In this section, we describe the proposed algorithm in detail. The following notation is used through the discussion of the algorithm. Let G_1 and G_2 be the two groups of measurements, with ranks $n \times p$ and $n \times q$ respectively, observed on the same set of objects, n. The ith column of G_1 is denoted by $p^{(i)}$, likewise, the ith column of G_2 is denoted by $q^{(i)}$.

Definition 1. The set $\{p^{(1)}, \ldots, p^{(m)}$, where $m \leq n\}$, has a priori-based within-group correlation, if $\forall i, j \in m : within\_Group(p^{(i)}, p^{(j)}) \geq \beta_{WG}$.

Definition 2. Suppose that $G_1 s_i = \{p^{(1)}, \ldots, p^{(m)}$, where $m \leq n\}$ has a priori-based within-group correlation for group G_1 and $G_2 s_j = \{q^{(1)}, \ldots, q^{(l)}$, where $l \leq n\}$ has a priori-based within-group correlation for group G_2, the groups $G_1 s_i$ and $G_2 s_j$ have Between_Groups correlation if
Between_Groups$(G_1 s_i, G_2 s_j) \geq \theta_{BG}$.

β_{WG} and θ_{BG} are the threshold parameters for the within-group and the between-groups correlations, respectively. In other words, these parameters control the strength of the correlations to be discovered in each group separately and jointly. Increasing the values for β_{WG} and θ_{BG} threshold values means that only stronger correlations in the groups and across the groups will be discovered.

Definition 3. Let $G_1(i, j)$ be a data point in G_1 that is found through the intersection of the ith row and the jth column (*variable*). Let the projection distance for this point on the line be denoted by $pd(G_1(i, j))$. The sum of the square distances (SSD) for the data points and the variables that are considered for fitting the linear model is computed as follows:

$$SSD = \sum_{i=1}^{n} \sum_{j=1}^{P} d(G_{1i}, j, pd(G_1(i, j))) \qquad (11.1)$$

The goal is to find a line segment that minimizes the total squared distances of all the data points to the line.

The LPC-KR algorithm works in a two step process. In order to obtain the correlations within each group of variables, a linear model is fitted to each feature pair, $p^{(i)}$ and $p^{(j)}$. The sum of the square distances for all the data points is computed from the linear model that is fitted for each feature pair (see Algorithms 1 and 2). In fact, we divided the sum of the square distances for each linear model by $\sqrt{2}$, we call the new value as $dist(p^{(i)}, p^{(j)})$.

Algorithm 1: *Compute_within_Group_Correlation*

Input: X: feature dataset of dimensionality $n \times p$.
α: a parameter that controls the accepted scores of correlations.
Output: *Correl_List*: a list containing the subsets of features that are correlated.
Ranks: projection indices of the correlated features on the fitted linear model.
Algorithm:
$P = \text{variables}(X)$
for each pair of variables $i, j \in P$ **do**
$\quad [sqr\_dist, proj\_Ind] = Fit\_Linear\_Model(p^{(i)}, p^{(j)})$
$\quad dist(p^{(i)}, p^{(j)}) = \frac{\sum sqr\_dist}{\sqrt{2}}$
end for
$\beta_{WG} = \alpha * \frac{\sum_{i=1}^{n} dist(p^{(i)}, p^{(j)})}{n}$
$Index = 1$
for each pair of variables $i, j \in P$ **do**
$\quad$ **if** $dist(p^{(i)}, p^{(j)}) < \beta_{WG}$ **then**
$\quad\quad Correl\_List(Index) = p^{(i)} \cup p^{(j)}$
$\quad\quad Ranks(Index) = proj\_Ind(p^{(i)}, p^{(j)})$
$\quad\quad Index = Index + 1$
$\quad$ **end if**
end for
for each pair of subsets $s_i, s_j \in Correl\_List$ **do**
$\quad [sqr\_dist, proj\_Ind] = Fit\_Linear\_Model(s_i, s_j)$
$\quad dist(s_i, s_j) = \frac{\sum (sqr\_dist)}{\sqrt{s_i + s_j}}$
$\quad$ **if** $dist(s_i, s_j) < \beta_{WG}$ AND $(s_i \cup s_j) \notin Correl\_List$ **then**
$\quad\quad Correl\_List(Index) = s_i \cup s_j$
$\quad\quad Ranks(Index) = proj\_Ind(s_i, s_j)$
$\quad\quad Index = Index + 1$
$\quad$ **end if**
end for

Once we get the $dist(p^{(i)}, p^{(j)})$ for all the features pairs, we compute β_{WG}, the threshold for the within-group correlations. Only those pairs having the sum of the square distances less than the threshold, β_{WG}, are passed for further analysis. The threshold β_{WG} is computed as follows:

$$\beta_{WG} = \alpha * \frac{\sum_{i=1}^{n} dist(p^{(i)}, p^{(j)})}{n} \tag{11.2}$$

Hence, the β_{WG} is set automatically after getting the sum of the square distances for all the feature pairs. Once this threshold is determined, it will be fixed for all other possible combinations of the features. The α parameter is tuned by the user where the higher the value of α, the higher the value of β_{WG}. As the value of α parameter increases, less significant correlations are considered for further analysis. Next, we consider fitting optimum linear models using more features. In fact, we consider constructing linear models from all the possible combinations of the feature pairs that have the $dist(p^{(i)}, p^{(j)})$ less than the β_{WG} threshold. The sum of the square error is computed again for the linear models generated from the subsets of the correlated features. In each iteration, we test the possibility of having the correlation

---

Algorithm 2: *Fit_Linear_Model*

Input: X: feature dataset of dimensionality n x p
Output: *Optimal_Linear_Model* fitted to the data.
sqr_dist: projection distance of the data.
proj_Ind: projection indices of the data points on the fitted linear model.
Algorithm:
$X\_1^{st}\_PC = First\_Principal\_Component(X)$
Optimal_Linear_Model $= PC\_Segment(X\_1^{st}\_PC)$
sqr_dist $= Projection(X, Optimal\_Linear\_Model)$
proj_Ind $= Rank\_Data(X, Optimal\_Linear\_Model)$

Algorithm 3: *Compute_Kendall_based_Between_Groups* correlations

---

Input: *Ranks_Group1* and *Ranks_Group2*: The ranks for all of the subsets having
within-Group correlations from Group1 and Group2, respectively.
θ_{BG}: Threshold for the accepted degree of the between groups correlation.
Output: *Cross_Corr_Scores*: Cross-correlation matrix based on Kendall's rank correlation.
Cross_Corr_Variables: the corresponding correlated subsets of highly correlated
within-group features from the two groups.
Algorithm:
Index=1
for each pair of subsets of correlated features $(r_i, r_j), r_i \in Ranks\_Group1$ and
$r_j \in Ranks\_Group2$ **do**
    Kendall_corr = compute_Kendall_Correlation(r_i, r_j)
    if *Kendall_corr* $> \theta_{BG}$ **then**
        Cross_Corr_Variables(Index) $= r_i \cup r_j$
        Cross_Corr_Scores(Index) $=$ *Kendall_corr*
    end if
end for
Sort *Cross_Corr_Scores* in descending order and maintain the corresponding
Cross_Corr_Variables

---

between two already identified correlated subsets. This process continues until either reaching a specific size of the subsets or having the size equals to the number of the features. In order to find a good line that models the data, we use segments of the first principal component that are bounded by $3\sigma/2$ from the mean of the whole dataset.

Kendall's ranking correlation evaluates the degree of association between two sets of ranks given on the same set of variables [1] (see algorithm 3). The range for Kendall's tau scores is $[-1, 1]$. A value of 1 indicates a perfect positive agreement, hence, the two rankings will be the same. A value of 0 indicates that the two rankings are completely independent, whereas, a value of -1 indicates a perfect negative agreement. As a consequence, an increase in the magnitude of the Kendall's tau means an increase in the agreement between the rankings.

The Kendall's ranking correlation coefficient is given by the following formula:

$$\tau = \frac{n_c - n_d}{n(n-1)/2} \tag{11.3}$$

where n_c is the number of concordant pairs and n_d is the number of discordant pairs. The denominator yields to the total number of pairs of the samples. When there are ties in the observations, τ_b is used:

$$\tau_b = \frac{n_c - n_d}{\sqrt{F(u_i) F(v_i)}} \tag{11.4}$$

Where

$$F(u_i) = n(n-1)/2 - \sum_{i=1}^{u} u_i(u_i - 1)/2 \tag{11.5}$$

Here, u_i is the number of observations tied at a particular rank of the first sample and v_i is the number of tied observations at a rank of the second sample. It is worthwhile to mention that we mean by correlation the preservation of the order. Additionally, we believe that discovering relationships between groups of correlated features from each dataset (the within-group correlated features) may reveal significant hidden information in many disciplines.

Datasets

In this section, we present the results of the LPC-KR algorithm on two biological studies.

Nutrigenomic Dataset

The nutrigenomic dataset comes from a nutrition study in mouse [15]. Forty mice were undertaken as the biological units with two different sources of information:

- Gene expression of 120 genes measured in liver cells.
- Concentration of 21 hepatic fatty acids (FA).

Moreover, these biological units are cross-classified according to the following two factors:

- Genotype: Wild-type (WT) versus PPAR deficient mice (PPAR).
- Diet: five diets were used depending on the FA compositions (*REF, COC, SUN, LIN and FISH* diets).

These two groups of variables were analyzed separately in [15]. Using the LPC-KR algorithm, we were able to discover significant correlations between the variables in each group. The top ranked significant correlated FA are shown

Table 11.4 The five top within-group correlations for the FA using the LPC-KR algorithm

Correlated FA	Score
C16.1n.7, C18.1n.7, C18.3n.6, C14.0, C16.0	0.98
C18.0, C16.1n.9, C16.1n.7, C18.1n.7, C18.1n.9	0.94
C18.3n.3, C20.3n.3, C16.0, C18.3n.6	0.89
C14.0, C16.1n.9, C16.1n.7, C18.1n.9, C18.1n.7	0.89
C18.1n.7, C18.3n.6, C20.3n.9	0.86

Table 11.5 The five top within-group correlations for the genes using the LPC-KR algorithm

Correlated genes	Score
BACT, C16SR, Lpin3, c.fos, TRb	0.99
ACC1, BACT, C16SR, TRb, c.fos	0.98
ADISP, BIEN, C16SR, Lpin3, c.fos	0.94
Lpin3, TRb, c.fos, UCP3	0.89
X36b4, C16SR, AM2R	0.85

in Table 11.4. The scores in the table represent the degree to which the subset of the variables agree on the rankings. Similarly, the most significant correlated genes are shown in Table 11.5. More interestingly, most of these correlations were also found using RCCA. However, RCCA does not provide a measure of the strength of these correlations. Hence, no ranking for the correlated variables is provided by RCCA.

Figure 11.2 shows examples of the strongest correlations found by the LPC-KR algorithm when applied on the nutrigenomic dataset. In particular, the top strong within-group correlations for the nutrigenomic dataset using the proposed approach are shown. The first three plots are from the first dataset (the gene expression) while the last three plots are from the second dataset (FA).

For the cross-correlation, we did not find a significant ranking of the correlation that is preserved between the subsets of the correlated features from the two sources. These results are also consistent with the findings from RCCA as we also were not able to obtain such results from RCCA. Therefore, we performed another experiment in which we found correlated genes only and then applied the cross-correlation between the FA and the correlated genes. The top most significant correlations are shown in Table 11.6.

Multidrug Dataset

The multidrug resistance data comes from a pharacogenomic study [19]. Sixty cancer cell lines were studied on which the following two sets of variables were measured:

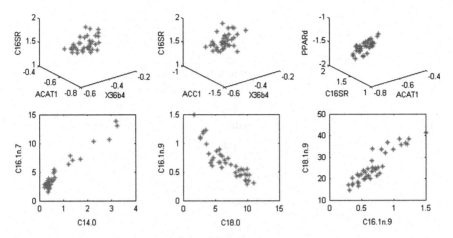

Fig. 11.2 The strongest within-group correlations for the nutrigenomic dataset using the LPC-KR algorithm. The first three plots are obtained from the first dataset (the gene expression dataset) while the last three plots are obtained from the second dataset (the FA dataset)

Table 11.6 The five top cross-correlations for the FA and the correlated genes using the LPC-KR algorithm

FA	Correlated genes	Score
C20.1n.9	ADISP, BIEN, C16SR, BIEN, C16SR, Lpin3, c.fos	0.50
C16.0	AOX, C16SR	0.49
C18.2n.6	C16SR, BSEP, BIEN	0.46
C20.2n.6	BIEN, C16SR, TRb, c.fos	0.44
C18.3n.3	ACC1, BSEP, C16SR	0.35

- The expression of 47 human ABC transporters measured in the 60 cell lines.
- The activity of 853 anti-cancer drugs, chosen from 1,429 anti-cancer drugs, tested against the cells.

Since we are not interested here to impute missing values, variables which have missing values were excluded.

It is worthy to mention that in the datasets used here, it cannot be assumed that the variation in one dataset is caused by the variation in the other dataset, which justifies the use of CCA and RCCA for comparing the results with the proposed algorithm. Using the LPC-KR algorithm, we were able to find correlations between the genes and the corresponding drugs. We compare the results obtained for this dataset with the ones obtained using RCCA [12]. Table 11.7 shows some selected genes and the corresponding correlated drugs that are discussed in [12]. While most of the correlations that are found using RCCA are highlighted using the proposed algorithm, our algorithm was successful to extract additional correlations between

Table 11.7 The cross-correlations for four selected genes and the correlated drugs using the LPC-KR algorithm

Gene	Correlated drugs
ABCC2	690,434, 602,617, 628,507, 670,762, 690,432
ABCA9	602,617, 642,061, 628,507, 690,434, 690,432, 670,762, 602,617, 670,766
ABCA5	643,915, 690,434, 690,432, 628,507, 602,617, 670,762, 670,766

Table 11.8 The top five most significant within-group correlations in the genes dataset

Correlated genes
ABCA1, ABCA9, ABCB7
ABCA9, ABCA3, ABCB5, ABCB7
ABCA8, ABCA9, ABCB7, ABCB5
ABCA5, ABCA6, ABCB7

Table 11.9 The top five most significant within-group correlations for the drug dataset

Correlated drugs
17,275, 25,154, 690,434, 628,507
670,762, 690,434, 690,432, 670,766, 628,507
602,617, 628,507, 17,275, 25,154
658,450, 670,762, 670,766, 628,507
670,762, 690,434, 690,432, 670,766, 628,507

the genes and the drugs that were not found using RCCA. Tables 11.8 and 11.9 show the most significant within-Group correlations found in the genes dataset and the drugs dataset, respectively.

Figure 11.3 shows the robustness of the LPC-KR algorithm through discovering the correlations in the presence of the outliers in the data. This Figure shows the within-group correlation between three genes found by our algorithm, namely, ABCA1, ABCA9 and ABCB7. Although there are outlier points, the algorithm is able to capture the relationships between the three mentioned genes. Finally, the proposed algorithm is flexible according to the application needs. In other words, if the goal of the application is to identify the within-group correlations for one group but not the other and then to find the cross-correlations between the data sources, then this simply means to ignore detecting the within-group correlations for that particular dataset.

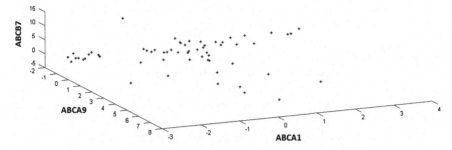

Fig. 11.3 The strongest correlation found by the LPC-KR algorithm in the genes dataset of the multiDrug dataset

Discussion

The identification of complex multivariate relationships is necessary with the availability of multiple phenotypic or genotypic measures. The current work focuses on inspecting the relationship between two sets of variables only. In many applications, there is a need to study the correlation of more than two datasets at the same time. The ability to conduct multi-'omics' analysis would allow the generation of biological hypotheses to be tested. For example, finding a strong correlation between transcriptomic or proteomic data can serve as a confirmation for the discovery of an induced response to a treatment, whereas the lack of a strong correlation can help in detecting experimental errors [16, 24].

Furthermore, finding the correlation between the multiple data sources can facilitate the integration process. The advent of high-throughput technologies enables the generation of huge amount of genomic data. However, most of these data sources are noisy and incomplete. How to effectively integrate heterogeneous data sources is a major challenge. Many studies strongly suggested that the integration of knowledge at different levels in the cascade from genes to proteins and further to metabolic fluxes at a genomic-scale is a powerful tool for understanding the interaction between the individual components in the living systems [24]. Therefore, the integration of multiple sources of information, the multi-"omics" approach, is essential to form a precise picture of living micro-organisms.

Conclusion

We proposed the LPC-KR algorithm, a novel algorithm to find the within-group and the between-groups correlations based on the local principal components and the Kendall's ranking. The use of the proposed algorithm tends to be relevant to a wide variety of applications where the data is noisy. Moreover, in high dimensional contexts, when there is a need to identify the correlations between the correlated groups of variables, the LPC-KR algorithm produced promising results for different 'omics' datasets. Future work includes the extension of the LPC-KR algorithm to find the associations between more than two heterogeneous data sources. Finding the correlation between multiple data sources can be helpful in resolving the mystery of other research problems such as gene function prediction [4, 5]. We also plan to apply the LPC-KR algorithm in the context of data fusion for other biomolecular datasets of other problem domains and applications. Additionally, we intend to provide visual analysis of the highly correlated features so that the interpretation of the correlations can be illustrated using an interactive environment.

References

1. Abdi H (2007) Kendall rank correlation. In: Salkind NJ (ed) Encyclopedia of measurement and statistics. Sage, Thousand Oaks, pp 508–510
2. Agarwal S, Sengupta S (2009) Ranking genes by relevance to a disease. In: Proceedings of the 8th annual international conference on computational systems bioinformatics, Stanford, CA
3. Alaydie N, Fotouhi F (2011) Unraveling complex relationships between heterogeneous omics datasets using local principal components. In: Proceedings of the IEEE information reuse and integration (IEEE IRI), Las Vegas, pp 136–141
4. Alaydie N, Reddy CK, Fotouhi F (2011) A bayesian integration model of heterogeneous data sources for improved gene functional inference. In: Proceedings of the ACM conference on bioinformatics and computational biology (BCB), Chicago, pp 376–380
5. Alaydie N, Reddy CK, Fotouhiand F (2012) Exploiting label dependency for hierarchical multi-label classification. In: Proceedings of the Pacific-Asia conference on knowledge discovery and data mining (PAKDD), Kaula Lumpur, pp 294–305
6. Correa N, Li YO, Adali T, Calhoun VD (2008) Canonical correlation analysis for feature-based fusion of biomedical imaging modalities to detect associative networks in schizophrenia. IEEE J Sel Top Signal Process 2(6):998–1007. Special Issue on fMRI Analysis for Human Brain Mapping
7. Correa NM, Li YO, Adali T, Calhoun VD (2009) Fusion of fmri, smri, and eeg data using canonical correlation analysis. In: ICASSP '09: proceedings of the 2009 IEEE international conference on acoustics, speech and signal processing. IEEE Computer Society, Washington, DC, pp 385–388. doi:http://dx.doi.org/10.1109/ICASSP.2009.4959601
8. Frank IE, Friedman JH (1993) A statistical view of some chemometrics regression tools. Technometrics 35(2):109–135
9. Gittins R (1985) Canonical analysis: a review with applications in ecology. Springer, Berlin
10. Golugula A, Lee G, Master SR, Feldman MD, Tomaszewski JE, Speicher DW, Madabhushi A (2011) Supervised regularized canonical correlation analysis: integrating histologic and proteomic measurements for predicting biochemical recurrence following prostate surgery. BMC Bioinform 12:483
11. González I, Déjean S, Martin PGP, Baccini A (2008) CCA: an R package to extend canonical correlation analysis. J Stat Softw 23(12):1–14
12. González I, Déjean S, Martin P, Gonçalves O, Besse P, Baccini A (2009) Highlighting relationships between heterogeneous biological data through graphical displays based on regularized canonical correlation analysis. J Biol Syst 17(2):173–199
13. Hotelling H (1936) Relations between two sets of variates. Biometrika 28:321–377
14. Lé Cao KA, Martin P, Robert-Granié C, Besse P (2009) Sparse canonical methods for biological data integration: application to a cross-platform study. BMC Bioinform 10:Article 34

15. Martin PGP, Guillou H, Lasserre F, Déjean S, Lan A, Pascussi J, SanCristobal M, Legrand P, Besse P, Pineau T (2007) Novel aspects of ppará-mediated regulation of lipid and xenobiotic metabolism revealed through a nutrigenomic study. Hepatology 45(3):767–777
16. Nie L, Wu G, Culley DE, Scholten JC, Zhang W (2007) Integrative analysis of transcriptomic and proteomic data: challenges, solutions and applications. Crit Rev Biotechnol 27(2):63–75
17. Parkhomenko E, Tritchler D, Beyene J (2009) Sparse canonical correlation analysis with application to genomic data integration. Stat Appl Genet Mol Biol 8:1–34
18. Rustandi I, Just MA, Mitchell TM (2009) Integrating multiple-study multiple-subject fmri datasets using canonical correlation analysis. In: Proceedings of the MICCAI workshop: statistical modeling and detection issues in intra- and inter-subject functional MRI data analysis, London, pp 1–8
19. Szakács G, Annereau JP, Lababidi S, Shankavaram U, Arciello A, Bussey K, Reinhold W, Guo Y, Kruh G, Reimers M, Weinstein J, Gottesman M (2004) Predicting drug sensitivity and resistance: profiling abc transporter genes in cancer cells. Cancer Cell 6:129–137
20. Vinod HD (1976) Canonical ridge and econometrics of joint production. J Econom 4(2): 147–166
21. Wiesel A, Kliger M, Hero AO (2008) A greedy approach to sparse canonical correlation analysis. Submitted to ArXiv, http://arxiv.org/abs/0801.2748
22. Wold H (1966) Estimation of principal components and related models by iterative least squares. In: Krishnaiaah PR (ed) Multivariate analysis. Academic, New York
23. Zhang W, Li F, Nie L (2009) Integrating multiple 'omics' analysis for microbial biology: application and methodologies. Microbiology 156:287–301
24. Zhang W, Li F, Nie L (2010) Integrating multiple 'omics' analysis for microbial biology: application and methodologies. Microbiology 156(Pt 2):287–301

Chapter 12
Towards Collaborative Forensics

Mike Mabey and Gail-Joon Ahn

Abstract Digital forensic analysis techniques have been significantly improved and evolved in past decade but we still face a lack of effective forensic analysis tools to tackle diverse incidents caused by emerging technologies and the advances in cyber crime. In this paper, we propose a comprehensive framework to address the efficacious deficiencies of current practices in digital forensics. Our framework, called Collaborative Forensic Framework (CUFF), provides scalable forensic services for practitioners who are from different organizations and have diverse forensic skills. In other words, our framework helps forensic practitioners collaborate with each other, instead of learning and struggling with new forensic techniques. In addition, we describe fundamental building blocks for our framework and corresponding system requirements.

Introduction

Computer crime has swiftly evolved into organized, and in some cases state sponsored, cyber warfare. The tools digital forensic examiners currently use are too limited to take on the challenges that are rapidly approaching their forensic cases. Before long, fundamental changes in the industry will make many of the forensic techniques used today obsolete [15]. Although many contributing elements can be identified, the heart of the problem is that current digital forensic examinations are

A preliminary version of this paper appeared under the title "Towards collaborative forensics: Preliminary framework" in Proc. of the IEEE International Conference on Information Reuse and Integration (IRI), 2011. All correspondences should be addressed to Dr. Gail-Joon Ahn at gahn@asu.edu

M. Mabey · G.-J. Ahn (✉)
Laboratory of Security Engineering for Future Computing (SEFCOM), Arizona State University, Tempe, AZ 85281, USA
e-mail: mmabey@asu.edu; gahn@asu.edu

too time-inefficient. The three principal causes of this inefficiency are summarized as follows:

Software Limitations: Single workstation computers have served as the primary tool of our society's computing needs for a long time. With the evidence data sets being as large as they are, a single computer simply does not have the resources to deliver sophisticated analysis results in a timely manner.

Size of Evidence Data: Today a 1 TB hard drive can be purchased for about US$60 and the average hard drive cost per GB is less than US$0.10 [6]. Such low cost makes terabyte-sized systems commonplace among even non-tech-savvy consumers. With such a proliferation of huge storage systems filled with user data, examiners are confronted with a mountain of stored data to work through [31]. The problem is compounded when the situation involves a redundant array of independent disks (RAID) [34] or network attached storage (NAS) unit shared among individuals or employees.

Increased Examiner Workload: As if insufficient tools and large datasets were not enough, digital crime continues to increase in popularity [17, 24, 25], naturally resulting in more investigations. Furthermore, state-sponsored cyberwar promotes the development of increasingly sophisticated software. Simply trying to keep up with the latest methods of penetration, exfiltration, and attack is insufficient to accommodate the pace of digital crime.

In addition, when cases become backlogged, only those designated as more urgent are worked on, potentially leaving suspects' co-conspirators at large and capable of making more victims out of innocent people.

Motivation

The challenges above can be greatly reduced by a secure and robust infrastructure that facilitates *collaborative forensics* [18, 27], which we define as the willful cooperation between two or more forensic examiners during any step in the forensics process, for the benefit of sharing specialized knowledge, insight, experience, or tools. By this we mean to indicate a process and system through which multiple examiners perform their work, using a common interface that provides the means for carrying out all steps of the examination process as well as providing mechanisms for collaboration between the users.

Two advantages of collaboration are of particular interest to us. First, collaboration allows people to draw from others' expertise, which is invaluable when working on problems of a diverse nature or when the problem set of a job constantly changes. Second, collaboration is a method of spreading a workload, which results in less time needed for the job to be completed.

Consider the following hypothetical scenario which illustrates a need for a better method of collaboration. While investigating a case with multiple computational and storage devices that are uncommon, Bob, who is the lead examiner, determines that by soliciting the aid of two subject matter experts that he trusts, the devices could be successfully examined for evidence of interest. However, when Bob makes the request to his supervisor to obtain assistance from these experts, she informs him that the compensation expenses of the experts' consultation fees plus travel costs is too great to justify with the current budget. Bob must find a way to either make do with only one of the experts or to eliminate the travel expenses. Bob needs an effective means of collaborating with these experts remotely.

Similar to the above scenario, it is already quite common for evidence seizure to yield a variety of digital evidence, such as a mix of Windows, Linux, and Mac computers, as well as cell phones, GPS devices, gaming consoles, etc. Since examiners must be certified to work on a particular type of evidence (depending on the investigating agency), such a workload must be split up among personnel. Since there is no tool which can accommodate all evidence types, the evidence presentation lacks uniformity in format and structure.

While many generic collaboration solutions exist today, none of them have been crafted specifically for the needs of the digital forensics industry. To be truly effective, a collaborative forensics infrastructure should maintain the strict privacy and integrity principles the discipline demands, while also giving examiners the flexibility to communicate however is best for the situation. This demands a level of robustness that is simply not offered by collaboration tools at present.

Beyond just communication, collaboration also implies a sharing of resources. For a proper exchange of data (whether it be files needing to be analyzed or the results of an analysis), there must first be a uniform representation of that data, and then a common storage space solution where all collaborators can keep their resources secure. This will require the establishment of standards to ensure that all parties can access and interpret the data. Means to efficiently manage resources will also be needed.

If examiners are to collaborate on a large scale, it will also be crucial for this infrastructure to provide vast amounts of computing power, which is best accomplished through some distributed processing method. Ideally, a distributed processing solution would also include scalable resources. Because there is not a single technological solution that will properly meet this need for all organizations, there must be a generic way to interface for such processing resources.

To best facilitate collaboration among examiners, a collaborative forensics solution should not be limited to supporting its use on a small number of operating systems. This would hinder the collaboration process and may exclude experts who could offer potentially crucial insight.

The rest of this paper is organized as follows. We first discuss the progress made by others in related fields in section "Related Work". In section "CUFF: Collaborative Forensic Framework" we provide the architecture of our solution, which is an abstraction of the most essential components. We then introduce all other necessary components and provide details on how to realize our framework in section "Realization of CUFF". Section "Conclusion" concludes this paper by summarizing our contributions and discussing our future work.

Related Work

The nature of our work is such that it brings together aspects of other, previously completed works which we discuss here by topic.

General Digital Forensics: Two challenging types of evidence that forensics examiners need to be able to analyze at times are Redundant Array of Independent Disks (RAID) storage systems and drives protected with encryption. In [34], Urias and Liebrock attempted to use a parallel analysis system on RAID storage systems, and documented the issues and challenges they faced with that approach. Similarly, multiple methods of properly handling the challenges presented by encrypted drives have been presented by Casey and Stellatos in [5] and by Altheide et al. in [2].

Distributed Processing for Forensics: With distributed processing in use so much today and in so many distinct settings, it is natural to think of using it to divide the workload of digital forensics processing. Several years ago, when the use of distributed processing was not yet as common as it is today, Roussev and Richard proposed a method for moving away from single workstation processing for forensic examination to a distributed environment [31]. A few years later, Liebrock et al. proposed improvements upon Roussev and Richard's system in [21], which introduced a decoupled front-end to a parallel analysis machine.

In [32], Scanlon and Kechadi introduced a method for remotely acquiring forensic copies of suspect evidence which transfers the contents of a drive over a secure Internet connection to a central evidence server. While this effort is a step for the better in terms of making evidence centrally accessible, it is difficult to see the direct utility of such an approach without accompanying software or analysis techniques to take advantage of storing the evidence on a server. Furthermore, the presented approach relies on either using the suspect's Internet connection to upload the image or images, or the use of a mobile broadband connection. Given the relatively abysmal upload speeds for current mobile broadband when dealing with data sets that are hundreds of gigabytes or even a few terabytes large, this approach will continue to be prohibitively inadequate.

Forensics Standardizations: Garfinkel has made great efforts to create standards to improve the overall digital forensic examination process. Garfinkel et al. presented the details of a forensic corpora in [16] with the purpose of giving researchers a systematic way to measure and test their tools. Garfinkel took this a step further in [13] with his work to represent file system metadata with XML. Finally, in [15] Garfinkel put forth a challenge to researchers and developers everywhere to take note of the current industry trends and take them head on with innovative forensic solutions that match the properties of emerging technologies.

Storage: Since our realization of our framework is built upon a cloud, we also consider work done by researchers to address some of the issues related to shared storage in a cloud. Du et al. proposed an availability prediction scheme for sharable objects, such as data files or software components, for multi-tenanted systems in [8]. In [36], Wang et al. introduced a middleware solution to improve shared IO performance with Amazon Web Services [3]. Increasing the security of the data stored in a cloud has been improved upon by Liu et al. in [22] and by Zhao et al. in [38].

In addition to the above subject areas, there also appears to be a trend toward supporting collaboration mechanisms in digital forensics tools such as FTK 3 [11]. But, to the best of our knowledge, there has yet to be a single system which can satisfy all the functionalities set forth in section "Introduction" in a truly robust manner.

CUFF: Collaborative Forensic Framework

Based on the features and requirements necessary to achieve collaborative forensics as enumerated in section "Introduction" and the work presented in [23], this section describes our framework, called Collaborative Forensic Framework (CUFF), and elaborates what mechanisms are needed to facilitate these features. As illustrated in Fig. 12.1, our framework consists of four core components (i) to mediate communication between components in the system, (ii) to coordinate the distributed analysis processing, (iii) to maintain the shared storage space, and (iv) to provide a basic interface to the system for the user interface. While a precise set of APIs for these four components may vary for the deployment setting, they should always fulfill specific foundational operations and always have the same basic interactions with the other components. We now discuss these two points in context of each component:

Analysis Block: This component is the workhorse of the system, and in truth all other components are simply in place to either provide an interface to it, or to facilitate its proper function. The Analysis Block is composed of a controller as well as all processing resources. Ideally, the processing resources would be quite substantial and capable of handling a continuous inflow of analysis jobs of significant size. The controller will receive a large number of analysis requests, and is expected to enqueue and dequeue each job request in an organized and efficient manner, which should also be fault-tolerant and maintain a high level of responsiveness. Because it is in charge of maintaining the queue of jobs, the controller oversees the processing resources and ensures that they are used properly according to a selected method of prioritizing the jobs.

Storage: This component keeps track of all acquired disk images, the analyses of their contents, comments and notes from users, and related information all need to be kept for performing forensic tasks. To do this, it must accept incoming data streams of acquired disk images, and strictly maintain the integrity of the data through validation of the original checksums. Requests for getting and putting data to and from the storage component will come at a high rate, particularly

Fig. 12.1 Each of the
components in CUFF fulfill
one of the four main
objectives of the system. All
inter-system communication
passes through the Cuff Link,
and the end user only
interacts with the user
interface component

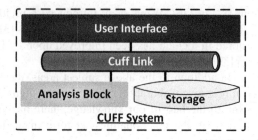

from the processing resources in the Analysis Block, so the storage component's
response time needs to be controlled. To maximize reusability, a generic method
of transferring data to and from the storage unit should be used such that distinct
data types (such as analysis results, user comments, and communications between
users) will not need any specialization made to the system. In coordination with
whatever access control mechanism is implemented, the storage component also
maintains strict confidentiality of the data it stores. The storage component must
also be flexible enough to allow temporary and/or limited access to case data for
subject matter experts conducting consultation work, allowing them to collaborate
with those directly responsible for the case.

User Interface: This is the access portal through which all the system's
features are made available. More specifically, the user interface supports evidence
acquisition, allows users to view the structure and contents of files, accepts requests
for specific analyses to be performed on files or groups of files, and provides a means
for users to communicate and share data and information with each other.

Cuff Link: This component mediates communication between all other components in the system. It validates parameter input and stores location information
for each of the other components. Also, since it is the component that manages
the forensic process, it is responsible for assigning examiners jobs and notifying
supervisors when the work on a case has been completed. The Cuff Link maintains
order in the system by dictating the available APIs for each of the other components.
It also simplifies the implementation of other components by reducing the number
of connections they must make down to one.

Realization of CUFF

In this section, we describe how to realize the CUFF framework using commercial
off-the-shelf (COTS) software and open source tools. For each component, we
address the desired functionality, some of the challenges associated with achieving
such functionality, and what tools and software meet these challenges and why.

It is highly desirable for an implementation of CUFF to be easily accessible by
the users that will collaborate through it, to have scalable resources, and to have

built-in redundancy for fault-tolerance. While it would be possible to implement CUFF as a set of desktop applications that communicate with other remote installations through a peer-to-peer networking architecture, such an approach would be difficult to monitor and assure that all connected parties strictly abide by the rules of evidence.

To achieve the system-wide features we desire, we have selected to build upon a cloud-based infrastructure, deploying each of the components as virtual machine (VM) instances. Using a cloud architecture has many obvious advantages. One advantage is that VM instances can be spawned quite easily, improving the scalability as well as the reliability and recovery time of all the components of the system. A second advantage is derived from the fact that each of CUFF's features are made accessible through various web services, including a web interface that can be accessed and used by all authenticated users. Although most of the web services in the system are only accessible internally, the use of web standards increases the composability of the system.

While several cloud architectures exist, OpenStack [29] stands out as one built for a high level of flexibility and scalability while also exporting an API compatible with Amazon EC2 and S3 services [3], hence allowing the use of the widely-used euca2ools [10] set of cloud administration tools.

We now elaborate on our implementation of each of CUFF's components. Although much of this section is dedicated to discussing a messaging protocol (section "Scheduling Analysis Jobs"), we would propose that efficient collaboration among forensic examiners depends heavily on the intelligent appropriation of the analysis resources, which begins with the scheduling of their use. Hence, this is a core component to address properly as we work towards our goal of facilitating collaboration.

Cuff Link

As stated earlier, the Cuff Link provides a couple of key functions for the overall system. It mediates communication, manages the forensics examination flow, validates input, and exposes an API for the other components.

One thing that must be taken into consideration is that not all communication types used in CUFF have the same behavior. Some types of Internet traffic are difficult to stop and process before sending it on to its intended destination, such as uploading or downloading files. However, with other types of traffic there is no difficulty in intercepting, processing, and then forwarding the messages being sent, such as requests for certain evidence files to be analyzed.

With this in mind, it would not be wise to impose a single method of handling communication. Rather, the Cuff Link uses multiple technologies appropriate for the type of messages being handled. Because of this, it was necessary to divide the functionality of the Cuff Link such that it acts as a layer of abstraction in

Fig. 12.2 Inter-component
communication passes
through the Cuff Link, which
is deployed in multiple
locations to provide the layer
of abstraction necessary for
the various components

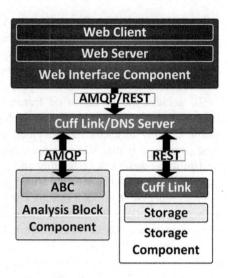

multiple locations. This is illustrated in Fig. 12.2 where an element of the Cuff Link is running on the Storage component.

To accommodate the communication types that cannot be interrupted (which is limited to traffic to and from the Storage component), the Cuff Link first provides a domain resolution through Domain Name System (DNS) server, which translates URLs into IP addresses. This makes it easy for other CUFF components to send traffic to a destination without knowing its exact location. The component making a request only needs to specify the generic name for the destination server, such as http://cuff.storage.example. The Cuff Link DNS server can then resolve the name to the appropriate server.

Typically, this kind of action would require that the URL http://cuff.storage. example be registered with some authoritative entity that stores all official URLs. However, because we have configured the Cuff Link as a primary master name server for the domains used within CUFF and specified that the system's components should query the Cuff Link before any other servers, such URLs are resolved within the system without making an external DNS query. This does require that any CUFF components that need to be accessed by this means have their IP address associated with their appropriate domain by the Cuff Link. Once this has been done, however, the DNS server can also potentially perform some level of load balancing among available servers by rotating which server's IP address it uses as the resolution of the URL.

The second thing the Cuff Link does to accommodate communication with the Storage component is to leverage a Representational State Transfer (REST) web service on the Storage component. REST web services allow for certain actions (in this case uploading and downloading files) to be specified in the URL of the web request, using the type of web request (POST, GET, DELETE, etc.) as one factor for interpreting what action should be taken. For example, a GET request in the form http://cuff.storage.example/listing/2398-56-1-9125 is interpreted by first removing the base URL, leaving listing/2398-56-1-9125, which is a request for the evidence listing for the case number 2398-56-1-9125.

Each different type of web request is interpreted in a specific way. Within the logic of these web services, we are able to perform the input validation and mediation necessary for other components to access storage resources. Additionally, by adding the appropriate filters, we can manage the forensics examination flow by noting when certain events take place and taking action. For example, when a new device image is being uploaded, the Cuff Link can easily recognize this event and perform a predefined action, such as notify the appropriate supervisor that the new case needs to be assigned to an examiner.

The communication in CUFF that is of the type that can be easily interrupted before reaching its destination is typically being sent to or from the Analysis Block (traffic of this type are discussed in more detail in section "Scheduling Analysis Jobs"). As messages are sent to the Analysis Block, they are first sent to the Cuff Link and checked to ensure that the analysis request is well-formed and that the specified Analysis Block is within a reachable domain. This would be the mechanism whereby multiple deployments of CUFF could share analysis resources.

Storage

Similar to the communication in the system, there are two types of storage needs in CUFF. First, because it is built on a cloud, there is a need for some way to store the VM images that run in the system. This storage need is distinct because VM images are large, rarely change, but also may be needed to start up an instance very quickly.

Second, because cloud instances cannot store any persistent data within the image itself, all data must be stored in a container suited for the particular purpose of being temporarily attached to an instance and storing any data that needs to be preserved. Examples of this type of data includes evidence images, evidence analysis results, and database files. Evidence images will need to always be accessed in a read-only mode to preserve their integrity. Furthermore, the rules of evidence dictate that the system have a means of conducting logging and auditing on the access of any stored data in the system.

To accommodate these features, we take advantage of the two storage facilities available from the OpenStack architecture. As shown in Fig. 12.3, these facilities are distinct, but together they satisfy the needs of our framework. The first is Swift, an object storage component that, when used in connection with Glance OpenStack's image service, can provide discovery, registration, and delivery services for virtual disk images through a REST web interface. As such, Glance will act as the image registry for the system.

The second storage facility we use is volumes, which are similar in functionality to Amazon's Elastic Block Storage [3]. Each volume is labelled with a universally

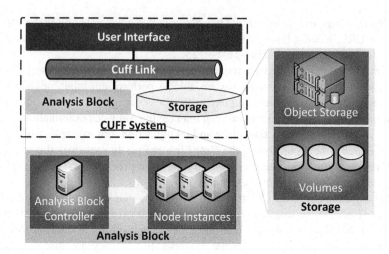

Fig. 12.3 The Analysis Block and Storage components are composed of multiple parts, each filling a separate role

unique identifier (UUID)[1] that distinguishes it from other volumes. The primary use of these volumes will be to store evidence images and analysis results. Typically, a separate volume will be created for each device uploaded to the system. If a hard drive is seized that contains multiple partitions, each partition may also be stored on a separate volume, to be determined by the examiner when uploading the evidence to the system. Analysis results will be stored on volumes separate from the evidence to which they pertain, but will store the UUID of the corresponding evidence volume to keep the two connected.

In order to maintain the integrity of evidence images stored in volumes, a snapshot is taken of each volume immediately after the upload is complete. This essentially makes the original volume read-only because, although changes are technically allowed to the volume, all write operations are saved in a "child volume" that is separate from the original and can be easily discarded when the volume is no longer being accessed by an instance.

One challenge that arises from doing automated, distributed analysis is finding an efficient means of referring to and transferring portions of evidence images (e.g. files or file segments). This is inherently a storage issue, because it is the Storage component that provides access to this data. And while it is true that because we have made snapshots of the evidence image volumes, we can technically attach the root volume to multiple instances in a read-only fashion, this still requires that

---

[1]UUIDs are 128-bit numbers that are used in distributed systems to uniquely identify information. The assurance that a UUID is in fact unique is derived from the number of theoretically possible numbers, which is about 3×10^{38}. Because of this, UUIDs are used to identify the volumes in the system.

```
29   <fileobject>
30     <filename>README.txt</filename>
31     <id>2</id>
32     <filesize>43</filesize>
33     <partition>1</partition>
34     <alloc>1</alloc>
35     <used>1</used>
36     <inode>6</inode>
37     <type>1</type>
38     <mode>511</mode>
39     <nlink>1</nlink>
40     <uid>0</uid>
41     <gid>0</gid>
42     <mtime>1258916904</mtime>
43     <atime>1258876800</atime>
44     <crtime>1258916900</crtime>
45     <byte_runs>
46       <run file_offset='0' fs_offset='37376' img_offset='37888' len='43'/>
47     </byte_runs>
48     <hashdigest type='md5'>2bbe5c3b554b14ff710a0a2e77ce8c4d</hashdigest>
49     <hashdigest type='sha1'>b3ccdbe2db1c568e817c25bf516e3bf976a1dea6</hashdigest>
50   </fileobject>
```

Fig. 12.4 This portion of a DFXML file shows how a single file object is stored with all its metadata. In the case where a file is fragmented in the disk image, multiple `<run>` tags will be contained under the `<byte_runs>` section

the instance have access to the entire image. An approach that allows for concise data transfer and thorough data representation would be better.

Garfinkel's Digital Forensics XML (DFXML) representation for file system metadata [13, 14] is just such an approach. We employ DFXML in CUFF to aid in improving the efficiency and standardization of how CUFF stores and transmits data. DFXML provides a standard way of representing and accessing the contents of an imaged drive by using an XML file to store the offsets and lengths of all "byte runs" (file fragments) on the disk, thereby acting as an index for the image. Using this DFXML file, an entity can access specific files by simply specifying the byte runs of the file and concatenating the returned results. An example of how a file's information is stored in a DFXML file is shown in Fig. 12.4.

One issue we discovered in working with DFXML is that Garfinkel's tool [12] for creating DFXML files from acquired disk images was that the tool currently only produces a simple Document Type Definition (DTD) specification for each DFXML document, which doesn't allow for type validation. To help encourage the adoption of DFXML as a standard, we have created an XML schema detailing tag hierarchy and complex data types. Using this schema to validate an image's file system representation, any digital forensic tool can reliably use this standard in its interactions with the disk image. We believe such a schema will help developers of forensic tools to be more willing to adopt this data format as a standard, because they have the assurance of precise data types with any DFXML file.

Analysis Block

As stated previously and as depicted in Fig. 12.3, there are two types of components that make up the Analysis Block, the Controller and the Nodes. The Analysis Nodes act as a network of VM instances that can be used in two different ways. First, nodes can be used as a means to perform distributed, automated analysis. In this case, a node is sent files to be analyzed, and the tool is executed from the command line, performing the requested analysis in an automated fashion. Because analysis node images are virtual machines, they can be configured to run a wide selection of operating systems, maximizing platform compatibility.

The other way of using the nodes is to manually interact with them and exercise fine-grained control over the work performed. A node is sent the files and the specified program begins execution, but the node does not indicate to the program to begin analyzing the files. Instead, the node enters a waiting state until the user accesses it remotely from the system's dashboard. At this point, the user is in complete control of the node and can perform whatever functions are necessary.

Since it is required that all inter-component communication in the system go through the Cuff Link, communication is to be standardized and regulated through the use of agents which run on all nodes in the system. While all node agents will be programmed with a standard set of communication protocols, each distinct analysis node's agent will be customized to the analysis programs being hosted on that image. This allows the agent to store whatever parameters necessary to interface with the programs as well as retrieve the analysis results. Because much of the implementation for these nodes will be the same for all node types, this improves the ability to flexibly support new file systems, operating systems, analysis algorithms, and so forth.

Forensic Flow

The most important feature of the entire system is the fact that it accommodates the main tasks of any digital forensic investigation. Since most of these tasks involve the Analysis Block in some way, we discuss the connection of each task to the Analysis Block.

1. *Acquisition*: When a user is uploading a new evidence image to the system, the destination volume for that image is mounted to a VM instance crafted specifically for handling this task. During the upload, the instance generates checksums of the image, which are validated against the checksums of the original device, and then stored for later use during evidence validation after operations are performed on the image. Finally, the instance takes a snapshot of the volume to effectively seal it from further changes.
2. *Validation*: In order to guarantee the integrity of images and files in the system, Analysis Nodes are utilized to calculate and validate the checksums before and after every data transmission.

3. *Discrimination*: By creating a VM image that can use sets of checksums of known good files (such as the Reference Data Set provided by the National Institute of Standards and Technology [28]), the system can highlight those files which are unknown for the examiner, effectively eliminating an extensive number of files they need to look at.

To support such an event-based forensic workflow and accommodate relevant workflow management features in CUFF, we consider existing approaches on a web-based workflow systems [7, 20, 26]. Especially, we believe workflow modeling approaches [9, 33] would help design and govern forensic flow and related tasks in CUFF. In addition, BPEL (business process execution language) would be another candidate to articulate a particular forensic flow for facilitating web-based events [19].

Scheduling Analysis Jobs

One of the merits of the Analysis Block's design is that it not only provides a collection of resources for analyzing evidence, but also does so in a very generic fashion, making it very reusable. The Analysis Block Controller (ABC) is indifferent to both the nature of the analyses to be performed as well as what the requirements are for the operating system or software used to perform the work.

While constructing a generic controller, we realized that the system had a great need for scheduling automated analysis jobs, so we created a set of utilities suited to accommodate this need. Our scheduling utilities have three specific purposes. The first purpose is to package information regarding analysis jobs for the entities in the system that will carry out the work. The information packaged includes the type of analysis to be carried out, the location of the subject of the analysis (i.e. the files to be analyzed), and some sort of ordering or priority information for the analysis subject.

The second purpose of the utilities is to create a channel by which the information described above can travel from the user who inputs it to its end destination, meaning the Analysis Node that will perform the analysis specified in the job information. Creating this channel implies that there is a path defined for the job that passes through multiple components of the CUFF system.

The third and final purpose of the utilities is to queue jobs according to the ordering or priority specified in the job information, and then to distribute jobs to available nodes upon receipt of an assignment request.

A few significant properties of these objectives emerge upon examination that should be highlighted. As job information is packaged, a data encapsulation method must be chosen that is standard and efficient. The efficiency of both passing the data along the defined path through the system and interpreting it is important for preventing the utilities from becoming a bottleneck, especially since there is a one-to-many relationship between the Analysis Block Controller and the Analysis Nodes. No upper bound is imposed on the number of nodes in the system, nor is there any restriction on the configurations of the nodes, which again emphasizes the importance of using standard data formats. Since the nodes submit requests for job assignments, the scheduling utilities do not preempt the work of nodes. Finally, as the utilities distribute jobs, care must be taken to prevent starvation of jobs with lower ordering or prioritization.

Multiple approaches for ordering or prioritizing can be adopted depending on what is most important for the deployment domain. One approach would be to calculate the resource demands of each job on the system using the order of complexity for each of the available analysis tools, an estimated turnaround time for a small baseline job, and the size proportion difference between the baseline job and that of a queued job request. With these values, CUFF could prioritize jobs so that those jobs with a significant workload on the system are either spread out among jobs with a lesser demand or are delayed until off-peak hours.

A second approach would be to assign priority based on the importance of the case of which it is a part. At times, one investigation will be more pressing than all others currently being worked on. In such a scenario, the case that has a higher level of criticality should be given priority over other analysis work being done in the system. By giving the user the ability to specify what criticality level a certain case has been given, jobs related to that case can be allotted more time for being analyzed by the system resources.

In our deployment of CUFF, we have implemented the second prioritization approach. We reiterate that this scheduling scheme is specifically for automated analysis. In other words, it is purposed for when users submit batches of requests to analyze data segments which will then be carried out without any further input from users. We anticipate examiners will interact more closely with VM instances in the cloud on occasion, but that is a use case distinct from the one we address here.

To begin describing the behavior of the utilities, we first identify how we have satisfied the purposes of the utilities as set forth earlier. First, the container format used for all messages is JavaScript Object Notation (JSON), which is both easily transmitted and easily interpreted from this notation to programming objects and vice versa. Second, to satisfy the needs for a path through the system components, a queuing mechanism, and a distribution method, we use RabbitMQ [30], an implementation of the Advanced Message Queuing Protocol (AMQP) [1]. RabbitMQ is a messaging broker, which allows for a common yet generic method for passing messages between components by creating queues for messages, producers that put messages into queues, and consumers that take messages out of the queues.

Figure 12.5 shows the sequence of how messages travel through CUFF using RabbitMQ. The process is initiated at step 1, when the user submits a batch of analysis requests to be done for a case. In step 2, each request is processed by the web server and is reformed to the format understood by RabbitMQ, such that the list of files for a single analysis request is stored in the body of the message, as are the criticality of the request and the tool or algorithm to be used on the files. If the tool or algorithm needs specific command line parameters, these are also stored in the body of the message. After the message has been properly crafted, it is passed

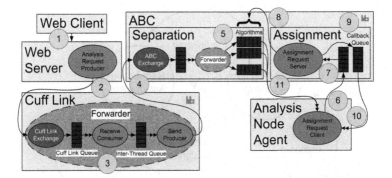

Fig. 12.5 The path of job request messages being passed through CUFF. *Single-headed arrows* indicate a message being sent to the broker, and *double-headed arrows* indicate a message being retrieved from the broker. Components with the *RabbitMQ logo* in the *top right* corner are running the messaging server

to the Analysis Request Producer. From this point on the message is in the care of the broker until it is delivered to an Analysis Node.

In step 3, the message is sent to the Cuff Link that is running a forwarder utility. In a deployment of CUFF that does not interact with other deployments, this utility is fairly insignificant because it simply passes messages on to the Analysis Block Controller. However, for deployments that interact with each other and allow jobs from one organization to be analyzed on another deployment, this is the mechanism that would be responsible for directing messages to the other deployment's Cuff Link. The forwarding of messages in this manner would depend on the name server of the first deployment knowing how to resolve the domain names of any connected deployments.

After a message has been received by the appropriate Cuff Link, it is forwarded to the Analysis Block Controller in step 4. In step 5 each message is put into a queue with messages that have both an equivalent criticality level as well as the same analysis type. Messages remain in these queues until retrieved by an Analysis Node Agent.

Before we proceed, it is appropriate that we discuss the behavior of Analysis Node Agents. As illustrated in Fig. 12.6, each Analysis Node follows a specific set of state transitions which are governed by the agent running on the node. During most of a node's time running in the cloud, it will be working on an analysis task for a job that it has been assigned. When the job is done, the agent sends the results to the Storage component and submits a job assignment request. An assignment indicates to the agent from which queue to take a job. Upon requesting a job from a particular queue, the agent will either be informed the queue is empty, in which case a subsequent assignment request would be made, or it will have the necessary information to retrieve the files from the Storage component and begin the analysis.

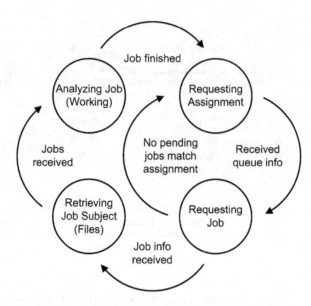

Fig. 12.6 The state transitions for Analysis Node Agents

In step 6, the Analysis Request Client segment of the node agent sends a job request message to the Analysis Request Server on the ABC. During a course of step 7, all assignment request messages are stored in a queue and are processed in the order they were received. The Analysis Request Server then utilizes a read-only interface to the job queues to evaluate the best candidate for the node in step 8.

Next, in step 9, the Analysis Request Server puts this information into the callback queue that was specified as part of the message body from step 6. It is noted that although it technically fulfills the purpose of a queue, we have designed our use of the callback queue to store at most one element. The reason for this is that job description messages sent to it will only be in response to an assignment request message, which will only be sent to the ABC when the node has completed a previous analysis job, at which point it takes step 10 and consumes the contents of the callback queue. Hence, the callback queue is only used because it is required by the broker.

Finally, having received an assignment, the node agent takes one of the jobs from a queue in step 11. At this point, the agent can get the files from the Storage component and begin the analysis.

In addition, for handling the assignment request messages, each message contains the necessary information for the ABC to make an appropriate job assignment, namely, the types of analyses the node can perform as well as the desired level of criticality. This turns out to be quite a critical element in this scheme, because it is the node agent that requests what criticality level the job should have that is assigned to it. This means that the anti-starvation requirement is satisfied in the implementation of the node agent, which keeps track of the quantities of jobs *completed* for each distinct criticality level. Then, before the agent submits an assignment request, it first compares the ratios of completed jobs for each criticality level with the ratio specified by the system administrator and selects the most outlying level to include in the request.

Evaluation of Scheduling Utilities

The overall viability of CUFF as a digital forensics analysis framework depends on its ability to distribute the work of analyzing evidence by scheduling nodes to be responsible for smaller atomic portions of the analysis work. Therefore, to demonstrate that our method of scheduling jobs is also viable, and to support our claim that the Analysis Block Controller functions efficiently and is scalable enough to facilitate collaboration between examiners, we present our set of tests which simulate real analysis jobs being assigned to nodes and executed.

In terms of execution profile, the procedure of accepting and separating job request messages (steps 1–5 in Fig. 12.5) is remarkably different from the procedure of assigning jobs to nodes (steps 6–11 in Fig. 12.5). The former will occur in bursts of batches as practitioners submit groups of jobs to the system and will not have a continual inflow. The latter will be a steady disbursement of jobs one at a time to nodes as they become ready. Because of such a difference, it is less important that the separation procedure be time-efficient and more important that it provide reliable delivery of every single message to the Analysis Block, whereas the assignment procedure should be likewise reliable but also expeditious to manage queued jobs and respond to each assignment request from nodes so as to minimize their wait time between analyses for the greatest possible throughput.

One challenge in evaluating the performance of the scheduling utilities is the fact that processes are running on completely separate VM instances in the cloud and hence have separate system clocks. For the separation procedure, this proved to make it prohibitively difficult to produce reliable travel times since the path of a single message is linear and does not return to its origin. Even with a Network Time Protocol (NTP) service running on the Cuff Link to try to keep all the components' times synchronized, impossible (i.e. negative) travel times continued to plague our results which are on the order of thousandths of seconds.

The assignment procedure is different, however, because the Analysis Node initiates the request *and* is the final destination, allowing for very reliable measurements that are obtained from the same system clock. Because of this, we will only present the empirical results of the assignment process.

To test how well the assignment process facilitates collaboration, we will equate certain actions of practitioners to the process of automatically retrieving, analyzing, and sharing the analysis results of a task as they are carried out by an Analysis Node. We affirm that this comparison is acceptable for the reason that, whenever the occasion calls for it, practitioners will manually perform these same operations by taking control of an Analysis Node. One difference between the two scenarios is that nodes only retrieve and work on one analysis task at a time. To accommodate

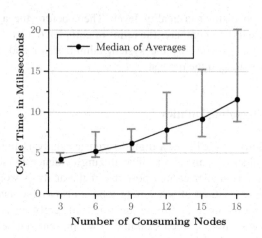

Fig. 12.7 The minimum, maximum, and median values for sets of averages where each set contains average execution times for a number of concurrently running nodes

Table 12.1 Precise numbers for the evaluations illustrated in Fig. 12.7. Numbers are given in milliseconds

Consumers in group	Minimum average	Median average	Maximum average
3	3.8295	4.31941	5.0408
6	4.5067	5.24674	7.6002
9	5.1649	6.19420	7.9581
12	6.1907	7.89824	12.4222
15	7.0317	9.24481	15.2574
18	8.8711	11.55450	20.1397

this difference, we consider the behavior of groups of nodes that may be coupled with an organization or team of practitioners. In this way, the nodes are not limited in their capacity to collaborate since they can logically pool their resources and results.

To help make the nodes' behavior more realistic, each of the job analysis messages has been given between 5 and 15 fake file descriptors. When an Analysis Node retrieves a job, it simulates the load of processing each file by sleeping for 5 ms per file before continuing with its normal execution.

In our test, we created groups of Analysis Node consumers in multiples of three. Timing mechanisms were implemented to measure the completion of steps 6–11 from Fig. 12.5, which we call a "request cycle." Each consumer made 2,000 synchronous requests[2] with an average cycle time calculated for each set of 100 requests. Minimum, maximum, and median values of all nodes in the group were then calculated as illustrated in Fig. 12.7 and as detailed in Table 12.1.

---

[2]Here we mean that each node made synchronous calls while all the nodes ran asynchronously.

We recognize that the evaluations we have presented here focus on a single component in a complex system comprised of many other elements that could have a significant effect on the scalability of our framework. However, with many of these other elements of CUFF still in development, we chose to demonstrate that the most fundamental of all the components is an appropriate method that will facilitate other components' with a high level of reliability and reuse. In doing so, we believe CUFF's abilities can be further extended to take on increasingly realistic analysis tasks.

User Interface

The main purpose of the user interface is to provide a means for the users to take advantage of all of CUFF's features. These features fall into three main categories: evidence browsing and communication, analysis management, and storage management.

Evidence browsing (extraction) is the task that takes more of an examiner's time during the forensic process than any other task. During this stage of work, the examiner looks through the file system of the acquired evidence, identifies files to be analyzed, studies the results of analyses, and makes decisions based on those results. This is the phase when collaborating with colleagues and subject matter experts is the most beneficial, so it is logical to combine the browsing tools with the collaboration tools into one interface.

We have created a simple web interface with the Google Web Toolkit that demonstrates one way in which these tools can be combined. As depicted in Fig. 12.8, the left pane provides means for navigating evidence, the user's contacts, and the communication files connected with the case that is currently open. The evidence navigation section is populated by deriving the original file system structure from the DFXML file of the evidence image.

The right side of the interface shows the contents of the selected file, a detailed listing of the currently selected directory, and a space for adding comments about the evidence. At this time, this approach of adding comments is the primary means of collaboration that we have implemented into our system. These comments are stored with the case metadata and analysis results.

We initially considered implementing a more sophisticated, near-real-time communication mechanism by adopting the Google Wave Operational Transformation algorithm [35]. However, due to the complexity of implementing this algorithm outside its intended use for a deployment of "Wave in a Box" [37] and because of its recent transitory state to become an Apache incubation project [4], that implementation effort still needs further investigation.

During the extraction phase, examiners also need a way to specify what forensic analysis needs to be performed on which files. To do this, the examiner needs access to something that presents the available analysis tools and algorithms for the files that have been selected. Figure 12.9 is gives an idea of what such an interface would

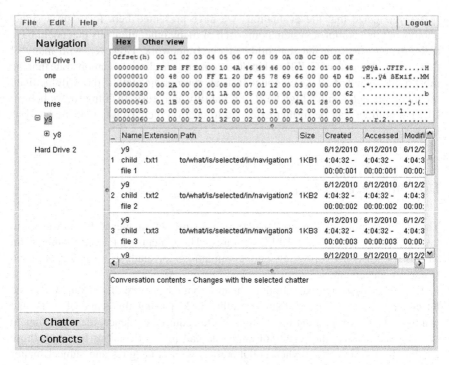

Fig. 12.8 This simple web interface allows users to browse the contents of evidence and communicate with each other

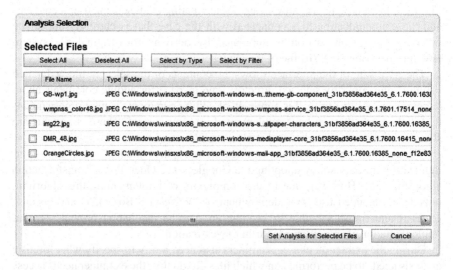

Fig. 12.9 Using this simple tool in CUFF, users will be able to specify evidence to be analyzed and check on its progress

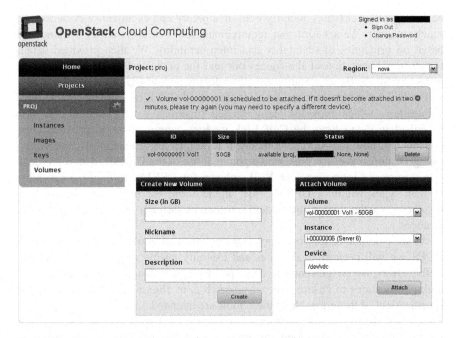

Fig. 12.10 A screen shot of the OpenStack dashboard immediately after connecting a volume to a running instance as /dev/vdc

look like. In the dialog presented to the examiner, the files that have been previously been marked to be analyzed in the evidence browsing window are listed. From this list the examiner can manually select files, select all the files, deselect all the files, select by file type, or select by a regular expression filter. Once the desired files have been selected, the examiner can then click on "Set Analysis for Selected Files" to choose from a list of available analysis algorithms and tools, after which the analysis jobs will be queued into the system.

Because storage volumes are needed for new evidence images and evidence analysis results, there must be some way for the user to execute the operations of creating volumes and attaching them to instances, at least until such processes can be fully automated by the system. One simple solution to performing these tasks is to utilize the web dashboard provided by OpenStack, which is shown in Fig. 12.10. While using this dashboard for all volume operations will be a bit tedious for jobs of any substantial size, it does provide the needed functionality.

Conclusion

In this paper we have discussed the trends of computer crime and the tools to combat those crimes. From these trends we have determined that collaboration among examiners through a secure and robust system would give them a significant advantage to successfully identify both inculpatory and exculpatory evidence in a timely manner. We set forth our requirements for such a system in a framework based on principles of scalability and interoperability. We then provided details for an implementation of the framework and the additional components that are necessary for the basic operations of a live deployment of CUFF.

For this extended work, we have implemented CUFF on the OpenStack cloud architecture, which provides many needed functions for the system. We also described in detail how the Cuff Link mediates communication between components and how the Storage component leverages the strengths of OpenStack's storage features. We also presented a potential use of the DFXML data representation format and introduced our XML schema for DFXML to enhance reliability of data types within a DFXML file. In addition, we proposed our approach to scheduling the use of the system's resources through an efficient messaging protocol.

As we continue to improve upon our implementation of all the components in CUFF, we will perform evaluations and usability testing on our system. As part of this effort, we are currently in correspondence with law enforcement agents in multiple locations to ensure that our research is in alignment with the needs and specifications of those for whom these tools are intended.

Another aspect we will consider as we continue our work on this framework is issues dealing with multi-cloud scenarios. We will be exploring means of securely connecting multiple deployments together so as to allow for sharing of resources and analysis tools to a much higher level without compromising the system's compliance with the rules of evidence.

References

1. Advanced message queuing protocol (amqp) project home (2013). http://www.amqp.org/
2. Altheide C, Merloni C, Zanero S (2008) A methodology for the repeatable forensic analysis of encrypted drives. In: EUROSEC '08: proceedings of the 1st European workshop on system security, Glasgow. ACM, New York, pp 22–26. doi:http://doi.acm.org/10.1145/1355284. 1355289
3. Amazon web services (2013). http://aws.amazon.com/
4. Apache wave incubating project home (2012). http://incubator.apache.org/wave/
5. Casey E, Stellatos GJ (2008) The impact of full disk encryption on digital forensics. SIGOPS Oper Syst Rev 42(3):93–98. doi:http://doi.acm.org/10.1145/1368506.1368519
6. Cost of hard drive storage space (2013). http://ns1758.ca/winch/winchest.html
7. Denning PJ (1996) Workflow in the WEB. In: Fischer L (ed) New tools for new times: electronic commerce. Future Strategies, Lighthouse Point
8. Du J, Gu X, Reeves DS (2010) Highly available component sharing in large-scale multi-tenant cloud systems. In: Proceedings of the 19th ACM international symposium on high performance distributed computing, HPDC '10, Chicago. ACM, New York, pp 85–94. doi:http://doi.acm. org/10.1145/1851476.1851487. http://doi.acm.org/10.1145/1851476.1851487
9. Dumas M, Hofstede AHMt (2001) Uml activity diagrams as a workflow specification language. In: Proceedings of the 4th international conference on the unified modeling language, modeling languages, concepts, and tools, Toronto. Springer, London, pp 76–90. http://dl.acm.org/ citation.cfm?id=647245.719456
10. Euca2ools user guide (2013). http://www.eucalyptus.com/docs

11. Forensic toolkit (ftk) (2013). http://accessdata.com
12. Garfinkel SL Afflib.org open source computer forensics software – fiwalk (2012). http://afflib. org/software/fiwalk
13. Garfinkel S (2009) Automating disk forensic processing with Sleuthkit, XML and Python. In: IEEE systematic approaches to digital forensics engineering, Berkeley, pp 73–84. doi: 10.1109/SADFE.2009.12
14. Garfinkel S (2010) Aff and aff4: where we are, where we are going, and why it matters to you. In: Sleuth kit and open source digital forensics conference, Chantilly
15. Garfinkel SL (2010) Digital forensics research: the next 10 years. Digit Investig 7(Suppl 1): S64–S73. The proceedings of the tenth annual DFRWS conference doi:10. 1016/j.diin.2010.05.009. http://www.sciencedirect.com/science/article/B7CW4-50NX65H-B/ 2/19b42d7f2ccc4be6794c5a1330a551bb
16. Garfinkel S, Farrell P, Roussev V, Dinolt G (2009) Bringing science to digital forensics with standardized forensic corpora. Digit Investig 6(Suppl 1):S2–S11. The proceedings of the ninth annual DFRWS conference. doi:10.1016/j.diin.2009.06.016. http://www.sciencedirect.com/ science/article/B7CW4-4X1HY5C-3/2/090ebc16025d598c775d87c8abbb7ae5
17. Higgins KJ (2010) Zeus attackers deploy honeypot against researchers, competitors. DarkReading. http://www.darkreading.com/insiderthreat/security/attacks/showArticle.jhtml? articleID=228200070
18. (ISC)^2 US Government Advisory Board Executive Writer's Bureau (2010) Do punishments fit the cybercrime? Infosecurity. http://www.infosecurity-us.com/view/12029/do-punishments-fit-the-cybercrime-/
19. Juric MB (2010) Wsdl and bpel extensions for event driven architecture. Inf Softw Technol 52:1023–1043. doi:http://dx.doi.org/10.1016/j.infsof.2010.04.005. http://dx.doi.org/10.1016/ j.infsof.2010.04.005
20. Krishnakumar N, Aheth A (1995) Managing heterogeneous multi-system tasks to support enterprose-wide operations. Distrib Parallel Databases 3(2):155–186
21. Liebrock LM, Marrero N, Burton DP, Prine R, Cornelius E, Shakamuri M, Urias V (2007) A preliminary design for digital forensics analysis of terabyte size data sets. In: SAC '07: proceedings of the 2007 ACM symposium on applied computing, Seoul. ACM, New York, pp 190–191. doi:http://doi.acm.org/10.1145/1244002.1244052
22. Liu Q, Wang G, Wu J (2010) Efficient sharing of secure cloud storage services. In: 2010 IEEE 10th international conference on computer and information technology (CIT), Bradford, pp 922–929. doi:10.1109/CIT.2010.171
23. Mabey M, Ahn GJ (2011) Towards collaborative forensics: preliminary framework. In: 2011 IEEE international conference on information reuse and integration (IRI), Las Vegas, pp 94–99. doi:10.1109/IRI.2011.6009527
24. Menn J (2010) Fatal system error: the hunt for the new crime lords who are bringing down the internet, 1st edn. PublicAffairs, New York
25. Menn J (2010) US experts close in on google hackers. http://www.cnn.com/2010/BUSINESS/ 02/21/google.hackers/index.html
26. Miller JA, Palaniswami D, Sheth AP, Kochut KJ, Singh H (1998) Webwork: meteor's web-based workflow management system. J Intell Inf Syst 10:185–215. doi:10.1023/A: 1008660827609. http://dl.acm.org/citation.cfm?id=290056.290067
27. Moraski L (2011) Cybercrime knows no borders. Infosecurity. http://www.infosecurity-us. com/view/18074/cybercrime-knows-no-borders-/
28. National software reference library (2009). http://www.nsrl.nist.gov/Downloads.htm
29. Openstack project home (2013). http://www.openstack.org
30. Rabbitmq project home (2013). http://www.rabbitmq.com
31. Roussev V, Richard GG III (2004) Breaking the performance wall: the case for distributed digital forensics. In: The proceedings of the fourth annual DFRWS conference, Baltimore
32. Scanlon M, Kechadi MT (2009) Online acquisition of digital forensic evidence. Lecture notes of the institute for computer sciences, Social informatics and telecommunications engineering, vol 31, pp 122–131. Springer, Berlin/Heidelberg

33. Sharp A, McDermott P (2001) Workflow modeling: tools for process improvement and application development, 1st edn. Artech House, Inc., Norwood
34. Urias V, Hash C, Liebrock LM (2008) Consideration of issues for parallel digital forensics of raid systems. J Digit Forensic Pract 2(4):196–208. http://www.informaworld.com/10.1080/15567280903140953
35. Wang D, Mah A, Lassen S (2010) Google wave operational transformation. Version 1.1. http://wave-protocol.googlecode.com/hg/whitepapers/operational-transform/operational-transform.html
36. Wang J, Varman P, Xie C (2010) Middleware enabled data sharing on cloud storage services. In: Proceedings of the 5th international workshop on middleware for service oriented computing, MW4SOC '10, Bangalore. ACM, New York, pp 33–38. doi:http://doi.acm.org/10.1145/1890912.1890918. http://doi.acm.org/10.1145/1890912.1890918
37. Wave in a box announcement (2010) http://googlewavedev.blogspot.com/2010/09/wave-open-source-next-steps-wave-in-box.html
38. Zhao G, Rong C, Li J, Zhang F, Tang Y (2010) Trusted data sharing over untrusted cloud storage providers. In: 2010 IEEE second international conference on cloud computing technology and science (CloudCom), Indianapolis, pp 97–103. doi:10.1109/CloudCom.2010.36

Chapter 13
From Increased Availability to Increased Productivity: How Researchers Benefit from Online Resources

Joe Strathern, Samer Awadh, Samir Chokshi, Omar Addam, Omar Zarour, M. Ozair Shafiq, Orkun Öztürk, Omair Shafiq, Jamal Jida, and Reda Alhajj

Abstract With the rapid growth of data on World Wide Web, this paper presents researchers with an analysis that summarizes data collection and evolution features in the World Wide Web. We have reviewed a large corpus of published work to extract the research features supported by advanced Web features, i.e., blogs, microblogging services, video-on-demand web sites and social networks. We have presented summary of our review and analysis. This will help in further analysis of the evolution of communities using and supporting the features of the continuously evolving World Wide Web.

Introduction

The World Wide Web (WWW) continues to grow at an unpredictable rate. The first decade of the new millennium has seen the birth of so-called "Web 2.0" services through which massive amounts of data are continuously generated at high rate. Much of this data are user generated. The once-complex task of identifying and categorizing web communities is even more complex.

In this seemingly endless flood of data, researchers interested in studying a specific phenomenon first need to start by identifying a suitable data source. For

J. Strathern · S. Awadh · S. Chokshi · O. Addam (✉) · O. Zarour · M.O. Shafiq · O. Öztürk · O. Shafiq
Department of Computer Science, University of Calgary, Calgary, AB, Canada
e-mail: omaddam@gmail.com

J. Jida
Department of Informatics, College of Science, Lebanese University, Tripoli, Lebanon

R. Alhajj
Department of Computer Science, University of Calgary, Calgary, AB, Canada

Department of Computer Science, Global University, Beirut, Lebanon

T. Özyer et al. (eds.), *Information Reuse and Integration in Academia and Industry*,
DOI 10.1007/978-3-7091-1538-1_13, © Springer-Verlag Wien 2013

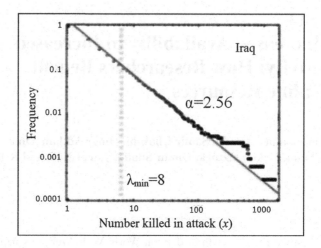

Fig. 13.1 Statistical data gathered from news articles

instance, researchers studying the patterns of how breaking news spread first need to identify a data source (such as a social network) and ensure that source is suitable for the purpose of their study. The data related to the identified source is then analyzed for effective knowledge discovery that covers the domain to be investigated.

In this paper we undertake the task of trying to present the research community with a categorization of some Web 2.0 services and features found in each service. Our hope is that the categorization will help researchers jump-start their work by providing a research-guided categorization. This work is in no way exhaustive, and is only intended as a starting point. As the evolution of the World Wide Web continues, continuous future work is needed to maintain the relevance of the results of this study.

Next we present our motivation for conducting this research, followed by survey of relevant work, and present our findings followed by conclusions.

Motivation

The WWW appears to be an ever-growing repository of information. Data is flowing in from variety of sources and need to be analyzed for maximizing the benefit to users who are interested in figuring out the best usage of the data to at least compensate for the effort of collecting the data. This wealth of data can aide every group of domain experts in a specific fiend covered by the data, e.g., computer scientists, sociologists, psychologists, and even security forces analyze, understand, and theorize about the real world. One example is the work of Bohorques et al. [2] in which they used raw statistical data gathered from news articles, NGO's, and cable news and resulted in the graph shown in Fig. 13.1. To the authors, this seemingly ordered distribution of the number of causalities killed in attack (x) to the frequency of attacks was surprising. When they repeated their work in other conflicts (such as Afghanistan, Senegal, and Colombia), the same distribution appeared. This allowed the authors to present a formula that could help answer questions such as why the conflict in Iraq continues until today.

Such power of raw data motivated us to ask what can Web 2.0 services tell us about the world. The main research question this paper tries to answer is what types of raw data can micro-blogging, blogging, social networks, and video web sites support research in, and how we can use the information collected from these information resources in a meaningful and useful way to increase the productivity of the raw data while having increase in availability.

Survey and Analysis

This section describes in detail our analysis of the features and formation of communities over the World Wide Web from Blog, Microblogging, Video sharing and Social networks.

Blog

Blogs are a popular source of a large amount of information that is posted and accessed daily. "As the amount of available information and its 'dispersion' among many related blogs increases, it becomes more difficult to get a complete picture of the public opinion on a particular topic" [18]. This is why we present some of the applications of blog mining in research and to solve some practical problems.

In [6], De Choudhury et al. explore the possibility of whether blog communications can be correlated to stock market movement. If such a correlation exists, corporations can identify the moods of clients after the release of a new product, for example. Furthermore, such a correlation, if it exists, can help create targeted advertising for clients. The authors develop a model to study and analyze such correlation. The model was then applied activity in the blogosphere and the stock market. The stocks of Apple, Google, Microsoft, and Nokia were used in the study and the results were encouraging. This is not the only study pointing at the blogosphere as a source for data on the movement in the stock market to (see [20] for another example).

Blogs can also be used as an accurate measure of public opinion with relation to movies, music, and so on. The authors of [18] took movies as a case study, with possibility to easily modify the approach for music. In the case of movies, the authors were able to show a significant correlation between "the amount of buzz a movie generates and its critical or financial success" (Fig. 13.2).

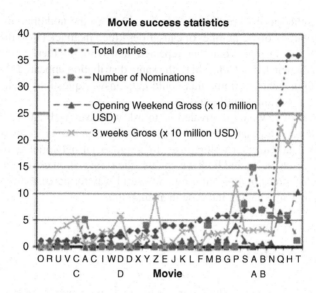

Fig. 13.2 Entry, nomination and gross statistics for each movie

The role the blogosphere can play in education does not seem to be obvious. Shaohui and Lihua [16] for instance, hypothesizes about the potential role blogs can play in education, but the results are not clear. The other question to be asked is whether blogs have been used in education. Also, the answer to that question seems unknown (Fig. 13.3).

Microblogging Services

Microblogging services, represented by Twitter for example, focus on sharing very short updates. The phenomenal success of Twitter and the hundreds of millions of users around the world make the service an attractive source of data for research.

The types of research that can be done in microblogging sites are similar to those that can be done with blogs (see [1, 19] for example), but microblogging sites provide a few added advantages. The first is that those shared "updates" are usually time-sensitive, which potentially makes microblogging communities a source to study how breaking news, as an example of a time-sensitive topic, spread in populations. In [14], the authors present Buzzer, a real-time news recommendation system. Combining Twitter chatter and user's RSS feeds preferences, Buzzer can recommend news articles of interest to the user, in real-time, as the articles are published. The approach the authors use to rank pages in the recommendation engine can be modified, of course, but the relevance of this work is that it provides evidence that Twitter, with input about users' preferences (i.e. what kind of news they are following and/or interested in), can be used to bring news articles from around the web, in real-time, to readers.

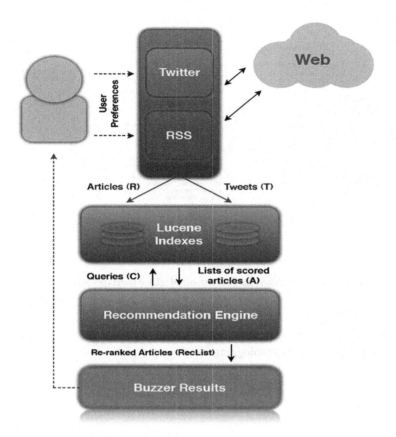

Fig. 13.3 Buzzer back-end architecture

Another feature that researchers can exploit is user-generated, geographically-referenced (georeferenced) updates. Services such as Twitter have been shown to be a useful source of georeferenced data for geographically relevant research. There are two major ways for users to geo-tag their updates. One is manually mention where they are when they publish the update. The other is the use of a GPS-enabled mobile device (e.g. smartphone or laptop) to geo-tag the update. In [7], the authors successfully demonstrate the effectiveness of using *tweets* to track the spread of wild fire.

The paper has covered the application of Twitter as a source of spatial-temporal information for crisis events, and used a major wild fire in France as a case study. The analysis of the temporal dimension showed that user-generated content was accurate and synchronized to actual events. This was not true, however, for when the forest fire started. The media broke the story before users, which makes the use of Twitter as a way to break news questionable. After that stage, Twitter proved effective following the progress of fire over time. It should be noted that only 20 % of content was user-generated original content. The rest was referencing other URLs.

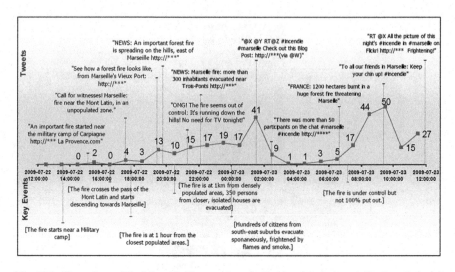

Fig. 13.4 Chronology of the Marseille Fire, number of related tweets per hour and selected tweets' contents

The following two figures from [7] are included below to demonstrate the accuracy the data gathered from microblogging sites.

Video Sharing

Video sharing is another feature for which behavior of communities has been surveyed and analyzed in terms of Self-Expression, Education, Marketing, Geotracking, Medicine, Financial, Counter-Terrorism and Politics.

Self-Expression/Art

In [11] researchers explored the influence of user generated input upon the online video site, YouTube. Classifying each studied video in a range between either professional or user-generated, they worked towards a goal of isolating the methods required to support access to these materials once they are publicly released. They created a research agenda to find unique authoring mechanics to aid in a user having more self-expression in the creation of their videos, and worked towards finding new ways to present this media. Taking a random sampling of 100 videos uploaded in 2008, they analyzed the audio, video, and popularity and found some interesting trends (Figs. 13.4–13.6).

Previously, the researchers had felt user-generated content was the least viewed due to poor editing and a short length. Their research found some user-generated

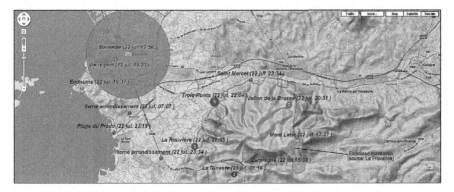

Fig. 13.5 Location, frequency and time of the first citation of place names cited in tweets, and estimated total burnt

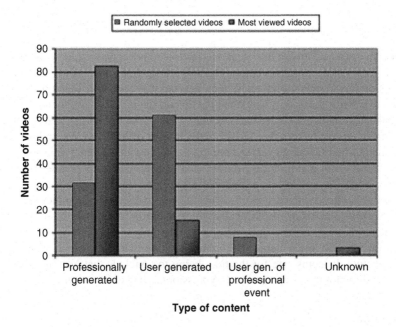

Fig. 13.6 Type of movie content

videos that did extremely well to disprove this. A father's recording of his daughter gained more than five million views. However, this seemed to be an exception to the rule, and the vast amount of popular content on YouTube comes from a professional realm as opposed to user generated.

From this research paper, we can draw our own conclusions about using YouTube as a research source for studying forms of self-expression. The previously mentioned research paper states that user generated videos on YouTube were not very popular with the online community as a whole, and because of this we can

Fig. 13.7 Videos watched vs. students

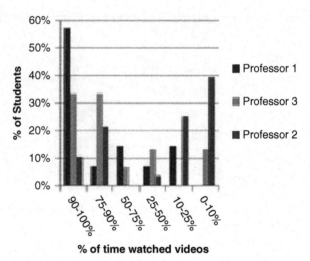

% of time watched videos

expect the vast majority of user generated videos to never be viewed. If these videos are never viewed, the web community will slowly find little reason to post their videos online, knowing that unless they get lucky, no one will watch their videos. The paper states that it is possible people upload these videos simply to share with a smaller sub-network of the web, including their friends and associates, yet they explained several factors that would make it very difficult for researchers to use YouTube to find out about self-expression in online videos. One primary reason is the difficulty they had in finding these videos. Other than by popularity of a broad search, YouTube does not have a simple way to browse these videos for examples of user-generated content, making it much more difficult to examine any sort of self-expression in them. Additionally, since many users upload for only a small sub-network, they can give out exclusive rights to these videos, blocking access to them for not only the general public, but researchers in the topic as well. Due to these factors, it seems safe for the time being to conclude that YouTube is not an ideal medium for the research of self-expression/art in web communities (Fig. 13.7).

Education

In [3], researchers give students 21 YouTube videos on programming in Java, and study how if affected their work. Noticing only about 20–30 % of students do their assigned readings, the researchers noticed that the student demographic spend much more time online watching videos instead of reading, and therefore decided to try to present their material in a new manner. Making short videos to keep their attention, the researchers recorded audio and video for the video lectures, and posted them on YouTube for the students as an alternative to doing readings from a textbook. They found that out of three professors, the one that did the least lecturing and most in class hands-on support had his students watch the videos and learn the most from them.

The example of YouTube videos as an education tool is one of many that can prove YouTube can be effectively researched for its educational value. Through the posting of informational videos, and studying the education received by watching them, researchers should be able to draw results on the effect of these videos as opposed to other mediums. This example explicitly showed how videos could be used as an alternative to reading as an educational tool, but researchers could draw many more results from similar studies. Sites like YouTube give public access to this knowledge, and by letting users access it in their web browsing, researchers can study the spread of information. One further example mentioned in the paper was that when they posted these videos on YouTube, it was visited by several members outside their class, especially in the 13–17 year old demographic. Another element researchers would be required to consider is the simple effect of visual cues on video sharing sites to assist in the education of their viewers. Researchers could use this information to study why people may choose to use videos as an educational tool, and what effect this would have upon video based web communities.

Marketing/Ads

The work described in [8] outlines a new method for pop-up advertising in videos. It suggests that instead of YouTube's method of overlay ads during the video, you detect a set of positions before streaming the video and associate ads with those positions. This would give relative ads during that video that could interest the viewer, and maximize the effect of the advertisement.

With the vast amounts of videos one can obtain from the web, and viewing how many times the most popular ones have been watched, it is clear that online videos, especially in web communities such as YouTube, are extremely popular. Web video popularity advents an opportunity by providing a new medium for advertisers to reach their audience. The development of AdOn and other alternate methods of advertising in these videos can demonstrate to researchers how important of a medium web videos is becoming. By analyzing how advertisements are done in the online video community, researchers can find many of the latest and unique techniques advertisers will choose to implement in order to sell their products. Programs like Ad-On are even able to adapt and change in order to optimize the product being advertised to the user watching the video. This is a relatively new idea, that's effectiveness can be researched so that the method can be fine-tuned and improved. Just like movies, television, and radio, web-videos are becoming a very important medium for advertising, and with that comes the possibility for a great amount of research to improve our methods and designs.

Geotracking

YouTube is used as a resource in the paper [4] in order to improve a user's video browsing based upon their geographical interests. These researchers developed GeoTracker, a tool that uses geospatial representation and a temporal presentation

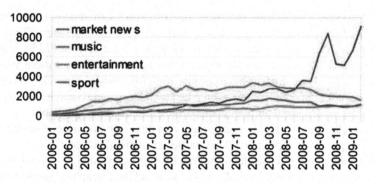

Fig. 13.8 Recent geographical trends

in order to help users spot relevant RSS feed updates as quickly as possible. Once it finds these relevant RSS updates, they are pin pointed to a map and are given key words and tags. GeoTracker then uses the RSS feed tags to search popular video sites, such as YouTube and Google Video, to find related clips and help in any sort of geo-analysis the user intends to do, even streaming it to their mobile device (Fig. 13.8).

By giving visual feedback to important and recent geographical trends, tools like Geotracker can use video streaming sites to enhance their ability to geo-analyze. This method will allow research into geo-analysis to now use video-streaming communities as a prime tool, and as such, it can be researched to find out more about the geotracking topic. Researches can view these RSS feeds, see what videos are being sent to geo-analyst, and find trends and patterns in how they are able to use this data, and how useful this data ends up being to them. For instance, researchers may be able to see that whenever a natural disaster occurs around the world, a geo-analyst can receive a streaming video from it, notice a key element in its appearance, and use that information to warn nearby area of the disasters path. Similarly, by receiving videos related to a specific place at a certain time, geo-analysis can be done anywhere in the world instead of having to go to that spot to examine it. If researchers could prove these means as effective for geo-analysis, it could greatly cut down the costs required to geo-analyze and otherwise optimize the field, increasing its contributions to society.

Medicine

In a medical letter titled "YouTube as a source of information on Immunization: A Content Analysis" [10], a researcher studied YouTube videos that related to either immunization or vaccines. Extracting information from these videos based upon comments and ratings, the researchers found that negative videos, or ones that portrayed immunization negatively, were more highly rated and commented upon. Many of these negative videos even contradicted the reference standard.

Based upon this researcher's work on immunization and how it is presented on video sites like YouTube, it can be safe to conclude it is not a good medium to visit or research for information on medicine, unless you desire to study the perceived opinion of the medicine. The researcher, in the letter, warns Clinicians that patients may be ill-informed about certain immunization from sources like YouTube, and that these video-steaming sites will often be quite critical of immunization. Since content on video web communities if often not regulated, it can be quite difficult for users to discern fact from fiction, and in the field of medicine this could have harsh repercussions. Some videos do seem to report the facts, and the previous research claims these videos were often public service announcements and never contradicted the reference standard, these videos seemed infrequent and unpopular in the web community. These facts will all work together to prove that, for the time being, the video web community is not an effective way for researcher's to study things in the field of medicine due to misinterpreted information.

Financial

In [17] researchers examine content publishing habits of financial news topics and determine the trends in the financial market area. Through various analysis of financially related YouTube videos, the researchers were able to conclude that numerous reputable financial news agencies are now using YouTube as a medium and submitting video content. This helps to prove the reliability and quality of these financial videos, as the sources the upload them are themselves reliable. They also notice how this medium was barely used years ago, and is growing quite strong in the coming years, with no sign of its progress slowing down.

This paper puts a vast amount of study, research and time into proving the reliability of the sources that upload financial information to YouTube. With their results proving that these resources are indeed reliable, stemming from the fact they come from reliable financial companies like Bloomberg, Associated Press and CBS. Research proved that these companies are constantly posting financial videos on sites such as YouTube, and the amount of videos posted seems to only increase as time goes on. Additionally, by studying the trends of stock market and financial news posts on YouTube over a period of time, the researchers were able to prove a sharp incline in the number of videos being uploaded. With more and more of this reliable information being posted on YouTube, it becomes an even better web community to analyze in order to research in the topics of finance. The only issue that could arise in researching finance with YouTube comes from the difficulty of finding valid videos, which can be countered by introduction a search by a series of tags, simple to do over the long term but a fair bit of overhead work for a short quick analysis.

Counter-Terrorism

Hsinchun et al. [9] is a research paper that aims to study terrorist activities on the web, especially in sites like YouTube. Their previous research found that certain terrorist extremist videos are tagged on YouTube, and can be classified in a variety of severities. Their research states that although YouTube aims to filter out inappropriate videos, it can often be days before these videos are tagged and removed, due to the sheer volume of videos uploaded. Through both videos linked you YouTube from other pages, and the videos directly found on YouTube, the researchers were able to find several videos related to Jihadist activities, ranging from explosive devices to Al-Qaeda recruitments.

The vast majority of these videos were linked from blogs that had known affiliations with terrorist activities. Yet this research describes various ways to find and isolate these videos, which can be of extreme importance to anyone researching counter-terrorism and stopping terrorist activities. By researching where these blogs and sites are coming from, and who is uploading these videos onto sites like YouTube, as well as finding more efficient ways of removing them once uploaded, researches can work hard to eliminate the web, especially video web communities, from being popular gathering places for terrorist activities. Research and analysis of certain videos can even determine additional methods and strategies used by terrorist groups to isolate and attack their targets. The researchers themselves suggested YouTube find more efficient ways to monitor uploaded content, and stated that since the Jihadist information is displayed visually, their videos have a much greater impact upon the viewer and need to be blocked from public viewing as quickly as possible. While it is important to note that much of this information may only be coming from Jihadist supporters as opposed to the group itself, they are still working to spread around Jihadist information and do a similar role as some Jihads. By examining these videos to find out more about terrorism, and finding ways to block these videos from being viewed by the public, YouTube and other video streaming sites can be effectively used by researchers to counter terrorism and other extremist Jihad groups in the global sphere.

Political

Mustafaraj et al. [13] explores the impact YouTube and other streaming video websites had upon the result of the 2008 election. Researchers analyzed things like video submission date, view count, ranking, keywords, political messages in the video, and comments to discover the degree of impact the web had upon the election. Through YouTube, BarackObama.com and JohnMcCain.com, they found that political groups were the most common to post videos, as opposed to simply supporters of the political group. Most advertisement videos were negative against their opponent, and that upload timing seemed to always be right before the election, and within weeks these rose in popularity.

A vast number of people visit the internet daily, and because it is quickly becoming a large medium for information, it seems only natural the politics are discussed in it as well. With the popularity of the US election, research has shown us that dozens are videos were uploaded to sites like YouTube, and ended up being viewed by millions in a short time frame. With this large amount of traffic, it would be very easy for researchers to study YouTube and other sites in the video-streaming web community in order to analyze its effect on politics. For example, now users can watch political debates and see politicians speak without having to wait for the news; they can simply log onto their computer and watch a pre-recorded video of it. This is bound to have a profound effect upon the voting population, and can easily be researched to find common trends and patterns. Additionally, it could be worth researching the differences between how politicians act online vs. otherwise, and see if they decide to present themselves in a different manner. However, the previously mentioned researchers noticed that although certain videos ranked higher, trends were tough to notice because most viewers would only watch the already top-ranked videos. In respect to the 2008 US election, it is important to notice that every major politician knew the role of the internet on their voters, and were all online to some degree. One factor research does notice, is certain sites, like YouTube, seemed to have a political bias in the videos that were posted, and like any bias, must be kept in mind while doing research to keep things objective. Research also suggests that due to the vast amount of views political videos received in this time, it is likely they had a strong effect on the outcomes of the election, proving such videos are reliable sources, and can deserve research in proving their effect on the viewer population.

Social Networks

Formation of social network is another important behavior of the formation and evolution of communities over the Web. The analysis for this has been described in terms of activities like Sports, Education, Music and Health.

Sports

In [12], the authors try to show how student athletes at a large university use Facebook differently than fellow students. These differences include the size of their networks, their usage of the website as a whole, and perceptions about their audience. They are often considered on-campus celebrities or the representatives of the university. Because of these differences, the on-campus celebrity athletes have a higher percentage of being watched compared to other students. Hence, they have a higher status and will receive more comments than other students on Facebook.

The researchers did a basic content analysis of the student athletes' pages to get a good idea what goes on their page. As well, they collected data from a large U.S. university and conducted two surveys, one for the athletes and the other for the students. The response rate for the athletes survey was 27 % (202 students), while the response rate for student one was 21 % (419 students). Both surveys were conducted 8 months apart and judging by previous work, the time difference had no strong effect on the results. The final results were given to the coaches and the student support staff.

The results showed that most student athletes rated their overall Facebook experience as positive. Even though they did see risks and rewards in using it, they felt that they represented themselves well through their profiles. The athletes use the site to either coordinate their activities or keep in touch with fans. This is completely based on group norms and the popularity of the sport though. As predicted before, their network size is large. The researchers showed their results in tables. The table highlighted student athlete experiences on Facebook.

Education

In [5], the researchers are trying to show that Computer Science lecturers in South Africa are using Facebook as an academic tool to enhance their teaching. The way students engage and interact with their instructors has changed tremendously over the years because of technology advances. Initially used only for social interaction, students soon started forming study groups on Facebook for academic purposes. Members in these groups create posts to share knowledge with other students. Hence, peer-to-peer learning and the level of engagement increase.

The researchers distributed an online questionnaire to professors in both the Information Systems and Computer Science departments, and 45 of the questionnaires were completed. The study was limited. Meaning, the questions were unknown to the professor beforehand and no demographic data was collected. There were eight questions in the questionnaire.

The questionnaire asked the professors what they do on Facebook and how they felt about the social networking website. The results showed that many instructors do not have a Facebook account and the majority who do have one only use it for social purposes, not academic. Hence, they do not participate in a group related to their teaching/research areas. One reason for this is that they may want to maintain their professional image and not gain strong relations with other students. Even though most instructors have not applied for online social-networking tool in their teaching, most do believe that they (Facebook for example) can be used as an academic tool for teaching. However, most professors would not use one because they already have dedicated "secure" website to interact with students.

With the successful research study of the impact of using a social network like Facebook as an education tool, we can conclude that social networks can be accurately studied for their educational value. The study itself showed that by giving the students a social network to communicate with, they had a tendency to co-operate and work with each other a little more. Researchers would be able to view this co-operation, and study on how different the interaction is from typical classroom interaction, as well as factoring in the ease of access to it. They could also research on how, if they give instructors access to the same community, they could evaluate student interaction and even moderate it, preventing cheating, plagiarism, and more. A final example of the topic that could be studied using this research into Facebook as an educational tool is how a student would view their teacher through a social networking site. They could study if the student began to view the professor as less professional, or if it would simply be a great way to ask the professor questions outside of class time.

Music

By analyzing on a dataset from the social-networking site Last.fm [15], the researchers want to determine the music preferences of people and how they change over time. They proceed by extracting data from each of the users and building/clustering a graph of similar users. By doing this, they obtain groups of people with similar music preferences. Once this is done, they label all these clusters and show how these clusters evolve over time. This includes how new clusters emerge, die, merge and split from other clusters.

From the Last.fm website, the researchers were able to obtain the user listening behaviour over the next 4 proceeding months. The site provides for each user and interval a list of the top artists whose songs are played the most. Once this was done, they conducted experiments using data from 16 intervals to determine the parameters e and n for the clustering procedure. Finally, they apply the incremental DENGRAPH algorithm to obtain the results.

Their final analysis showed that DENGRAPH detects and obtains groups of users with similar music taste by clustering their profiles. Some of these groups overlap and some of them are separated. If they overlap, they are considered more similar because they have tags in common. If they are separated, the groups have no similarity. In addition, they were able to observe with their incremental procedure approach the growth, decline, creation and removal of new clusters, and the merge and splits of other clusters as well.

With the research proving direct links between music and social network sites, it opens up many possible research opportunities. The one suggested in this paper is important, as by following and studying user's music preferences over a long range of time, they can determine and discern patterns and trends certain people, or even types of people, may follow. Since music is considered a very personal topic by many, there is no more important source to query than the listeners themselves, and this research paper helps to prove that through a social network site like Facebook, users are willing to publicly share their tastes and opinions of music. Further research could delve into proving things like links between user age and music genre, through a query or data mining of a social network web site. Lastly, another topic researchers would be able to study with the use of social networks are how relationships are formed and strengthened based upon similar, or even possibly different, musical tastes.

Health

The researchers for this area of study are trying to explore whether the main features from a social networking site that can be used to help ease interventions for Health Behaviour Change. Using qualitative methods, this helps increase social support to interventions. For this study, five Norwegian citizens (three men and two women) were used and the average age was 60 years old. The method used to collect data was computer-assisted interviews, which each participant had to complete. An interview guide was created per person consisting of open-ended questions about social networks. The questions were mainly focused on the participant's on views and experience navigating through network sites such as Facebook and MySpace. During these interviews, the responses by the people were constantly analyzed.

These results show that staying in touch family and friends in social networks seems more important than staying in touch with distant friends/strangers. In essence, a network with a few close relationships gives more social support than a network of more distant relations. Social networks are an easy way to keep in touch with close friends and their whereabouts, especially if you don't see them often. Because of all these benefits, the features on these sites could be used to ease social support in health behaviour change interventions.

No graphs or visuals were shown to support or show these results. The researchers even state that more quantitative research is needed to show if social-networking features can ease interventions. Social support networks are vital to a person wellbeing and health, and this research paper proves that through a social network site like Facebook, users can build up these social support networks. This would open up many opportunities for research into social support networks, particularly how they are formed inside the constructs of a web community. Additionally, researchers could find very interesting information about the formation, dissolution, strengthening and weakening of social support networks through online communities like Facebook as opposed to real life situations. Another topic that this research proves Facebook can be scientifically studied would be how much emotional and structural support an individual could gain from an online friend in Facebook, communicating through mainly text, and a real life friends, with many more sources available to them such as phone, in person, and more. Researchers could study the differences in willingness to support an online friend in Facebook versus a real life friends, and see if there is a greater physical connection to meeting them in person.

Results

From the survey of works above, we can summarize our findings in the following table (Table 13.1). Note that the table is not exhaustive, nor complete. The undertaking of classifying features of web services will require future continuous work. The following table is meant to provide an idea of how such work can be useful for researchers.

Table 13.1 Summary of results

Feature	Microblogging	Blogosphere	Video	Social networks
Georeferencing	Y	Y	Y	?
Breaking news	Y	?	?	?
Politics/current affairs	Y	Y	Y	Y
Gaming	?	?	?	Y
Movies	?	?	?	Y
Music	?	?	?	Y
Research/education	?	?	Y	Y
Geneology/personal history	?	?	?	?
Counter-terrorism/attack	?	Y	Y	?
Jobs/workplace	?	?	?	Y
Food/health	?	?	N	Y
Sports/athlets	?	?	?	Y
Travel/tourism	?	Y	?	Y
Marketing/ads	Y	?	Y	Y
Self-expression/art	?	?	N	?

The results summary table is an easy to use visualization for researchers, where there is a 'Y' if the web service could be used for such research in the same row, 'N' if it could not, and we put '?' for ones where we could not find published research supporting that. This table can be used in one of two ways:

1. Using a more complete table, a researcher interested in studying self-expression can avoid services such as YouTube, a result we think is counter-intuitive but can save valuable research time and resources. On the other hand, a researcher who is interested in how studying the spatiotemporal spread of news can confidently use a Twitter dataset, knowing that the results they will obtain are relevant.
2. Researchers can easily identify areas where research is needed. Where there is '?' can continue to indicate a gap in our knowledge where research could be done.

Conclusions

In this paper we attempted to analyze a corpus of published researched that uses some of the most recent advances in the World Wide Web (WWW), to extract information and provide insights in different aspects of its evolution. With the WWW growing rapidly, we provide researchers with a visualization of what features some of the most recent advances can support research in.

Some questions arise from this paper. Which advancements are better for the features supported by all services of the Web? Whether there is a way to rank those services or not is interesting, as YouTube may be the best source for raw data when it comes to politics and current affairs, even though all types of technology we looked support the same feature. Also, where there is overlap, as in the case of politics, would the use of a combination of services be better than using only one? All these questions are open ended. However, our analysis takes the first step in analyzing and categorizing the evolving features.

References

1. Admati A, Pfleiderer PC (2001) Disclosing information on the internet: is it noise or is it news? Technical report, Graduate School of Business, Stanford University, …
2. Bohorquez JC, Gourley S, Dixon AR, Spagat M, Johnson NF (2009) Common ecology quantifies human insurgency. Nature 462(7275):911–914
3. Carlisle MC (2010) Using YouTube to enhance student class preparation in an introductory Java course. In: Proceedings of the 41st ACM technical symposium on computer science education (SIGCSE'10), Milwaukee, 10–13 Mar 2010. ACM, New York
4. Chen YR, Di Fabbrizio G, Gibbon D, Jora S, Renger B, Wei B (2007) Geotracker: geospatial and temporal RSS navigation. In: Proceedings of the 16th international conference on world wide web (WWW'07), Banff, 08–12 May 2007. ACM, New York
5. Colete C, de Villiers C, Roodt S (2009) Facebook as an academic tool for ICT lecturers. In: Proceedings of the 2009 annual conference of the Southern African computer lecturers' association (SACLA'09), Eastern Cape, 29 June–01 July 2009. ACM, New York
6. De Choudhury M, Sundaram H, John A, Seligmann DD (2008) Can blog communication dynamics be correlated with stock market activity? In: Proceedings of the nineteenth ACM conference on hypertext and Hypermedia (HT'08), Pittsburgh. New York, p 55
7. De Longueville B, Smith RS, Luraschi G (2009) OMG, from here, I can see the flames!: a use case of mining location based social. In: Proceedings of international workshop on location based social networks, Seattle
8. Guo J, Mei T, Liu F, Hua X (2009) AdOn: an intelligent overlay video advertising system. In: Proceedings of the 32nd international ACM SIGIR conference on research and development in information retrieval (SIGIR'09), Boston, 19–23 July 2009. ACM, New York
9. Hsinchun C, Thoms S, Tianjun F (2008) Cyber extremism in Web 2.0: an exploratory study of international Jihadist groups. In: IEEE international conference on intelligence and security informatics (ISI 2008), Taipei, 17–20 June 2008, pp 98–103
10. Keelan J, Pavri-Garcia V, Tomlinson G, Wilson K (2007) YouTube as a source of information on immunization: a content analysis. J Am Med Assoc (JAMA) 298(21):2482–2484. doi:10.1001/jama.298.21.2482. Retrieved 29 Apr 2010
11. Kruitbosch G, Nack F (2008) Broadcast yourself on YouTube: really? In: Proceeding of the 3rd ACM international workshop on human-centered computing (HCC'08), Vancouver, 31–31 Oct 2008. New York
12. Lampe C, Ellison NB (2010) Student athletes on facebook. In: Proceedings of the 2010 ACM conference on computer supported cooperative work (CSCW'10), Savannah, 06–10 Feb 2010. ACM, New York
13. Mustafaraj E, Metaxas PT, Grevet C (2009) The use of online videos in the 2008 U.S. congressional elections. In: International conference on computational science and engineering (CSE'09), Vancouver, 29–31 Aug 2009, vol 4, pp 320–325
14. Phelan O, McCarthy K, Smyth B (2009) Using twitter to recommend real-time topical news. In: Proceedings of the third ACM conference on recommender systems (RecSys'09), New York, p 385
15. Schlitter N, Falkowski T (2009) Mining the dynamics of music preferences from a social networking site. In: Social network analysis and mining (ASONAM 2009), Athens

16. Shaohui W, Lihua M (2008) The application of blog in modern education. In: 2008 international conference on computer science and software engineering, Wuhan, pp 1083–1085
17. Sykora MD, Panek M (2009) Financial news content publishing on youtube.com. In: 3rd international workshop on soft computing applications (SOFA'09), Szeged, 29–30 July 2009, pp 99–104
18. Tirapat T, Espiritu C, Stroulia E (2006) Taking the community's pulse, one blog at a time. In: Proceedings of the 6th international conference on web engineering, Palo Alto. ACM, p 176
19. Tumarkin R, Whitelaw RF (2001) News or noise? Internet postings and stock prices. Financ Anal J 57:41–51
20. Wuthrich B, Permunetilleke D, Leung S, Cho V, Zhang J, Lam W (1998) Daily prediction of major stock indices from textual WWW data. In: Proceedings of the 4th international conference on knowledge discovery and data mining, New York, pp 364–368

Chapter 14
Integration of Semantics Information and Clustering in Binary-Class Classification for Handling Imbalanced Multimedia Data

Chao Chen and Mei-Ling Shyu

Abstract It is well-acknowledged that the data imbalance issue is one of the major challenges in classification, i.e., when the ratio of the positive data instances to the negative data instances is very small, especially for multimedia data. One solution is to utilize the clustering technique in binary-class classification to partition the majority class (also called negative class) into several subsets, each of which merges with the minority class (also called positive class) to form a much more balanced subset of the original data set. However, one major drawback of clustering is its time-consuming process to construct each cluster. Due to the fact that there are rich semantics in multimedia data (such as video and image data), the utilization of video semantics (i.e., semantic concepts as class labels) to form negative subsets can (i) effectively construct several groups whose data instances are semantically related, and (ii) significantly reduce the number of data instances participating in the clustering step. Therefore, in this chapter, a novel binary-class classification framework that integrates the video semantics information and the clustering technique is proposed to address the data imbalance issue. Experiments are conducted to compare our proposed framework with other techniques that are commonly used to learn from imbalanced data sets. The experimental results on some highly imbalanced video data sets demonstrate that our proposed classification framework outperforms these comparative classification approaches about 3–16 %.

C. Chen (✉) · M.-L. Shyu
Department of Electrical and Computer Engineering, University of Miami, 1251 Memorial Drive, Coral Gables, FL, USA
e-mail: c.chen15@umiami.edu; shyu@miami.edu

T. Özyer et al. (eds.), *Information Reuse and Integration in Academia and Industry*, DOI 10.1007/978-3-7091-1538-1_14, © Springer-Verlag Wien 2013

Introduction

The success and affluence of social media networks in the Internet have enabled the sharing and distribution of a huge amount of multimedia data in the forms of videos, images, etc. The abundance of multimedia data poses an urgent need on effectively and efficiently searching, indexing and retrieving the data which are of interest to the end users. For example, effective goal detection [6, 7, 20] in a large collection of soccer videos is helpful to the fans who are very interested in the fantastic goals made by the soccer players. Under this circumstance, the goal shots are regarded as positive data instances and the rest of the shots are regarded as negative data instances. TRECVID [21] semantic indexing task is another example in which each video shot is required to be indexed for different semantic concepts. It is a common strategy to build a binary-class data set for each semantic concept where the positive class is composed of the video shots that contain the specified semantic concept and the remaining video shots are categorized into the negative class. Both of the aforementioned examples can be addressed by adopting binary-class classification approaches to detect and rank the video shots related to the positive class.

Binary-class classification aims to separate one target class from a mixture of other non-target classes based on some separation rules or properties. By default, the data instances belonging to the target class are called the positive data instances, and all data instances belonging to the non-target classes as a whole are considered as the negative data instances. However, many popular learning algorithms encounter difficulties when they are directly deployed into these detection tasks because of the so-called data imbalanced issue [14]. In a binary-class data set, the data imbalance issue is usually represented by the negative class dominating the positive class. In details, the size of the positive class is much smaller than that of the negative class. In this case, the majority class is the negative class and the minority class is the positive class. It is not uncommon to see the ratio between the minority class and the majority class on the order of 100:1, 1,000:1, or even 10,000:1. Most of the popular learning algorithms such as Support Vector Machines (SVM) [24] and Neural Networks [19] assume that their models are built on a balanced data set. However, this assumption is often violated in real-world applications. Without any strategy to handle the data imbalance problem, these classification algorithms tend to predict all data instances as the members of the majority class since the learning algorithm is biased towards the majority class. For example, within a data set where 0.1 % of the data instances are the positive data instances and 99.9 % are the negative data instances, all data instances are probably predicted to be negative. This is because that such a misclassification of positive instances only produces a tiny prediction error (probably the minimum prediction error) by the adopted classification algorithm. However, usually these positive data instances are more important than the negative ones, as can be seen by the previous two examples. Therefore, these important positive data instances will most likely be incorrectly predicted in an imbalanced data set.

The data imbalance issue has attracted attentions from many research communities. In Year 2000, the Association for the Advancement of Artificial Intelligence (AAAI) [13] called for a workshop about learning from imbalanced data sets. The International Conference on Machine Learning as well as Association for Computing Machinery Special Interest Group on Knowledge Discovery and Data Mining Explorations (ACM KDD Explorations) also held some similar workshops on the topic of learning from imbalanced data sets [2, 4]. Since then, many algorithms and frameworks have been proposed to handle the data imbalance issue. He and Garcia [11] provided a comprehensive survey of the state-of-the-art solutions to this issue as well as the standardized evaluation metrics to measure the effectiveness for imbalanced data learning.

To address such a data imbalance issue, we propose a novel binary-class classification framework that integrates the semantics information in the multimedia data and the clustering technique in this book chapter. For the binary-class data set built for a target concept, the original training data set is first divided into a positive class subset and a negative class subset, in which the positive class subset is composed of all the training data instances containing the target concept and the negative class subset consists of the remaining data instances. On account of the original imbalanced data set, where the negative class dominates the positive class, the negative class subset is further divided into many negative groups by either clustering or holding out some other non-target concept classes within the original negative class subset so that the ratio of the data size between each negative group and the positive class subset is not large. Therefore, the data groups generated by combining each negative group and positive class subset does not suffer from the data imbalance issue. For each balanced group, a subspace model is trained and optimized. Finally, the subspace models trained on all data groups are integrated with the subspace model built on the original imbalanced data set to form an integrated model which is able to render a better classification performance than the subspace model trained on the original data set alone.

This chapter is organized as follows. Section "Related Work" introduces the related work. The details of the proposed classification framework is illustrated in section "The Proposed Framework". Section "Experiment" demonstrates the setup and results of the comparative experiment, and finally section "Conclusion and Future Work" concludes this chapter and explores some future directions.

Related Work

A number of techniques can be applied to address the data imbalance issue. Data sampling is a common technique to learn from an imbalanced data set. The idea of sampling is to adjust the ratio between the positive data instances and the negative data instances that are used for training the classification models by reducing the number of negative data instances and/or by increasing the number of positive data instances. Therefore, data sampling can be further divided into oversampling and undersampling [1].

Oversampling aims to add more positive data instances to the original imbalanced data set so that the number of the positive data instances is comparable with the number of the negative data instances. New positive data instances can be generated either by simply replicating existing positive data instances (called random oversampling) or by syntactical sampling of the positive (minority) data instances (called Synthetic Minority Oversampling TEchnique (SMOTE)). The idea of oversampling is quite straightforward, that is, to balance the ratio between the number of the positive data instances and the number of the negative data instances without losing any information related to the data instances of both positive and negative classes. However, random oversampling by replicating the positive data instances from the original data set could lead to the overfitting problem, as indicated by Mease et al. [18]. The other oversampling method like SMOTE generates each syntactical positive data instance $X^{(new)}$ between two existing data instances, as shown in Eq. (14.1).

$$X^{(new)} = (1 - \varepsilon) \cdot X^{(i)} + \varepsilon \cdot \hat{X}^{(i)}, \tag{14.1}$$

where $X^{(i)}$ is an arbitrary positive data instance and $\hat{X}^{(i)}$ is randomly picked from the K-nearest neighbors of $X^{(i)} \cdot \varepsilon$ is a random variable between 0 and 1. Similar to random interpolation, it is reasonable to assume that there is a data instance that lies between two existing data instances if they are close to each other. However, over-generalization seems to be a major issue for SMOTE. Therefore, some adaptive synthetic sampling algorithms [10, 12] were proposed to consider the information about neighboring data instances, such as their class labels.

Different from oversampling, undersampling balances the ratio between the positive class and the negative class by removing the data instances belonging to the negative (majority) class. The way that undersampling tries to balance the data set is quite simple and sometimes it is effective. However, some important negative data instances that represent the characteristics of the negative class could be discarded during the undersampling process and the training model could thus be compromised. Data sampling methods directly manipulate the data instances by either increasing or reducing the size of a specified class.

On the other hand, boosting methods handle the data imbalance issue in a different way. The boosting methods acknowledge that the training models built from an imbalanced data set might be not good, but consider the use of an appropriate "re-weighting" of these weak training models to lead to a good classification result. Boosting methods combine weak learning models to reduce the negative influence caused by the data imbalance problem. Among them, AdaBoost [8] is a representative boosting algorithm, which reweighs the training data instances and models iteratively during the training phase by minimizing the prediction error produced by an ensemble of the training models. In the classification phase, the class label of each testing data instance is determined by the voting of these weighted ensemble models. AdaBoost is proved to be effective in many real-world applications. However, the major drawback of AdaBoost as well as other boosting methods is that they usually require a time-consuming iteration process to find the optimal weights for the ensemble models.

There are also algorithms that integrate both boosting methods and sampling methods. For example, SMOTEBoost [3] is built by combining SMOTE and Adaboost.M2 algorithm. SMOTEBoost interactively uses SMOTE at each boosting step and the learning of the positive (minority) class is gradually strengthened and emphasized during the iterative steps. Another approach is the DataBoost-IM [9] method that aims to utilize the boosting procedure to ensure the predictive accuracy values of the positive class and the negative class are both satisfactory. To prevent the training models from overfitting, JOUS-Boost [18] uses the Adaboost algorithm together with over/under-sampling and jittering of the training data.

Another category of approaches that address the data imbalance problem are the cost sensitive learning methods [15, 16, 25, 27]. In these methods, the cost is associated with the misclassification of the positive data instances and the negative data instances are different. In the case where the positive class is dominated by the negative class, the misclassification of the positive data instances should be given a larger cost than that of misclassifying the negative data instances. Studies from [17, 27] showed that cost sensitive learning is able to render better performance than the sampling methods. Algorithms like Cost Sensitive Decision Tree and Cost Sensitive Neural Networks are well studied. However, cost sensitive learning can also be integrated with the other classifiers. One of the problems of cost sensitive learning is the configuration of the cost matrix. Although it is obviously that misclassifying a data instance of the minority class should be given a larger cost, one question arises when it comes to determine how larger the cost value should be. Therefore, it is still a challenging task to find a suitable cost matrix for the cost sensitive learning methods when they are used in an imbalanced data set.

The Proposed Framework

In our previous work [5], a clustering-based subspace modeling method called CLU-SUMO was proposed. CLU-SUMO utilizes K-Means clustering to build K negative data groups from the original negative training subset. Each negative data group is combined with the original positive training subset to generate K training data groups. Subspace modeling method (SUMO) is used to build models on each training data group as well as the original imbalanced data set to predict the ranking scores (soft label) for each testing data instance. Next, a combination of these ranking scores are compared with a decision threshold (the threshold is 0 in CLU-SUMO) to predict the final label of the testing data instance. The CLU-SUMO framework has shown to improve the classification performance with the help of clustering the negative data instances [5].

In this chapter, we further enhance the CLU-SUMO classification framework by integrating semantics information and clustering in the construction of a set of balanced data groups to address the data imbalance issue for multimedia data.

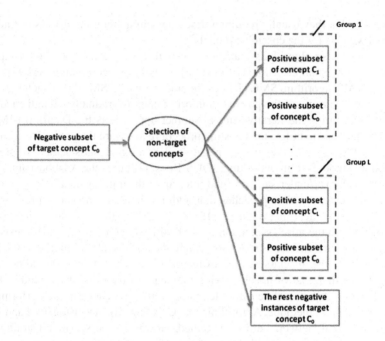

Fig. 14.1 Generation of balanced training subsets by class selection with the utilization of semantics information

In our proposed Class Selection and Clustering based SUbspace MOdeling method (CSC-SUMO), the following enhancements are achieved.

- Speed up the model training procedure. In our proposed framework, the clustering step is applied after some non-target concept classes are held out as negative data groups. The idea behind such a hold-out strategy is that those data instances of the non-target class usually share some common data characteristics and semantics. Since the purpose of applying a clustering method is to find data groups whose data instances share similar data characteristics, from the view of semantics, it is reasonable to regard each non-target concept class as one negative data group though the intra-group similarity cannot be guaranteed to be as small as the one generated by a clustering method.
- Some of the generated data groups hold semantic meanings. Each non-target class corresponds to a particular concept. Therefore, the generated rules that rely on these concepts can help to interpret their meanings. Furthermore, the semantic relationship between concepts can potentially be utilized to help improve the detection results of the target concept.

The proposed CSC-SUMO classification framework consists of three procedures: the generation of balanced training subsets by class selection (as shown in Fig. 14.1), the generation of balanced training subsets by clustering

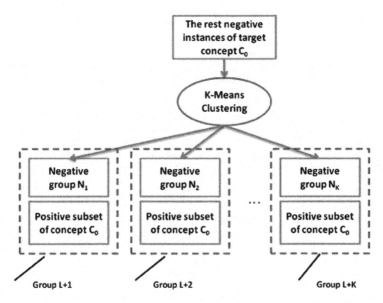

Fig. 14.2 Generation of balanced training subsets by clustering

(as shown in Fig. 14.2), and integrated subspace modeling and classification (as shown in Fig. 14.3).

During the first procedure, a number of non-target concepts are selected based on the following pre-defined criteria which are chosen via domain knowledge and empirical studies.

- The ratio of the selected non-target concept class to the target concept class should fall within the interval of [0.5, 2];
- The overlapping of non-target concept class and target concept class should be below 1 %;
- The overlapping between the selected non-target concept classes must below 50 %.

The first criterion ensures that each group in Fig. 14.1 is balanced. The second criterion requires the non-target concept class to overlap with the target concept as small as possible, considering that too much overlapping could make it hard to learn separation rules from the generated balanced groups. The third criterion aims to reduce the number of groups generated by the first procedure. If the overlapping between two non-target concept classes is large, then it is not necessary to generate a data group for each of them since one non-target concept class is already enough to describe the majority of the data instances belonging to the other concept class. Since the selected non-target concept classes may not cover the whole negative subset of the target concept, the size of the remaining negative data instances should be small, which will be the input to the second procedure to cluster them into several data groups.

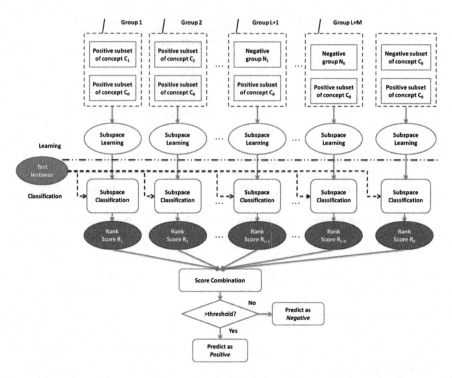

Fig. 14.3 Integrated subspace modeling and classification

The advantages of utilization class label information lie in two folds. First, the efficiency of the clustering-based binary classification framework is enhanced. Second, some negative subsets have semantic meanings, which provides a way to facilitate to interpret the generated rules. On account of this, we propose a new clustering-based binary-class classification framework that integrates both the clustering technique as well as semantic partitioning of negative class to handle the imbalanced data sets.

In the second procedure, K-Means clustering method is used to cluster the remaining negative data instances after the first procedure to form more data groups. This procedure is the same as the one proposed by Chen and Shyu [5]. Till procedure 2, each negative data instance is assigned to one or more data groups since the data groups generated from the first procedure may have some overlapping negative data instances (i.e., those data instances belonging to two or more selected non-target concept classes).

All the balanced data groups and the original imbalanced training data set are trained and optimized by the Subspace Modeling (SUMO) method, as shown in Fig. 14.3. The learning and classification (with the ranking scores) of SUMO is briefly introduced in Code 1 and Code 2, which corresponds to the "Subspace Learning" part and "Subspace Classification" part in Fig. 14.3. Please note that in order to reduce the iterative loops, the parameter β is not used in the learning phase of SUMO as in [5]. The definitions of the functions used in Code 1 and Code 2 are shown as follows.

Definition 1 (function Z). For an $m \times n$ matrix $A = a(i, j)$ and a $\rho \times n$ matrix B,

$$Z(B, A) = \begin{bmatrix} (B(1, :) - \mu(A))/s(A) \\ \cdot \\ \cdot \\ \cdot \\ (B(\rho, :) - \mu(A))/s(A) \end{bmatrix}$$

where $\mu(A) = [\mu_1(A), \ldots, \mu_n(A)]$ and $s(A) = [s_1(A), \ldots, s_n(A)]$ are calculated by Eqs. (14.2) and (14.3), respectively.

$$\mu_j(A) = \frac{1}{m} \sum_{i=1}^{m} a(i, j), j = 1, 2, \ldots, n \qquad (14.2)$$

$$s_j(A) = \sqrt{\frac{1}{m-1} \sum_{i=1}^{m} (a(i, j) - \mu_j(A))^2}, j = 1, 2, \ldots, n \qquad (14.3)$$

It can be observed that $Z(A, A)$ is the z-score normalization of A.

Definition 2 (SVD). The standard SVD (Singular Value Decomposition) is shown in Eq. (14.4).

$$A = U \Sigma V^T, \qquad (14.4)$$

The SVD function of an $m \times n$ matrix A produces $\lambda(A)$ and $PC(A)$, where $\lambda(A)$ is the positive diagonal elements of $\Sigma^T \Sigma$ sorted in a descending manner. In other words, $\lambda(A) = \{\lambda_1(A), \ldots, \lambda_\theta(A) | \lambda_1(A) \geq \lambda_2(A) \geq \cdots \geq \lambda_\theta(A) > 0\}$. $PC(A)$ is the eigenvectors from V that correspond to the sorted $\lambda(A)$.

Definition 3 (function PCP). Suppose there are an $m \times n$ matrix $B = \{b(i, j)\}$ and eigenvectors $PC(A) = \{PC_1(A), \ldots, PC_\theta(A)\}$, where $PC_i(A)$ is an $n \times 1$ vector, $i = 1, \ldots, \theta$, as defined in Definition 2. The Principal Component Projection (PCP) of B on PC(A) is defined as follows.

$$PCP(B, A) = \{B * PC_1(A), \ldots, B * PC_\theta(A)\}. \qquad (14.5)$$

Equation (14.5) shows that $PCP(B, A)$ is an $m \times \theta$ matrix. If $PCP_{(x,y)}(B, A)$ is used to denote the element of $PCP(B, A)$ at the x-th row and y-th column, then $PCP_{(x,y)}(B, A)$ is the projection of the x-th row vector of B on y-th eigenvector of $PC(A)$.

Definition 4. Based on Definitions 2 and 3, we can further define the score function $Score(B, A, pl) = [Score_1(B, A, pl), \ldots, Score_x(B, A, pl), \ldots, Score_m(B, A, pl)]^T$, where $Score_x(B, A, pl)$ is defined in Eq. (14.6).

$$Score_x(B, A, pl) = \sum_{y=1}^{pl} \frac{PCP_{(x,y)}(B, A) \times PCP_{(x,y)}(B, A)}{\lambda_y(A)}, \tag{14.6}$$

where pl can be any integer between 1 and θ.

CODE 1: SUMO: LEARNING PHASE

1   **Input**:
    (1) A set of training data instances Tr
    (2) Training labels
2   **Output**: $pl^{(opt)}$, $\mu(TrP)$, $\mu(TrN)$, $s(TrP)$, $s(TrN)$, $\lambda(TrP)$, $\lambda(TrN)$, $PC(TrP)$, $PC(TrN)$

---

3   Divide Training data set Tr into positive class TrP and negative class TrN according to the training labels.
4   Apply normalization function Z and SVD to positive and negative classes and derive the projected data $PCP(Tr, PC(TrP))$ and $PCP(Tr, PC(TrN))$.
5   Iteratively search pl to optimize the F1-Score of the learning model.
6   Output $pl^{(opt)}$ corresponding to the best F1-score, $\mu(TrP)$, $\mu(TrN)$, $s(TrP)$ and $s(TrN)$, $\lambda(TrP)$, $\lambda(TrN)$, $PC(TrP)$ and $PC(TrN)$.

CODE 2: SUBSPACE MODELING: CLASSIFICATION PHASE

1   **Input**:
    (1) Testing data instance $Ts[i]$, $i = 1$ to ω (the total number of testing data instances)
    (2) Output from the learning phase: $pl^{(opt)}$, $\mu(TrP)$, $\mu(TrN)$, $s(TrP)$, $s(TrN)$, $\lambda(TrP)$, $\lambda(TrN)$, $PC(TrP)$, $PC(TrN)$
2   **Output**: ranking score of $Ts[i]$

---

3   Derive the projected testing data instance by applying Z function and subspace projection to calculate $Score(Ts[i], TrP, pl^{(opt)})$ and $Score(Ts[i], TrN, pl^{(opt)})$.
4   Let $S = Score(Ts[i], TrN, pl^{(opt)}) + Score(Ts[i], TrP, pl^{(opt)})$
5   Output $(Score(Ts[i], TrN, pl^{(opt)}) - Score(Ts[i], TrP, pl^{(opt)}))/S$ as the ranking score of $Ts[i]$

For a testing data instance $Ts[i]$, the generated ranking scores from the subspaces are combined by a Score Combination module to produce a final ranking score. The final ranking score $R_{final}[i]$ of $Ts[i]$ is calculated by Eq. (14.7).

$$R_{final}[i] = (L + K) \cdot R_0 + \sum_{j=1}^{L+K} e^{(-(1+\|Ts[i]-C_j\|))} \cdot R_j, \tag{14.7}$$

Table 14.1 An example of training data instances

Instance ID	Attribute 1	Attribute 2	$\cdots$	Attribute 120	Class label
1	0.50861	0.50584	$\cdots$	0.42221	0
2	0.44957	0.46049	$\cdots$	0.39756	0
3	0.4168	0.549	$\cdots$	0.43015	0
4	0.50199	0.48082	$\cdots$	0.39877	0
...	...	...	$\cdots$	...	...
10000	0.42924	0.56815	$\cdots$	0.017	1
10001	0.4448	0.48015	$\cdots$	0.016	1
...	...	...	$\cdots$	...	...

Table 14.2 The centroid of each negative group

Centroid ID	Attribute 1	Attribute 2	$\cdots$	Attribute 120
C_1	0.45888	0.46478	$\cdots$	0.49454
C_2	0.4407	0.50273	$\cdots$	0.45169
C_3	0.46194	0.49503	$\cdots$	0.47173
...	...	...	$\cdots$	...
C_{14}	0.33237	0.22438	$\cdots$	0.49799

where C_j is the centroid of the j-th negative data group generated either from the first or the second procedure, and $|| \cdot ||$ stands for the norm operation. If $R_{final}[i]$ is larger than a threshold value, then $Ts[i]$ is predicted as positive. Otherwise, $Ts[i]$ is predicted as negative. In the experiment, this threshold value is set to 0.

A running example is given as follows. Assume that the concept to be retrieved is "Car" (i.e., target concept). An example of the input training data instances is shown in Table 14.1, where the instances with class label 1 are positive, which contain the concept "Car"; while those with class label 0 are negative, which are irrelevant to the concept "Car". In the learning phase, suppose Instances 1 and 2 also contain semantic concept "meeting". Assume that the concept "meeting" satisfies the pre-defined criteria to be a negative group (G_1), then Instances 1 and 2 are assigned to the negative group G_1. For convenience, in this example, there is only one negative group formed by the non-target class which is the negative group containing concept "meeting". The remaining negative instances with class label 0 (such as Instances 3 and 4) are clustered into several negative groups ($G_2, \cdots$, and G_{14}) using the K-Means Clustering method, assuming K is 13 here. The centroids of $G_1, G_2, \cdots$, and G_{14} are $C_1, C_2, \cdots$, and C_{14}, respectively (see Table 14.2).

Next, the positive group which consists of all instances whose class labels are 1 is combined with $G_1, G_2, \cdots$, and G_{14} separately to form new binary datasets D_1, $D_2, \cdots$, and D_{14}. Let the original dataset be D_0. In the final step of the learning phase, one subspace model is trained on each binary dataset by following the steps in CODE 1 (e.g., applying normalization in line 4, searching the optimal pl value in line 5, and etc.). For example, the subspace model M_0 is built on D_0, M_1 is on D_1, and so on.

Table 14.3 An example of testing data instances

Instance ID	Attribute 1	Attribute 2	...	Attribute 120	Class label
1	0.42898	0.54476	...	0.40614	N/A
2	0.41305	0.4928	...	0.46485	N/A
3	0.47003	0.48959	...	0.46499	N/A
4	0.35064	0.54878	...	0.49799	N/A
...	...	...	...	...	...

Table 14.4 The ranking scores of testing data instances from different subspace models

Instance ID	M_0	M_1	M_2	...	M_{14}
1	−0.0833	0.2732	0.5213	...	0.1535
2	−0.0821	0.1738	0.4691	...	0.1909
3	−0.1383	0.1686	0.5779	...	0.2380
4	−0.0074	0.4092	0.6705	...	0.2925
...	...	...	...	...	...

In the testing phase, each testing data instance $Ts[i]$ is input into all subspace models built in the learning phase to get the ranking scores from all subspace models by following the steps in CODE 2 (e.g., applying subspace projection and calculating $Score(Ts[i], TrP, pl^{(opt)})$, and $Score(Ts[i], TrN, pl^{(opt)})$ in line 4, deriving the ranking score of $Ts[i]$ in line 6, etc.). For example, $Score_0[i]$ is $Ts[i]$'s ranking score from model M_0, $Score_1[i]$ is $Ts[i]$'s ranking score from model M_1, and etc. Table 14.3 shows an example of the testing data instances. The ranking score for each testing data instance from all subspace models are listed in Tables 14.4 and 14.5 displays the final ranking scores calculated by Eq. (14.7) and the corresponding predicted labels ("1" for positive and "0" for negative) using 0 as the decision threshold.

Experiment

To show the effectiveness of our proposed framework, experiments are conducted using the public available data sources. The proposed framework is also compared with other popular approaches that are commonly used to handle imbalanced data sets. The setup of the experiment are illustrated in section "Experimental Setup" and the results are shown and discussed in section "Experimental Results".

Experimental Setup

The data sets used for the experiment are from MediaMill Challenge Problem [22], which contains 85 h of news video data [23]. The data set in Experiment 1 of

Table 14.5 The final ranking scores of testing data instances

Instance ID	Final score	Predicted label
1	−0.8785	0
2	−2.1424	0
3	−4.6432	0
4	0.3738	1
...	...	...

Table 14.6 The positive and negative training data instance ratio for the selected concepts

ID	Concept	Positives (P)	Negatives (N)	P-to-N ratio
19	Car	1, 509	29,484	0.051
22	Military	1, 283	29,710	0.043
23	Vegetation	1, 198	19,795	0.040
24	Sports	1, 166	29,827	0.039
26	Graphics	897	30,096	0.030
29	People_marching	597	30,396	0.020
30	Soccer	517	30,476	0.017
34	Screen	475	30,518	0.016

the MediaMill Challenge Problem is used in our experiment, in which the low-level features and class labels are represented by sparse vectors. The training data set and testing data set are divided in advance by the provider. The training data set is composed of a total of 30,993 data instances with 120 attributes; while there are 12,914 data instances in the testing data set with the same number of attributes. A number of concepts corresponding to an imbalanced binary-class data set are selected. The information related to these concepts are shown in Table 14.6. The Positive to Negative (P-to-N) ratio of these concepts varies between 0.016 and 0.051. Therefore, such imbalanced data sets are suitable to evaluate the effectiveness of the proposed framework.

In the experiment, all classifiers take the same training and testing data sets and the performance from all classifiers is evaluated in terms of F1-score which is the harmonic mean of precision and recall, as shown in Eq. (14.8).

$$F1 = \frac{2 \cdot Precision \cdot Recall}{Precision + Recall} \tag{14.8}$$

For CSC-SUMO, K is carefully chosen so that the ratio of positive data instances to negative data instances is on average 1:2, balancing the positive and negative classes in the generated data groups.

With regard to the classification algorithms used for performance comparison, a list of popular approaches such as Adaboost with C4.5 algorithm (Adaboost), Cost Sensitive Decision Trees (CostDTree) and classic re-sampling method are used, which are available in Weka [26]. The cost matrix CM used by Cost Sensitive Decision Tree is shown below.

Table 14.7 Performance of classification on concept "Car"

Classifier	Precision (%)	Recall (%)	F1 (%)
CSC-SUMO	20.28	45.56	28.07
CLU-SUMO	25.42	31.59	28.17
Adaboost	48.20	12.00	19.20
CostDTree	18.30	21.70	19.80
ResampleLG	28.39	26.76	27.55

Table 14.8 Performance of classification on concept "Military"

Classifier	Precision (%)	Recall (%)	F1 (%)
CSC-SUMO	23.98	42.24	30.59
CLU-SUMO	26.10	34.94	29.88
Adaboost	32.60	5.30	9.10
CostDTree	17.90	17.10	17.50
ResampleLG	16.32	68.59	26.37

Table 14.9 Performance of classification on concept "Vegetation"

Classifier	Precision (%)	Recall (%)	F1 (%)
CSC-SUMO	10.50	67.11	18.16
CLU-SUMO	7.75	83.97	14.20
Adaboost	39.10	7.20	12.10
CostDTree	14.00	16.40	15.10
ResampleLG	37.08	11.02	16.99

$$CM = \begin{bmatrix} 0 & 1 \\ \omega & 0 \end{bmatrix}$$

where ω is set to the negative to positive ratio for each target concept. For a re-sampling method, a logistic regression model is trained on the re-sampled training data set and later is used for predicting the class labels of testing data set. This method is denoted as Re-sampling with Logistic Regression Model (ResampleLG). The re-sampling percentage is tuned according to different data sets. We also compare the proposed method with our previous work (clustering-based subspace modeling method (CLU-SUMO) [5]). The clustering number of CLU-SUMO is chosen based on empirical studies and varies for different concepts.

Experimental Results

The experimental results on the selected eight concepts are shown from Tables 14.7–14.14. The average F1 scores for all classifiers including CSC-SUMO are shown in Table 14.15. The results show that the proposed CSC-SUMO framework outperforms all the comparative approaches in terms of F1 measure (about 3–16 % improvement on average).

Table 14.10 Performance of classification on concept "Sports"

Classifier	Precision (%)	Recall (%)	F1 (%)
CSC-SUMO	24.62	33.23	28.28
CLU-SUMO	22.57	34.42	27.26
Adaboost	58.50	11.30	18.90
CostDTree	11.50	20.80	14.80
ResampleLG	18.50	31.45	23.30

Table 14.11 Performance of classification on concept "Graphics"

Classifier	Precision (%)	Recall (%)	F1 (%)
CSC-SUMO	45.69	60.13	51.92
CLU-SUMO	30.47	61.69	40.80
Adaboost	75.60	28.30	41.20
CostDTree	34.00	37.40	35.60
ResampleLG	35.35	50.78	41.86

Table 14.12 Performance of classification on concept "People_marching"

Classifier	Precision (%)	Recall (%)	F1 (%)
CSC-SUMO	30.79	24.95	27.57
CLU-SUMO	14.24	67.92	23.55
Adaboost	36.70	3.40	6.20
CostDTree	18.20	18.90	18.50
ResampleLG	9.89	75.23	17.48

Table 14.13 Performance of classification on concept "Soccer"

Classifier	Precision (%)	Recall (%)	F1 (%)
CSC-SUMO	71.88	60.53	65.71
CLU-SUMO	80.00	52.63	63.49
Adaboost	75.00	55.30	63.60
CostDTree	9.10	65.80	15.90
ResampleLG	12.80	42.11	19.63

Table 14.14 Performance of classification on concept "Screen"

Classifier	Precision (%)	Recall (%)	F1 (%)
CSC-SUMO	64.15	13.88	22.82
CLU-SUMO	88.00	8.98	16.30
Adaboost	82.40	5.70	10.70
CostDTree	6.00	11.40	7.90
ResampleLG	9.62	23.67	13.68

Table 14.15 Average F1 on all concepts

Classifier	Mean F1 (%)
CSC-SUMO	34.14
CLU-SUMO	30.78
Adaboost	22.63
CostDTree	18.14
ResampleLG	23.34

The performance of ResampleLG method seems to be unstable. For example, for some concepts like "Car", the F1 value of ResampleLG is slightly worse (about 0.5 %) than CSC-SUMO. However, for concept "Soccer", the F1 value of ResampleLG is much smaller than CSC-SUMO. This is due to the fact that Resampling methods often require an appropriate selection of sampling percentage, which has a large impact on the prediction quality of the classifiers. However, it is often hard to determine such an appropriate sampling percentage.

With regard to CostDTree, there is an inherent problem related to the configuration of the cost matrix. Similar to the re-sampling method, it is also difficult to build a cost matrix that can always render satisfactory classification results. Adaboost method is able to provide better results than CostDTree. However, it requires a time-consuming model training process in order to achieve better results. In the situation when the training time is a major concern, Adaboost may have its limitations.

As shown in our previous work [5] that the weighted voting of all subspace models can improve the classification results. This is mainly because that these K subspace models were built on balanced data sets, and each balanced learning model could learn the patterns belonging to the positive class accompanied by a proportion of data instances of the original negative subset. The selection of K definitely will have an influence on the final classification results. On one hand, a small K value does little help to improve the classification results in terms of F1-measure. On the other hand, a large K value may increase the number of involved training models and could cause the overfitting problem, since too few negative data instances are trained in each subspace model. Besides, compared the results of CSC-SUMO with those of CLU-SUMO, it is interesting to observe that the generation of negative groups in a combination manner between semantic information and clustering seems better than in a purely clustering manner, which implies the semantic information can be utilized to build balanced subsets from the original dataset to improve the effectiveness of semantic concept detection on an imbalanced dataset.

Conclusion and Future Work

This book chapter introduces a novel binary-class subspace modeling classification framework. Our proposed framework utilizes both the video semantics information of the non-target concept class (for class selection) and the K-means clustering method to divide the negative training subset into $L + K$ different negative data groups. Each negative group is combined with the positive training subset to construct $L + K$ new balanced data groups, each of which is trained using the subspace modeling methods. From the experimental results, our proposed framework shows its effectiveness by producing competitive results against the other comparative learning methods for handling the imbalanced data sets.

For the future work, several directions will be investigated to increase the robustness of the framework. First, experiments pertain to the influence of the cluster size K on the performance of the proposed framework should be conducted. Second, an appropriate classification threshold of CSC-SUMO should be determined dynamically to bring robustness to the proposed framework. The number of selected non-target concepts of each fold in the first procedure could also differ for the target concept class. Therefore, an effective strategy to adaptively determine such an important threshold with respect to each target concept class will be developed.

References

1. Batista GE, Batista RC, Monard MC (2004) A study of the behavior of several methods for balancing machine learning training data. ACM SIGKDD Explor Newsl 6(1):20–29
2. Chawla NV, Japkowicz N, Kolcz A (2003) Workshop learning from imbalanced data sets ii. ACM SIGKDD Explorations Newsletter. In: Proceedings of the ICML'2003 workshop on learning from imbalanced data sets, Washington DC, Aug 2003
3. Chawla NV, Lazarevic A, Hall LO, Bowyer KW (2003) Smoteboost: improving prediction of the minority class in boosting. In: Proceedings of the seventh European conference on principles and practice of knowledge discovery in databases, Cavtat-Dubrovnik, Sept 2003, pp 107–119
4. Chawla NV, Japkowicz N, Kolcz A (2004) Editorial: special issue on learning from imbalanced data sets. ACM SIGKDD Explor Newsl 6(1):1–6
5. Chen C, Shyu M-L (2011) Clustering-based binary-class classification for imbalanced data sets. In: The 12th IEEE international conference on information reuse and integration (IRI 2011), Las Vegas, Aug 2011, pp 384–389
6. Chen S-C, Shyu M-L, Zhang C, Luo L, Chen M (2003) Detection of soccer goal shots using joint multimedia features and classification rules. In: Proceedings of the fourth international workshop on multimedia data mining, Washington, DC, Aug 2003, pp 36–44
7. Chen S-C, Shyu M-L, Zhang C, Chen M (2006) A multimodal data mining framework for soccer goal detection based on decision tree logic. Int J Comput Appl Technol, Special Issue on Data Mining Applications 27(4):312–323
8. Freund Y, Schapire R (1996) Experiments with a new boosting algorithm. In: Proceedings of the 13th international conference on machine learning, Bari, July 1996, pp 148–156
9. Guo H, Viktor HL (2004) Learning from imbalanced data sets with boosting and data generation: the databoost im approach. ACM SIGKDD Explor Newsl 6(1):30–39
10. Han H, Wang WY, Mao BH (2005) Borderline-smote: a new over-sampling method in imbalanced data sets learning. In: Advances in intelligent computing, Hefei, pp 878–887
11. He H, Garcia EA (2009) Learning from imbalanced data. IEEE Trans Knowl Data Eng 21(9):1263–1284
12. He H, Bai Y, Garcia EA, Li S (2008) Adasyn: adaptive synthetic sampling approach for imbalanced learning. In: IEEE international joint conference on neural networks, Hong Kong, June 2008, pp 1322–1328
13. Japkowicz N (2000) Learning from imbalanced data sets. In: Proceedings of association for the advancement of artificial intelligence, Austin, July–Aug 2000, pp 10–15
14. Japkowicz N, Stephen S (2002) The class imbalance problem: a systematic study. Intell Data Anal 6(5):429–450
15. Liu XY, Zhou ZH (2006) The influence of class imbalance on cost-sensitive learning: an empirical study. In: Sixth international conference on data mining (ICDM'06), Hong Kong, Dec 2006, pp 970–974

16. Maloof MA (2003) Learning when data sets are imbalanced and when costs are unequal and unknown. In: Proceedings of the ICML'2003 workshop on learning from imbalanced data sets, workshop learning from imbalanced data sets II, Washington, DC, Aug 2003
17. McCarthy K, Zabar K, Weiss GM (2005) Does cost-sensitive learning beat sampling for classifying rare classes? In: Proceedings of the 1st international workshop on utility-based data mining, Chicago, Aug 2005, pp 69–77
18. Mease D, Wyner AJ, Buja A (2007) Boosted classification trees and class probability/quantile estimation. J Mach Learn Res 8:18–36
19. Moya M, Hush D (1996) Network constraints and multi-objective optimization for one-class classification. Neural Netw 9(3):463–474
20. Shyu M-L, Xie Z, Chen M, Chen S-C (2008) Video semantic event/concept detection using a subspace-based multimedia data mining framework. IEEE Trans Multimed 10(2):252–259
21. Smeaton AF, Over P, Kraaij W (2006) Evaluation campaigns and TRECVid. In: ACM international workshop on multimedia information retrieval (MIR06), Santa Barbara, Oct 2006, pp 321–330
22. Sneok C, Worring M, Gemert J, Geusebroek J, Smeulders A (2006) The challenge problem for automated detection of 101 semantic concepts in multimedia. In: ACM multimedia, Santa Barbara, Oct 2006, pp 421–430
23. The mediamill challenge problem (2005). Available at http://www.science.uva.nl/research/mediamill/challenge/data.php
24. Vapnik V (1998) Statistical learning theory. Wiley, New York
25. Weiss GM (2004) Mining with rarity: a unifying framework. ACM SIGKDD Explor Newsl 6(1):7–19
26. Witten IH, Frank E (2005) Data mining: practical machine learning tools and techniques, 2nd edn. Morgan Kaufmann, San Francisco
27. Zadrozny B, Langford J, Abe N (2003) Cost-sensitive learning by cost-proportionate example weighting. In: Third international conference on data mining (ICDM'03), Melbourne, FL, Nov 2003, pp 435–442

Index

T. Özyer et al. (eds.), *Information Reuse and Integration in Academia and Industry*,
DOI 10.1007/978-3-7091-1538-1, © Springer-Verlag Wien 2013

Printed in the United States
By Bookmasters